Social Welfare

Social Welfare

A History of the American Response to Need

SEVENTH EDITION

June Axinn

Professor Emeritus, University of Pennsylvania

Mark J. Stern

University of Pennsylvania

Boston   New York   San Francisco   Mexico City
Montreal   Toronto   London   Madrid   Munich
Paris   Hong Kong   Singapore   Tokyo   Cape Town   Sydney

Senior Series Editor: *Patricia Quinlin*
Series Editorial Assistant: *Nakeesha Warner*
Marketing Manager: *Laura Lee Manley*
Production Supervisor: *Liz Napolitano*
Editorial-Production Services: *Connie Strassburg*
Composition Buyer: *Linda Cox*
Manufacturing Buyer: *Debbie Rossi*
Electronic Composition: *GGS Book Services*
Cover Administrator: *Joel Gendron*

For related titles and support materials, visit our online catalog at www.ablongman.com

Between the time Website information is gathered and then published, it is not unusual for
some sites to have closed. Also, the transcription of URLs can result in unintended typograph-
ical errors. The publisher would appreciate notification where these errors occur so that they
may be corrected in subsequent editions.

Library of Congress Cataloging-in-Publication Data

Axinn, June.
    Social welfare: a history of the American response to need / June Axinn, Mark J. Stern.—
7th ed.
        p. cm.
    Includes bibliographical references and index.
    ISBN-13: 978-0-205-52215-6
    ISBN-10: 0-205-52215-7
    1. Public welfare—United States—History—Sources. 2. Social service—United States—
History—Sources. 3. Child welfare—United States—History—Sources. I. Stern, Mark J.
II. Tilte.

HV91. S6235 2007
361.60973—dc22

                                                                                2007010168

Printed in the United States of America.

10 9 8 7 6 5   RRD-VA   11 10

For Sidney Axinn
and
David and Sadye Stern

BRIEF CONTENTS

CONTENTS

6 The Depression and the New Deal: 1930–1940   173

PREFACE

This book has gone through many stages. Initially, the volume was planned as a collection of historical documents with brief introductory statements. The documents were to be materials pertinent to an understanding of the development of social welfare policies and programs in the United States. As work progressed, it became clear that the documents did not always support long-established interpretations found in popular secondary sources. The introductory statements got longer and longer as what we found became more intriguing. The core of the book is now the historical narrative. The documents included have been chosen to illuminate the history.

The seventh edition of *Social Welfare: A History of the American Response to Need* examines the most current social welfare issues in historical perspective. Chapter 9 has been revised to cover the period from 1992 to 2007. It looks at the main thrusts of social welfare policy emphasized by the Republican majority in Congress and examines their impact on the poor and the oppressed in the United States. Earlier editions analyzed the beginnings of the "turn to the right" of the 1980s. This new edition explores the effects of the drive to reduce federal spending for public programs further and to turn control and responsibility for social welfare over to the states and the private sector.

As in every period treated in the book, from the colonial era to the present, social welfare policy is put into economic, demographic, and political contexts. The accelerating shift to a postindustrial economy with its accompanying loss of manufacturing jobs and the increasing bifurcation of income and wealth, set the background for the weakening safety net.

The introduction and the historical chapters have been revised and expanded to include new sections on the treatment and status of Native Americans, immigration policy, historical ambivalence about family roles and income support for single women, and attitudes toward the aging.

Successive editions of this book have been used by graduate students in the social work program of the University of Pennsylvania. Thanks go to all of them for their thoughtful contributions.

Many colleagues both in social work and in related fields have been particularly helpful. It is especially pleasant to acknowledge June's niece, Amy Hirsch, of Community Legal Services of Philadelphia, and son, David Axinn, formerly director of Blair County Legal Services of Altoona, Pennsylvania, and now a partner in the firm of Cohen and Axinn, Hollidaysburg, Pennsylvania. They have each made insightful comments and suggestions from their frontline positions. We thank June's daughter, Constance Johnson, who as legal research analyst at the Law Library of Congress was of invaluable bibliographic aid.

We thank the publisher's reviewers for their thoughtful suggestions and comments: Beverly Edwards, Jackson State University; David Fauri, Virginia Commonwealth University; Michael Reisch, University of Michigan; and Michael Wolf-Branigan, George Mason University.

The first two editions of *Social Welfare* were coauthored by Hal Levin, one of our most treasured colleagues. Although Hal died in 1983, his name appeared as a coauthor of the book for the next sixteen years. His contribution to the book—especially its attention to the historical development of social administration—remains considerable.

During the last years of Hal's life, Mark Stern joined the faculty of the University of Pennsylvania School of Social Work. For a short period, the three of us enjoyed our collaboration, which included developing an understanding of the impact of the rise of conservatism on social welfare, as well as more mundane pursuits, like agreeing on a place to eat lunch. After Hal's death, we continued this work which appeared in *Dependency and Poverty: Old Problems in a New World* (Lexington Books, 1988) and regular discussions of history and contemporary social welfare.

Most of all we express our deep appreciation to our spouses, Sidney Axinn and Susan Seifert. Their wit, humor, and support make all things possible.

June Axinn
Mark J. Stern

June Axinn died in May 2006 while we were in the midst of revising the book for the seventh edition. I have retained June as the senior author because her scholarship remains the foundation of the book.

Mark Stern
December 2006

Social Welfare

1

Introduction

This volume is a history of social welfare in the United States. Its special concern is the American response to the needs of the poor and the oppressed. It explores values and attitudes, as well as the political and economic forces that have brought about particular social welfare policies and programs at any one time.

The goals of social welfare programs derive from the goals of the larger society for itself and from the view that society holds of itself and of its various members. In turn, decisions about who is "truly" needy and how they are to be helped bear upon economic development, political organization, social stability, and family integrity. Social welfare programs involve a redistribution of resources—from the "haves" to the "have nots." This nation has been reluctant to do that, holding instead to a faith in laissez-faire and individualism. The country has valued the private economy over the public, and individual autonomy over collective choices.

Because social welfare goals touch core ideologies, they polarize Americans. Priorities for funding programs for older people or children, for example, vie with each other and with programs meant to encourage work among employables. Further, priorities regarding older people or children may conflict with traditions of self-help among family members and consequently lead to programs that discourage acceptance of needed help.

Decisions need to be made about the nature of social welfare programs. Should help be offered in cash, goods, or services? Rent supplements or public housing? Should major cash transfer programs be tied to workforce participation? Are money payments to be joined to counseling services and changes in personal behavior? Is help in one's own family or community preferable to institutional care? Need the extension of health care benefits be tied to insurance mechanisms? Simultaneously, decisions about benefit levels and, equally important, terms of entitlement must relate closely to the purposes for which programs have been devised. The extent to which potential beneficiaries are viewed as claimants, recipients, clients or consumers suggests not only the intent of the program but also the extent to which eligibility factors will deter or invite. For example, in the late 1990s, the number of Americans receiving public assistance fell by nearly two-thirds even as poverty remained largely unchanged.

Additional decisions are inherent in efforts to implement social welfare programs and to establish a coherent welfare system. The sheer land size of the United States, the size and diversity of its population—as well as legal and social traditions related to volunteerism, to separation of church and state, to states' rights, and to local responsibility—all complicate legislative and administrative decisions in social welfare matters. Which programs should be government funded and administered and at which level of government? Which programs should be both funded and administered by voluntary and/or proprietary organizations? What is the appropriate public/private mix for the delivery of social services? What should be the degree of consumer participation in program design and service delivery? The list of policy and program decisions to be made is not yet complete.

The history of social welfare is paralleled by and enmeshed with the growing professionalism of those who administer social services—that is, with the history of the social work profession. The early development of the public and voluntary sectors of social welfare was accompanied by the development of purveyors of service seemingly appropriate to the purposes of each: both the overseer of the poor and the lady bountiful. Historical evolution has led to professionalization in both the public and the private sectors. In both sectors there have been and still are philosophical differences leading to quite different program positions and social strategies. Those social workers who emphasize the structural and institutional causes of social problems seek programs establishing governmental responsibility for meeting needs and develop coalitions for reform and institutional change. On the other hand, those who emphasize the individual causation of social problems have moved to develop and use psychological theory and therapy. Historical cleavages continue to divide social welfare generally and social work in particular.

This book emphasizes the meaning of social welfare for the family as a unit and for family members as individuals. The assumption is that the family is the basic organizing device of modern society and that all social policy decisions impinge on family well-being. In this sense, then, social policy and family policy are essentially one. The fact that the United States has no governmental family policy, no social policy that overtly supports family life as a goal in itself, highlights the discrepancies and dilemmas that have marked the American approach to social welfare. Society's interest in the family has not resulted in a stated, widely accepted goal for family welfare. Efforts to clarify such a goal through the calling of a White House Conference on Families in the 1970s, for example, were marked by confusion, dissension, and delays. The controversy of gay marriage that arose in 2004 underlined that the very definition of family was being challenged by the decisions of individuals and couples who had previously existed in a shadow world.

From the beginning, a separate channeling of "family" welfare and child welfare, originating with English Poor Laws, and, therefore, at one with the fabric of an English colonial milieu, divided social welfare responses for the worthy, impotent poor—the disabled and children—from those for the unworthy—the able-bodied poor. The incorporation of the English Poor Laws into the legislative framework of American colonial governments differentiated those who were unable to work from those who were potentially employable. Poor Law programs were vitally concerned with those who were employed and who might be in danger of "falling into pauperism." The family was effective to the degree that it maintained the social order and the economic viability of its individual members. To a considerable extent, social welfare programs for poor people in the twentieth century were characterized by this same orientation.

The essential worthiness of children and the importance of nurturing their potential for social and economic contribution led to stated, public concern for their well-being as members of families and eventually to grudging recognition of the needs of families. The twentieth century was proclaimed the Century of the Child, and pressures to make the label stick resulted in the calling of the first White House Conference on Children in 1909 and to a positive statement of public policy in regard to child care. Home and family life were declared to be society's goal for children, an enunciation of the rights of children. Economic necessity, many felt, should not require that a mother leave her childcare responsibilities for work outside the home. Time and reality have demonstrated more and more ambivalence of policy and practice in child welfare. The "Century of the Child" came to a close with one-fifth of U.S. children living in poverty.

Now, as in the past, welfare programs are fragmented and disparate. Efforts to develop a coherent family policy and an integrated income maintenance system have foundered. Budgetary constraints and concern with the recent growth in the number of single-parent families shape efforts to "reform" welfare. Budgetary concerns are a powerful force pushing to decrease expenditures. The increased labor force participation of all women—single and married, mothers and the childless—weakens the argument for governmental support of mothers as homemakers. But the desire to increase labor force participation of single mothers implies increased expenditures—for job training, employment counseling, and day care. Throughout this volume, attention is given to the place of women in the contemporary social and economic structure and in the family. The book traces the process by which the able-bodied poor—a label applied to poor men of the eighteenth and nineteenth centuries—came, in our own time, to signify poor women.

The needs of the aging now receive great attention in the United States. But concern for the welfare of our older citizens was not consistent before the Great Depression. Thus, in the late nineteenth century there was special attention paid to the needs of older white men who were veterans, but by the time of the Great Depression the aging were one of the poorest groups in American society. The chapters that follow will trace the evolution of the policy that has given the aging, particularly older white men, some relative advantage within the social welfare system.

The social welfare needs of two groups, veterans and blacks, are given special analysis to demonstrate two extremes in social policy in the United States. History shows the assignment of veterans to special consideration for social welfare benefits as a result of their unique social and economic contribution through service in the armed forces. So much value has been placed on this contribution that benefits initiated for veterans have tended to set precedents for benefits later extended to others.

For peoples of color—blacks, Hispanics, Native Americans, and Asian Americans, a very different picture emerges. Native Americans were oppressed by white invaders from the very first, and their treatment shames us still. Much of our attention is focused primarily on the largest of these groups, African Americans. This group has suffered the dual difficulties of color and class, of racial discrimination and poverty. Like other people of color, they have been assigned a social and economic role that has assured their vulnerability to the risks of industrial society and to extended need. Simultaneously, the assignment of that peculiar economic and social role has been used to rationalize the denial of economic and social justice that might have enabled them to meet their needs. Even when government adopted policies that attempted to address past discrimination, the social and economic inequality of African Americans has proven resistant to change.

It should be noted that the assignment of special roles to veterans and to minorities has been based on considerable agreement in the general population. Interestingly, most of the poor have concurred with the special treatment of these groups and with the general expectation that families support themselves.

Nativist attitudes existed in the United States from the very first days. The treatment of Native Americans is one example. In the colonial period, Benjamin Franklin had major concerns about the German language and culture spreading in Pennsylvania, and the Federalists worried about the Irish and French. Despite the large immigration of the nineteenth century, the period from the late 1830s to the mid-1850s was markedly anti-Catholic, and anti-Asian sentiment dominated immigration legislation the last quarter of the century. Nativist dominance triumphed in the twentieth century, with legislation against all immigrants in 1924 and anti-Semitism prevailing during the 1930s and 1940s. The entry of millions of new immigrants since the 1970s has again provoked two persistent reactions: a cosmopolitan belief that immigrants enrich American society and a defensive fear that they will steal jobs and dilute the "national character" (itself a product of generations of immigration).

Over the years these principles were implemented in accordance with the country's economic realities. Prior to 1990, as the country became richer, social welfare programs expanded, regardless of which political party was in power. The disparate treatment of different groups persisted, but policies became more generous for all.

The low level of individual economic output relative to the level of production needed during the colonial period permitted little choice in regard to ability or willingness to work. The well-being, the very existence, of the colonies depended upon the maximum contribution of each of the colonists. Such dependence, supported by a view of human beings as inherently evil and easily seduced into idleness and pauperism, resulted in a policy of coercive alternatives to relief—the workhouse, indenture, apprenticeship, contracting out, and so on.

In contrast, the contemporary economy has an unprecedented capacity to produce consumer goods. Our society has now achieved a stage of development in which there is more labor than needed for simple maintenance, and therefore more choice is possible in formulating policy and devising programs for those who are less productive. The growth of social welfare expenditures in the twentieth century reflects the increased ability of society to meet the social welfare needs created through the industrial process and its impact on family structure. The greater freedom to choose notably appears in the separation of money payments to public assistance recipients from socially controlling services. Nevertheless, recurring periods of recession and inflation make it clear that the ability to finance welfare programs is finite, that the economy continues to require an allocation of "scarce" productive resources among competitive uses. And to the extent that this is true, the goals of money payment programs will continue to influence the choice of benefits offered and the terms of entitlement to these services.

An examination of the history of the American response to dependency gives evidence that morality and ideology follow upon technological and economic reality. The colonial perception of work as moral and idleness as immoral may be challenged, in an affluent society, by a concept of entitlement to protection from society's hazards and by a view of poverty as immoral. The postindustrial economy offers a new challenge to the linkage of income and benefits to work effort. The current emphasis on the immorality of not working comes at a time of a basic change in the nature of our market economy, as low-paying, unstable service jobs are replacing the more permanent manufacturing employment of a previous era. A Labor Department study finds that, despite a slight decrease from the high displacement rates of the 1980s, 8 million people, of whom 3.6 million had been working for their employers for three years or more, were downsized from 1995 to 1997. About one-fourth of these long-tenured displaced workers were not able to find full-term employment. Of those who did find work, one-fourth suffered substantial wage cuts—20 percent or more.[1]

Not only are wages in the service sector less adequate to support families, but these jobs offer fewer benefits. These changes would seem to support the expansion of social welfare programs, but instead we are retreating from our help to the working poor. The resistance to change suggests the strength of the ideological overlay inherited from an earlier economy of severe scarcity we need to resolve value conflicts, if policy and program decisions relevant to today's various families are to be made.

Even a cursory historical review of social welfare policies and programs demonstrates that political decisions about family welfare have been economically based. Overall, the family has been seen as a unit to be supported, if such support achieves economic independence for its members. When the family seems unlikely to support itself conventional political wisdom has leaned toward the denial of public support. The hypothesis that family welfare policies and programs are economically based suggests again the numerous questions to be answered before benefits can be determined.

No exact formula is available for achieving an integrated response to the questions. Nevertheless, this volume assumes that decisions leading to the formulation of social policies and programs for families result from the interaction of four factors:

1. The level of output
2. The perception of social institution's effectiveness
3. The view of human nature
4. The historical heritage

The level of productivity, of output, of a particular society lends obvious constraints to choices about the uses of that output. These constraints are quite real. High levels of output and affluence increase the possibilities for choice; and the degree of equality in a society can, and indeed often does, increase as national income rises. At the same time that wealth makes some redistribution possible, it also makes it psychologically necessary; our concept of what might be a tolerable level of poverty varies with gross national product. Still, the United States has not been a generous or equalitarian nation. Far beyond the demands of economic reality, the nonproductive have been subjected to poverty programs that in the end maintain the poor only minimally.

The view that is held of the effectiveness of society's functioning strongly influences the initiation and development of social welfare programs. If society believes itself to be operating effectively, and if most people feel they do well within the system, then those who find it hard to survive can be looked upon as individual failures. In such circumstances, the approach to the poor and to poverty issues is by way of remedial, residual programs aimed at uplifting the failures, at changing them to look like the rest of us. On the other hand, when society is considered to be operating ineffectively, the demand is for institutional change. The response to the severe, localized unrest of the 1960s was the War on Poverty, which consisted of educational, employment, legal, and social services aimed at helping individuals to become more effective participants in the labor market. In contrast, government responded to the widespread unemployment crisis of the Great Depression with the permanent social insurance programs of the Social Security Act, which altered the income distribution system and helped it become more effective in meeting the needs of individuals and families.

The commonly held view of human nature unquestionably contributes to the nature of the response to human need. A belief in the superiority of any group in the population—indeed, any racial, ethnic, religious, or sexual hierarchical ordering—becomes a basis for discrimination and exploitation. Certainly, the history of social welfare in the United States reflects this in its insistence on blaming the victims. In the nineteenth century, Americans used Social Darwinism to rationalize greed; more recently, sociobiology has filled the same function.

If people are seen as basically lazy, as shiftless, even sinful, then social welfare programs are devised to deter. A nineteenth-century listing of the causes of dependency highlighted individual character flaws and argued that the help given the poor by organized charity aggravated the problem. The dominant nineteenth-century response to dependency was the organization of friendly services aimed at pushing the poor individual, and by extension the family, above the need for relief. Alternatively, if people are considered essentially good (that is, ambitious), the response to need is more likely to be guided by the offer of incentives and the development of programs that provide opportunity for self-advancement.

Historically, both views of the human condition, as reflected in the treatment of the poor, have been held. The poor have been considered both blessed and condemned by God, both virtuous and sinful, both lazy and ambitious. And these contrasting views have been held simultaneously. In connection with the family, for example, the prevailing nineteenth-century view of Charity Organization Society leaders that family members had to be deterred from a base, inherited instinct for pauperism was countered by Settlement House Movement leaders' conviction about the constructive force of human aspiration. To the former, pauperism—its effects upon the individual, the family, and society—was a disease worse than death, and hunger and starvation were to be endured for its exorcism. To the latter, poverty resulted from the denial of opportunity, and pressure was exerted for legislative reform designed to affirm and expand an inherent core of human dignity.

The need for resolution of value conflicts seems especially clear as we move toward revisions in our welfare system. The federalization of adult categories of public assistance—Old Age Assistance, Aid to the Needy Blind, and Aid to the Permanently and Totally Disabled—on January 1, 1974, and the rejection by Congress of proposals by Presidents Nixon and Carter to replace the Aid to Families with Dependent Children (AFDC) category of public assistance, demonstrate enduring, contradictory views of human nature and the force of history on the shape of social welfare. Public acceptance of the Supplemental Security Income Program for the worthy, adult, nonworking poor highlights, by contrast, the suspicion with which we continue to view the needy family with employable members.

The rejection of Nixon's Family Assistance Plan and Carter's Better Jobs and Income Proposal was especially significant considering their belief in the therapeutic value of work. The fact that the proposals were steeped in adherence to the work ethic did not dispel the fear that adding the "working poor" to the welfare rolls would lead to widespread moral decline. The link between work and the receipt of income security benefits was not strong enough to dispel the threat to our economic system that Congress saw in a guaranteed annual income—no matter how low that income was. We are again at a period where the drive is "to change welfare as we know it." The success of conservative welfare reform during the 1980s and 1990s ended efforts to balance support for the work ethic and for providing a decent standard of living to even our poorest citizens. Rather, by 1996, government used punitive regulations to prevent millions of eligible families from even applying for aid.

The impact of cultural bias is clear throughout our history. The Poor Laws, as they developed in England during the longtime move away from agriculture to factory production, were an effort to deal with disjuncture and the conflict in that society between feudal lords and an emerging industrialism. The adoption of the Poor Laws for use by the American colonies represented the imposition of laws that were culturally appealing but in some aspects inappropriate to the American territorial and agricultural scene. The renewed vigor with which the Poor Laws were administered during the post-Civil War period demonstrates again the significance of historical heritage. The reliance upon family responsibility and local settlement as requirements for financial relief was detrimental not only to industrial expansion but also to family welfare. The importance of mobility and of the nuclear family to successful urbanization and industrialization went unheeded, and the country was bemused by welfare measures that eased but did not eliminate the hazards of the new society. The racially discriminatory application of the Poor Law principles to the freed slaves was touted as a base for helping blacks achieve the independent status of fellow American citizens.

The significance of history to an understanding of social welfare policies and programs can be demonstrated further by the pattern of administration devised for their operation. Federal, state, and local relationships have varied from program to program in accordance with concepts of local responsibility and states' rights. We increasingly hear calls for decentralization and the movement of power and responsibility back to the states. It is becoming clear, however, that—despite the innovative efforts of a few states—overall, service will lose by this renewed deference to states' rights and to the abandonment of federal standard-setting guidelines.

In summary, the congruence of technology and the level of output, the view of society, the view of human nature, and the historical heritage will determine the kinds of social policy decisions reached. This does not mean that these four factors contribute equally at any given moment. The very fact that the family, from the point of view of public policy, has been considered primarily an economic unit suggests that the degree to which each factor will exert influence on policy will depend upon existing economic conditions. The response to human need during the 1930s was remarkably different from the response to need during the high employment era of the 1960s. And yet both were periods during which need per se was widely recognized and civil disorder threatened. The past and the present must be understood in order to make any predictions for the future.

This volume is organized around historical time periods and gives a description of the economic, political, and cultural situation for each. When appropriate, regional differences are described. The book examines social welfare programs and institutions through the use of legislative documents, judicial decisions, administrative rulings, and statements of public and voluntary social welfare leaders. Reference is made to these documents in the text; documents that represent historical turning points are given in original form.

DOCUMENT: Introduction

The document that accompanies this introductory chapter is an Act for the Relief of the Poor, better known as the Poor Laws of 1601, passed by the English Parliament during the forty-third year of the reign of Queen Elizabeth. It is the only document in this book not derived from the American experience. Its inclusion is based on the tremendous and lasting influence that the Poor Laws have had upon social welfare policy and programs, first in the American colonies and subsequently in the United States.

Underlying the provisions of the Act for the Relief of the Poor are those features that have been identified as Poor Law principles. The overriding importance of work and workforce participation were primary. In providing support for the needy, individual and family responsibility came first. The act sets forth the qualifications for the selection of overseers of the poor, their duties and accountability. In addition, the act details the provisions to be made for various categories of poor persons and the ways in which benefits are to be funded and administered.

The Poor Laws of England and western Europe were a reaction against economic dependency and a statement that those who could earn a living were expected to do so. Those who were incapable of working were to be provided for, either by relatives if possible, or by the local community. But those who were able to work, should. A primary concern with the work effort has dominated U.S. social policy throughout the years.

At the end of the twentieth century, the influence of the Poor Laws on the American response to need has become stronger than at any time since the colonial period. The legislation originally devised to deal with the upheavals of the shift from feudalism to an industrial society is providing a base for social welfare as we move from an industrial to a service economy.

THE

STATUTES AT LARGE,

From The

Thirty-ninth Year of Q. Elizabeth,

TO THE

Twelfth Year of K. Charles II. inclusive.

To which is prefixed,

TABLE containing the TITLES of all the STATUTES during that Period.

VOL. VII.

DANBY PICKERING, of Gray's Inn, Esq;

Reader of the Law Lecture to that Honourable Society.

Edited by Joseph Bentham, CAMBRIDGE, Printer to the University; Charles Bathurst, at the Cross-Keys, opposite St. Dunstan's Church in Fleet-Street, London 1763.

CUM PRIVILEGIO.

An Act for the Relief of the Poor, 43 Elizabeth, 1601

Be it enacted by the authority of this present parliament, That the church-wardens of every parish, and four, three or two substantial householders there, as shall be thought meet, having respect to the proportion and greatness of the same parish and parishes, to be nominated yearly in *Easter* Week, or within one month after *Easter*, under the hand and seal of two or more justices of the peace in the same county, whereof one to be of the *quorum*, dwelling in or near the same parish or division where the same parish doth lie, shall be called overseers of the poor of the same parish: and they, or the greater part of them, shall take order from time to time, by and with the consent of two or more such justices of peace as is aforesaid, for setting to work the children of all such whose parents shall not by the said church-wardens and overseers, or the greater part of them, be thought able to keep and maintain their children; and also for setting to work all such persons, married or unmarried, having no means to maintain them, and use no ordinary and daily trade of life to get their living by: and also to raise weekly or otherwise (by taxation of every inhabitant, parson, vicar and other, and of every occupier of lands, houses, tithes impropriate, propriations of tithes, coal-mines, or saleable underwoods in the said parish, in such competent sum and sums of money as they shall think fit) a convenient stock of flax, hemp, wool, thread, iron and other necessary ware and stuff, to set the poor on work: and also competent sums of money for and towards the necessary relief of the lame, impotent, old, blind, and such other among them, being poor and not able to work, and also for the putting out of such children to be apprentices....

***

III. And be it also enacted, That if the said justices of peace do perceive, that the inhabitants of any parish are not able to levy among themselves sufficient sums of money for the purposes aforesaid; That then the said two justices shall and may tax, rate and assess as aforesaid, any other of other parishes, or out of any parish, within the hundred where the said parish is, to pay such sum and sums of money to the church-wardens and overseers of the said poor parish for the said purposes, as the said justices shall think fit, according to the intent of this law: (2) and if the said hundred shall not be thought to the said justices able and fit to relieve the said several parishes not able to provide for themselves as aforesaid; Then the justices of peace at their general quarter-sessions, or the greater number of them, shall rate and assess as aforesaid, any other of other parishes, or out of any parish, within the said county for the purposes aforesaid, as in their discretion shall seem fit.

***

IV. And that it shall be lawful, as well for the present as subsequent church-wardens and overseers, or any of them by warrant from any two such justices of peace, as is aforesaid, to levy as well the said sums of money, and all arrearages, of every one that shall refuse to contribute according as they shall be assessed, by distress and sale of the offender's goods, as the sums of money or stock shall be behind upon any account to be made as aforesaid, rendering to the parties the overplus; (2) and in defect of such distress, it shall be lawful for any such two justices of the peace to commit him or them to the common gaol of the county, there to remain without bail or mainprize until payment of the said sum, arrearages and stock: (3) and the said justices of peace, or any one of them, to send to the house of correction or common gaol, such as shall not employ themselves to work, being appointed thereunto, as aforesaid: (4) and also any such two justices of peace to commit to the said prison every one of the said church-wardens and overseers which shall refuse to account, there to remain without bail or mainprize until he have made a true account, and satisfied and paid so much as upon the said account shall be remaining in his hands.

***

V. And be it further enacted, That it shall be lawful for the said church-wardens and overseers, or the greater part of them, by the assent of any two justices of the peace aforesaid, to bind any such children, as aforesaid, to be apprentices, where they shall see convenient, till such man-child shall come to the age of four and twenty years, and such woman-child to the age of one and twenty years, or the time of her marriage; the same to be as effectual to all purposes, as if such child were of full age, and by indenture of covenant bound him or her self. (2) And to the intent that necessary places of habitation may more conveniently be provided for such poor impotent people; (3) be it enacted by the authority aforesaid, That it shall and may be lawful for the said church-wardens and overseers, or the greater part of them by the leave of the lord or lords of the manor, whereof any waste or common within their parish is or shall be parcel, and upon agreement before with him or them made in writing, under the hands and seals of the said lord or lords, or otherwise, according to any order to be set down by the justices of peace of the said county at their general quarter-sessions, or the greater part of them, by like leave and agreement of the said lord or lords in writing under his or their hands and seals, to erect, build, and set up in fit and convenient places of habitation in such waste or common, at the general charges of the parish, or otherwise of the hundred or county, as aforesaid, to be taxed, rated and gathered in manner before expressed, convenient houses of dwelling for the said impotent poor; (4) and also to place inmates, or more families than one in one cottage or house; one act made in the one and thirtieth year of her Majesty's reign, intituled, *an act against the erecting and maintaining of cottages,* or anything therein contained to the contrary notwithstanding: (5) which cottages and places for inmates shall not at any time after be used or employed to or for any other habitation, but only for impotent and poor of the same parish, that shall be there placed from time to time by the church-wardens and overseers of the poor of the same parish, or the most part of them, upon the pains and forfeitures contained in the said former act made in the said one and thirtieth year of her Majesty's reign.

***

VII. And be it further enacted, That the father and grandfather, and the mother and grandmother, and the children of very poor, old, blind, lame and impotent person, or other poor person not able to work, being of a sufficient ability, shall, at their own charges, relieve and maintain every such poor person in that manner, and according to that rate, as by the justices of peace of that county where such sufficient persons dwell, or the greater number of them, at their general quarter-sessions shall be assessed; (2) upon pain that every one of them shall forfeit twenty shillings for every month which they shall fail therein.

***

VIII. And be it further enacted, That the mayors, baliffs, or other head officers of every town and place corporate and city within this realm, being justice or justices of peace, shall have the same authority by virtue of this act, within the limits and precincts of their jurisdictions, as well out of sessions, as at their sessions, if they hold any, as is herein limited, prescribed and appointed to justices to the peace of the county, or any two or more of them, or to the justices of peace in their quarter-sessions, to do and execute for all the uses and purposes in this act prescribed, and no other justices of peace to enter or meddle there: (2) and that every alderman of the city of *London* within his ward, shall and may do and execute in every respect so much as is appointed and allowed by this act to be done and executed by one or two justices of peace of any county within this realm.

***

X. And further be it enacted by the authority aforesaid, That if in any place within this realm there happen to be hereafter no such nomination of overseers yearly, as if before appointed, That then every justice of peace of the county, dwelling within the division where such default of nomination shall happen, and every mayor, alderman and head officer of city, town or place corporate where such default shall happen, shall lose and forfeit for every such default five pounds, to be employed towards the relief of the poor of the said parish or place corporate, and to be levied, as aforesaid, of their goods, by warrant from the general sessions of the peace of the said county, or of the same city, town or place corporate, if they keep sessions.

***

XI. And be it also enacted by the authority aforesaid, That all penalties and forfeitures beforementioned in this act to be forfeited by any person or persons, shall go and be employed to the use of the poor of the same parish, and towards a stock and habitation for them, and other necessary uses and relief, as before in this act are mentioned and expressed; (2) and shall be levied by the said church-wardens and overseers, or one of them, by warrant from any two such justices of peace, or mayor, alderman, or head officer of city, town or place corporate respectively within their several limits, by distress and sale thereof, as aforesaid; (3) or in defect thereof, it shall be lawful for any two such justices of peace, and the said alderman and head officers within their several limits, to commit the offender to the said prison, there to remain without bail or mainprize till the said forfeitures shall be satisfied and paid.

***

XII. And be it further enacted by the authority aforesaid, That the justices of peace of every county or place corporate, or the more part of them, in their general sessions to be holden next after the feast of *Easter* next, and so yearly as often as they shall think meet, shall rate every parish to such a weekly sum of money as they shall think convenient; (2) so as no parish be rated above the sum of six-pence, nor under the sum of a halfpeny, weekly to be paid, and so as the total sum of such taxation of the parishes in every county amount not above the rate of two-pence for every parish within the said county; (3) which sums so taxed shall be yearly assessed by the agreement of the parishioners within themselves, or in default thereof, by the church-wardens and petty constables of the same parish, or the more part of them: or in default of their agreement, by the order of such justice or justices of peace as shall dwell in the same parish or (if none be there dwelling) in the parts next adjoining.

***

XV. And be it further enacted, That all the surplusage of money which shall be remaining in the said stock of any county, shall by discretion of the more part of the justices of peace in their quarter-sessions, be ordered, distributed and bestowed for the relief of the poor hospitals of that county, and of those that shall sustain losses by fire, water, the sea or other casualties, and to such other charitable purposes, for the relief of the poor, as to the more part of the said justices of peace shall seem convenient.

***

XVI. And be it further enacted, That if any treasurer elected shall willfully refuse to take upon him the said office of treasureship, or refuse to distribute and give relief, or to account, according to such form as shall be appointed by the more part of the said justices of peace; That then it shall be lawful for the justices of peace in their quarter-sessions, or in their default, for the justices of assize at their assizes to be holden in the same county, to fine the same treasurer by their discretion; (2) the same fine not to be under three pounds, and to be levied by sale of his goods, and to be prosecuted by any two of the said justices of peace whom they shall authorize. (3) Provided always, That this act shall not take effect until the feast of *Easter* next.

***

XVII. And be it enacted, That the statute made in the nine and thirtieth year of her Majesty's reign, intituled, *An act for the relief of the poor*, shall continue and stand in force until the feast of *Easter* next; (2) and that all taxations heretofore imposed and not paid, nor that shall be paid before the said feast of *Easter* next, and that all taxes hereafter before the said feast to be taxed by virtue of the said former act, which shall not be paid before the said feast of *Easter*, shall and may after the said feast of *Easter* be levied by the overseers and other persons in this act respectively appointed to levy taxations, by distress, and by such warrant in every respect, as if they had been taxed and imposed by virtue of this act, and were not paid....

Notes

1. U.S. Bureau of Labor Statistics, *Worker Displacement, 1995–97*. August 19, 1998.

2

The Colonial Period: 1647–1776

The earliest white settlers of New England came to North America to establish the ideal religious community, "a city upon a hill," that would provide an example for European reform. Yet, as soon as they arrived, they were confronted with a set of realities that forced them to adapt their ways. A radically different ecology, complex relationships with Native Americans, and different economic and demographic realities forced them to tailor the institutions they had brought from England—including the Poor Laws—to these new realities.

As early as 1647, at the first session of its colonial legislature, Rhode Island announced the Elizabethan Poor Law principles that stressed, most importantly, public responsibility for relief for the poor who could not work, and work for the able-bodied:

> It is agreed and ordered by this present Assembly, that each towne shall provide carefully for the relief of the poor, to maintain the impotent, and to employ the able, and shall appoint an overseer for the same purpose. Sec. 43 Eliz. 2[1]

Needy widows and their children would receive aid but were expected to help with their own support by working. Those judged able to work and those who had worked in the past were expected to support themselves through work. They were not generally eligible for public aid even though they might be poor, despite working.

Considering the severe economic and physical privations of the early settlers, it is not surprising that public responsibility for relief should have been buttressed by those other principles of English Poor Law: local responsibility, family responsibility, and the residency requirement of legal settlement. These principles had been evolving in England and western Europe for some 200 years and had been codified in 1601 in the most famous of all pieces of poor-relief legislation, An Act for the Relief of the Poor, 43 Elizabeth.[2]

The principle of local responsibility made public aid the domain of small units of government. Family responsibility originally denoted the legal obligation of support that adults had for their minor children and grandchildren and for their aged parents. Settlement, added in 1662, made a designated period of residence a requirement for the receipt of assistance. Settlement—the fact that only residents of a particular community were entitled to aid—was a response to the new economic realities of early modern Britain. Population growth had combined with new commercial opportunities to push a large share of the rural population off the land. Although the emergence of textile and mining industries offered new opportunities, the supply of labor outstripped the new demand. The ultimate effect was the creation of a large class of mobile labor—vagabonds, beggars, and tramps—who were no longer tied to a particular locality. These sturdy vagabonds, the beggars, and the unemployed poor, whose numbers and potential for civil disorder loomed frighteningly large, were people caught in the middle of forces beyond their control. They were people in need; and the Poor Laws, in providing public relief, were designed to meet—and control—their needs.

The terms upon which relief was offered reflected much more than the interests of the poor. Parliament was subject to conflicting pressures. The owners of large farms wanted to ensure the availability of local, low-cost, seasonal workers; the emerging industrialists needed to encourage the migration of factory labor; town officials wanted to minimize the need to levy taxes to support the homeless. The decision of Parliament to make local settlement an eligibility condition for relief reflected the power of the landed gentry. In supporting this interest the government provided an incentive for labor to remain on the farms—the risk of leaving was clear. At the same time, they were able to satisfy the towns' concern for minimizing local costs. Furthermore, by limiting the mobility of the poor, government could respond to the interest of landowners and of industrialists in maintaining law and order.

In accordance with the Act of Settlement of 1662, newcomers could be returned to their place of legal residence even though there was no actual application for assistance.

> That it shall and may be lawful upon complaint made by the churchwardens or overseers of the Poor of any Parish ... for any two Justices of the Peace ... where any Person or Persons are likely to be chargeable to the Parish shall come to inhabit ... to remove and convey such Person or Persons to such Parish where he or they were last legally settled....[3]

By 1795, power had shifted. There had been marked industrialization during the eighteenth century. As urban centers grew and immigration increased, the Poor Laws were amended. Efforts to control relief costs were more urgent. Behavioral restrictions on relief recipients increased, and punishment, including whipping for not working, became more widespread. Residency requirements were made stiffer, but the penalties for vagrancy eased. A passport system was introduced, permitting increased mobility of labor between communities. The changes represented the victory of industry and commerce over agriculture.

The Poor Laws in the Colonies

Although the long evolution of the Poor Laws in England served both as a hindrance and an aid to the process of commercial development, that evolution was always contingent on the availability of masses of workers. The climate of the

American colonies was strikingly different. There was no persistent unemployment problem; no mass of employables had been pushed off the land; no industries existed to pull workers into towns; no pool of workers awaited hiring. Initially there was neither an economic reason nor a law-and-order reason to reduce mobility; and, in fact, since land was freely taken, economic interest—societal and individual—might have encouraged movement. The rationale for the adoption of the Poor Laws rested on other grounds.

In the main, those colonists who were potential recipients of relief were the poor who were largely incapable of self-support: the ill, the disabled, the elderly, orphans, and widows with young children. Widows and their children made up a large percentage of the poor—as high as half in some towns.[4]

Frequent wars, in part a response by Native Americans to the invasion of their land by the settlers; recurring epidemics of smallpox, dysentery, measles, and yellow fever; major uncontrollable fires; high childbirth mortality rates; the hazards of fishing and the consequent loss of life at sea—all gave rise to economic need. These risks to which the colonists were subject were ones for which all held common concern. The colonists were small bands of individuals joined together in enterprises whose success depended upon the contribution and well-being of each. The smallness of their numbers made it possible to keep friendly, public watch over individual misfortunes. Their isolation made this public watch over community affairs a matter of individual self-interest. The Poor Laws ensured individual and public protection. Those settled colonists known to be in need through no fault of their own could be helped with cash relief in their own homes or in the homes of neighbors. Relief for people in home—that is, family—settings was well regarded because of the order and stability such settings promised for the community as a whole.

In seventeenth-century New England, the modern boundaries between "public" and "private" and "church" and "state" would have made little sense. Community leaders sought to ensure that sinful behavior was suppressed, including "idleness" which in an agricultural society could threaten everyone's well-being. At first, there was no voluntary sector to respond to people's troubles. The Scots Charitable Society was established in Boston in 1657.[5] In 1713, the Friends Almshouse was established in Philadelphia to provide relief for poor Quakers.[6] In 1724, the Boston Episcopal Society was formed,[7] and in 1767, the Society of House Carpenters was organized in New York.[8]

These societies were an early representation of the variety of religious and ethnic groups resulting from an increasing flow of immigrants, as well as a representation of the commercial interests of the colonists. But as might be expected, the resources of these societies were very limited. Other resources were similarly hindered. The church, a helpful force in England, was too poor—and too congregationally fragmented—to take on very much in the colonies. Thus, in many respects, the Poor Laws seemed a rational approach to a severe problem. The laws offered some support to the disabled, but they also served as a deterrent to the able-bodied who might consider not working. The specific provisions regarding settlement and family responsibility limited the number of inhabitants for whose relief the town might be called upon to accept responsibility.

In a situation of such economic scarcity and of such threatening welfare measures, the family (and its structure) was a central force for maintaining economic, social, and political stability. Even at the close of the seventeenth century, 90 percent of the colonists were farmers, and their farms were isolated, small, and poorly equipped. For the most part, these farming families had to supply their own food, clothing, and equipment, as well as their own education, entertainment, and health care. Family governance was hierarchical—generally with the husband in command. Women were not entitled to vote, had little part in governance, and lived in patriarchal families. Indeed, even their clothing was designed to show their sexual subordination.[9] Within this structure, all persons made valued contributions. Men and boys cleared fields, farmed, cut wood, and trapped. Women and girls spun thread, engaged in weaving, turned cloth into clothes, and took responsibility for myriad internal household chores. Men and women together worked to produce and to improve whatever implements, utensils, furniture, and weapons were needed for self-sufficiency. Since large families were a necessity, childbearing was viewed as a productive contribution to the family economy. If the husband were killed or disabled, the wife moved naturally into the family and economic role he had held. In English colonies, more than in Spanish or Portuguese colonies, women in the colonial period could—and did—hold property, run small businesses, and work for wages.[10]

During the eighteenth century, even as the colonies became more firmly established and the colonists benefited from improved technology, expanding commercial activities and shipbuilding, and increased trade with the native population, home manufactures continued to flourish. Their pursuit was increasingly encouraged by official efforts to maintain colonial independence and to ward off the economic stringencies of trade restrictions and embargoes imposed as disputes between the colonies and London grew in intensity. Improvements in the spinning wheel—particularly after 1765,* when the invention of the spinning jenny made it possible for a person to spin eight to ten yarns simultaneously—made possible some home production for market sale. With men continuing to concentrate on farming, the newly oriented home manufacturing fell largely to women. In effect, women—and children—began to expand a function that had long been theirs, and did so in their own homes so that their work was easily integrated into family life. Contemporary dependence upon, and respect for, women's work is demonstrated in a number of occurrences. In 1750, Boston opened a group of spinning schools for female children. In 1751, the Society for Encouraging Industry and Employing the Poor was founded to promote the manufacture of woolen cloth and to employ "our own women and children who are now in great measure idle."[11] The Massachusetts Province Laws of 1753–1754 supported the manufacturing of linen, again with the employment of women and children in mind:

> The number of poor is greatly increased ... and many persons, especially women and children, are destitute of employment and in danger of becoming a public charge.[12]

---

*Interestingly, 1765 was also the year in which the English Parliament passed the Stamp Act, that major stimulus to conflict between the colonists and England.

The colonies welcomed home manufacturing and the employment it provided. Poor rates could be lessened, and employment could be offered to women and children who might otherwise be "useless, if not burdensome, to society."[13] Shortages resulting from the gathering revolutionary storm could be diminished.

The dire language of the Poor Laws and of subsequent legislation designed to ensure their rigorous administration rested on cultural as well as economic factors. The popularity of spinning schools and the enthusiastic attendance at and participation in spinning bees sponsored by New England townships in the years preceding the Revolutionary War suggest the extent to which the essential isolation of the colonists had "produced a home-bred, home-living, and a home-loving people—a people who found both their employment and their pleasure in their own and their near neighbor's home."[14] This internalization of pleasure in work would later be labeled "the work ethic." A fuller explanation of the meaning and operation of the Poor Laws must take account of the moral underpinnings provided by Puritan Calvinism.

The New England colonists had emigrated to escape religious persecution and to seek freedom to worship in accordance with their own religious beliefs. The result was a unity of church and "state" peculiarly suited to New World conditions. The stark need for labor in New England required that the colonists operate with regard for the common store of wealth—that is, for profit in their joint enterprise—but they also operated out of religious necessity with regard for individual, private control of resources. With individual status and economic reward a manifestation of predestined grace, the Puritan work ethic was a conceptually useful tool for minimizing what was publicly, communally available to maximize individual and family wealth and well-being. Although poverty could not be equated with unworthiness, it could suggest—especially if public relief was necessary—a character and moral flaw that dared not be pampered for the common welfare and for the individual's state of grace. Giving, within reason, was encouraged; but charity reflected a concern for the salvation of the rich—the stewards of God's wealth—more than a concern for the poor. Despite the family's usefulness, the impetus to maximize individual and family well-being did not center on the individual as a family member or on the individual family as a unit. When a family was in trouble, the concern was to save its potentially productive members. Hence, there developed such social welfare measures as farming out, indenture, and apprenticeship, which provided a family structure for governance and a means for productivity.

Poor Law provisions for public aid took no cognizance of the family as a social entity to be helped. Indeed, the provisions for relief established categories of individuals—the young, the old, the disabled, and the able-bodied. By implication the family consisted of a number of individuals living together for the purpose of ensuring self-support and, by extension, avoiding the necessity for support by taxpayers. Hindsight would suggest that the term "family responsibility" is a misinterpretation of Poor Law intent; for the laws designated relative, rather than family, responsibility for support. Such designation was perhaps quite purposeful at a time when financial independence, worthiness, and divine reward were perceived as facets of individually achieved success. In this context, the family that could not maintain financial independence was not simply unsuccessful but actually dangerous, both economically and morally. Such families could not by example, precept, or education be expected to prepare the young for adult, independent living. The colonists, therefore, provided for the binding out of children as apprentices for "better educateing of youth in honest and profitable trades and manufactures, as also to avoyd sloath and idleness wherewith such young children are easily corrupted"[15] and required that in addition to a trade, children learn to "read and understand the principles of religion & the capitall lawes of this country."[16] These were preventive measures designed to protect children from the contagion of parental failures.

Unattached, neglected, or dependent children could be placed with persons willing to take responsibility for their care and who would educate and train them for a useful calling. Persons assuming such responsibility for children were expected to recoup their expenses from the child's work. Thus, indenture and apprenticeship were preventions against the danger of pauperism and ensured that children were immediately and potentially profitable to themselves and to the community.

Apprenticeship reflected colonial society's concern with the home life, the work life, and the Christian life of the child. Ideally, each child would grow up "under some orderly family government"[17] that provided support and an opportunity for learning both for economic and religious salvation. When the natural family did not provide these essentials, apprenticeship to a contracted family was an alternative that often eased the burden on the public treasury.

> If after warning and admonition given by any of the Deputies; or Selectmen, unto such Parents or Masters, they shall still remain negligent in their duty, in any the particulars aforementioned, whereby Children or Servants may be in danger to grow Barberous, Rude or Stubborn, and so prove Pests instead of Blessings to the Country; That then a fine of ten shillings shall be levied on the Goods of such negligent Parent or Master, to the Towns use, except extreme poverty call for mitigation of the said fine.
>
> And if in three months after that, there be no due care taken ... then a fine of twenty shillings to be levied....
>
> And Lastly, if in three months after that, there be no due Reformation of the said neglect, then the said Selectmen with the help of two Magistrates, shall take such children and servants from them, and place them with some Masters for year, (boyes till they come to twenty-one, and girls eighteen years of age) which will more strictly educate and govern them according to the rules of this Order.[18]

Apprenticeship was used for economy and for control. New England colonies varied in practice, but all reacted to the economic hardships of the wars with the native population and the increase in the number of poor families by looking toward an expansion in indenture and apprenticeship for job training, religious training, and education. The emphasis for Native American children, apprenticed to the English, was particularly on Christian education and the imposition of European religious beliefs on the native population.[19]

The practice of indenturing the children of the poor did not always occur without protest. When the British government sent a large group of Palatine German refugees to Manhattan in 1710, Governor Robert Hunter issued an order to apprentice the children to families in faraway Westchester, Long Island, and Rhode Island, to keep them off public support. The parents, despite illness and destitution, protested the separation and loss.[20]

Children of poor parents—both in and out of the almshouse—were subject to bonding and indenture. Complaints about cruel treatment and lack of appropriate education and job training increased as the eighteenth century progressed.[21]

The counterparts of the systems of indenture and apprenticeship for children were the systems of indenture contracting or farming out for adults. In accordance with colonial welfare legislation, overseers of the poor were empowered "to take effectual care that ... persons of able body living within the same town or precincts thereof (not having estates otherwise to maintain themselves) do not live idly or misspend their time loitering, but that they be brought up or employed in some honest calling, which may be profitable unto themselves and the public."[22]

To the end that individuals be profitable to themselves and to the common wealth, indenture contracts enforced labor by sentencing potential paupers to servitude, sometimes to a master of their own choosing and sometimes to an assigned master. Under farming out, the adult poor could be turned over to the bidder willing to contract, at the lowest charge to the community, to take on the care of paupers and to put them to work. Such care might permit the individual to remain home. Assistance to the elderly, under this formulation, was quite flexible. It ranged from care in a private home for those who were feeble all the way to assistance in finding employment if the older person were capable of working.[23]

By the middle of the eighteenth century, cities began to build almshouses to replace individual homes for those poor who were either very old, disabled, or seriously ill. As demand for help rose, cash relief and noninstitutional help became harder to obtain. Urban poverty and unemployment increasingly meant commitment to a privately owned workhouse, a publicly owned house of correction, a poor farm, or an almshouse where care or "proper" punishment and hard labor could more easily be administered. The first almshouse was established in Rensselaerswyck, New York, in 1657. Plymouth ordered the construction of an almshouse in 1658, and Boston did the same two years later.

The early development of workhouses and almshouses—welfare mechanisms that were both sophisticated and expensive—was a response to the rapid population growth experienced by the colonies and of the increased financing ability to be found in some colonies. Occasionally, where towns could not afford such institutions, private philanthropists made contributions to the public effort.[24]

The popularity of indenture as a means of dealing with dependency was indicative of the transition to a "free" labor system in which employers were free to hire and fire as they saw fit and workers had to find a "buyer" for their labor. The new mobility of the population in the late seventeenth and early eighteenth centuries placed strains on all forms of established authority. Community leaders could not regulate people as they moved in and out of town. Even Colonial authorities were challenged to cope with a hard-to-follow population of floating laborers. The "binding" of labor to a particular authority was one means of slowing this mobility and the social disorder it might breed.

Colonial welfare legislation stressed the provision of indoor relief; that is, care offered in homes other than one's own or in institutions. Nevertheless, the seasonally unemployed might benefit from tax remissions, and the overseers of the poor could legally provide outdoor relief—money payments to persons permitted to remain in their own homes because their poverty resulted from physical disability, widowhood, or old age. Taxes were collected for the latter purpose. Frequent wars coupled with postwar recessions created increased demands for help. In crises, private philanthropy supported the practice of outdoor relief by the provision of such items as blankets and stockings. During the severe winter of 1761–1762, the Quakers in Philadelphia distributed fuel stamps—"tickets of recommendation"—to be redeemed for wood.[25]

Even worthiness had its limits. The stigma of poverty was not reserved for the underserving. In 1718, a statute of the Province of Pennsylvania made it obligatory that every person receiving public relief "upon the shoulder of the right sleeve … in open and visible manner, wear … a large Roman P. together with the first letter of the name of the county, city or place whereof such poor person is an inhabitant, cut either in red or blue cloth, as by the overseers of the poor, it shall be directed and appointed."[26] In New York, relief recipients were required to wear badges enscribed with the large letters "N.Y."[27]

The coercive work features of the Poor Laws and the meagerness of relief provisions were indirectly, as well as directly, deterring. Not only did the laws spell out the kinds of care that might be made available to those who applied, but they also directed the overseers to seek out those whose situations or ways of living portended financial burden for the community. Direct deterrence was enhanced by the Poor Law principle of family responsibility requiring that "the father and grandfather and the mother and grandmother and the children of every poor, old, blind, lame, and impotent person, or other poor person not able to work … shall at their own charges relieve and maintain every such poor person as the justices of the peace … shall order and direct."[28] The overt demand that relatives support each other in time of need was covertly strengthened by the general awareness of the alternatives.

The Poor Laws were designed to protect those who held legal claim to settlement in particular localities. They offered protection against strangers who threatened the stability—namely, the morality and physical safety—of a society singularly concerned with order and wary of new ways and different cultures. In regard to strangers, the Poor Laws demonstrated most clearly their law-and-order nature. The requirement of settlement for public assistance—for example, forty days in New York, three months in Massachusetts, a year in North Carolina—clarified the absence of local responsibility for outsiders.

As the eighteenth century went on, residency requirements became even stricter. In New York, for example, the time needed to establish settlement rose to a year and the annual rental value required more than doubled, increasing from five pounds to twelve pounds a year.[29] Beyond that, "warning out" the practice of expelling "strangers" became more common. Strangers were carefully screened. In the 1690s, as in the 1990s, the newcomer was suspect and major efforts were made to

(A) The Manager's Apartment   (B) The House of Employment

The Bettering House. This is a view of the House of Employment, the Almshouse, and the Pennsylvania Hospital, which were built in 1766–1767 in Philadelphia. The three buildings comprised a complex devoted to the problems of the poor. The Manager's apartment strategically separated the workhouse from the poorhouse. (Letters added for identification.)

The Historical Society of Pennsylvania

reduce the potential costs of support for immigrants. Those few who could ensure their financial independence and future contribution to the community were permitted to remain and to acquire settlement. More frequently they were escorted beyond local geographical jurisdictions.

The low numbers of the reported poor in the early years of the eighteenth century are deceptive. They did not usually include people receiving temporary relief—and there were many in winter. Nor did they include the "near poor" and those needy but ineligible people, displaced Indians and nonresidents who were poor but excluded from aid. Even with the small number who received help, the cost of aid made up a large part of the total budget and sometimes even exceeded total tax receipts.[30] The colonists were concerned with the threat to economic survival posed

(C) The Almshouse   (D) The Pennsylvania Hospital

by possible drains on the public treasury resulting from the potentially poor and sick outsider. This fear often outweighed the value of labor skills the stranger might bring.

Additional evidence that the protection of society, rather than the care of the poor, dictated the writing of the colonial Poor Laws is offered by the fact that the laws contain no expression of concern for the poor beyond the concise statements of provision for their care. The laws do, however, make explicit the rights and duties of the overseers of the poor and spell out in detail methods for selecting and appointing overseers, their taxing powers, their responsibilities, their accountability—as well as the penalties to which they were subject if they performed improperly. The laws indicate that the tasks of the overseers were considered onerous. In Pennsylvania, for example, the overseers were appointed to a one-year term of office but, on penalty of having to serve a second year or pay a heavy fine, were required to set forth the names of their successors.[31]

Conquest, Expansion, and Population Growth: Native Americans, Immigration, and Slavery

In New England, the township became the unit of colonial Poor Law administration, and, as might be expected, the major foci of administrative practice implementing welfare legislation were work and religion. Although they were adapted to local conditions and to variations of religious tenets, colonies outside of New England also adopted the poor-relief system of England.

The colonists, whether Anglican as in Virginia, Puritan as in Massachusetts Bay, or Catholic as in Maryland, were English in their political and social heritage.* The English character of these colonial enterprises was enhanced by the fact that they were essentially private enterprises. All were financed through private capital raised by such investment organizations as the London and Massachusetts Bay companies or, as in the case of Maryland, by individual landowners ready to risk their own fortunes. In either instance, royal support was given in the form of charters or land grants. Colonization was a reflection of England's longtime process of democratization, industrialization, and commercialization forged within the military and political struggles of older powers. Along with that came a view of the resident population as uncivilized, barbarous, and consequently without rights to their land or even their lives. Their success derived from a combination of patriotism, profit seeking, religious fervor, and belief in the superiority of English culture.

The newcomers to America were not just settlers; they were conquerors. The English and the Europeans attacked and conquered the resident population in many ways, both direct and indirect. Combat played a major role. Guns, armor, horses, ships, and strong forts were all factors in the conquest of the native population. The forced resettlement of Native Americans was common. Native Americans were pushed from their communities. Despite royal decrees of protection and endless promises of security, they were marched westward, leaving the most valuable and useful land to the victors.

The weakening of the native population through the introduction of firearms, alcohol, and new and fatal diseases was another aspect of the story. Europeans—the Spanish in Florida and the Southeast, the English in New England—brought diseases that took a heavy toll on the native population. Smallpox, measles, and mumps arrived with the Europeans and frequently decimated the indigenous population.

Even the introduction of "friendly" trade played a part. Native hunters and traders were frequently cheated and robbed. More than that, the competition for the goods to be acquired, the lure of alcohol, English tools, cloth, and guns, led to destructive intratribal warfare.

The end result of colonization was to dispossess the Native Americans from their land and from their government. Many were killed; some were enslaved. Those

---

*The Dutch settled New Amsterdam in 1609 and set up a church system of poor relief. By 1664, however, New Amsterdam came under English rule, and with its new English name, New York's relief efforts were changed to a public, Poor Law, system.[32]

remaining lost sovereignty and ownership of their property through conquest, through trading, and by way of negotiated treaties.[33]

The process of establishing colonies was not, however, an easy task for the newcomers. The colonists shared a common experience of hardship and scarcity in America. The severity of the New England winter, the "horrid snow" described by Cotton Mather,[34] was counterpart to the unexpected, unbearable heat that brought death to one-half of the Virginia settlers during their first summer in America. Captain John Smith, a leader of the Virginia Company, wrote, "Nothing can be expected thence, but by labor."[35] In the South, as in the North, the Poor Laws constituted a reasonable response to a situation in which financial disaster and death seemed imminent and which, in fact, did produce social and physical disabilities.

The intent of the original colonists to settle permanently in the New World was strengthened by the rapid addition of new settlers and new settlements. The English revolution that led to the overthrow of King Charles I in 1649, the establishment of the Puritan Commonwealth, and the restoration of the monarchy in 1660 spurred emigration, especially of those who were seeking freedom and purity of religion. The emigrants to New England were of all classes of English society and consisted of whole families and individuals ready to establish homes and families in the new country.

The Restoration, and the emigration of Puritans it sparked, foreshadowed the dominance of Puritanism in colonial America. Later, French Huguenots and Scot Calvinists emigrated to Carolina as a result of religious persecution and trade restrictions. The possibilities for religious and political freedom and for economic stability brought additional settlers—Welsh, Jews, Swiss—and the colonial population soared. By 1640, more than 27,000 Englishmen were scattered through Massachusetts, Connecticut, Rhode Island, New Hampshire, Maine, Maryland, and Virginia. In 1690, there were 200,000 inhabitants; by 1710, there were 350,000; and in 1760, 1.5 million people lived in the thirteen colonies, representing many parts of Europe and Africa. The numbers of Africans grew from the original twenty brought in 1619 to 16,700 in 1690; 44,900 in 1710; and 325,000—22 percent of the population—in 1760.[36]

European population growth in the New England colonies was controlled by the factors that led to their founding. The colonists were bound by a common set of religious and ethical motivations and, for the most part, had underwritten the expenses of their passage and of supplies through the purchase of shares in a joint enterprise. The New England colonies, despite official ties to England, were essentially independent and used their independence to accept and reject immigrants on the basis of religious beliefs and potential for economic self-sufficiency. A predominantly free labor system developed.

A different pattern evolved in the South, reflecting the different base for settlement and the economic base that developed. Virginia was settled solely as a commercial enterprise. A large number of its settlers were working-class Englishmen who paid for their passage through indenture contracts, a four- to seven-year commitment to work. In 1625, documents show that 487 people—almost

40 percent of Virginia's population—were indentured servants.[37] The South grew as it developed tobacco and prospered with the establishment of plantations. Some Native Americans were enslaved for service in Florida and Georgia; some were traded in the Caribbean islands. The first blacks to come to Virginia came as indentured workers. As servants and as freemen, they had much in common with their white counterparts in terms of status and problems. By 1661, however, slavery was institutionalized, and by the eighteenth century slaves were the base of the labor force.

With New England practicing selectivity in the acceptance of immigrants and the South relying increasingly upon the use of slave labor, immigrants were quite naturally funneled into the Middle Atlantic colonies. Large numbers were unable to pay for their passage and came under contracts of indenture. It is estimated that two-thirds of the settlers in Pennsylvania came under such provisions of servitude. German and Scotch–Irish families who arrived during the eighteenth century came as "redemptioners," people who had made a down payment on passage and who used the promise of work as collateral for the balance. Indentured servitude resulted for those who defaulted.

By the close of the colonial period, British North America had prospered. When Georgia was declared a crown colony in 1752, all thirteen American colonies were formal geographic and political entities. Between 1700 and 1776, a great deal of cultural, social, political, and economic change occurred. Population growth had occurred not only by natural increase but also by way of immigration. The resulting intermingling of various religious, ethnic, and racial groups lent a cosmopolitan air to such identifiable urban centers—all busy ports of trade and entry—as Boston, New York, Philadelphia, and Baltimore. The regular plying of sailing vessels between North America and the European continent brought not only economic returns to all but also, to the upper classes, the latest turns of fashion in dress, belles lettres, and social amenities. The establishment of active legal and political ties between the separate colonies and London and the frequent exchange of representatives this required lent additional encouragement to the maintenance of continental social graces, at the same time that the separation of the American and European continents presented the colonies with opportunity for self-government.

The colonies took an early interest in expanding schooling because their leaders believed that the population should be able to read the *Bible*. A college—soon to be called Harvard—was established at Cambridge in the Massachusetts Bay Colony as early as 1636. By the mid-eighteenth century, William and Mary, Yale, the University of Pennsylvania, Princeton, Brown, Rutgers, and Dartmouth were all established. The ties of communication among the colonies were fostered by a flood of printed materials and broadsides and the practice of letter writing. Newspapers proliferated, and the instituting of a mail service, carried regularly by 1732 between Massachusetts and Virginia, was additionally encouraging to writings of all kinds.

The many changes that marked colonial life at the end of the period led to sharpened class differences. By the time of the American Revolution, many colonials were already third- and fourth-generation Americans. By the middle of the eighteenth century, a new elite, based on commercial success, had come to dominate both Northern and Southern society. Beneath this class existed a group, again largely Protestant, of middle-class farmers, artisans, small tradesmen, and laborers in the fledgling manufacturing establishments. Alongside and below this group existed another large group—non-English, frequently non-Protestant, sometimes nonwhite, and almost always without property.

Different bases for prosperity for the North and South resulted in different views of people and of their need for social welfare programs. New England and the Middle Atlantic colonies shifted from sole dependence upon farming and fishing to home manufacturing, shipbuilding, and trading. These colonies were sufficiently urbanized to add the risks of a market economy to those of colonial frontier life. Problems of dependency increased with the influx of poorly paid immigrants and with the growing numbers of disabled men resulting from the wars of European powers in America and from wars with Indians. Particularly stark were the needs of elderly and disabled blacks, who had been freed as a way of avoiding their care in old age.[38] These factors, combined with an economy of scarcity and with a growing population, made the enforcement of the Poor Laws attractive to town governments.

In the South, the introduction of slavery and the continued reliance upon a farm economy prevented the development of a large, free, laboring class. If the large plantation holdings of Virginia contrasted sharply with small tenant farmer holdings of Carolina, the two were, nevertheless, joined in a feudal system that created a degree of economic security. The milder climate, the availability of fertile land, and the mixture of less austere religious sects fostered a warmer, more favorable view of the free man. As early as 1728, William Byrd, a prosperous and educated gentleman who served on a commission set up to run the dividing line between Virginia and North Carolina, observed the way of life in North Carolina:

> Surely there is no place in the World where the inhabitants live with less labour . . . by the great felicity of the Climate, the easiness of raising Provisions. . . . Indian Corn is of so great increase, that a little Pains will Subsist a very large Family with Bread, and then they may have meat without any pains at all, by the Help of the Low Grounds, and the great Variety of Mast that grows on the Highland.[39]

While such ease of living might have led to laziness and an "Aversion to Labor," as Byrd feared, the fact was that it also led to greater tolerance of human misfortune—again for free men. By the middle of the seventeenth century, Virginia had adopted both the Poor Laws and apprenticeship to provide for poor free men: white and black, orphans, illegitimate children, and mulatto children of white women. The original resident population—Native Americans—were for the most part excluded from these arrangements. There was no recognition of any social welfare needs that Native Americans, slaves, or indentured servants might have, and it was left to these groups to develop their own informal self-help mechanisms.

BOSTON, April 20*th*, 1773.

SIR,

THE efforts made by the legiſlative of this province in their laſt ſeſſions to free themſelves from ſlavery, gave us, who are in that deplorable ſtate, a high degree of ſatisfacton. We expect great things from men who have made ſuch a noble ſtand againſt the deſigns of their *fellow-men* to emſlave them. We cannot but wiſh and hope Sir, that you will have the ſame grand object, we mean civil and religious liberty, in view in your next ſeſſion. The divine ſpirit of *freedom*, ſeems to fire every humane breaſt on this continent, except ſuch as are bribed to aſſiſt in executing the execrable plan.

WE are very ſenſible that it would be highly detrimental to our preſent maſters, if we were allowed to demand all that off *right* belongs to us for paſt ſervices ; this we diſclaim. Even the *Spaniards*, who have not thoſe ſublime ideas of freedom that Engliſh men have, are conſcious that they have no right to all the ſervices of their fellowmen, we mean the *Africans*, whom they have purchaſed with their money ; therefore they allow them one day in a week to work for themſelve, to enable them to earn money to purchaſe the reſidue of their time, which they have a right to demand in ſuch portions as they are able to pay for (a due appraizment of their ſervices being firſt made, which always ſtands at the purchaſe money.) We do not pretend to dictate to you Sir, or to the honorable Aſſembly, of which you are a member : We acknowledge our obligations to you for what you have already done, but as the people of this province ſeem to be actuated by the principles of equity and juſtice, we cannot but expect your houſe will again take our deplorable caſe into ſerious conſideration, and give us that ample relief which, *as men*, we have a natural right to.

BUT ſince the wiſe and righteous governor of the univerſe, has permitted our fellow men to make us ſlaves, we bow in ſubmiſſion to him, and determine to behave in ſuch a manner, as that we may have reaſon to expect the divine approbation of, and aſſiſtance in, our peaceable and lawful attempts to gain our freedom.

WE are willing to ſubmit to ſuch regulations and laws, as may be made relative to us, until we leave the province, which we determine to do as ſoon as we can from our joynt labours procure money to transport ourſelves to ſome part of the coaſt of *Africa*, where we propoſe a ſettlement. We are very deſirous that you ſhould have inſtructions relative to us, from your town, therefore we pray you to communicate this letter to them, and aſk this favor for us.

In behalf of our fellow ſlaves in this province, And by order of their Committee.

PETER BESTES,
SAMBO FREEMAN,
FELIX HOLBROOK,
CHESTER JOIE.

For the REPRESENTATIVE of the town of *Thompſon*

Broadside Letter from Four Slaves, Asking to Return to Africa, 1773, Boston
The New York Historical Society, New York City

Challenge to the Poor Laws

The Poor Laws were a product of a society that used the legal system to constrain a dynamic population during a time of social change. In America, as in England, efforts at control increasingly were at odds with the speed of change. For many in authority, the response to the Poor Laws' ineffectiveness was to make them more restrictive. Yet, for others, the alternative conclusion was that the entire effort to help the poor was counterproductive. For them, the effort to help the poor would make poverty more attractive. Anticipating later generations of "welfare reformers," Benjamin Franklin argued for the abolition of the Poor Laws. As Franklin saw it, the cause of poverty was of the individual's own making; the social system worked well, the growing wealth of the upper classes was justified, and an assumption of social responsibility would inevitably aggravate the problem by fostering further dependency.

> I have sometimes doubted whether the laws peculiar to England, which *compel the rich to maintain the poor*, have not given the latter a dependence, that very much lessens the care of providing against the wants of old age.
>
> I have heard it remarked that the *poor* in *Protestant* countries, on the continent of Europe, are generally more industrious than those of *Popish* countries. May not the more numerous foundations in the latter for relief of the poor have some effect towards rendering them less provident? To relieve the misfortunes of our fellow creatures is concurring with the Deity; it is godlike; but, if we provide encouragement for laziness, and supports for folly, may we not be fighting against the order of God and Nature, which perhaps has appointed want and misery as the proper punishments for, and cautions against, as well as necessary consequences of, idleness and extravagance? ...
>
> However, as matters now stand with us, care and industry seem absolutely necessary to our well-being. They should therefore have every encouragement we can invent, and not one motive to diligence be subtracted; and the support of the poor should not be by maintaining them in idleness, but by employing them in some kind of labour suited to their abilities of body, as I am informed begins to be of late the practice in many parts of England, where workhouses are erected for that purpose. If these were general, I should think the poor would be more careful, and work voluntarily to lay up something for themselves against a rainy day, rather than run the risk of being obliged to work at the pleasure of others for a bare subsistence, and that too under confinement.[40]

Franklin's view highlights a belief in the responsibility of people for their own welfare in an ordered society that rewards industry and thrift. Franklin rationalized poverty and inequality in income distribution:

> Much malignant censure have some writers bestowed upon the rich for their luxury and expensive living, while the poor are starving, & c.; not considering that what the rich expend, the labouring poor receive in payment for their labour. It may seem a paradox if I should assert, that our labouring poor do in every year receive *the whole revenue of the nation;* I mean not only the public revenue, but also the revenue or clear income of all private estates, or a sum equivalent to the whole....

In support of this position I reason thus. The rich do not work for one another. Their habitations, furniture, cloathing, carriages, food, ornaments, and every-
thing in short, that they or their families use and consume, is the work or produce of
the labouring poor, who are, and must be continually, paid for their labour in producing the same.[41]

Some went so far as to argue that, for the market economy to function, individual earned income should never be supplemented. This would compel labor force
participation and ensure a supply of workers willing to perform menial, difficult, and
unpleasant tasks.

It seems to be a law of nature, that the poor should be to a certain degree improvident, that there may always be some to fulfil the most servile, the most sordid, and
the most ignoble offices in the community. The stock of human happiness is
thereby much increased, whilst the more delicate are not only relieved from
drudgery, and freed from those occasional employments which would make them
miserable, but are left at liberty, without interruption, to pursue those callings
which are suited to their various dispositions, and most useful to the state. As for
the lowest of the poor, by custom they are reconciled to the meanest occupations,
to the most laborious works, and to the most hazardous pursuits; whilst the hope
of their reward makes them cheerful in the midst of all their dangers and their
toils.[42]

By the end of the Colonial era, the poor and unfortunate were no longer seen as
an organic part of the social order. Often they were literally "outsiders"; addressing
their problems was no longer the responsibility of respectable citizens. As Americans
began to consider the meaning of "liberty" and "equality" in their political thought,
these words meant little for the poor—"free" and enslaved—whose well-being was increasingly marginalized.

Veterans: A Special Class

Welfare measures for veterans, however, differed from those applied to the general
population. The English "Acte for Reliefes of Souldiours" of 1593 set the tone for
colonial legislation. It had recognized both the special services and special needs of
disabled soldiers and sailors and provided relief for this group *as a right* on the basis
of disability, with payments scaled to military pay. As early as 1624, the colony of Virginia passed similar legislation. In 1636, Plymouth Colony declared that any soldier
injured in defense of the colony was entitled to support.

That in case necessity require to send forces abroad, and there be not volunteers sufficient offered for the service, then it be lawfull for the Governor and [his] assistants
to presse [men into service] in his Majesties name...provided that if any that shall
goe returne mamed & hurt, he shall be mayntayned completely by the Colony
duringe his life.[43]

Other colonies followed the precedent, and by 1777 all but Connecticut had made special provisions for veterans. The entitlement to these provisions did not carry the onus of pauperism and, equally important for the future, carried no requirement of local settlement. Colonies, not towns, were responsible for financing and administration. The pattern was so well accepted that the Continental Congress in 1776 adopted a report of the Committee on Disabled Soldiers and Sailors recommending to the states pensions for invalid and disabled veterans.[44] This special attention to veterans, and in some instances to other persons identified as the "unsettled poor," broke ground for eventual contributions by the states and by the federal government to social welfare.

Of more immediate interest, however, is the logic by which the colonies selected veterans for preferential treatment—domiciliary care, pensions for elderly and disabled veterans, and outdoor relief for widows and children of veterans. This selection for special treatment was, after all, consistent with the colonial view of humanity. Veterans had participated in an unusual kind of work. In doing so, they had made an extraordinary contribution to the commonwealth at the same time that they had made visible their own individual worth. Certainly such work and such worthiness were not to be deterred in a society where their special services were so badly needed.

Discussion Questions

1. To what extent is Benjamin Franklin's criticism of the Poor Laws similar to the rationale for restrictions on public assistance today?
2. What might contemporary child welfare workers learn from the experience in apprenticing out orphans and other dependent children during the seventeenth and eighteenth centuries?
3. American slavery emerged before Americans had come to embrace democratic ideals. By the time of the American Revolution, what ethical challenges would the expansion of these ideals cause?

DOCUMENTS: The Colonial Period

The two documents selected to illustrate the thrust of social welfare during the colonial era are *An Act of Supplement to the Acts Referring to the Poor* (Massachusetts Bay, 1692) and the contract of indenture entitled *The Binding of Moses Love* (1747). The documents illustrate legislative and judicial actions taken to achieve societal stability and individual well-being. For society and the individual, the actions were protective and preventive and called upon a family unit to perform the functions of a social welfare institution. Where no natural family existed to support members in need, a substitute family was found. The number of colonists was very small and the community itself functioned in part as an extended family.

An Act of Supplement expresses governmental concern for all the inhabitants of Massachusetts Bay. The Act explicitly states that its provisions extend beyond those who receive public alms; its intent is to ensure that all single persons under the age of twenty-one years live "under some orderly family government." The significance of such an assurance stems from the nature of a society in which government and family mirrored one another in their responsibility to fulfill God's plan that people work and produce. Both were organized in a fixed hierarchical structure to which each individual had been called to an assigned place. Fulfilling one's responsibility within the structure was a duty to oneself, to the community, to God. Family government was protective of the individual who might be tempted to fall away from that responsibility and protective of the community that would bear the cost of such a fall. The family model reinforced the Puritan values of work and frugality as religious observances. In a society of scarcity, such a joining of religious and secular concerns was particularly felicitous.

The Binding of Moses Love demonstrates that the colonists observed the human condition with a certain solicitousness. Moses Love was bound out when only two years and eight months of age. The indenture contract is concerned with avoiding future dependency of the children of the poor. Support, education, and employability are the long-term goals. All in all, the rights and responsibilities bestowed on Moses Love's master are those of a parent. As indicated in the *Act of Supplement,* this discharge of governmental and familial responsibilities toward children generally endeavored "to defend them from any wrongs or injuries" and to prepare them for economic self-sufficiency in adulthood.

The ACTS AND RESOLVES, Public and Private

of the

PROVINCE OF THE MASSACHUSETTS BAY:

CHAPTER 14.

AN ACT OF SUPPLEMENT TO THE ACTS REFERRING TO THE

POOR,

&c.

1692–3, ch. 28, & 7

Whereas the law for the binding out poor children apprentice is misconstrued by some to extend only to such children whose parents receive almes; for explanation whereof—

Be it declared and enacted by His Excellency the Governour, Council and Representatives in General Court assembled, and by the authority of the same,

Selectmen or overseers of the poor to bind out poor children, &c.;

[Sect. 1.] That the selectmen or overseers of the poor in any town or district within this province, or the greater part of them, shall take, order and are hereby impowred from time to time, by and with the assent of two justices of the peace, to set to work, or bind out apprentice, as they shall think convenient, all such children whose parents shall, by the selectmen or overseers of the poor, or the greater part of them, be thought unable to maintain them, (whither they receive almes or are chargeable to the place or not), so as that they be not sessed to publick taxes or assessments, for the province or town charges; male children till they come to the age of twenty-one years, and females till they come to the age of eighteen years, or time of marriage: which shall be as good and effectual in law, to all intents and purposes, as if any such child were of full age, and by indenture of covenant had bound him or herself, or that their parents were consenting there [un] to: provision therein to be made for the instructing of children so bound out, to read and write, as they may be capable. And the select-

—to inquire into the usage of such as they bind out.

men or overseers of the poor shall inquire into the usage of children bound out by themselves or their predecessors, and endeavour to defend them from any wrongs or injuries.

And, for the better preventing of idleness, and loose or disorderly living,—

Be it further declared and enacted by the authority aforesaid,

Selectmen or overseers of the poor to set to

[Sect. 2.] That the selectmen or overseers of the poor, or the greater part of them, be and are further impowred, by and with the assent of two justices of the peace, to set to work all such persons, married or unmarried, able of body, having no means to maintain them, that live idlely and use or exercise no ordinary and daily lawful trade or business to get their living by. And no single person of either sex, under

No single person under twenty-one years old to live out of family government.

the age of twenty-one years, shall be suffered to live at their own hand, but under some orderly family government; nor shall any woman of ill fame, married or unmarried, be suffered to receive or entertain lodgers in her house. And the selectmen or overseers of the poor, constables and tythingmen, are hereby ordered to see to the due observance of this act, and to complain and inform against any transgressions thereof to one or more justices of the peace, or the court of general sessions of the peace, who are hereby respectively required and impowred, upon due conviction of the offender or offenders for living idely or disorderly, contrary to the true intent of this act, to commit or send such offenders to the house of correction or work-house, there to remain and be kept to labour, until they be discharged by order of the court of general sessions of the peace, unless such person or persons so complained of shall give reasonable caution or assurance, to the satisfaction of the justice or court, that they will reform: provided, this act shall not be construed to extend to hinder any single woman of good repute from the exercise of any lawful trade or imployment, for a livelihood, whereto she shall have the allowance and approbation of the selectmen or overseers of the poor, or the greater part of them, any law, usage or custom to the contrary notwithstanding: *provided,*—

[Sect. 3.] This act shall continue in force for the space of three years next coming, and to the end of the session of the general assembly next after. *[Passed November 27; published December 3.]*

Volume I. Boston: Wright & Potter, Printers to the State, 1869.

***

THE BINDING OF MOSES LOVE, 1747

This Indenture made the fourteenth day of September Anno domini 1747 by and between Luke Lincoln, Benja Tuckor, Nathall Goodspeed and John Whittemor all of Leicester in the Covnty of Worcester select-men of sd Leicester on the one part, Matthew Scott of Leicester aforesaid yeoman on the other part Wittnesseth that the above sd selectmen by virtue of the Law of this province them Impowering & with the assent of two of the Majesties Justices of the Peace for sd Covnty hereto annexed to put and bind out to the sd Matthew Scott & to his heirs Execvtors & Adminrs as an Apprentice Moses Love a Minor aged two years and Eeight Months with him & them to Live and dwell with as an apprentice dureing the term of Eighteen years and fovr months (viz) untill he shall arrive to the age of twenty-one years—he being a poor Child & his parants not being well able to support it. Dureing all which the sd apprentice his sd Master his heirs Execvtors & Adminrs shall faithfully serve at such Lawfull imployment & labovr as he shall from time to time Dureing sd term be Capable of doing and performing & not absent himself from his or their ser-vice without Leave & In all things behave himself as a good & faithful apprentice ought to do and the sd Matthew Scott for himself his heirs Execvtors & Adminrs do Couenant promise and grant to & with the above sd selectmen of Leicester aforsaid & with their successors in the office or trust of selectmen of Leicester aforsaid & Inbehalf of sd apprentice that he the sd Matthew Scott his heirs Execvtors & Adminrss shall & will Dureing the term aforsd find and provide for the sd apprentice sufficient Cloathing meet drink Warshing and Lodging both in Sickness & in health & that he will teach him or cavse him to be tavght to read & write & siffer fiting his degree if he be Capable of Learning and at the Expiration of the term to Dismiss him with two suits of apparril one to be fitt for Lords days In Wittness where of the partyes to these present Indentvrs haue Interchangably set their hands & seals the day and year first written. Signed sealed & Delivered in presence of

    Steward Southgate
    John Brown

Luke Lincoln (seal)
Benja Tucker (seal)
John Whittemor (seal)

New England Historical and Genealogical Register, Boston, 1880, Vol. XXXIV, p. 311.

Notes

1. *Records of the Colony of Rhode Island and Providence Plantations in New England*, Vol. 1, 1636–1663 (Providence: A. Crawford Greene and Brother, State Printers, 1856), 1:184–185.
2. Danby Pickering, ed., *The Statutes at Large from the Thirty-Ninth Year of Q. Elizabeth to the Twelfth Year of K. Charles II, Inclusive* (Cambridge: Bentham & Bathhurst, 1763), 7:30–37.
3. The Act of Settlement of 1662 may be found in *An Acte for the Better Reliefe of the Poor of the Kingdom. The Statutes at Large from the First Year of King James the First to the Tenth Year of the Reign of King William the Third* (London: Basket, Woodfall and Straham, 1763), 3:243–247.
4. William P. Quigley, "Work or Starve: Regulation of the Poor in Colonial America," *University of San Francisco Law Review.* Fall 1996, p. 41.
5. Katherine D. Hardwick, *As Long As Charity Shall Be a Virtue* (Boston: 1964), p. 5. *John Adams* by Page Smith. Copyright © 1962 by Page Smith. Reprinted by permission of Doubleday & Company, Inc., 1964.
6. Thomas J. Scharf and Westcott Thompson, *History of Philadelphia, 1609–1884* (Philadelphia: L. H. Everts, 1884), pp. 1452–1453.
7. Hardwick, op. cit., p. 8.

8. Raymond A. Mohl, "Poverty in Early America, A Reappraisal: The Case of Eighteenth-Century New York," *New York History*, Vol. L, January 1969, p. 19.

9. David Hackett Fischer, "Growing Old in America," in Jill Quadagno, *Aging, the Individual and Society: Readings in Social Gerontology* (New York: St. Martin's Press, 1980), pp. 34–45.

10. Carl N. Degler, *At Odds: Women and the Family in America from the Revolution to the Present* (Oxford: Oxford University Press, 1980), p. 194.

11. Edith Abbott, *Women in Industry: A Study in American Economic History* (New York: D. Appleton, 1909), p. 21.

12. *Province Laws* (Mass.), 1753–1754.

13. Quoted in Abbott, op. cit., p. 33.

14. Milton T. Rolla, *Household Manufacturers in the United States, 1640–1860* (Chicago: University of Chicago Press, 1919), p. 6.

15. Act XXVII, October, 1646, in *The Statutes at Large: Being a Collection of All the Laws of Virginia from the First Session of the Legislature in the Year 1619*, William Waller Henning, ed. (New York: Piser and Russell, Printer, 1846), 1:336.

16. *Records of the Governor and Company of the Massachusetts Bay in New England*, Vol. 2, 1624–1629, 2:6.

17. *Acts and Resolves, An Act of Supplement to the Acts Referring to the Poor*, Province of the Massachusetts Bay, 1703.

18. William Brigam, ed., *The Compact with the Charter and Laws of the Colony of New Plymouth, and so on*. This contains *The Book the General Laws of the Inhabitants of the Jurisdiction of New Plymouth, and so on*. To be found in Marcus Wilson Jernegan, *Labouring and Dependent Classes in Colonial America, 1607–1783* (Chicago: University of Chicago Press, 1931), pp. 98–99.

19. Jernegan, op. cit., pp. 102, 233–234.

20. Robert E. Cray Jr., *Paupers and Poor Relief in New York City and Its Rural Environs, 1790–1830* (Philadelphia: Temple University Press, 1988), pp. 42–43.

21. For details of legislation and parental reactions, see Cray, op. cit., pp. 79–81, and Jernegan, op. cit., pp. 84–115.

22. *Acts and Resolves*, Province of Massachusetts Bay, 1692.

23. For a discussion of the application of the Poor Laws to the elderly in colonial society, see Jill S. Quadagno, "Policies toward the Elderly," in David Van Tassel and Peter N. Stearns, eds., *Old Age in a Bureaucratic Society* (Westport, Conn.: Greenwood Press, 1986), pp. 129–136.

24. Scharf and Thompson, op. cit., p. 1450.

25. Gary B. Nash, "Poverty and Poor Relief in Pre-Revolutionary Philadelphia," *William and Mary Quarterly*, Third Series, Vol. 33, January 1976, pp. 12–13.

26. *Statutes at Large of Pennsylvania, 1682–1801*, Vol. 3, chap. 238.

27. Mohl, op. cit., pp. 8–9.

28. *Statutes at Large of Pennsylvania*, 1682–1801, Vol. 2, chap. 154.

29. Raymond A. Mohl, *Poverty in New York: 1783–1825* (New York: Oxford University Press, 1971), p. 57.

30. Ibid., p. 42.

31. *Statutes at Large of Pennsylvania*, op. cit., Vol. 3, pp. 76–77.

32. David M. Schneider, *The History of Public Welfare in New York State, 1609–1866* (Chicago: University of Chicago Press, 1938), pp. 9–44.

33. For an excellent review of this process, see Francis Jennings, *The Invasion of America: Indians, Colonialism, and the Cant of Conquest* (New York: W. W. Norton, 1976), and *500 Nations*, television production by Jack Leustig, Vol. 3, "Clash of Cultures," and Vol. 5, "Cauldrons of War" (Burbank, Calif.: TIG Productions, 1994).

34. Cotton Mather, A Letter [An Horrid Snow], 10d. X m. 1717. To be found in Norman Foerster, ed., *American Poetry and Prose* (New York: Houghton Mifflin, 1934), pp. 79–80.

35. Jeannette P. Nichols and Roy F. Nichols, *The Growth of American Democracy* (New York: Appleton-Century, 1939), p. 16.

36. U.S. Department of Commerce, Bureau of the Census, *Historical Statistics of the United States: Colonial Times to 1957* (Washington, D.C.: Government Printing Office, 1960), p. 756.

37. Merrill Jensen, ed., *English Historical Documents: American Colonial Documents to 1776* (London: Eyre and Spottiswoode, 1955), p. 480.

38. Schneider, op. cit., p. 87.

39. William Byrd, "The History of the Dividing Line" [Life in North Carolina], [March] 25 [1728]. To be found in Foerster, op. cit., pp. 87–92.

40. Letter to Richard Jackson, May 5, 1753, in *The Writings of Benjamin Franklin*, Vol. 3, 1750–1759, Albert Henry Smith, ed. (New York Macmillan, 1907), pp. 134–135, 137.

41. Ibid., "Essay on the Labouring Poor," Vol. 5, pp. 124–125.

42. Joseph Townsend, "A Dissertation on the Poor Laws By a Well-Wisher to Mankind," in *A Select Collection of Scarce and Valuable Economic Tracts*, J. R. McCulloch, ed. (London: Lord Overstone, 1859), pp. 397–449.

43. U.S. Congress, House Committee Print No. 4, *Medical Care of Veterans*, 90th Cong., 1st sess., April 17, 1967, p. 21. Printed for the use of the Committee on Veterans' Affairs.

44. Ibid., p. 28.

3

The Pre-Civil War Period: 1777–1860

The American Revolution was a political watershed for the United States. American society was in the middle of a social and economic transition that had begun by the end of the seventeenth century and would not be completed until the Civil War. The result of that process—the emergence of a liberal, capitalist society—would touch every part of American culture, from the work people did to the beliefs they held to the institutions they developed. It held particular significance for the poor and needy. Where in the eighteenth century, the poor were seen as an organic part of society; in the nineteenth century, they were increasingly cast as *deviants*—outside the "normal" social order and in need of "reform." During the years from the Revolution to the Civil War, well-off Americans alternated between an optimistic hope that they could improve the poor by changing their environment and a pessimistic fear that only by containing the poor could they prevent them from pulling down the entire society. Whether in hope or fear, the actions of the powerful during these years did little to address the fundamental problems faced by the poor or the social and economic inequality that were at the root of these problems. Yet, one piece of unfinished business left over from the Revolution could not be avoided. The issue of slavery and race—the foundation of American prosperity and the greatest challenge to its political creed—slowly but inexorably overshadowed all other issues. Ultimately the nation was forced to endure its greatest tragedy so that the "peculiar institution" of American slavery could be eliminated.

With their declaration of independence from England and the beginning of the Revolutionary War, the now independent states established a loose confederation for governance. But the Articles of Confederation gave the new central government little power. James Madison, predicting its failure, cited the confederation as "nothing more than a treaty of amity of commerce and of alliance between...independent and Sovereign States."[1] It was too weak to deal with the political and economic crises of the early postwar years.

The Articles of Confederation had promised a "perpetual union" of the states, but post-Revolutionary War disorganization and disruption highlighted the need for even closer and more effective political ties. The Federal Convention, which sat at Philadelphia from May 25 to September 17, 1787, drafted a new constitution for the states, and the United States government began to function on March 4, 1789, with the commencement of the first presidential term.

The Declaration of Independence, the Articles of Confederation, and the Constitution were based on limited democratic ideals. In the colonies, only adult, white men of property were eligible to vote. Slowly, by the middle of the nineteenth century, the property requirements were eliminated. Most white men could vote, but women, blacks, and Native Americans could not. Tribes were ruled to be "domestic dependent nations" and Native Americans were thus considered aliens, not citizens. Even the census—the official enumeration of the population of the United States, which was the basis for the number of representatives of each state in Congress—counted slaves as three-fifths of a person; Native Americans did not count at all.[2]

The Preamble of the Constitution of the United States cited the promotion of "the general welfare" as one of the reasons for forming the new government. Nevertheless, there was no mention of social welfare concerns among the carefully enumerated powers of the government's legislative body, the Congress. Since the Constitution specifically reserved to the states such powers as had not been delegated to the central government, providing for the social welfare needs of families and individuals remained the responsibility of the separate states, much as it had been the responsibility of the separate colonies. A "public–private partnership" of local government and charities was the typical means of addressing want and deprivation.

The years between the ratification of the Constitution of the United States and the outbreak of the Civil War were years of major political, economic, and social changes. These changes were accompanied by, and in turn furthered, rapid population growth, enormous geographical expansion, mechanization of farm and factory, and heated political and ideological struggles. By the turn of the century, the country had already lost the mark of a colonial dependent; by 1860, the country could be considered a world power. The pre-Civil War period was one of excitement and turmoil, expansion and recession, opportunity and frustration, exhilaration and discontent. It was a period of rapid change necessarily affecting the welfare of individuals and families.

Population growth, composition, and movement make up one aspect of the pre-Civil War transformation.[3] In 1790, families had many children and the ordinary life span was quite short. One result was that less than 2 percent of the population was 65 or older and the median age was only sixteen. Those who survived until old age were revered by the colonists. At public meetings the best seats were assigned to the oldest men, then the oldest women. Wealth, race, and gender counted, but age was the primary consideration.

By 1860, however, the age distribution had shifted; old age was less of a rarity and the median age of the population rose to about twenty years old. Seniority was no longer the basis for preferential seating in meeting houses, and, by the end of the century, wealth became the dominant basis of preference. Clothing styles for men reflected the shift in generational power. Wigs were replaced by hairpieces to make men look younger; jackets were cut to be narrow at the waist and broad at the shoulders, with straight backs. For women, more revealing styles came much later—not until the 1920s. Throughout the nineteenth century, the desire to hide women's bodies and demonstrate their sexual subordination prevailed over the glorification of youthful styles.[4]

The racial structure had changed too. In 1800, 19 percent of the population was nonwhite; by 1860, that percentage had dropped to about 14 percent, or 4,521,000 persons, of whom 3,954,000 were slaves. And the country had become more urban. In 1800, only 6 percent of the population lived in urban areas; by 1860, almost 20 percent did so.

The total population of the country (excluding Native Americans, who were not counted) numbered 3,929,000 in 1790, the year of the first U.S. census. By 1800, the population had risen by 34 percent to about 5,297,000, of whom 1,002,000—19 percent—were nonwhite and 322,000—6 percent—lived in urban areas. By 1830, on the eve of massive migrations, especially from Ireland and Germany, the total population stood at 12,901,000. By 1840, it reached 17,120,000; in 1850 it was 23,261,000 and in 1860, it was 31,513,000.

Population growth had been the result of several factors, including resident births and the purchase, annexation, and cession of populated territories. The most important cause of the population explosion, however, was the extraordinary wave of immigration beginning during the 1830s, when 538,381 immigrants arrived in the United States. Immigration rose to 1,427,337 during the 1840s and peaked during the 1850s with the arrival of 2,814,554 individuals. Even the Civil War did not deter migrants; 2 million immigrants arrived during the 1860s.

Of the total of 1,427,337 immigrants to the United States during the 1840s, nearly 900,000 arrived from Ireland and 400,000 from Germany. Spurred by famine in the former and political repression in the latter, immigration from these two countries continued at extremely high levels during the 1850s, when together they accounted for 87 percent of immigrants. Almost all the immigrants landed at entry points between Baltimore and Boston, and most remained in the northern section of the country, where they congregated in cities. The Irish, coming primarily from a background of peasant farming, with little education, moved into canal and railroad construction, domestic service, and the developing textile industry. The Germans were more likely to be farmers or skilled artisans and moved more quickly into steadier and better paying jobs.

Whether from Ireland or Germany, the immigrants were perceived as a threat to resident Americans. They were foreign and Catholic in an essentially Protestant country. Moreover, they came at a time of initial industrial conflict. The sudden availability of workers ready to take employment at lower than generally accepted wages and the introduction, by German immigrants especially, of radical political philosophies upset American labor and industry alike. Further, many of the immigrants arrived in need of immediate employment or emergency financial aid. The addition of newcomers to the rolls of public charges provoked opposition and agitation against them.

By the end of Washington's second term, anti-immigrant feeling was strong. The Naturalization Act of 1795 had increased the residence requirement for naturalization for free, white persons to five years from the two previously specified. Three years later, the Alien and Sedition Acts legislated fourteen years for residency, required registration of all aliens, and gave the president the power to expel any alien deemed dangerous. Although most of this legislation was repealed and residence requirements returned to the five-year level, the early years of the republic showed deep distrust of foreigners. Ethnicity as well as race played a part in the social policies of the United States from the very beginning. In the 1850s, the Know-Nothing party, built on anti-immigrant, anti-Catholic, and anti-black feelings, became a major force in many regions.[5]

Although population growth between 1790 and 1860 was most spectacular in the northern areas of the country—growth occurred in the South as well. In 1850, the population of the fifteen states (Delaware, Maryland, Virginia, North Carolina, South Carolina, Georgia, Florida, Alabama, Mississippi, Louisiana, Tennessee, Kentucky, Missouri, Arkansas, and Texas) was about 10 million, of whom 3 million were slaves. This slave population was an increase from the 1.5 million counted in 1820. During the years between 1820 and 1850, the number of free blacks had increased from 234,000 to 434,000. By 1860, the African American population stood at 4.5 million, of which 4 million were slaves. The continuing increase in the slave population was due primarily to births, since opposition to slavery had succeeded in cutting off slave trade. As early as 1774, the Continental Congress had prohibited further importation of slaves into the colonies after December 1, 1775. This prohibition was not entirely successful, and the question was again debated at the Federal Convention of 1787, where, as part of the compromises reached in forming the United States and writing the Constitution, it was agreed that the further importation of slaves would cease after January 1, 1808. Although the slave population was ignored in public and involuntary social welfare measures, its effect upon the well-being of the country, as reflected in economic and social reform activity, was enormous.

As the black and white population grew, the Native American population was devastated. Wars, diseases, broken treaties, the loss of homeland, and the destruction of the game upon which they were dependent for food and clothing all took their tolls. The Creeks, Seminoles, Cherokees, and countless other tribes were in dire trouble. Many were pushed out of the East and beyond the Mississippi to live. The reservation replaced the range, at an enormous cost in population, lifestyle, and culture for the native population.

Population growth prior to the Civil War was matched by territorial expansion. Territorial additions included the Northwest Territory secured by treaty with Great Britain in 1783, the Louisiana Purchase from France in 1803, the Florida Purchase from Spain in 1819, the Texas Annexation in 1845, the Oregon and Mexican Territories secured by treaties with Great Britain and Mexico in 1846 and 1848, respectively, and the Gadsden Purchase from Mexico in 1853. Thus, by 1860, the country's land area reached to the Pacific Ocean, and its northern and southern borders were fixed. The thirteen original states had increased to thirty-three. In 1790, the original thirteen states contained 94 percent of the total population. Only 250,000 of a total population of 4 million persons lived in the land west of the boundaries of these states. In 1860, half the population lived in trans-Appalachian regions[6] despite the heavy European immigration into the Northeast. The rapid increase in the number of states admitted to the Union was due not only to the existence of already populated centers in territories acquired by the young country, but also to the intense, deliberate development of the territories as part of the struggle between proponents and opponents of slavery.

Although the western expansion and development was encouraged on ideological grounds, political decisions concerning it were determined by economic reality. The invention of the cotton gin in 1793 had made cotton production a base of the Southern economy and slavery the most profitable form of labor. The economy of New England was shaped by the introduction of the spinning jenny and the power loom, bringing together the processes of spinning and weaving under one roof and requiring a larger scale of operation than the cottage. Cotton land in the South was held by plantation landlords who controlled extensive acreage, and a large permanent labor supply could be used profitably year-round. The textile factories of the North were smaller operations, their need for labor, more seasonal. As a group these industrialists required the availability of a large but free labor force, a group for which they need feel no responsibility during off-seasons or periods of recession.

The New England and Southern states quite naturally moved to opposing sides on questions related to territorial expansion and to the acceptance of new states into the Union. The cultivation of cotton lent itself not only to the use of slave labor but also to the creation of large plantations, essentially an enclosure system in the tradition of the English manor. Ever-larger enclosures were desired, and the search for improved climate and fertility led westward. The assumption of the South was that western lands would be needed for cotton planting and, therefore, that these lands must, as far as possible, be open to the use of slave labor. New England, with its concern for a large, readily available supply of free labor, was initially opposed to territorial expansion because of the threat such expansion represented to the retention of an adequate labor pool in New England.

Labor requirements led New England and the South—that is, the industrialists and plantation owners who controlled the economic destinies of the areas—to opposing views on other issues. The matter of land grants constituted one such issue. The federal government's policy in regard to selling public lands became increasingly flexible and generous during the pre-Civil War period. Originally, the government's policy was to sell only large tracts of land, a policy that was favorable to large landholders. In 1800 and again in 1820, the government reduced the minimum number of acres required for purchase. This policy, which encouraged small landholders, was further liberalized in 1832 with recognition of the "right of preemption," a right that permitted squatters to take possession of land without a cash down payment and to pay for it later.

The period of recession that followed the War of 1812 helped to encourage migration to the West. This migration, seemingly about to reduce the population of the Northeast at the very beginning of its era of industrial revolution, led to a conservative approach to the homestead question. As industrialization proceeded, however, and as the inflow of immigrants dissipated concern about the labor supply, the region's interest shifted to securing western lands as free lands to be purchased easily by workers who were discontented with the conditions of the factory system or by workers who were unemployed during industrial crises. The fact that the shift was pressured by the self-interest of laborers highlighted the freeman-versus-slave aspect of this North–South controversy.

The tariff question was also one that found New England and the South pitted against each other. The Northern manufacturing states were in severe competition, with Great Britain in particular, to buy their raw material—cotton—and to sell their products—textiles. Understandably, the North sought high-tariff protections against the importation of foreign-made goods. The South, on the other hand, seeking high prices for raw cotton and low prices for finished products, favored low tariffs and competition among industries, domestic and foreign. The tariff struggle continued until the outbreak of the Civil War; to the extent that it led to the Doctrine of Nullification—the right to nullification by a state of federal tariff legislation—it was a significant cause of the outbreak of hostilities.

The mechanization of cotton production in the South and the industrialization of the production of cotton goods in the New England states were the base of expansion for all sections of the country.

In 1792, the year before the invention of the cotton gin, the annual production of cotton was about 6,000 bales. In 1794, the year after the cotton gin's invention, production rose to 17,000 bales. By 1800, 73,000 bales were being produced, and by 1860, 3,841,000 bales.[7] Just as the South's production of raw cotton outstripped the country's production of all other agricultural products, New England's production of finished cotton goods outstripped the country's manufacture of all other goods. The value of cotton products, which stood at $46 million in 1840, rose to $116 million in 1860.[8] Simultaneously, the needs of these two areas spurred the development of the Middle Atlantic states, which produced farm commodities, meat and dairy products, lumber, and other necessities. In addition, the Middle Atlantic states became the shipping and banking centers for the country. Truly, the South, New England, and the Middle Atlantic states were closely joined, and the tie that bound was made of cotton. The digging of canals and building of railroads opened the West, an important factor in its own right, but additionally so in view of the way in which its resources served to strengthen the dependence of the other areas, one upon the other.

The rise of King Cotton extinguished the hope that African American slavery would die a "natural" death. At the end of the revolution, Northern whites who objected to slavery could tell themselves that it was an archaic institution that could not survive long in an independent nation. With the rise of cotton, slavery became the bedrock of the entire American economy. It would take a bloody social conflict to bring it to an end.

Labor and Economic Security

The economic realities that led the South and New England to different solutions to the questions of labor supply had inevitable consequences for the social well-being of their workers. To speak of workers in the South is to speak largely of slaves and, therefore, to speak of no public social welfare programs. Free blacks were left to help themselves. Self-help among the slaves was common but the very fact of being owned left with the owner the responsibility for maintaining his property in working order. An apologist for slavery defined it as a "system of labor which exchanges subsistence for work."[9]

> Slavery makes all work, and it insures homes, food and clothing for all. It permits no idleness, and it provides for sickness, infancy, and old age. It allows no tramping or skulking, and it knows no pauperism.[10]

Outside the plantation, there were stretches of territory cultivated by small farmers without slave labor. These "hardy yeomen" occupied areas generally not suitable to growing cotton, but quite suitable for raising cattle and for cultivating corn and wheat. As a class, they were prosperous and independent. There remained only the poor whites, also farmers, but because they were landless or owned the most worthless, worn-out land, their subsistence was most precarious. Nevertheless, they were not directly subject to the economic fluctuations created by the commercialization of agriculture.

Despite the overall picture of self-sufficiency, there were Southerners who found themselves in need. The poor whites, although generally capable of independence, were one such group. But in developing Southern towns, there were others—abandoned and orphaned children, mulattoes, freed slaves. A warmer, more accepting approach to need carried over from colonial days. In a situation of relatively little need, the approach to it was characterized by noblesse oblige.

Destitution in the North during the pre-Civil War period was more directly related to urbanization, industrialization, and the development of the factory system. In 1791, the year of Hamilton's *Report of Manufacture*, household manufacture of wool and cotton cloth was occurring in all of the states and could still be characterized as "a vast scene."[11] The first successful cotton mill, using the principle of the spinning jenny, had already been put into operation in Pawtucket, Rhode Island, and by 1809 there were sixty-two mills operating in New England, with twenty-five more in the process of construction.[12] New England had thus become the textile manufacturing center of the country. The introduction of the power loom in the factory at Waltham, Massachusetts, was the impetus for further development.

The large-scale production of cotton textiles required, first of all, the construction of factories so expensive that their costs had to be borne by absentee owner-investors. Operation of the factories required the recruitment of large numbers of workers to towns. In New England, the workers recruited during the early years of industrialization were young women from farm families living in surrounding areas. To attract these young women, the factory owners erected dormitories or saw to the development of boarding homes, where social, religious, and educational activities for workers could be planned and supervised. The combined offer of work, religion, and learning was peculiarly a New England tradition and was an enormously successful recruitment device.[13]

The growing ease with which young women were recruited for factory work paralleled the rise of commercial farming, the decline of the household manufacturing of cloth, and the transfer to the market of services formerly performed at home. The reality of large families as a liability could, for the moment, be mitigated by the fact that girls could earn wages for use in an increasingly monied society. Harriet Martineau, a traveler to the United States in 1835, reported her visit to "the corporate factory-establishment at Waltham":

> Most of the girls live in houses provided by the corporation, which accommodate from six to eight each. When sisters come to the mill, it is a common practice for them to bring their mother to keep house for them and some of their companions, in a dwelling built by their own earnings. In this case, they save enough out of their board to clothe themselves, and have their two or three dollars a week to spare. Some have thus cleared off mortgages from their fathers' farms; others have educated the hope of the family at college; and many are rapidly accumulating an independence.[14]

These young recruits were white, Protestant, and native born. Later, as immigration swelled the ranks of job seekers, they would be replaced by whole families of foreign and Catholic extraction. At that point, native-born women moved into such occupations as teaching. If financially able, they moved into a new genteel ethos of homemaking.

America's first industrial workers were not a social class; the young women who worked in factories eventually left to marry or pursue other work. By the 1830s, however, they had been replaced by a more permanent groups of workers—often immigrants—whose prospects for advancement were limited. The risks that we associate with industrialization—unemployment, disability, and displacement—became a new reality on the social landscape.[15]

The success of the textile factories fostered the development of other manufactures required for the maintenance of that industry and that industry's employees. The "factory system" was applied to other industries and spread rapidly throughout the New England and Middle Atlantic states, with the result that centers of considerable size, offering employment to males as well as females, to skilled as well as unskilled laborers, developed. Whereas 202,000 persons lived in urban centers in 1790, 6.2 million were living in cities in 1860. The growth of older cities demonstrates what was happening. For example, the census of 1790 recorded the largest urban centers as having populations numbering 25,000 to 50,000. The census of 1860 showed the largest centers to have populations numbering 500,000 to 1 million.[16] New York City's population grew from 123,000 in 1820 to 805,000 in 1860; Philadelphia's jumped from 112,000 in 1820 to 562,000 in 1860; Boston's went from 43,000 to 177,000 and Baltimore's from 62,000 to 212,000 during the same years.[17] In addition, many new cities sprang up, not only in New England and the Middle Atlantic states but in the West and the South as well.

Industrialization and urbanization led to many problems for which social welfare measures—particularly financial aid—were necessary. Mobility and wage labor increasingly became requirements for family security. With extended kinship ties frequently broken by distance and with adults away from home at work, families were more and more subject to forces beyond their control and dependent upon services supplied from outside the family unit. The hazards of the developing market economy in which families depended on wages and in which industrial competition kept wages low and employment uncertain, were aggravated by a series of economic depressions—one, 1815 to 1821; another, 1837 to 1843; still another, 1857 to 1859. Only the years 1850 to 1856 showed vigorous, sustained recovery. The long stretch between 1815 and 1859 was a difficult time for individuals and families who were not physically or psychologically free to move to the open lands and opportunities of the West. These people included immigrant families physically and financially exhausted by their journey; disabled veterans of the War of 1812, the Mexican War, and the Indian Wars; the ill and disabled; children who had been orphaned or abandoned; and older people who had no children or spouses to support them and who found themselves forced into involuntary retirement because of ill health or unemployment.

The Reform Movements

The emergence of large reform movements during the antebellum period represented a split vision of American society. On the one hand, many movements associated with the middle class saw their society as fundamentally sound, but in need of some improvement around the margins. On the other hand, other movements raised the fear that America was corrupt at its core. With the rise of evangelical Protestantism after the "second Great Awakening" of the 1820s, this conviction that Americans needed to attack sin propelled a variety of movements against alcohol, prostitution, and other forms of vice. Ultimately, this same sensibility would drive the movement to abolish slavery.

Much of the response to unemployment and inequality of income distribution took the path of "reform" activities. Such activities supported a view of the basic soundness of the economic order at the same time that they demonstrated new convictions about the potential for change of individuals and of aspects of the social structure. As early as 1827, with the formation of the Mechanics' Union Trade Association in Philadelphia, an effort was made to organize all skilled artisans. Although attempts at a combined national association failed, labor entered the depression starting in 1837 with at least five national trade unions: cordwainers, comb makers, carpenters, weavers, and printers.[18] These unions, and the workers' political parties that developed during the 1830s, demanded action in regard to a number of reform and protection issues:[19]

1. Equal and universal free education
2. The availability of public lands for settlement
3. The deprecation of child labor and apprenticeship abuses
4. Restrictions on competitive prison labor
5. Better working conditions for women
6. Establishment of a ten-hour workday without any decreases in wages
7. Governmental control of currency
8. The right to organize
9. Provision of jobs for the unemployed in public works programs

They did not demand a change in basic property relationships, but they did demand a larger share of the product of the existing economic system.

By the beginning of the Civil War, the labor movement had generally collapsed. To some extent this failure was due to the fact that labor's success in achieving a liberal land policy meant that frustrated employees could, in sufficient numbers, leave behind their reasons for discontent. Failure to unionize workers was also due to organized corporate and judicial opposition.

Whatever hardships labor suffered, the promise of a new world for common people seemed real enough. Industrialization had fostered the development of a middle class—skilled workers and artisans, merchants, owners of small manufacturing enterprises, and professional and service entrepreneurs. Similarly, westward migration had produced large numbers of small, independent landowners. It appeared to resident Americans and immigrants alike that the country's economic growth and geographic expansion were of their own making, that their own toil and adventuresomeness had produced a situation in which dreams could come true. Thus, what developed was a view of humanity as flawed but, nevertheless, as self-determining and perfectible. The colonial view of man as predestined to damnation gave way to a view of people as having the power to change, if properly led. The easing of economic pressures was accompanied, therefore, by a more optimistic view of human nature. The new age of reason meant that individuals could respond to the godliness of their own nature and could control their own destinies, including economic and social welfare.

With the election of Andrew Jackson to the presidency in 1828, Jacksonian democracy symbolized the possibility of egalitarianism and a spur to its further achievement. Reform of individuals was the process by which the achievable was to be achieved.

Areas of reform activity included the extension of suffrage, temperance, more effective poor relief, humane treatment for the insane, rehabilitation of criminals, child saving, and, of course, the drive for the abolition of slavery. A large part of the reform effort centered on free public education as a weapon in the battle for egalitarianism, for democracy. Horace Mann labeled education "the great equalizer of the conditions of men—the balance-wheel of the social machinery."[20] For Native Americans, "education and conversion usually went hand in hand," with religious conversion the dominant force.[21] Only through education could the rich and poor be brought together.

> Now surely nothing but universal education can counterwork this tendency to the domination of capital and the servility of labor.... But, if education be equably diffused, it will draw property after it by the strongest of all attractions: for such a thing never did happen, and never can happen, as that an intelligent and practical body of men should be permanently poor. Property and labor in different classes are essentially antagonistic; but property and labor in the same class are essentially fraternal.[22]

There was widespread agreement that "universal and complete" education "would do more than all things else to obliterate factitious distinctions in society." Democracy could be real if the poor could be made the equal of the rich. Education could instill the means and will to make it so.

This drive for education was left to the states for development and moved from New England to the West, where Jacksonian political democracy was most advanced. The Middle Atlantic states—New York, Pennsylvania, New Jersey, and Delaware—experienced more difficulty, but by midcentury these states had permissive statutes allowing for the establishment of schools by localities. In the South, no statewide systems of public education were in operation before the Civil War. For the country as a whole, however, an "educational consciousness" had been achieved.

The opening of the West must be credited with the rapid advance of white male suffrage.

As people went westward and formed new states, they made new constitutions. In the western country there were few great differences in wealth ... much the same state of poverty and hope. Naturally, under such conditions ... all were equally capable of bearing the responsibility of voting or governing. The new states of the days after the War of 1812, Indiana, Illinois, Alabama, and Missouri, provided white manhood suffrage though Mississippi clung to a tax provision.[23]

In the East, where urbanization was bringing large numbers of people together for effective, collective action, demands for the vote were heard. Connecticut liberalized its suffrage qualifications in 1818. Massachusetts followed in 1820. In 1821, New York legislated universal male suffrage, even for free blacks if they owned property. Other states followed and "male political democracy" became a reality.

Women did not achieve legal and political equality with men, but the reform period was the beginning of a long campaign for women's rights. In 1848, the first Women's Rights Convention was held in Seneca Falls, New York. A "Declaration of Sentiments," modeled after the Declaration of Independence, was adopted. Women demanded equal civil and political rights and began the long struggle for suffrage.

Not so clearly recognized was the effect of industrialization and urbanization upon the economic structure of the family. The technological revolution, which gained such momentum during the pre-Civil War period, spelled the beginning of a decline in farming as a chief means of support and the virtual end of the family system of manufacturing. Not only had wages, per se, become a basic means of family support, but these wages were being earned away from home. From this economic reality evolved separate worlds for men and women. All that went on outside the home—particularly in the areas of work and politics—was the world of men. For the middle class, the world of women centered in the home, the family, and the church. The pastoral letter read on July 28, 1837, from the pulpit of all Congregational churches in New England described a proper woman operating in her "proper sphere."

The appropriate duties and influence of women ... are unobtrusive and private. ... When the mild, dependent, softening influence of women upon the sternness of man's opinion is fully exercised, society feels the effects of it in a thousand forms. The power of woman is in her dependence, flowing from ... that weakness which God has given her for her protection, and which keeps her in those departments of life that form the character of individuals and of the nation.[24]

Women became involved in reform movements—temperance, suffrage, and the abolition of slavery. They moved from a concern for the rooting out of individual imperfections that would lead to unhappy family living to a demand for explicit political recognition and power, and then to larger social issues.

The American Society for the Promotion of Temperance was founded in 1826 and engaged in widespread propaganda against intemperance. The Temperance Movement involved itself in social and political activities, and by 1860 it boasted a membership of a number of formal social groups and more than a million individuals. One state (Maine) had voted for prohibition. The Temperance Movement would become more vocal and politically stronger after the Civil War, but the attention given to the problem during the prewar period was evidence of a growing concern about the relation of drinking to unemployment and to pauperism.

Spurred by the growth in corn production by the pioneer farmers of the Ohio River Valley and the burgeoning distilling industry of the East, whiskey became abundant and cheap—and whiskey drinking something of a national pastime for men, women, and children.[25] During the first three decades of the nineteenth century, annual per capita consumption increased to more than five gallons. After 1830, as a result of the Temperance Movement and of stiff federal taxation, it dropped to less than two gallons per capita.[26] Before that, however, the proliferation of unregulated taverns that encouraged drinking, particularly on the part of male laborers, aggravated perceptions of social chaos and disorder in the lower class, especially immigrants. The loss of time from work because of drunkenness on the part of the male breadwinner and the habit of spending time at the saloon on payday were real threats to family well-being. The unavailability of adequate jobs for women made them dependent upon men for the family's support. The physical abuse that often accompanied the drinking added to the urgency of temperance as "a matter of women's rights as well as a religious and humanitarian reform."[27]

During the 1830s and 1840s, thousands of local and state temperance societies were formed with the intention of regulating or prohibiting the sale of liquor. While these societies generally had women's auxiliaries appended, an independent women's gesture was made when Amelia Bloomer founded the newspaper, *The Lily*. In her first editorial, Mrs. Bloomer wrote:

> It is WOMAN that speaks through the LILY. It is upon an important subject, too, that she comes before the public to be heard. Intemperance is the great foe to her peace and happiness.[28]

Tales of victimized women, of victimized families, led Mrs. Bloomer and *The Lily* to an alliance with those more specifically focused on women's rights.

The efforts of *The Lily* were not isolated. Middle- and upper-class women, spurred by evangelical fervor and optimism, turned to a variety of moral reform movements—like the crusade against prostitution. It was not difficult to see these moral reform efforts as a thinly-veiled criticism of dominant male culture. Although only a small minority of women would move from this criticism to overt feminism, the moral reform efforts of the antebellum era are a critical stage in the emergence of a distinctive women's perspective in social welfare.

The Temperance Movement addressed itself to the economic costs of drinking and also served as a reflection of the crusading, religious spirit of the era, an era of striving for perfection and beauty as a response to the reality and harshness of a changing society. The democratic, educated, temperate, spiritual individual was the ideal; and reform activity was an acknowledgment of human perfectibility as well as a spur to the accomplishment of aspirations. For some, the reality of the larger world seemed too oppressive and they withdrew to such utopias as Brook Farm or Walden Pond or to the intellectual and metaphysical world of transcendentalism. For others, the reform of people, and of institutions that damped their progress, was cause enough for the good fight.

The assurance of opportunity and liberation to fulfill human and societal potential underlay the zeal of adherents to particular causes and comprised the moral force that brought Quakers, Transcendentalists, free blacks, activist women, and reformers of all types together in the abolitionist cause. The new religious humanitarianism, the growing democratic thrust, and the moral force surrounding black uprisings on behalf of freedom made abolition the central and urgent core of the Northern reform movement. Concurrently, in the South, the principles of Jeffersonian democracy and its apologetic approach to slavery lost out to an aggressive ideological defense. The egalitarianism and humanistic spirit of the North and West were rejected. Leadership passed from the moderate Virginians to the extremists of South Carolina, and eventually the aristocratic view representing the interests of a small group of planters prevailed. The white South united in an effort to maintain and extend slavery.

Abolitionism pulled together many strands of the reform era. An optimistic view of human nature—perfectionism—made the existence of human bondage that much more obnoxious. If the solution to the "labor" problem of the North were expanded opportunity for free labor, then the expansion of slavery into the West was intolerable. Although Southerners often chided the North for its treatment of the poor, Northerners continued to see the extension of a liberal, capitalist social order as the solution to most of the nation's ills. Ultimately, this vision could not be reconciled with the enslavement of 4 million human beings.

Institutions, Almshouses, and Paupers

For the most part, reform during the pre–Civil War period was geared to the reform of individuals—not to reform of systems—and the effort was to find an environment in which individual changes might be encouraged. The memorials written by pioneer reformer Dorothea L. Dix to encourage provisions for the construction of hospitals for the insane exemplified contemporary efforts to help people fulfill their potential through the use of specialized facilities. Institutions for the insane, for children, for the disabled, and for the poor were particularly important in this regard, since they offered attention to classified needs and surcease from worldly instability. Dix wrote about "the mischiefs which result alike from religious, social, civil, and revolutionary excitements,"[29] excitements that characterized the pre–Civil War period and that were deemed responsible for the increase in mental illness. In the same vein, society was held responsible for an increase in crime and pauperism. The economic growth, geographic expansion, and extension of political democracy that had created a world of opportunity had also created a world of change, insecurity, and temptation. A society laying claim to a belief in human perfectibility but given to the creation of environmental and human disorders must provide order—and cure—for both. Institutions were thought to do just that.

During the pre-Civil War period, thirty-two hospitals for the insane were built. The expectation that they and other specialized institutions would, or could, cure both human and societal ills was burdensome indeed. Speaking particularly of the insane, Dix said:

> To confine the insane to persons whose education and habits do not qualify them for this charge, is to condemn them to mental death....
>
> Under well-directed hospital care, *recovery is the rule—incurable* [italics in original] permanent insanity the exception....
>
> But cure alone...is not the sole object of hospital care....Of vast importance is the secure and comfortable provision for...the incurable insane. Their condition... is susceptible of amelioration, and of elevation to a state of comparative comfort and usefulness.[30]

Professional and humane treatment could cure, especially if that treatment were offered in an ordered, stable milieu, a milieu that provided the sick individual with relief from excitement and with a sense of dignity. At the least, it would ameliorate symptoms. In either case, the conviction that individuals were capable of self-perfection required that they be treated as though they might perfect themselves. The institution became the answer to the individual's ailment and, simultaneously, in its exemplification of needed reform, the answer for society's ills.

The development of specialized institutions for dependent populations often began in the private sector, but generally its advocates ultimately looked to government for financial support. Dorothea Dix's Memorial to Congress in 1848 asking that 5 million acres of public land be given to the building of institutions for the insane was a challenge to the federal government to support reform. In time, Congress passed a bill allocating 10 million acres, taking cognizance of the needs not only of the insane, but also of the blind and the deaf. President Pierce's veto in 1854 denied the federal government's responsibility for the social welfare of the country. In so doing, however, the veto upheld the historic responsibility of the states in matters of social welfare, when people could not sustain their own social well-being through self-endeavor or private charity.

> I readily and, I trust, feelingly acknowledge the duty incumbent on us all as men and citizens, and as among the highest and holiest of our duties, to provide for those who, in the mysterious order of Providence, are subject to want and to disuse of body or mind; but I can not find any authority in the Constitution for making the Federal Government the great almoner of public charity throughout the United States.... And if it were admissable...I can not avoid the belief that it would in the end be prejudicial...to the noble offices of charity....
>
> If the several States, many of which have already laid the foundation of munificent establishments of local beneficence, and nearly all of which are proceeding to establish them, shall be led to suppose...that congress is to make provision for such objects, the fountains of charity will be dried up at home....[31]

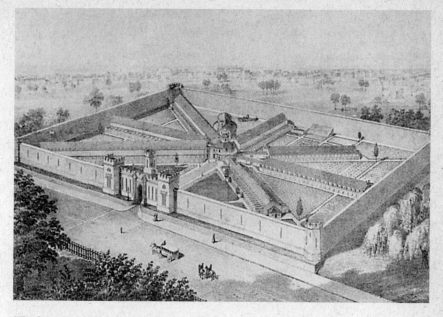

The State Penitentiary for the Eastern District of Pennsylvania
The Pennsylvania Prison Society

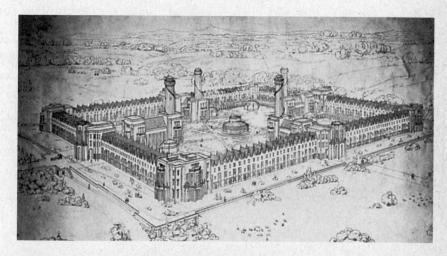

*Robert Owen's Community at New Harmony, Indiana—A Plan. The design of the East-
ern State Penitentiary and of Robert Owen's New Harmony in Indiana are remarkably
similar. Both reflected the era's belief in the value of the well-ordered environment. The
design for the New Harmony community was never realized; the penitentiary, however,
was occupied in 1829—the last inmate removed in 1971.*
The Indiana Historical Society Library

The Pierce veto reinforced the pattern of state responsibility and of private charity dominance in social welfare. Only in regard to veterans did the federal government maintain direct responsibility for a group of disabled citizens. By 1790, Congress had taken over financial support for disabled veterans, veterans' widows, and orphans of veterans. Pensions were established for those groups during the Revolutionary War and were extended without serious questioning to participants of the War of 1812, the Seminole Indian Wars, and the Mexican War of 1846–1848. Benefits to able-bodied veterans of each war were eventually granted. The pensions were small and the numbers of veterans covered were few because of the time that had elapsed between each war's end and congressional action. Nevertheless, the precedent of some benefits regardless of economic need was established. Some of the needy elderly received cash support in this form.

For most people, however, economic need continued to be viewed as an individual aberration. The view of poverty and of the plight of families in need changed very little from that of the colonial period. Welfare legislation passed by the founding states had represented the carrying over of colonial, provincial law; welfare legislation of subsequently admitted states was ideologically similar. Unemployment and sharp increases in relief roles reconfirmed the ultimate responsibility of government for the relief of individual suffering but, at the same time, fostered an expanded definition of the responsibility of relatives, one for the other. In most northeastern and north central states, grandchildren were added to the list of legally responsible relatives; in many states, brothers and sisters were added. The humane conviction that the poor were an inescapable obligation meant the provision of minimal, survival relief. But, more than ever, the view was that relief should be unnecessary and that government was obligated to minimize the cost to the taxpayer for the care of the poor. Only the legislation of the southern and western states tempered this view with any concern for the "comfort of the poor" or with legislation less restrictive than that of New England.

The more restrictive approach of the northeastern and north central states seems quite natural considering the fact that the crises in unemployment and the rise in relief expenditures were chiefly felt there. In his 1824 report on the relief and settlement of the poor, John V. N. Yates, secretary for New York State, wrote that "populous places have at all times, been burdened with a larger proportion of paupers, than places where a thin or scattered population is found."[32] At the time of the report, well over half the population of the country was still living on the Atlantic Coast. The beginning influx of immigrants, who tended to remain in eastern cities, aggravated the reaction to public outdoor relief giving, since they frequently were among the unemployed. Indeed, what appears to be an overreaction to public outdoor relief giving—New York City, for example, with a population of 203,000, had expended only $16,000 in 1830[33]—might have been a veiled stance against immigrants. Similarly, the influx of foreigners strengthened the argument that relief giving be left to benevolent societies and to the rich. The uncertainty of private charity was in itself considered a virtue, for it instilled in the newcomer that most American of all values, independence. Furthermore, private charity preserved a Puritan value—the need of the rich to give charity.

The view that individuals were responsible for their poverty did not go completely unchallenged. Thomas Paine as early as 1792 and Mathew Carey in 1833 both saw poverty as related to the malfunctioning of the economic system. Paine urged the abolition of the Poor Laws and the establishment of a system of pensions, family allowances, subsidized education, and guaranteed employment.

> By the operation of this plan, the poor laws, those instruments of civil torture, will be superseded, and wasteful expense of litigation prevented. The hearts of the humane will not be shocked by ragged and hungry children, and the persons of seventy or eighty years of age, begging for bread. The dying poor will not be dragged from place to place to breathe their last, as a reprisal of parish upon parish. Widows will have a maintenance for their children, and not be carted away, on the death of their husbands, like culprits and criminals; and children will no longer be considered as increasing the distresses of their parents. The haunts of the wretched will be known, because it will be to their advantage, and the number of petty crimes, the offspring of distress and poverty, will be lessened. *The poor, as well as the rich, will then be interested in the support of government, and the cause and apprehension of riots and tumults will cease.*[34] [italics in original]

Mathew Carey, a renowned pamphleteer on political and economic matters, responded to the charge that the poor rates and the aid of private philanthropy demoralize the poor and lead to corruption of pride in independence. His "appeal to the wealthy of the land" was written to refute "certain pernicious errors" that prevailed respecting the situation of the poor:

1. That every man, woman, and grown child, able and willing to work may find employment.
2. That the poor, by industry, prudence, and economy, may at all times support themselves comfortably, without depending on eleemosynary aid....
3. That their suffering and distresses chiefly, if not wholly arise from their idleness, their dissipation, and their extravagance.
4. That taxes for the support of the poor, and aid...by charitable individuals... are pernicious, as...they foster their idleness and improvidence, and thus produce, or at least increase, the poverty and distress they are intended to relieve.[35]

Through comparisons of average annual wages and subsistence expenses for workers in selected occupations, Carey demonstrated the inevitable gaps between income and need—the necessity for financial supplementation. He demonstrated further that only 549 paupers had been supported with outdoor relief—that most suspected form of relief—in Philadelphia in 1830, and that the aid granted had averaged 46 1/4 cents per week—less than 7 cents per day. Pointing up how many of those supported were either families with children, the disabled, or the aged, Carey argued that the poor rates and the aid of benevolent societies "far from producing the pernicious effects ascribed to them are imperiously necessary." Rather than look to the poor as the cause for the rise in poor rates, he concluded that one must look to the workings of a market economy in a society becoming increasingly dependent upon machines "for the low rate of wages is the root of mischief."

> A cause has been steadily and powerfully operating to increase the poor rates.... I mean the rapid and oppressive reduction of wages, consequent on the wonderful improvements in machinery. Manual labour succumbs in the conflict with steam and water power; and everything that supersedes the demand for that labour must increase competition, lower wages; produce distress and ... increase the poor rates.[36]

The arguments of Paine and Carey did little to improve programs for the poor. They did, however, help to prevent the abolition of public relief despite the powerful forces aligned against it. The retention of the Poor Laws was rationalized on the basis of humaneness, even by some who believed them to be unnecessary. So distinguished a leader as Josiah Quincy—congressman, mayor of Boston, and chairman of a state committee to study the pauper laws—considered the Poor Laws "too deeply rivetted in the affections, or the moral sentiment of our people to be loosened by theories, however plausible."[37]

The physically disabled aside, public and private sources generally agreed that the causes of poverty were to be found in individual character flaws and in organizations that encouraged and promoted dependency. New York's Society for the Prevention of Pauperism was founded "to investigate and as far as possible to remove the causes of mendicity; to devise plans for ameliorating the condition of the poor and wretched, and to secure their successful operation."[38] The society successfully petitioned the Corporation of the City to appoint five members of that body to the Board of Managers of the society, thus encouraging the board "to calculate upon municipal countenance and aid." The first annual report (1818) of the society listed the causes of poverty as ignorance, idleness, intemperance, and imprudence (especially to marry). The report listed the following as tending to aggravate the causes of poverty: lotteries, pawnbrokers, houses of ill fame, and the numerous charitable institutions. Although public relief and private benevolence did admittedly relieve some misery and suffering, the long view of the society, as expressed by its president and its chairman of the Committee to Prepare a Report on the Subject of Pauperism, was that giving and taking help encouraged the tendency to idleness and extravagance on the part of the poor, relaxed their need for industry, and eventually diminished that "wholesome anxiety to provide for the wants of a distant day, which alone can save ... from a state of absolute dependence, and from becoming a burden to the community."[39]

New York City had already erected "buildings for eleemosynary purposes, at an expense of half a million dollars, and ... [was being called upon] for the annual distribution of 90,000 dollars more."[40] Failure to find a solution to the burgeoning expense of supporting an increasing number of paupers was frightening:

> Without a radical change in the principles upon which public alms have been usually distributed, helplessness and poverty would continue to multiply—demands for relief

would become more and more importunate, the numerical difference between those who are able to bestow charity and those who sue for it, would gradually diminish, until the present system must fall under its own irresistible pressure, prostrating, perhaps, in its ruin, some of the pillars of the social order.[41]

The agreement that pauperism could be prevented and cured only by erecting "barriers against the encroachments of moral degeneracy" fostered a review of contemporary relief practices and a search for barriers that could, at one and the same time, save the poor from pauperism and the rich from taxation. Voluntary organizations, such as the New York Society for the Prevention of Pauperism and the Associations for Improving the Condition of the Poor that developed later in several large cities, sought "to remove the various causes of mendicity" primarily through friendly advice. The Association for Improving the Conditions of the Poor and its successors during the nineteenth century did little to reduce want. Indeed, they were often formed on the belief that treacherous paupers were taking advantage of less hard-hearted philanthropists. They did, however, propagate the view that the pauper should properly be excluded from the social order. If outdoor relief were abolished, they hoped, the pauper would have no alternative but to seek aid within the almshouse. The New York Society's Sub-Committee on Ignorance was charged as follows:

> This Committee shall report the number of children who do not attend any school; the number of adults who cannot read; the number of families and individuals who do not attend public worship; and the causes which prevent.[42]

Ignorance and the lack of religious fervor—in the eyes of the Association—reinforced pauperism.

Dissatisfaction with public outdoor relief, especially of the able-bodied, focused on its effectiveness in relieving or preventing poverty. Many believed that cash assistance promoted the very opposite of its intended purpose. So strongly was this view held that the state of Delaware prohibited local outdoor relief. Philadelphia abolished it from 1827 to 1839 and Chicago from 1848 to 1858. As for farming out and indenture, their abuses were notorious; and for some, indoor relief was no less suspect. Discussion was most intense where the problem was most serious, in the East. A series of state reviews of public relief giving developed, the most widely publicized of which were those of Massachusetts, New York, New Hampshire, and Pennsylvania. In their anxiety to ensure an appropriate work-spirit for the transient poor who might be employable, the reports tended to ignore the permanent poverty of children and the elderly who largely dominated relief rolls.

In 1821, Josiah Quincy's "Report of the Committee to whom was Referred the Consideration of the Pauper Laws of this Commonwealth" placed in "strong light the objections to the entire principle of our existing pauper laws" but despaired of the laws' being abolished. Among the committee's recommended principles for the operation of a relief system, two were particularly important:

1. That of all modes of providing for the poor, the most wasteful, the most expensive, and most injurious to their morals and destructive of their industrious habits is that of supply in their own families.
2. That the most economical mode is that of Alms Houses; having the character of Work Houses, or Houses of Industry, in which work is provided for every degree of ability in the pauper; and thus the able poor made to provide, partially at least for their own support, and also to the support, or at least the comfort of the impotent poor.[43]

In summary, the report stressed the responsibility of society to diminish pauperism and recommended the use of a single administrative mechanism, the almshouse, for doing so—"denying for the most part all supply from public provision, except on condition of admission into the public institution."[44]

In 1823, in response to rising costs of relief, the Senate and Assembly of the State of New York resolved that the secretary of state study and report on the expenses and operation of the Poor Laws in New York as well as in other states, for the purpose of suggesting improvements in the New York welfare system. Secretary Yates's report, submitted in February 1824, divided the poor of the state into "the permanent poor," that is, those who received support regularly during the year studied, and "the occasional poor," that is, those who received help during part of the year (perhaps briefly during the autumn and winter months). Of the first group, he found 6,896; and of the second, 15,215. Of the total of 6,896 permanent poor, only 1,789, "though not in the vigor of life," could be considered capable of earning their subsistence. Among the permanent poor not capable of earning their subsistence were 2,604 children under 14 years of age. Yates did not specify the number of families represented by the 6,896 individuals classified as permanent poor, but he did assert that 1,585 of the total were men who had been reduced to that state by drinking and "of consequence, that their families... were reduced to the same penury and want."[45]

In connection with the operation of the relief system in New York, the secretary reported four major findings: (1) that the poor, when farmed out, were frequently treated with barbarity and neglect, (2) that the education and morals of the children of paupers were almost wholly neglected, (3) that there was no adequate provision for the employment of the poor for the inculcation of industrious habits, and (4) that there was little attention being given to the disbursement of public funds appropriated for the support of the poor. As a single, total remedy for all these evils, Yates recommended the adoption of the "poorhouse plan" for every county of the state. In accordance with the plan, the one or more poorhouses to be erected in each county would be houses of employment where paupers might be "maintained and employed . . . in some healthful labor, chiefly agricultural, their children to be carefully instructed, and at suitable age, to be put out to some useful business or trade." As for sturdy beggars or vagrants—most likely the occasional poor—they were to be confined to penitentiaries connected to the poorhouses and subjected to a regimen of discipline consisting of "a rigid diet, hard labor, employment at the stepping mill, or some treatment equally efficacious in restraining their vicious appetites and pursuits."

The recommendations of the Yates report called for a separation of the worthy and unworthy poor: long-term care in houses of employment for the former and short-term penitentiary or workhouse confinement for the latter. The two types of houses were to be physically joined to form a system of almshouse care for the poor.

> Until a system . . . can be devised, which with economy and humanity, will administer relief to the indigent and infirm, incapable of labor, provide employment for the idle, and impart instruction to the young and ignorant, little hope can be entertained of meliorating the condition of our poor or relieving the community from the growing evils of pauperism.[46]

Thus the almshouse would be that particular institution given to the creation of an environment in which concern for the worthy poor and attention to their needs would militate against the development of pauperism in the individual and, by extension, in society. The unworthy occasional poor were to be handled quite differently, but not without attention to what they seemed to need, if they were to be saved from themselves.

Historically, the Yates report is significant, since it gained widespread attention and established indoor almshouse care as the major approach to the relief of the poor in the United States. In 1857, a state Select Senate Committee to Visit Charitable and Penal Institutions reported the existence of 55 almshouses, exclusive of the almshouses and poorhouses in New York and Kings counties.[47] Massachusetts listed 83 almshouses in 1824; there were 219 in 1860. By 1860, Pennsylvania had 31 county, in addition to local, almshouses. By 1860, Maryland had almshouses in all but one county, and that county was permitted use of the facility in Baltimore.[48]

As the Civil War approached, almshouse care was being used extensively throughout the United States. But condemnation of the "catchall almshouse" had begun. The condemnation might be traced to a failure to put into practice Yates's concepts of humane treatment and classification of the poor. In 1824, however, the almshouse seemed the obvious answer for all who deviated (or might deviate) from self-reliance—the impotent elderly or disabled, the potent able-bodied, and the eventually "potent" child. The emphasis in the Yates report upon saving the poor from pauperism and upon deterring the able-bodied from accepting relief, despite statistical evidence that the overwhelming numbers of the poor had been brought to their state by social and physical disabilities beyond their control, showed an inability to think beyond individual salvation to family welfare. Nowhere is this more evident than in the child-saving activities of the era.

Child Saving

Stirrings of dissatisfaction with almshouse care, especially for children, developed soon after the Yates report appeared. This dissatisfaction was based in part on the reform, crusading interests of the era. The period was one of growth of democratic concepts, of increased concern for individual self-realization. In child welfare this meant a new awareness of children as children—young people who must grow into adults able to participate in a democratic government. It seemed to the reformers that neither the undifferentiated almshouse nor the environment provided by the family—particularly the poor family—would provide the requisite discipline and education for children.

The "mischief" and "excitements" attributable to urbanization had led to social change and unrest. Self-realization and individual freedom were not to be confused with license and self-indulgence. Democracy was not to be extended to family life and the relaxation of parental authority. Fear of permissiveness in the care of children was aggravated by the growing presence of immigrants, who, it was thought, were unaware of traditional American child-rearing practices. The goal for a reformed American society was the return to the well-ordered "institutions" of the colonial era; for if children were to save the country for democracy, they must first be saved themselves.

Again, the institution—this time with specialized concern for dependent, neglected, and delinquent children—offered an approach that appeared to be both humane and salving for the individual, as well as a visible example of disciplined living for all families. That the children's institution, except as it attempted the achievement of order and stability, was not a model of colonial family life somehow went unobserved.

Institutions for children had appeared early on the American scene but were few in number until the nineteenth century. The first American institution for children was founded in 1729. This was a private institution for girls established in New Orleans by the Ursuline Sisters. The Bethesda House for Boys, founded in 1740 near Savannah, Georgia, was also privately supported. The first governmentally supported institution was established in 1790 in Charleston, South Carolina, and remained the only publicly funded institution for children until the turn of the century. The Charleston Orphan House was founded for the "Purpose of Supporting and Educating Poor Orphan Children, and Those of Poor, Distressed and Disabled Parents, Who are Unable to Support and Maintain Them."[49]

During the first half of the nineteenth century, the number of children's institutions increased rapidly, so that by 1851 there were seventy-seven. An additional forty-seven were built prior to 1860.[50] Most of these institutions were orphan asylums or simply asylums for dependent children; some were houses of refuge, reformatories for delinquent children. Most were privately controlled by religious, social, or foreign-born national groups, but many were the beneficiaries of state subsidies. The first private institution to receive a state subsidy was the Orphan Asylum of New York, which was granted a subsidy by an act of the state legislature in 1811. Similar grants were made in other states. The New York (City) House of Refuge and the Philadelphia House of Refuge were opened in 1825 and 1828, respectively. Both were supported by a combination of city appropriations, state subsidies, and voluntary contributions. By 1860, the system of state subsidies was greatly extended. Institutions wholly supported by public funds were also developed, generally to meet the needs of special classes of children. The Boston House of Reformation established in 1826 was the first reformatory for juveniles funded by a municipality. The first state reform school, the House of Refuge for Delinquent Boys, was established in Massachusetts in 1847. A School for Idiots, under the superintendency of Dr. Samuel Gridley Howe, was opened in 1848, also in Massachusetts. Similar publicly funded schools were opened in the next decade in Albany, New York; Columbus, Ohio; and Lakeville, Connecticut.

Institutional child care, as provided during the pre-Civil War period, gravitated toward an undemocratic and antifamily approach. Starting with distrust for the competence of poor parents, superintendents of children's institutions discouraged visits by parents except under severely restricting conditions. As for the actual care provided, in both orphan asylums and institutions for delinquents, the goal was submission and obedience on the part of the child. The Charleston orphan asylum saw itself as educating boys to become disciplined workers and citizens. The construction of houses of refuge for delinquent children spoke most pointedly to pre-Civil War concerns about the care of children. The delinquent child highlighted the "vicious tempers and habits" that could develop in an environment where authority and governance did not exact obedience and submission.[51] How easily the willful, offending child could become the adult criminal, the contributor to societal breakdown! The movement for institutions devoted to delinquent children was begun by the New York Society for the Prevention of Pauperism in 1819; the New York House of Refuge opened in 1826. By 1857, the number of such institutions had grown sufficiently to warrant a national convention of refuge superintendents.

Houses of refuge, like institutions for dependent, homeless children, offered a model for family home care, a combination of shelter, routine, and discipline. Isolated and shielded from outside, particularly from own-family influences, delinquent children were subjected to a "vigorous course of moral and corporal discipline" with the intent that they "be made tractable and obedient"[52] and, ultimately, good citizens. As indicated by the report of the investigation of the Philadelphia House of Refuge in 1835, the success of such an institution was thought to be measured by the extent to which its practices were a demonstration of parenting and parental responsibilities fulfilled.

> The inmates present a healthy appearance; their clothing is comfortable, and their fare is abundant and wholesome. Their labour is suited to their age and capacity—regular, but not severe. Their government ... is parental.—They have their regular hours of labour, and instruction; while every attention is paid to induce habits of industry, the greatest possible care is had for their intellectual improvement....
>
> To this unfortunate class, the advantages of this institution are peculiarly adopted. Here then vicious tempers and habits are restrained—their minds improved—principles of virtue inculcated; and not a few, who were on the broad road to ruin, have been rescued from destruction and prepared for usefulness....[53]

The model of "home life" offered by the house of refuge and by other child-caring institutions was semimilitary, characterized by discipline, training, and rehabilitation. The model was one in which the design of the institution and the imposition of a controlled, regulated environment were in themselves to effect needed reformation.

Thus, the realization of the goal of child saving through institutionalization meant mass, as opposed to individualized, care for children.

Despite the increase in special institutions for children, the unquestioned acceptance of institutional child care declined during the 1850s. This decline resulted partly from an inability to build specialized institutions in sufficient numbers to absorb the growing number of dependent, homeless, orphaned, and delinquent children. Economic uncertainty was increasing, and for adults without economic resources, there was little capacity to withstand these uncertainties and to support their children. In New York City alone, according to a police report in 1852, "there were an estimated 10,000 abandoned, orphaned, runaway children roaming the streets."[54] The catchall almshouse, rather than the specialized institution, remained the most available form of care for children.

Other factors contributed to a less positive view of institutional child care, including the rise of public education and the decline of opportunities for legal indenture and apprenticeship. The pattern of child-caring institutions had included a relatively short period of institutional housing during which education and re-education for orderly living were provided. Having satisfactorily completed this period of rehabilitation, the male child was placed out by the institution as an apprentice in a particular trade or occupation; the female child was indentured as a domestic servant. The spread of public, compulsory education made the educational efforts of child-caring institutions appear inadequate and unnecessary and, moreover, took the child back into the very community from which he was to have been saved. Similarly, the gradual disappearance of cottage industries not only meant the disappearance of work opportunities that could be selected and put under surveillance by the institution but also the disappearance of family care as an aspect of indentured apprenticeship. Simultaneously, increasingly heavy migrations from Europe, combined with stretches of economic recession to make for a surplus of adult workers, rendered child labor less profitable.

> As the apprenticeship system . . . passed away with the profound changes that occurred in industrial conditions, the indenturing of children underwent a change for the worse. The value of the instruction received from the "masters" became less, and the value of the services rendered by the children increased.[55]

The Children's Aid Society of New York was founded in 1853 by Charles Loring Brace for the purpose of effecting a new approach to child care. The circular announcing the formation of the society expressed the urgency of the task ahead.

> But a small part of the vagrant population can be shut up in our asylums. . . . The class increases. Immigration is pouring its multitudes of poor foreigners, who . . . leave young outcasts everywhere abandoned in our midst. For the most part . . . [they] grow up utterly by themselves. No one cares for them, and they care for no one. . . . Every cunning faculty is intensely stimulated. They are shrewd and old in vice when other children are in leading-strings.[56]

Conceptually, Brace was bent on saving children through the provision of education and shelter and, where necessary, through separation of children from parents.

Efforts to secure adequate and proper shelter for dependent children led Brace to the notion of foster home care:

> The workers...in this movement [foster home placement] felt from the beginning that "asylum-life" is not the best training for outcast children in preparing them for practical life. In large buildings, where a multitude of children are gathered together, the bad corrupt the good, and the good are not educated in the virtues of real life. The machinery, too, which is so necessary in such large institutions, unfits a poor boy or girl for practical handwork.[57]

Brace became convinced that foster home placement in an environment totally different from that of New York City was the only possible solution. That totally different environment turned out to be the West, where "the best of all Asylums for the outcast child . . . [would be] the farmer's home."[58] The fact that farm labor was in demand in the West and, therefore, that large numbers of children could be absorbed fit neatly with a romantic conception of country life. During the twelve-year period, 1853–1864, the Children's Aid Society of New York placed 4,614 children with western farmers. An even larger number were placed during the decade following the Civil War.[59]

The Society's efforts to place children in the West continued until after World War I. By the end, over 120,000 children had ridden the 'orphan trains.'

The apparent success of the Children's Aid Society led to the organization of other child-saving agencies employing similar placement methods—that is, removing dependent children from city environs, sometimes to the West, sometimes simply to the rural areas of a home state. The Church Home Society was founded in Boston in 1855, the Henry Watson Children's Aid Society in Baltimore in 1860, and the Home for Little Wanderers also in New York in 1861. With their emphasis upon child saving, these organizations, like institutions and almshouses, offered programs that did not individualize the child.

Retreat from the Almshouse

The Children's Aid Society advocacy of western emigration was only one part of a broader critique of institutional care during the years before the Civil War. Increasing state subsidy led to broader oversight of institutions. Ultimately, the gap between the promises of the moral entrepreneurs who created institutions and their reality led political and civic leaders to wonder if this was the best solution to the problems of a new democracy. In New York, the state Select Senate Committee to Visit Charitable and Penal Institutions made its report in 1857. The committee had been appointed

> to visit...all charitable institutions supported or assisted by the State, and all city and country poor and work houses and jails...to examine into the conditions of the said establishments, their...government, treatment, and management of the inmates, the conduct of the trustees, directors, and other officers...and all other matters whatever pertaining to their usefulness and good government.[60]

The Committee made its visits during the summer and autumn months when the "average number in the poor house is twenty-five percent less than in the winter" and made the following overall statement about what was found:

> The poor houses throughout the State may be generally described as badly constructed, ill-arranged, ill-warmed, and ill-ventilated. The rooms are crowded with inmates; and the air, particularly in the sleeping apartments, is very noxious, and to casual visitors, almost insufferable.[61]

Still further:

> The evidence taken by the committee exhibits such a filth, nakedness, licentiousness, general bad morals, and disregard of religion and the most common religious observances, as well as of gross neglect of the most ordinary comforts and decencies of life, as if published in detail would disgrace the State and shock humanity.[62]

The Committee recalled that almshouses had been originally designed to be "comfortable asylums for worthy indigence" and gave examples of how they had been permitted to become "unsuitable refuge for the virtuous poor, and mainly places of confinement for the degraded."[63]

The care of old people, of worthy adults who were suffering temporary reverses, of the insane, and of children was found to be especially outrageous. The committee recommended outdoor relief for worthy adults and specialized institutional care for children and the insane, the object being the removal of these classes from the almshouses.

> A...more efficient and economic auxiliary in supporting the poor, and the prevention of absolute pauperism, consists...in the proper and systematic distribution of *outdoor* relief. Worthy indigent persons should...be kept from the degradation of the poor house, by reasonable supplies of provisions...at their own homes.[64]

As for children:

> It is a great public reproach that they should ever be suffered to enter or remain in the poor houses as they are now mismanaged.
> The Committee most earnestly recommend[s] the establishment of special institutions for the purpose of maintaining and educating them by themselves, apart from the contaminations which now surround and vitiate them.[65]

It was recommended that the insane be removed to state asylums.

In Massachusetts, too, almshouse care was found wanting. A special committee was appointed in 1858 to "investigate the whole system of public charitable institutions of the Commonwealth." The committee found the system of state almshouses to have "grave disadvantages."

> For example: (1) partisan administration, (2) tendency of breaking up families to perpetuate dependency, (3) greater difficulty in placing children, (4) or finding work, (5) increased costs of transportation, (a) involved extra school and church facilities, (b) increased risks from fire and from moral and social contamination.[66]

The committee recommended that the almshouse system be abandoned at the earliest convenience.

The impetus for the attack on the Poor Law practice of outdoor relief and the subsequent rise in the use of almshouses and specialized institutional care was attributed to external factors and to individual behavior flaws.

The rise in immigration and the growth and increased crowding of cities created what was considered an unstable atmosphere, not conductive to mental health or stable labor-force behavior. The increased availability of alcohol and other forms of entertainment was a further factor believed to contribute to irresponsible behavior and poverty. In addition, the Poor Laws themselves, which provided a safety net for families in need, were judged to be part of the problem of rising incidence of need.

The response was the construction of many specialized institutions aimed at providing a stable environment for the poor and the mentally ill. The regularity of institutional life was to be a force for "cure" of those in need; the unpleasantness of life in the almshouse was to discourage the requests for assistance.[67]

Neither direct criticism of almshouse care, as in the New York and Massachusetts reports, nor indirect criticism, as implied in efforts to remove special classes of indigents, produced an immediate retreat from such care. The eruption of the Civil War was, certainly, a prime factor for the hiatus. Perhaps the nature of the population of inmates is even more telling. Although estimates vary widely, there is general agreement that more than half the inmates were foreign-born.[68] The probability is that most people agreed with Brace that these were "dangerous classes" and that fear rather than concern was the mark of public opinion. Almshouse care remained the dominant form of care for the poor until the Progressive Era of the late nineteenth century.

Discussion Questions

1. The early advocates of institutional responses to mental illness, crime, and poverty argued that these institutions would extract inmates from their 'natural' environment and place them in one in which rehabilitation was possible. How does this faith in institutionalization compare to contemporary experience with institutional care?
2. The Children's Aid Society's efforts to move thousands of working-class children to the Midwest is the most dramatic effort to remove children from what was considered a bad social and family environment. What alternative approaches might have been tried to help poor children then and now?
3. During the early nineteenth century, many religious individuals were motivated to save poor people through attacks on prostitution and alcohol. Ultimately, many of these reformers would move to crusades against slavery and women's oppression. How does this compare with the role of religion in social welfare and social reform activities today?

DOCUMENTS: The Pre-Civil War Period

Three documents have been selected to illustrate the tenor of social welfare during the pre-Civil War period: *The First Annual Report of the Society for the Prevention of Pauperism in New York City* (1816); *The Constitution and By-Laws of the Female Orphan Asylum of Portland, Maine* (1828); and President Franklin Pierce's *Veto of the Ten-Million Acre Bill,* the act granting public lands to the various states for the benefit of indigent persons (1854). The documents demonstrate several major themes:

1. That the causes of poverty are outside the economic system, and that poverty can be abolished through the reform of individuals
2. That institutions can serve as mechanisms for the rehabilitation of individuals and of the social order
3. That the development and administration of social welfare programs are local public and voluntary social welfare concerns, rather than a responsibility of the federal government

The managers of the Society for the Prevention of Pauperism in their First Annual Report give evidence of the change that had occurred in society's view of people. The Puritan doctrine of a fixed, preordained, predestined societal structure gave way to one in which achievement was limited only by failure to fulfill individual potential. It was the Age of Reason, and the will of God yielded to free will. The rational man could reach perfectibility, if he willed to do so. The problem for social welfare then, as for all institutions, was to create an environment in which individual reform and perfectibility were encouraged and could take place. The managers of the society were particularly frightened by the growth of pauperism, a condition they thought was easily fostered in a rapidly changing society if various internal and external forces went unheeded. The feared result was not only a detraction from individual potential, but from the fullest accomplishments of a whole society obviously on the path to perfection. The report of the managers demonstrates the extent to which rational human beings, freed of heavenly strictures, could rationalize the harsh treatment of the poor.

During the pre-Civil War era, institutions were founded to provide and demonstrate the well-ordered environmental setting in which human perfectibility could flourish. Children's institutions were particularly important in this regard, since the future of the country quite literally depended upon the kind of adults that children became. The Female Orphan Asylum of Portland, Maine, was established to "carry into effect *means* for the support, instruction and employment of female children, from three to ten years of age." The bylaws of the asylum demonstrate the premium placed upon stability and regularity in the daily lives of children. Their clothing, their fare, their instruction, and their activities are proscribed in rules and regulations so as to inculcate "habits of *order, neatness,* and *industry.*" Of equal importance was the prevention of parental interference "in the management of the children." Indeed, parents could not visit except in the presence of the asylum's governess. To be preferred was the parent's relinquishing all claim to the child, thus freeing the institution for its work. At the age of 11, the children were generally "placed out" with virtuous families; and the asylum followed their conduct and circumstances until they had reached 18.

President Pierce vetoed "the 10 million acre bill" in the belief that the bill would eventuate in the "transfer to the Federal Government the charge of all the poor in all the States." His decision to veto was based on the constitutional guarantee that those powers not specifically delegated to the United States by the Constitution were reserved for the states. Since he could find no specific delegation of authority for social welfare, the president interpreted the Constitution to mean that social welfare matters involved issues of states' rights and, therefore, required the exercise by each state of its own "police power" to provide for the welfare of its inhabitants. In addition to the constitutional question of states' rights, the president's decision was steeped in historical precedent by which programs to meet social welfare needs had long been the province of local and voluntary organizations. The veto was to sustain the tradition until the depression of the 1930s.

The First Annual Report of the Managers of the Society

for the Prevention of Pauperism in the City of New York

Read and Accepted October 26, 1818

To which is added:

A REPORT ON THE SUBJECT OF PAUPERISM,

dated February 4, 1818

The Managers of the Society for the Prevention of Pauperism
in the City of New York, REPORT

That their anticipation of the importance and difficulty of their duties has been fully realized. Their first efforts were necessarily directed to the development of the objects which they were appointed to consider. Though these objects were specified as far as practicable; though the nature of the duty allotted to the Board was pointed out, as well as the general aspect of the plan, such as the Managers should have in view, yet the basis only was laid, and it was their work to erect the superstructure. They were not at a loss for materials. These were more and more exhibited to them in the multifarious ramifications of their labours. But it was not an easy task to arrange them in proper order, and to dispose of them to advantage; it therefore required time, deliberation, and assiduity, to digest an effectual plan, and to take measures for rendering it subservient to the momentous purposes of the Society.

In order to investigate, and as far as possible to remove the various causes of mendicity; to devise plans for meliorating the condition of the poor and wretched, and to secure their successful operation, the Managers, immediately after their appointment, respectfully solicited the Corporation of this city to appoint five Managers from that body, agreeably to the 6th article of the constitution. The favourable result of this application warrants the Board to calculate upon municipal countenance and aid.

The 3d article of the By-laws declares that "each attending Committee shall consist of as many members of the Society as the Board may think necessary. They shall make rules, or by-laws, to govern themselves; keep a book, wherein they shall enter their proceedings, and report to the Board at every stated meeting, a summary of their proceedings, with their opinions on the most adviseable course for the Board to pursue relative thereto."

Nine Standing Committees were accordingly appointed, to carry into effect the views of the Managers, as stated in the following extract from the minutes:—

DISTRICTING COMMITTEE

This Committee shall consist of as many members of this Board as there are wards in the city, who shall form a general plan of operations;—and as soon after as possible each person shall, in his respective ward, associate with as many members of the Society as may be thought adviseable, who shall divide the ward into as many districts as they may think proper. These sub-committees shall embrace in their operations the duties specified on the 12th and 13th pages of the printed Report on the subject of Pauperism.

IDLENESS AND SOURCES OF EMPLOYMENT

The object of this Committee shall be to devise means for the employment of the poor.

INTEMPERANCE

This Committee shall inform the Board as to the number of places where ardent spirits are retailed in small quantities;—what quantity is drunk, with an estimate of its cost, and the class of citizens most subject to the vice of intemperance.

The Committee shall give opinions at large on every thing connected with this subject, including the law, police regulations, officers, & c. & c.

LOTTERIES

This Committee shall report the number of lottery offices in the city; the amount of money annually expended; the probable waste of time occasioned by lotteries; the usual percent advance on tickets; the extent of the evil arising from the insuring of tickets, how far the restraining laws are enforced, & c. & c.

HOUSES OF ILL FAME

This Committee shall report the probable number of houses of this description; families that live by prostitution; and in what particular the police regulations on the subject may be amended.

PAWN-BROKERS

This Committee shall report the number of pawn-brokers, their manner of doing business, and the best mode of correcting the evils arising therefrom.

CHARITABLE INSTITUTIONS

This Committee shall inform the Board as to the number in the city; the gross and annual amount of their funds, and the mode respectively adopted by them, in the distribution of charity to the poor.

GAMBLING

This Committee shall report the number and kinds of gambling houses, and their opinion as to the best mode of diminishing or suppressing them.

IGNORANCE

This Committee shall report the number of children who do not attend any school; the number of adults who cannot read; the number of families and individuals who do not attend public worship; and the causes which prevent. . . .

In the years 1788–1789, there were under the old system,

Paupers	7391
In the Hospital	894
—Penitentiary	446
—Orphan House	1000

Total 9731

In the year 1798–1799, when the new system was in operation, there were

Paupers	3090
In the Hospital	894
—Penitentiary	147
—Orphan House	600

Total 4731

Exhibiting a decrease in *one city* of 5026.

It is evident, therefore, that the object of the New-York Society for Preventing Pauperism is such as cannot, in the nature of things, be speedily accomplished. Habits and vices, which take their rise from the worst passions and propensities of men, however deplorable in their effects upon individuals and society, will yield to no sudden remedies. They must be supplanted gradually by the influence of appropriate agencies, by the assiduities of patient and persevering labour, by the constant and meliorating operations of benevolence. The measures pointed out in the document appended to this Report, are adapted ultimately to remove those evils which so much afflict society, and which the severest enactments of civil authority have been found unable to repress. Let the moral sense be awakened, and a moral influence be established in the minds of the improvident, the unfortunate, and the depraved; let them be approached with kindness and an ingenuous concern for their welfare; inspire them with self-respect, and encourage their industry and economy: in short, enlighten their minds, and teach them to care for themselves. These are the methods of doing them real and permanent good, and relieving the community from the pecuniary exactions, the multiplied embarrassments, and threatening dangers of which they are the authors. Happily, the object proposed by this institution is one which may be aided by every individual, whatever be his circumstances; though it prospectively demands the concurrence and patronage of all. The public is called upon not so much for pecuniary subscriptions and benefactions, as for friendly advice, for vigilant attention to the common good, for the adoption of wholesome opinions, and the exertion of a salutary influence. They who experience the ill effects of pauperism and its attendant evils, are urged, not to make fresh sacrifices and incur additional embarrassments, but to act upon the defensive, to employ the means of prevention, to check an inundation which threatens to overwhelm them. They are invited to adopt measures which cannot possibly be hurtful in any instance; which seem alone adapted to the end in view, which are required by the necessity of the case, and sanctioned by the results of experience.

The Managers consider the information which they have thus laid before the Society, of sufficient moment to encourage every member, and to stimulate the citizens generally, to give their utmost sanction and support to this truly benevolent institution, whose aim is to improve the temporal and moral condition of a considerable portion of this community.

Conscientiously engaged in so good a cause, let *all* rely on the blessing of that Almighty Father who "maketh his sun to rise on the evil and the good, and sendeth rain on the just and on the unjust."

MATTHEW CLARKSON, *President*

JOSEPH CURTIS, *Sec'y, pro tem.*
New-York, Oct. 26, 1818.

New York: Printed by J. Seymour, 49 John-Street, 1818.

***

REPORT
ON THE
SUBJECT OF PAUPERISM.

To the "New-York Society for the Prevention of Pauperism."

The Committee appointed to prepare a Constitution for the government of the Society, and a statement of the prevailing causes of pauperism, with suggestions relative to the most suitable and efficient remedies, Report,

That we entered upon the duties assigned us, under a strong conviction of the great importance of the subject of Pauperism. We were persuaded that on the judicious management of this subject depend, in a high degree, the comfort, the tranquility, and the freedom of communities.

We were not insensible of the serious and alarming evils that have resulted, in various places, from misguided benevolence, and imprudent systems of relief. We knew that in Europe and America, where the greatest efforts have been made to provide for the sufferings of the poor, by high and even enormous taxation, those sufferings were increasing in a ratio much greater than the population, and were evidently augmented by the very means taken to subdue them.

We were fully prepared to believe, that without a radical change in the principles upon which public alms have been usually distributed, helplessness and poverty would continue to multiply— demands for relief would become more and more importunate, the numerical difference between those who are able to bestow charity and those who sue for it, would gradually diminish, until the present system must fall under its own irresistible pressure, prostrating perhaps, in its ruin, some of the pillars of social order.

It might be long indeed before such a catastrophe would be extensively felt in this free and happy country. Yet it is really to be feared, as we apprehend, that it would not be long before some of the proximate evils of such a state of things would be perceived in our public cities, and in none, perhaps, sooner than in New-York. Although these consequences are but too apparent from the numerous facts which recent investigations have brought to light, particularly in Great Britain, and in some parts of the United States, yet we are very sensible of the difficulties attendant upon every attempt to provide an adequate remedy for poverty, and its concomitant wretchedness.

The evil lies deep in the foundation of our social and moral institutions; and we cannot but consider it as one of the most obscure and perplexing, and at the same time, interesting and imposing departments of political economy.

While there exists so great a disparity in the physical and intellectual capacities of men, there must be, in every government, where a division of property is recognized by law and usage, a wide difference in the means of support. Such, too, is the complication of human affairs, the numerous connexions, and close dependencies of one part upon another, it is scarcely to be presumed, and it would be extravagant to expect, that under the most moral, and the wisest civil regulation to which human society is susceptible of attaining, partial indigence and distress will not be experienced to an amount that will ever demand the exercise of Christian benevolence.

The great and leading principles, therefore, of every system of charity, ought to be, *First*, amply to relieve the unavoidable necessities of the poor; and, *Secondly*, to lay the powerful hand of moral and legal restriction upon every thing that contributes, directly and necessarily, to introduce an artificial extent of suffering; and to diminish, in any class of the community, a reliance upon its own powers of body and mind for an independent and virtuous support. That to the influence of those extraneous, debilitating causes, may be ascribed nine tenths of the poverty which actually prevails, we trust none will doubt, who are extensively acquainted with facts in relation to this subject.

The indirect causes of poverty are as numerous as the frailties and vices of men. They vary with constitution, with character, and with national and local habits. Some of them lie so deeply entrenched in the weakness and depravity of human nature, as to be altogether unassailable by mere political regulation. They can be reached in no other way, than by awakening the dormant and secret energies of moral feeling.

But with a view to bring the subject committed to our charge more definitely before the Society, we have thought it right, distinctly to enumerate the more prominent of those causes of poverty which prevail within this city; subjoining such remarks as may appear needful.

1st. IGNORANCE. Arising either from inherent dullness, or from want of opportunities for improvement. This operates as a restraint upon the physical powers, preventing that exercise and cultivation of the bodily faculties by which skill is obtained, and the means of support increased. The influence of this cause, it is believed, is particularly great among the foreign poor that annually accumulate in this city.

2d. IDLENESS. A tendency to this evil may be more or less inherent. It is greatly increased by other causes, and when it becomes habitual, it is the occasion of much suffering in families, and augments to a great amount the burden of the industrious portions of society.

3d. INTEMPERANCE IN DRINKING. This most prolific source of mischief and misery drags in its train almost every species of suffering which afflicts the poor. This evil, in relation to poverty and vice, may be emphatically styled the *Cause of Causes*. The box of Pandora is realized in each of the kegs of ardent spirits that stand upon the counters of the 1600* licensed grocers of this city. At a moderate computation, the money spent in the purchase of spirituous liquors would be more than sufficient to keep the whole city constantly supplied with bread. Viewing the enormous devastations of this evil upon the minds and morals of the people, we cannot but regard it as the crying and increasing sin of the nation, and as loudly demanding the solemn deliberation of our legislative assemblies.

4th. WANT OF ECONOMY. Prodigality is comparative. Among the poor it prevails to a great extent, in an inattention to those small but frequent savings when labour is plentiful, which may go to meet the privations of unfavourable seasons.

5th. IMPRUDENT AND HASTY MARRIAGES. This, it is believed, is a fertile source of trial and poverty.

6th. LOTTERIES. The depraving nature and tendency of these allurements to hazard money, is generally admitted by those who have been most attentive to their effects. The time spent in inquiries relative to lotteries, in frequent attendance on lottery offices, the feverish anxiety which prevails relative to the success of tickets, the associations to which it leads, all contribute to divert the labourer from his employment, to weaken the tone of his morals, to consume his earnings, and consequently to increase his poverty. But objectionable and injurious to society as we believe lotteries to be, we regard as more destructive to morals, and ruinous to all character and comfort, the numerous self-erected lottery insurances, at which the young and the old are invited to spend their money in such small pittances, as the poorest labourer is frequently able to command, under the delusive expectation of a gain, the chance of which is as low, perhaps, as it is possible to conceive. The poor are thus cheated out of their money and their time, and too often left a prey to the feelings of desperation: or, they are impelled by those feelings to seek a refuge in the temporary, but fatal oblivion of intoxication.

---

*Since this Report was written, the number of licenses has been very considerably reduced by the present chief magistrate of the city.

7th. PAWNBROKERS. The establishment of these offices is considered as very unfavourable to the independence and welfare of the middling and inferior classes. The artifices which are often practised to deceive the expectation of those who are induced, through actual distress, or by positive allurement, to trust their goods at these places, not to mention the facilities which they afford to the commission of theft, and the encouragement they give to a dependence on stratagem and cunning, rather than on the profits of honest industry, fairly entitle them, in the opinion of the Committee, to a place among the *causes of Poverty*.

8th. HOUSES OF ILL FAME. The direful effects of those sinks of iniquity upon the habits and morals of a numerous class of young men, especially of sailors and apprentices, are visible throughout the city. Open abandonment of character, vulgarity, profanity, &c. are among the inevitable consequences, as it respects our own sex, of those places of infamous resort. The effects upon the several thousands of females within this city, who are ingulphed in those abodes of all that is vile, and all that is shocking to virtuous thought, upon the miserable victims, many of them of decent families, who are here subjected to the most cruel tyranny of their inhuman masters—upon the females, who, hardened in crime, are nightly sent from those dens of corruption to roam through the city "seeking whom they may devour," we have not the inclination, nor is it our duty, to describe. Among "the causes of poverty," those houses, where all the base-born passions are engendered—where the vilest profligacy receives a forced culture, must hold an eminent rank.

9th. THE NUMEROUS CHARITABLE INSTITUTIONS OF THE CITY. The Committee by no means intends to cast an indiscriminate censure upon these institutions, nor to implicate the motives, nor even to deny the usefulness, in a certain degree, of any of them. They have unquestionably had their foundation in motives of true philanthropy; they have contributed to cultivate the feelings of Christian charity, and to keep alive its salutary influence upon the minds of our fellow-citizens; and they have doubtless relieved thousands from the pressure of the most pinching want, from cold, from hunger, and probably, in many cases, from untimely death.

But, in relation to these societies, a question of no ordinary moment presents itself to the considerate and real philanthropist. Is not the partial and temporary good which they accomplish, how acute soever the miseries they relieve, and whatever the number they may rescue from sufferings or death, more than counterbalanced, by the evils that flow from the expectations they necessarily excite; by the relaxation of industry, which such a display of benevolence tends to produce; by that reliance upon charitable aid, in case of unfavourable times, which must unavoidably tend to diminish, in the minds of the labouring classes, that wholesome anxiety to provide for the wants of a distant day, which alone can save them from a state of absolute dependence, and from becoming a burden to the community?

In the opinion of your Committee, and in the opinion, we believe, of the greater number of the best writers, of the wisest economists, and of the most experienced philanthropists, which the interesting subject of Pauperism has recently called into action; the balance of good and evil is unfavourable to the existence of societies for gratuitous relief:—that efforts of this nature, with whatever zeal they may be conducted, never can effect the removal of poverty, nor lessen its general amount; but that indigence and helplessness will multiply nearly in the ratio of those measures which are ostensibly taken to prevent them.

Such are the consequences of every avowal on the part of the public of a determination to support the indigent by the administration of alms. And in no cases are measures of this kind more prolific in evil, than where they are accompanied by the display of large funds for the purposes of charity; or where the poor are conscious of the existence of such funds, raised by taxation, and of course, as they will allege, drawn chiefly from the coffers of the rich.

How far these evils are remediable, without an entire dereliction of the great Christian duty of charity, is a problem of difficult solution. The principle of taxation is so interwoven with our habits and customs, it would, perhaps, in the present state of things, be impossible to dispense with it. But while our poor continue to be thus supported, to prevent the misapplication and abuse of the public charity, demands the utmost vigilance, the wisest precaution, and the most elaborate system of inspection and oversight.

To what extent abuses upon our present system of alms are practised, and how far the evils which accompany it are susceptible of remedy, we should not at present feel warranted in attempting to state. The pauperism of the city is under the management of five Commissioners, who, we doubt not, are well qualified to fulfil the trust reposed in them, and altogether disposed to discharge it with fidelity. But we cannot withhold the opinion, that without a far more extended, minute, and energetic scheme of management than it is possible for any five men to keep in constant operation, abuses will be practised, and to a great extent, upon the public bounty; taxes must be increased, and vice and suffering perpetuated.

LASTLY. Your Committee would mention WAR, during its prevalence, as one of the most abundant sources of poverty and vice, which the list of human corruptions comprehends. But as this evil lies out of the immediate reach of local regulation, and as we are now happily blessed with a peace which we hope will be durable, it is deemed unnecessary further to notice it.

Such are the causes which are considered as the more prominent and operative in producing that amount of indigence and suffering, which awakens the charity of this city, and which has occasioned the erection of buildings for eleemosynary purposes, at an expense of half a million of dollars, and which calls for the annual distribution of 90,000 dollars more. But, if the payment of this sum were the only inconvenience to be endured—trifling, indeed, in comparison would be the evils which claim our attention. Of the mass of affliction and wretchedness actually sustained, how small a portion is thus relieved! Of the quantity of misery and vice, which the causes we have enumerated, with others we have not named, bring upon the city, how trifling the portion actually removed, by public or by private benevolence! Nor do we conceive it possible to remove this load of distress, by all the alms-doing of which the city is capable, while the causes remain in full and active operation.

Effectually to relieve the poor, is therefore a task far more comprehensive in its nature, than simply to clothe the naked and to feed the hungry. It is, to erect barriers against the encroachments of moral degeneracy;—it is to heal the diseases of the mind;—it is to furnish that ailment to the intellectual system which will tend to preserve it in healthful operation.

But can a task of this nature come within the reach of any public or any social regulation? We answer, that to a certain, and to a very valuable extent, we believe it can. When any measure for the promotion of public good, or the prevention of public evil, founded upon equitable principles, is supported by a sufficient weight of social authority, it may gradually pass into full and complete operation, and become established upon a basis as firm as a law of legislative enactment. And in matters of private practice, reformation which positive statute could never accomplish, social and moral influence may thoroughly effect. . . .

To conclude, the committee has by no means intended, in the freedom with which it has thus examined the causes of pauperism, and suggested remedies, to encourage the expectation that the whole of these remedies can be speedily brought within the power and control of the society. A work of so much importance to the public welfare cannot be the business of a day; but we nevertheless entertain the hope, that if the principles and design of this Society shall, upon mature examination and reflection, receive the approbation of the great body of our intelligent fellow-citizens, and the number of its members be augmented accordingly, it will be able gradually to bring within its operation all the important measures suggested in this report. By what particular mode these measures shall be encountered, whether through the agency of large and efficient Committees of this Society, or by auxiliary societies, each established, for a specific purpose, under the patronage of the parent institution, and subordinate to its general principles, we leave to the wisdom and future decision of the Society.

On behalf of the Committee,
JOHN GRISCOM, *Chairman.*

New-York, Second month 4, 1818.

***

CONSTITUTION, BY-Laws, &c., of the

Female Orphan Asylum of Portland, Maine

ACT incorporating the Female Orphan Asylum

of Portland

STATE OF MAINE

In the year of our Lord one thousand eight hundred and twenty-eight.

AN ACT to incorporate the Female Orphan Asylum of Portland.

SECTION 1. *Be it enacted by the Senate and House of Representatives, in Legislature assembled,* That Sally M. Smith, Thankful Hussey, Mary B. Storer, Charlotte Andrews, Mary Radford, Mary B. Merrill, Elizabeth L. Fox, Elizabeth G. Atwood, Susan Richardson, Nancy Cushman, Marcia Hill, Alice Ilsley, Lois W. Dana, Susan E. Wood, and Eliza L. Goddard, their associates and successors be, and they hereby are, constituted a body politic and corporate by the name of the Female Orphan Asylum of Portland, with power to prosecute and defend suits at law; to have and use a common seal, to make and establish any by-laws for the management of their affairs, not repugnant to the laws of the State; to take and hold any estate, real or personal, for the purpose of supporting, instructing and employing female children, the first attention to be given to orphans; and to give, grant, bargain or sell the same; and with all the powers and privileges usually granted to other societies instituted for purposes of charity and beneficence.—*Provided,* that the value of the real estate of said corporation, shall never exceed forty thousand dollars, and the annual income of the whole estate of said corporation shall not exceed twenty thousand dollars.

SECTION 2. *Be it further enacted,* That the first meeting of said corporation shall be holden at such time and place, and be notified in such manner, as a majority of the persons named in this act shall direct.

SECTION 3. *Be it further enacted,* That the powers granted by this Act, may be enlarged, restricted, or annulled at the pleasure of the Legislature.

In the House of Representatives, February 16, 1828. This Bill, having had three several readings, passed to be enacted.

JOHN RUGGLES, *Speaker.*

In Senate, February 18, 1828. This Bill, having had two several readings, passed to be enacted.

ROBERT P. DUNLAP, *President.*

February 18, 1828, Approved.

ENOCH LINCOLN.

STATE OF MAINE

Secretary of State's Office,
Portland, February 20, 1828.

I hereby certify, that the foregoing is a true copy of the original, deposited in this Office.

ATTEST, A. NICHOLS, *Secy. of State.*

Shirley and Hyde, Printers

***

CONSTITUTION

OF THE

Female Orphan Asylum

OF PORTLAND

ARTICLE 1. This Society shall be called The Female Orphan Asylum of Portland, and being strictly a charitable Institution, no article shall be admitted into this Constitution, which shall recognize the peculiar sentiments of any particular denomination of Christians, but all shall be considered as enjoying equal rights and privileges.

ART. 2. The *object* of this Institution shall be to provide and carry into effect, *means* for the support, instruction and employment of female children, from three to ten years of age: the first attention to be paid to Orphans.

ART. 3. Any lady who shall subscribe and pay a sum not less than *two* dollars annually, shall become a member of said Society; her membership however to cease, whenever she shall refuse or neglect to pay said annual subscription.

ART. 4. The Society shall meet on the second Tuesday in September annually, for the purpose of electing by *ballot* a Treasurer, and a board to consist of fifteen managers: which board shall choose from among themselves a first and second Directress, a Secretary, and an Assistant Secretary if necessary: and they shall have power to fill their own vacancies.—Not *less* than *five* shall constitute a quorum for transacting business.

ART. 5. The Managers shall superintend the concerns of the Society, enact their own rules and by-laws; shall have the entire direction of the children committed to them; shall provide for them a suitable Governess; shall see that they are properly clothed, fed and instructed; shall determine where they shall be placed when their age and acquirements are such, as to render it proper for them to leave the Asylum; and in all respects exercise over them a *maternal care.*

ART. 6. The first Directress shall preside at all meetings, and in case of equal division give the casting vote. Upon any urgent occasion the first or second Directress, or in their absence the Secretary, or when requested in writing by twenty members of the Society, *any five* of the Managers shall call a special meeting of the Society, which shall be duly notified.

ART. 7. The Secretary shall register the names of the members; shall notify the meetings of the Society, by causing to be published in one or more of our newspapers the time and place of said meeting, at least seven days previous thereto; and shall record their transactions. She shall also meet with and record the proceedings of the Board. She shall receive all the *dues* of the Society, pay them over to the Treasurer, and at each stated meeting of the board, render an account of the sums thus received and paid over, and of such as still remain due.

ART. 8. The Treasurer shall always be a single woman of the age of twenty-one years or upwards; and shall give a bond with sufficient sureties. She shall meet with the Managers when necessary, and shall render to them and to the Society, a statement of its property, with her receipts and payments whenever requested.

ART. 9. All donations shall be reserved as a fund for *building*, and after that object is accomplished, shall go to the establishment of a *permanent fund.*

All subscriptions and the interest on donations, shall be appropriated to defray the annual expenses of the Society.

ART. 10. The Governess shall board the children committed to her care by the Managers, and instruct them in Reading, Writing, and Sewing, with the various branches of domestic employment, and shall make report of their conduct and improvement to the Managers, whenever requested.

ART. 11. The children shall be dressed in a plain manner and treated with kindness. If sick, they shall be visited by a regular physician, whose services shall be paid by the Society, when not rendered gratuitously.

ART. 12. The yearly *tax* shall be accounted *due* at the annual meetings of the Society.

ART. 13. Any alteration of this *Constitution*, not subversive of the *original object* of the Institution, may be made at any special meeting of the Society, called by the Managers for that purpose, by a vote of *two thirds* of the members present.

OFFICERS AND BOARD OF MANAGERS

For the year ending Sept. 1828

Mrs. Sally M. Smith, *First Directress,*
Mrs. Thankful Hussey, *Second Do.*
Mrs. Mary B. Storer, *Sec'ry.*
Mrs. Elizabeth L. Fox,
Mrs. Alice Ilsley,
Mrs. Eliza L. Goddard,
Mrs. Lois W. Dana,
Mrs. Susan Wood,
Mrs. Charlotte Andrews,
Mrs. Marcia Hill,
Mrs. Elizabeth G. Atwood,
Mrs. Mary S. B. Merrill,
Mrs. Mary Radford,
Mrs. Susan Richardson,
Mrs. Nancy Cushman,
Miss Lucretia Frothingham, *Treasurer.*

} *Managers.*

BY-LAWS

ESTABLISHED BY THE BOARD OF MANAGERS

April 1828

1. Regular Meetings of the Board of Managers shall be held on the first Tuesday in every month, for the purpose of attending to the concerns of the Society. These meetings shall be opened with prayer.

2. The first Directress shall preside at all meetings of the Board; and in case of equal division give the casting vote. In her absence the second Directress shall preside; and in the absence of both, a Moderator shall be chosen for the meeting.

The first Directress shall have power to call special meetings of the Board whenever necessary; and in her absence, the second Directress; and in the absence of both, the Secretary shall call a special meeting whenever requested by *three* Managers.

The special meetings of the Board shall be notified by the Secretary.

3. A collecting Committee shall be appointed annually by the Board of Managers, whose duty shall be to collect all the annual subscriptions to the Society, and pay them over to the Secretary.

This Committee shall consist of such a number as the Board shall from time to time think necessary.

4. When the Treasurer is required to attend any meeting of the Board, she shall be notified by the Secretary, four days previous thereto; and at every such meeting, she shall render an account of monies received, and paid out, and remaining in her hands. And at the end of every six months, she shall settle her accounts with a Committee to be appointed for that purpose by the Board.

5. All accounts against the Society, shall be laid before the Board of Managers, and if allowed, an order shall be drawn by the Secretary on the Treasurer for payment of the same; and no monies shall be paid without such an order, drawn in pursuance of a vote of the Board.

6. A Committee consisting of three Managers shall be chosen every quarter, whose duty it shall be, to examine into the circumstances of children proposed for admission into the Asylum; and also to inquire respecting those persons who may apply to take a child out of the Asylum; and they shall make report to the Board of Managers.

7. It shall be the duty of the Secretary, to place in the Managers' Room in the Asylum, the names of this Committee, with their places of residence.

8. A list of such children as are approved by the Board for admission into the Asylum, shall be kept by the Secretary; priority of application shall give right to admission, unless in the opinion of a majority of the managers at a regular meeting, the circumstances of a child shall require immediate relief.

9. No child shall be received into, or dismissed from the Asylum, or placed in any family, without a vote of the Board at a regular meeting.

10. No child shall be received into the Asylum, until its parents or relatives have relinquished all claim to it. Should, however, any child under the protection of the Society, be claimed by her connexions, she shall be returned to them, whenever all expenses incurred on her account are reimbursed.

11. No relative or friend shall interfere in the management of the children in the Asylum; or visit them except in the presence of the Governess; nor at any time, when their visits are disapproved by the Board.

12. At a suitable age, the children shall be placed in virtuous families, until the age of Eighteen, or marriage within that age; unless some other way for their gaining a livelihood should offer, which the Managers shall deem more eligible.

No child shall be placed out of the Asylum before she has attained to the age of *eleven* years, unless some special circumstance shall render it expedient.

13. In putting out the children, subscribers shall always have the preference. Every child on her leaving the Asylum, shall be supplied by the Society, with one suit of every day wearing apparel. And any person on taking a child, must provide all other clothing necessary for her.

14. A Committee shall be chosen from time to time, whose duty shall be, to make inquiry respecting the conduct and circumstances of the children placed out by the Managers; particularly to ascertain whether they are properly instructed, and treated with kindness; and report to the Board.

15. A Committee of two Ladies shall be chosen every month to provide for the house; to procure and attend to the clothes of the children, and to examine into their improvement; inquire respecting their treatment, and report at every meeting of the Board.

16. A sample of the Bread, meat, and other provisions used in the Asylum, shall be produced to the Board or monthly Committee, whenever required.

17. In case of sickness, the children shall be committed to the care of such Physicians as the Board shall direct.

18. Twenty-five subscribers in any town adjacent to Portland, shall be entitled to place a child in the Asylum, for so long a time as they pay their annual subscription.

19. The Governess shall always be a woman of piety. She shall be chosen by ballot; and a majority of the whole Board shall be necessary to constitute a choice.

20. No alteration in, or addition to, these By-Laws shall be made, unless two thirds of the whole Board of Managers shall concur, at a special meeting notified for that purpose four days previous thereto.

RULES AND REGULATIONS

FOR THE GOVERNMENT OF CHILDREN IN THE ASYLUM

1. All the children on the Sabbath, shall, if the weather permit, regularly attend public worship with the Governess, at such place as the Board shall direct; and during the intervals of worship, they shall read in the Bible and other religious books. They shall also attend the Sabbath School attached to the Society with which they worship.

It shall be the duty of the Governess to pay particular attention to their observance of the Sabbath, teaching them by precept and example, to reverence and keep it holy.

2. The Governess shall read a chapter in the Bible, and pray with the children every morning. She shall attend them at their meals, see that proper order is observed, and that grace is said before and after. She shall teach them to pay a sacred regard to truth, and to the performance of every moral duty; and shall give them such religious instruction as is suited to their age and capacity.

3. The Governess shall instruct the children in reading, writing, arithmetic, plain needle work and knitting.

Those who are old enough, shall mend their own clothes, and assist by weekly rotation, in the domestic business of the family. The Governess shall be particularly careful to educate them in habits of *order*, *neatness*, and *industry*.

4. The Governess shall not be absent a night from the Asylum, without permission from one of the Board.

She shall visit the children's rooms every night before going to bed. She shall not suffer any of the children to be absent from the Asylum, without special permission in writing from one of the Managers.

GENERAL DIRECTIONS

From the first of April to the first of October, the Children shall rise at six o'clock, say their Prayers, wash themselves, comb their hair, make their beds, and clean their chambers; breakfast at seven; play or work in the garden until nine, when the governess shall read a chapter in the Bible and pray with them; attend school until twelve, dine at one, play until two, attend school until five, after which, play one hour. In the evening say their Prayers, go to bed at eight, wash their feet every night.

From the first of October to the first of April, the Children shall rise at seven o'clock, say their Prayers, wash themselves, comb their hair, make their beds and clean their chambers;—breakfast at eight, attend prayers; school and play hours as before. In the evening, say their Prayers; go to bed at Seven; and wash their feet once a week.

BILL OF FARE

BREAKFAST

Sunday and Thursday mornings, tea, coffee, chocolate or shells, with bread. All other mornings, milk or milk-porridge and bread.

SUPPERS

Sunday nights, tea with bread and butter. All other nights bread, hastypudding, or rice with milk.

DINNERS

Fresh meat, salt beef and pork, salt fish, fresh fish, dried beans and peas, vegetables, and puddings.

CLOTHING

Factory Gingham or Calico for Summer, Bombazette for Winter.

The Society commenced their operations the first of April.

Their House is situated on the corner of Free and South Streets.

Mrs. ABIGAIL RICH, *Governess*.

Miss SARAH RICH, *Assistant*.

The present number of Children belonging to the Asylum, is ten.

At a late meeting of the Board of Managers it was *voted*, "that it is expected, no person will visit the Asylum except in company with one of the Managers, or without a written permission from one of them."

The necessity of such a regulation it is presumed, will be obvious to all; and the Managers take this opportunity to inform all interested in the Institution, that the House is open to inspection, and they will be happy to wait on those who wish to visit it.

FORM OF OBLIGATION

To be signed by a Parent or Guardian on surrendering a child or ward to the protection of the Female Orphan Asylum of Portland.

I, the Subscriber, do hereby surrender my daughter (or Ward) to the Managers of the Female Orphan Asylum of Portland, and to their successors in Office, and to their sole and exclusive care, guardianship and direction, to be by them exercised according to the Rules and Regulations of the Society aforesaid, until my said daughter (or Ward) shall have arrived at the age of eighteen years.

In witness, whereof, I have hereunto set my hand and seal, this   day of   in the year of our Lord, one thousand eight hundred and

SIGNED, SEALED AND DELIVERED IN
PRESENCE OF US,

***

PRESIDENT FRANKLIN PIERCE: VETO MESSAGE

An Act Making A Grant of Public Lands

to the Several States

for the Benefit of Indigent Insane Persons

Washington, *May 3, 1854*

To the Senate of the United States:

The bill entitled "An act making a grant of public lands to the several States for the benefit of indigent insane persons," which was presented to the Senate, the House in which it originated, with a statement of the objections which have required me to withhold from it my approval.

In the performance of this duty, prescribed by the Constitution, I have been compelled to resist the deep sympathies of my own heart in favor of the humane purpose sought to be accomplished and to overcome the reluctance with which I dissent from the conclusions of the two Houses of Congress, and present my own opinions in opposition to the action of a coordinate branch of the Government which possesses so fully my confidence and respect.

If in presenting my objections to this bill I should say more than strictly belongs to the measure or is required for the discharge of my official obligation, let it be attributed to a sincere desire to justify my act before those whose good opinion I so highly value and to that earnestness which springs from my deliberate conviction that a strict adherence to the terms and purposes of the federal compact offers the best, if not the only, security for the preservation of our blessed inheritance of representative liberty.

The bill provides in substance:

First. That 10,000,000 acres of land be granted to the several States, to be apportioned among them in the compound ratio of the geographical area and representation of said States in the House of Representatives.

Second. That wherever there are public lands in a State subject to sale at the regular price of private entry, the proportion of said 10,000,000 acres falling to such State shall be selected from such lands within it, and that to the States in which there are no such public lands land scrip shall be issued to the amount of their distributive shares, respectively, said scrip not to be entered by said States, but to be sold by them and subject to entry by their assignees: *Provided.* That none of it shall be sold at less than $1 per acre, under penalty of forfeiture of the same to the United States.

Third. That the expenses of the management and superintendence of said lands and of the moneys received therefrom shall be paid by the States to which they may belong out of the treasury of said States.

Fourth. That the gross proceeds of the sales of such lands or land scrip so granted shall be invested by the several States in safe stocks, to constitute a perpetual fund, the principal of which shall remain forever undiminished, and the interest to be appropriated to the maintenance of the indigent insane within the several States.

Fifth. That annual returns of lands or scrip sold shall be made by the States to the Secretary of the Interior, and the whole grant be subject to certain conditions and limitations prescribed in the bill, to be assented to by legislative acts of said States.

This bill therefore proposes that the Federal Government shall make provision to the amount of the value of 10,000,000 acres of land for an eleemosynary object within the several States, to be administered by the political authority of the same; and it presents at the threshold the question whether any such act on the part of the Federal Government is warranted and sanctioned by the Constitution, the provisions and principles of which are to be protected and sustained as a first and paramount duty.

It can not be questioned that if Congress has power to make provision for the indigent insane without the limits of this District it has the same power to provide for the indigent who are not insane, and thus to transfer to the Federal Government the charge of all the poor in all the States. It has the same power to provide hospitals and other local establishments for the care and cure of every species of human infirmity, and thus to assume all that duty of either public philanthropy or public necessity to the dependent, the orphan, the sick, or the needy which is now discharged by the States themselves or by corporate institutions or private endowments existing under the legislation of the States. The whole field of public beneficence is thrown open to the care and culture of the Federal Government. Generous impulses no longer encounter the limitations and control of our imperious fundamental law; for however worthy may be the present object in itself, it is only one of a class. It is not exclusively worthy of benevolent regard. Whatever considerations dictate sympathy for this particular object apply in like manner, if not in the same degree, to idiocy, to physical disease, to extreme destitution. If Congress may and ought to provide for any one of these objects, it may and ought to provide for them all. And if it be done in this case, what answer shall be given when Congress shall be called upon, as it doubtless will be, to pursue a similar course of legislation in the others? It will obviously be vain to reply that the object is worthy, but that the application has taken a wrong direction. The power will have been deliberately assumed, the general obligation will by this act have been acknowledged, and the question of means and expediency will alone be left for consideration. The decision upon the principle in any one case determines it for the whole class. The question presented, therefore, clearly is upon the constitutionality and propriety of the Federal Government assuming to enter into a novel and vast field of legislation, namely, that of providing for the care and support of all those among the people of the United States who by any form of calamity become fit objects of public philanthropy.

I readily and, I trust, feelingly acknowledge the duty incumbent on us all as men and citizens, and as among the highest and holiest of our duties, to provide for those who, in the mysterious order of Providence, are subject to want and to disease of body or mind; but I can not find any authority in the Constitution for making the Federal Government the great almoner of public charity throughout the United States. To do so would, in my judgment, be contrary to the letter and spirit of the Constitution and subversive of the whole theory upon which the Union of these States is founded. And if it were admissible to contemplate the exercise of this power for any object whatever, I can not avoid the belief that it would in the end be prejudicial rather than beneficial in the noble office of charity to have the charge of them transferred from the States to the Federal Government. Are we not too prone to forget that the Federal Union is the creature of the States, not they of the Federal Union? We were the inhabitants of colonies distinct in local government one from the other before the Revolution. By that Revolution the colonies each became an independent State. They achieved that independence and secured its recognition by the agency of a consulting body, which, from being an assembly of the ministers of distinct sovereignties instructed to agree to no form of government which did not leave the domestic concerns of each State to itself, was appropriately denominated a Congress. When, having tried the experiment of the Confederation, they resolved to change that for the present Federal Union, and thus to confer on the Federal Government more ample authority, they scrupulously measured such of the functions of their cherished sovereignty as they chose to delegate to the General Government. With this aim and to this end the fathers of the Republic framed the Constitution, in and by which the independent and sovereign States united themselves for certain specified objects and purposes, and for those only, leaving all powers not therein set forth as conferred on one or another of the three great departments—the legislative, the executive, and the judicial—indubitably with the States. And when the people of the several States had in their State conventions, and thus alone, given effect and force to the Constitution, not content that any doubt should in future arise as to the scope and character of this act, they ingrafted thereon the explicit declaration that "the powers not delegated to the United States by the Constitution nor prohibited by it to the States are reserved to the States respectively or to the people." Can it be controverted that the great mass of the business of Government—that involved in the social relations, the internal arrangements of the body politic, the mental and moral culture of men, the development of local resources of wealth, the punishment of crimes in general, the preservation of order, the relief of the needy or otherwise unfortunate members of society—did in practice remain with the States; that none of these objects of local concern are by the Constitution expressly or impliedly prohibited to the States, and that none of them are by any express language of the Constitution transferred to the United States? Can it be claimed that any of these functions of local administration and legislation are vested in the Federal Government by any implication? I have never found anything in the Constitution which is susceptible of such a construction. No one of the enumerated powers touches the subject or has even a remote analogy to it. The powers conferred upon the United States have reference to federal relations, or to the means of accomplishing or executing things of federal relation. So also of the same character are the powers taken away from the States by enumeration. In either case the powers granted and the powers restricted were so granted or so restricted only where it was requisite for the maintenance of peace and harmony between the States or for the purpose of protecting their common interests and defending their common sovereignty against aggression from abroad or insurrection at home.

I shall not discuss at length the question of power sometimes claimed for the General Government under the clause of the eighth section of the Constitution, which gives Congress the power "to lay and collect taxes, duties, imposts, and excises, to pay debts and provide for the common defense and general welfare of the United States," because if it has not already been settled upon sound reason and authority it never will be. I take the received and just construction of that article, as if written to lay and collect taxes, duties, imposts, and excises *in order* to pay the debts and *in order* to provide for the common defense and general welfare. It is not a substantive general power to provide for the welfare of the United States, but is a limitation on the grant of power to raise money by taxes, duties, and imposts. If it were otherwise, all the rest of the Constitution, consisting of carefully enumerated and cautiously guarded grants of specific powers, would have been useless, if not delusive. It would be impossible in that view to escape from the conclusion that these were inserted only to mislead for the present, and, instead of enlightening and defining the pathway of the future, to involve its action in the mazes of doubtful construction. Such a conclusion the character of the men who framed that sacred instrument will never permit us to form. Indeed, to suppose it susceptible of any other construction would be to consign all the rights of the States and of the people of the States to the mere discretion of Congress, and thus to clothe the Federal Government with authority to control the sovereign States, by which they would have been dwarfed into provinces or departments and all sovereignty vested in an absolute consolidated central power, against which the spirit of liberty has so often and in so many countries struggled in vain. In my judgment you can not by tributes to humanity make any adequate compensation for the wrong you would inflict by removing the sources of power and political action from those who are to be thereby affected. If the time shall ever arrive when, for an object appealing, however strongly, to our sympathies, the dignity of the States shall bow to the dictation of Congress by conforming their legislation thereto, when the power and majesty and honor of those who created shall become subordinate to the thing of their creation, I but feebly utter my apprehensions when I express my firm conviction that we shall see "the beginning of the end."

It is a marked point of the history of the Constitution that when it was proposed to empower Congress to establish a university the proposition was confined to the District intended for the future seat of Government of the United States, and that even that proposed clause was omitted in consideration of the exclusive powers conferred on Congress to legislate for that District. Could a more decisive indication of the true construction and the spirit of the Constitution in regard to all matters of this nature have been given? It proves that such objects were considered by the Convention as appertaining to local legislation only; that they were not comprehended, either expressly or by implication, in the grant of general power to Congress, and that consequently they remained with the several States.

The general result at which I have arrived is the necessary consequence of those views of the relative rights, powers, and duties of the States and of the Federal Government which I have long entertained and often expressed and in reference to which my convictions do but increase in force with time and experience.

I have thus discharged the unwelcome duty of respectfully stating my objections to this bill, with which I cheerfully submit the whole subject to the wisdom of Congress.

FRANKLIN PIERCE

Notes

1. James Madison, "Vices of the Political System of the United States," April 1787, *The Papers of James Madison*, Vol. 9 (Chicago: University of Chicago Press, 1975), p. 351.
2. Page S. Smith, *The Shaping of America: A People's History of the Young Republic* (New York: McGraw-Hill, 1980), Vol. 3, pp. 50–94; Charles A. Beard and Mary R. Beard, *A Basic History of the United States* (New York: The New Home Library, 1944), pp. 209–214; Roger Daniels, *Coming to America: A History of Immigration and Ethnicity in American Life* (New York: Harper Collins, 1990), p. 114.
3. U.S. Department of Commerce, Bureau of the Census, *Historical Statistics of the United States: Colonial Times to 1957* (Washington, D.C.: Government Printing Office, 1960) (hereafter cited as *Historical Statistics*).
4. David Hackett Fischer, "Growing Old in America," in Jill Quadagno, *Aging, the Individual and Society: Readings in Social Gerontology* (New York: St. Martin's Press, 1980), pp. 34–45.
5. Daniels, op. cit., pp. 112–118, 268–270.
6. Edward C. Kirkland, *A History of American Economic Life* (New York: F. S. Crofts, 1941), p. 144.
7. *Historical Statistics*, p. 302.
8. Walter W. Jennings, *A History of Economic Progress in the United States* (New York: Thomas Y. Crowell, 1926), Appendix, Table 7, "Development of Typical Manufactures," p. 759.
9. Vernon Louis Parrington, *Main Currents in American Thought* (New York: Harcourt, Brace, 1930), Vol. 2, *The Romantic Revolution in America*, p. 104. Quoted from William J. Grayson, *The Hireling and the Slave*, Preface, pp. xiv–xv.
10. Ibid.
11. Jennings, op. cit., p. 153. Quoted from *American State Papers, Series Finance*, Vol. 1, pp. 123–141.
12. Ibid., p. 166.
13. For a detailed description of the boarding house system, see Vera Shlakman, *Economic History of a Factory Town*, Smith College Studies in History, Vol. 20, Nos. 1–4 (Northampton, Mass.: Smith College, Department of History, Oct. 1934–July 1935).
14. Harriet Martineau, *Society in America* (London, 1837), 2:247–248. Quoted in Jennings, op. cit., p. 303.
15. For an interesting discussion of this point, see Thomas Dublin, *Women at Work* (New York: Columbia University Press, 1979).
16. *Historical Statistics*, p. 14.
17. S. E. Forman, *The Rise of American Commerce and Industry* (New York: The Century, 1927), pp. 195, 471.
18. Jennings, op. cit., pp. 295–297.
19. Ibid., pp. 300–310. See also Philip S. Foner, *History of the Labor Movement in the United States* (New York: International Publishers, 1947), pp. 143–166.
20. Horace Mann, *Education and Prosperity*, Old South Leaflet No. 144 (Boston: Directors of Old South Work, Old South Meeting House, 1848), p. 6.
21. Smith, op. cit., p. 197.
22. Mann, op. cit., p. 7.
23. Jeannette P. Nichols and Roy F. Nichols, *The Growth of American Democracy* (New York: Appleton-Century, 1939), p. 182.

24. "Pastoral Letter of the General Association of Massachusetts to the Congressional Churches under Their Care," reprinted in *The Liberator*, August 11, 1837.

25. For an in-depth study of drinking in the United States during the early decades of the nineteenth century, see W. J. Rorabaugh, *The Alcoholic Republic* (New York: Oxford University Press, 1979).

26. Ibid., pp. 8–9.

27. Judith Papachristou, *Women Together, A Ms. Book* (New York: Knopf, 1976), p. 19.

28. *The Lily*, January 1, 1848. Reprinted in Papachristou, op. cit., p. 20.

29. Dorothea L. Dix, Memorial, *Praying a Grant of Land for the Relief and Support of the Indigent Curable and Incurable Insane in the United States*, Miscellaneous Senate Document No. 150, 30th Cong., 1st sess., June 27, 1848, p. 213. Reprinted in *Poverty, U.S.A., On Behalf of the Insane Poor* (New York: Arno Press and *New York Times*, 1971).

30. Ibid., p. 25.

31. President Franklin Pierce, "Veto Message—An Act Making a Grant of Public Lands to the Several States for the Benefit of Indigent Insane Persons," May 3, 1854.

32. John V. N. Yates, *Report of the Secretary of State on the Relief and Settlement of the Poor*, p. 942. Reprinted in *Poverty, U.S.A., The Almshouse Experience* (New York: Arno Press and *New York Times*, 1971).

33. B. J. Klebaner, "Public Poor Relief in America 1790–1860" (Ph.D. diss., Columbia University, 1952), p. 329.

34. Thomas Paine, *The Rights of Man*, Part 2. Reprinted in *Basic Writings of Thomas Paine* (New York: Wiley, 1942), p. 253.

35. Mathew Carey, *Appeal to the Wealthy of the Land, Ladies As Well As Gentlemen, on Character, Conduct, Situation and Prospects of Those Whose Sole Dependence for Subsistence Is on the Labour of Their Hands* (Philadelphia: Stereotyped by L. Johnson, No. 6 George Street, August 15, 1833), pp. 3–34.

36. Ibid.

37. Josiah Quincy, *Report of the Committee to Whom Was Referred the Consideration of the Pauper Laws of This Commonwealth*, p. 7. Reprinted in *Poverty, U.S.A., The Almshouse Experience*, op. cit.

38. The Society for the Prevention of Pauperism in the City of New York, *The First Annual Report, to which is added A Report on the Subject of Pauperism* (New York: J. Seymour, 1818), p. 3.

39. Ibid., p. 16.

40. Ibid., p. 18.

41. Ibid., p. 12.

42. Ibid., p. 5.

43. Quincy, op. cit., p. 9.

44. Ibid., p. 10.

45. Yates, op. cit., pp. 941–942.

46. Ibid., p. 955.

47. *Report of Select Senate Committee to Visit Charitable and Penal Institutions*, 1857, New York Senate Document No. 8, 1857. Reprinted in Sophonisba P. Breckinridge, *Public Welfare Administration in the United States* (Chicago: University of Chicago Press, 1927), p. 149.

48. Klebaner, op. cit., pp. 73–74, 86, 89. For a discussion of the extension of the use of almshouses, see David J. Rothman, *The Discovery of the Asylum* (Boston: Little, Brown, 1971), pp. 180–205.

49. Grace Abbott, *The Child and the State* (Chicago: University of Chicago Press, 1938), 2:29.

50. Homer Folks, *The Care of Destitute, Neglected and Delinquent Children* (New York: Macmillan, 1911), pp. 52–55.

51. New York House of Refuge, *Second Annual Report*. Quoted in Rothman, op. cit., p. 215.

52. Rothman, op. cit., p. 214.

53. Report of the committee appointed to Visit and Examine into the Affairs and Management of the [Philadelphia] House of Refuge, *Hazard's Register of Pennsylvania, Devoted to the Preservation of Facts and Documents and Every Kind of Useful Information Respecting the State of Pennsylvania*, Vol. 15 (January–July 1835), ed. Samuel Hazard. Also to be found in Abbott, op. cit., 2:357–361.

54. Robert A. Bremner, *From the Depths: The Discovery of Poverty in the United States* (New York: New York University Press, 1956), p. 39.
55. Folks, op. cit., p. 41.
56. Edith Abbott, *Some American Pioneers in Social Welfare: Select Documents with Editorial Notes* (Chicago: University of Chicago Press, 1937), p. 132.
57. Charles Loring Brace, *The Dangerous Classes in New York* (New York: Wynkoop and Hallenbeck, 1880), pp. 224–266.
58. Ibid.
59. Henry W. Thurston, *The Dependent Child* (New York: Columbia University Press, 1930), p. 121.
60. *Report of Select Senate Committee*, 1857, op. cit., p. 149.
61. Ibid., p. 150.
62. Ibid., p. 154.
63. Ibid., pp. 153–154.
64. Ibid., p. 152.
65. Ibid., pp. 154, 155.
66. Breckinridge, op. cit., p. 142.
67. Michael B. Katz, *In the Shadow of the Poorhouse* (New York: Basic Books, 1986), pp. 16–19.
68. Klebaner, op. cit., passim; Rothman, op. cit., pp. 287–295.

4

The Civil War and After: 1860–1900

The Civil War and its aftermath were defining years in the history of social welfare and social work. At the end of the war, the nation undertook its most far-reaching effort at social reform as it attempted to "reconstruct" the South as a liberal, democratic society. Yet, the combination of Southern resistance and white racism defeated the experiment in a few years. In the wake of Reconstruction's failure, social activism was channeled into narrower and more limited endeavors. The Charity Organization and Settlement House movements grew out of this cautious approach to reform. Social work, which had its origins in these two movements, continued to share this caution. A focus on individual change over social reform, a distrust of the competence of the poor, and a preference for voluntary over government action would characterize social work over much of its first century.

These years were some in which science and invention progressed rapidly and created a base for growth in all sectors of the economy—transportation, communication, agriculture, mining, and manufacturing. Population increase, the discovery of additional natural resources, the extension of transportation, the development of new means of communication, the appearance of hundreds of new industries, the evolution of new forms of business organization, the growth of credit institutions, the concentration of economic power, and the beginning of effective organization of a free labor class were all components of the new wealth. Population doubled during the last thirty years of the century; gross national product rose from about $6.7 billion to an estimated $16.8 billion—about 2 1/2 times—which meant a substantial increase in per capita income.[1] Except for Native Americans, all groups of the population, all sectors of the economy, and all sections of the country shared this growth. But growth did not proceed uniformly, nor was it distributed equally, among industries, among regions of the country, or among population groups.

The war and the industrial development it hastened had laid the foundation for the acquisition of major fortunes, and the postwar railroad boom fostered the accumulation of individual wealth. Soon the formation of industrial corporations and trusts and the expansion of the stock market made it possible to extend and exploit the technological innovations of the period. The open display of affluence, of wild speculation and ruthlessness in business, and of widespread political immorality highlighted the precariousness of the lives of factory workers and tenant farmers and made the misery of the lives of the poor more bitter. Moreover, cyclical fluctuations brought panic, depression, and severe unemployment during the years 1873–1878 and 1893–1898. Population growth, the normal hazards of an increasingly industrial and urban society, and the recurring periods of economic depression resulted in expanding relief rolls. The country at large looked with envy and fascination upon the success of the rich and with despair and disapproval upon the failure of the poor.

For the North, the war brought prosperity. The increased output of war goods and rising prices for food and clothing stimulated the process of industrialization. Demand for labor was high; and the need for workers to fill newly created jobs, as well as the old ones left vacant by men away at war, meant continuing encouragement of immigration and steady expansion of the size of cities. The end of the Civil War and the return to civilian production furthered the process of industrialization and economic growth.

The war was a catalyst for Northern growth, but for the South it meant the devastation of land, property, transportation facilities, and credit institutions. While the Northeast and Midwest saw increasing concentration of property and wealth, the South experienced some breaking up of plantations and a decentralization of land ownership. While jobs were plentiful in the North, workers in the South—white and black—struggled to find employment and a means of self-support. The process of Southern reconstruction eventually led to the beginnings of industrialization and, of even more significance for the eventual shape of the Southern economy, to the simultaneous reestablishment of agricultural interests and the rise of tenant farming. The pattern that was to evolve was one of recovery and of growth, but of a growth rate much slower than the rest of the nation.

For the development of the West in the postwar period, the most important factors were the settlement and differential use of previously acquired Western territories. Dissatisfaction with the urbanization and industrialization of Northeastern states, and with the commercialization and tenant farm structure of agriculture in Southern states, led to the westward movement of population. As grazing was displaced by agriculture, cultivation of Western land increased. The westward trek was particularly responsive to periods of economic recession and labor unrest and to the pressures of integrating returning veterans and a constantly swelling number of immigrants into the population. In 1860 the five states immediately west of the Mississippi—Texas, Arkansas, Missouri, Iowa, and Minnesota—had only 15.3 million acres in improved farmlands. By 1880 these same five states had increased improved farmlands to 50 million acres; by 1910, to 87 million acres. An era ended in 1890 when the superintendent of the census wrote: "Up to and including 1880 the country had a frontier settlement but at present the unsettled area has been so broken into isolated bodies of settlement that there can hardly be said to be a frontier line."[2] In 1860, the area west of the Mississippi River included only seven states; by

1900, there were eighteen. By the turn of the twentieth century, the continental United States included 45 states and only three territories.

Population Changes

Territorial expansion and industrial and agricultural growth went hand in hand with growth and shifts in population. The country's overall population grew from 36 million in 1865 to 76 million in 1900, an increase of 40 million, or 111 percent.[3] The proportion of blacks in the total population remained comparatively stable— 13 percent in 1865 and 12 percent in 1900. For blacks and whites, life expectancy rose. A man born in 1860 could expect to live just past 38; a woman until 40.5 years. By 1900, white men were living over 48 years on the average, and white women, just past 51. The median age of the population increased from 19.4 in 1860 to 22.9 in 1900. The percentage of the aged in the population remained low, however, at only 4 percent, largely as a result of the large-scale immigration during the period.

Naturalization and Citizenship

The Homestead Act of 1862, the end of the Civil War, the opening of the Oregon territories, the development of new agricultural machinery to farm the prairies, and the gold rush all contributed to the westward movement. The Oklahoma land rush and the finishing of the transcontinental railroad to the Pacific coast accelerated the process.

The years after the Civil War saw the devastation of the Native American nations. The Western expansion of white settlers disrupted the economic, demographic, and social organization of Native American life. The American bison was hunted to near extinction as a way of eliminating the food supply of many native nations, and the U.S. government used almost any pretext to displace Native Americans from their land and destroy their capacity for an independent life.

There was a series of wars with Native Americans. Ranchers, settlers, and miners took over their lands. Chief Joseph of the Nez Perce had declared, "I will fight no more forever," and Geronimo of the Apache nation had become a prisoner. By the 1890s, nearly all Native American nations were conquered and located on reservations. In the course of three centuries, the population had been reduced by 90 percent. On reservations, Native Americans were subjects, not citizens. The Dawes Act of 1887 permitted naturalization for Native Americans not living on reservations. Those on reservations were considered members of another, dependent nation.[4]

In exchange for their land, tribal nations were at first settled on fertile ground. They were promised annual cash stipends and were to be taught how to live self-sufficiently as farmers on reservations. But the tribal nations were moved again and again to more barren areas. Most reservations had too little grazing land for buffalo, and the land was too unproductive to grow sufficient food. Added to this were the plagues, whiskey, and corrupt agents on both sides who stole supplies and sources of support. The result for most tribes was widespread poverty. In the words of President Rutherford B. Hayes in 1877:

> The Indians...have been driven from place to place. The purchase money paid...has still left them poor. In many instances, when they had settled down upon land assigned to them by compact and begun to support themselves by their own labor, they were rudely jostled off and thrust into the wilderness again. Many, if not most, of our Indian wars have had their origin in broken promises and acts of injustice on our part.[5]

Even sympathetic whites saw assimilation and the elimination of Native America's folkways as the only alternative to annihilation. With no recognition of tribal value systems, culture, or languages, Eastern reformers wanted to see Native Americans brought into the "mainstream." Children were taken from their parents and reservations and sent to military-style boarding schools, where they were forced to give up their traditions. Their hairstyles, dress, languages, food, and religions were westernized. After school, they were returned to their reservations. They were prepared for neither world.

The number of immigrants to the United States between 1865 and 1900 totaled 13 million, which constituted 32 percent of the increase in population during those years.[6] In the 1870s and early 1880s, they came largely from Great Britain, Scandinavia, and Germany and tended to move to the West. Toward the end of the nineteenth century, a new wave of immigration came from Russia, Austria-Hungary, Poland, and other parts of eastern Europe. The new immigrants went to the mines, steel mills, textile factories, and other manufacturing establishments of the Eastern seaboard. Businessmen welcomed them as cheap labor, but labor unions resented them as competition.[7]

The issue of immigration presented a complex dilemma for many Americans. On the one hand, since its founding as a "city upon a hill," Americans had seen their country as a beacon to the rest of the world. The United States was a nation of immigrants. How could it turn its back on that legacy? At the same time, the increase in Southern and Eastern European immigration added a racial element to the debate. Not only were immigrants poor and competing for jobs, but they did not share the cultural and genetic background of earlier generations. Anti-immigrant fervor fueled a wave of "scientific racism" in which scientists and pseudoscientists claimed to have discovered several European "races," each with different qualities and capacities. Darwin's theory of natural selection provided another pretext for differentiating groups. Rather than adding to America's diversity, the new immigrants posed a new battle for the "survival of the fittest."[8]

The Asian population, which had come to the United States in large numbers first during the California gold rush of 1848 and later as laborers recruited for the building of the railroads of the West, met with even more discrimination and more barriers. Immigration of Chinese, largely Cantonese and male, rose sharply during the period. With the completion of the rail system to the Pacific coast and the end of the need for a large supply of cheap laborers, economics and racism combined to decrease the Chinese presence.

Three Apaches at the Carlisle School. With the conquest of the Western tribes, federal policy during the late nineteenth century focused on "Americanizing" Native Americans. The Carlisle School in Pennsylvania became an important institution in this ill-conceived effort.
Denver Public Library

A series of legislative acts at the end of the nineteenth century first limited naturalization, then restricted immigration, and finally excluded the Chinese population in the United States.

In 1868, Congress adopted the Fourteenth Amendment to the Constitution, which was designed to protect the rights of the newly freed slaves. It declared that anyone born in this country was automatically a citizen. Although few Chinese had been born here, those who were had citizenship, as did their children, no matter where they were born. But Chinese, indeed all Asians, born abroad had no rights to citizenship at any time. Two years later, Congress passed the Naturalization Act of 1870, which limited naturalization to "white persons and persons of African descent." Asians and Native Americans were aliens, ineligible for citizenship.

Arguing that the Chinese were basically "inassimilable," the Chinese Exclusion Act was passed in 1882. In part, this act reflected the interests of organized labor and its fear of cheap labor. It built on a heavy layer of racial prejudice. The act excluded Chinese immigration of laborers (although not manufacturers), at first for ten years and then "permanently." Originally the act provided for Chinese workers going back to China to get readmission certificates. But in 1888, President Grover Cleveland canceled all certificates and prevented the readmission of many.[9]

Regional Shifts

Internal migration and immigration combined to change the social profile of the United States during the last half of the nineteenth century. As the cities grew larger, the majority of the population remained rural. In the countryside, the West and South continued to diverge even after the Civil War as tenancy and share-cropping ensnared the South in a cycle of "underdevelopment" that had profound implications for poor whites and African Americans.[10]

By the end of the century, large cities were no longer confined to the Atlantic coast. In 1860, there had been eight cities with populations over 100,000—four in the East, three in the Midwest, and one in the South. By 1900, there were thirty-three cities over 100,000—seventeen in the East, thirteen in the Midwest, three in the South, and three in the Far West.[11] Unquestionably, the process of urbanization had made great strides. In 1860, 20 percent of the country's territory had been defined as urban; by 1900, 40 percent. But this very fact emphasizes that in 1900 the country was, for the most part, still rural.[12]

The structure of rural life in the post-Civil War period changed in response to shifts in the organization of agriculture. The major crop of the prewar South was cotton, with some land devoted to tobacco and sugar. Ownership and control had been lodged primarily in a plantation system with slave labor. The postwar period saw the development of tenant farming, sharecropping, and some independent ownership of small farms. The average size of a farm in the South Atlantic states dropped from 352.8 acres in 1860 to 108.4 in 1900. Almost half the farms were tenant operated.[13] The high rate of tenancy prevented small farmers from improving their individual well-being or contributing to regional economic growth. Most tenants found themselves heavily in debt and dependent upon a rich landowner for credit and provisions. The oppression that resulted from this economic reality fueled a number of protest movements, including Populism. In the South, however, the ideology of white supremacy and the willingness of powerful whites to use violence prevented poor whites and blacks from effectively organizing for change.[14]

The postwar South saw some diversification of products, especially the development of corn as a cash crop and of fruit orchards. But this was small and largely confined to a group of independent white farmers. Cotton remained the staple. Familiarity, ready marketability, and, most critically, the dependence for capital on conservative credit sources prevented further diversification. Output of cotton was 4.5 million bales in 1861; by 1877, output was above prewar levels.[15] Recovery in cotton production both fueled and limited the postwar recovery of the Southern economy.

The West, too, saw major structural shifts. As in the South, the average size of a farm decreased; unlike the South, this was a response to a major change in output. The vast Western lands provided, first, an opportunity for raising cattle and sheep and, for growing wheat and corn. The availability of land resources for exploitation and for settling was particularly opportune at the close of the Civil War when the disjuncture created by unemployment due to necessary changeovers in war industries, troop demobilization, and continuing immigration could all be eased by movement westward. Additionally, this migration reflected a continuation of the attraction provided by the Homestead Act passed by Congress in 1862.

Migration was given further impetus by the completion of the first transcontinental railroad in 1869. Subsequently, through the use of land grants, Congress chartered the construction of the Northern Pacific to connect the Great Lakes with Puget Sound, the Southern Pacific and Santa Fe to tie the Mississippi Valley with the Pacific coast, and the Denver and Rio Grande to slice through the mountains of Colorado to Salt Lake City. The building of state-supported rival lines and of branch lines served to connect the states of the West with each other and the West with the East. In addition to being direct transportation links with Eastern markets, the railroads stimulated trade carried on ships operating from the Great Lakes and connecting with ports in New York State and in foreign countries. Grazing moved westward as more land came under cultivation.

Western crop acreage increased and, with the introduction of fertilizers, productivity rose. As a result, the country's production of wheat had jumped from 173 million bushels in 1859 to 600 million in 1900; the production of corn rose from 839 million bushels in 1859 to 2.7 billion in 1900.[16] With the value of wheat and corn exports up to $73 million and $85 million, respectively, by 1900, the West, in addition to being the breadbasket of the United States, had become a substantial supplier of foreign need.[17]

The opening of the West was speeded, too, by the discovery of and search for precious metals—gold, silver, and zinc—and soon by the realization of the existence of vast supplies of other extractives—copper, coal, iron ore, and petroleum. The rise in the value of mining from 1 percent of the nation's total output on the eve of the Civil War to 5 percent in the last year of the century was a mark of advancing Western enterprise as well as a base for Eastern industrialization.[18]

The recovery of the South and the settling and development of the West cannot be understood without awareness of their ultimate dependence upon the growth of manufacturing, particularly of Eastern manufacturing. In the country as a whole, the number of manufacturing establishments grew from 140,000 in 1860 to 208,000 in 1900. Between those same years, the number of employees grew from 1 million to 4.7 million—a 370 percent increase; the value of manufactured products from $1.8 billion to $11 billion—a 505 percent increase. Capitalization grew by 789 percent during these years. Manufacturing had become more capital-intensive, necessitating the eventual move toward larger units of manufacturing and decreased competition.[19] The value of manufacturing output rose by 515 percent from the period immediately preceding the Civil War to the end of the century. The value of agricultural output rose by 127 percent during the same period. Although both had increased in value, they had reversed positions in relative importance.[20] In 1900, the industrial heartland of the nation was still bounded by a parallel-ogram anchored by Boston and Baltimore to the east and Chicago and St. Louis to the west.

The dominance of the East in manufacturing is demonstrated by the fact that 67.3 percent of the country's manufacturing establishments were located in New England and the Middle Atlantic states in 1859. Although manufacturing grew in the Western states, the New England and Middle Atlantic states continued to account for 52.4 percent of all manufacturing enterprises at the end of the century.[21]

The Welfare of Soldiers and Veterans

During and immediately after the Civil War, the social welfare needs of soldiers and their families demanded attention in all sections of the country. During the war years, 2.3 million served in the Union forces, of whom 719,000 died and 280,000 were wounded—a casualty rate of 43 percent. Participants in the Confederate forces totaled 781,000, of whom 307,000 died and 100,000 were wounded—a casualty rate of 52 percent.[22] Whether for medical care, domiciliary care, or financial support, the needs of veterans were considered apart from the needs of the civilian population and as deserving of state and federal governmental support.

Federal legislation affording benefits to soldiers and veterans was passed first by Congress for the Union forces and, later, was confined to veterans of the Union. In July 1862, Congress enacted a pension system covering individuals disabled in the line of duty, as well as widows, children, and dependent relations of those who were killed. Efforts to encourage enlistment, such as the Enrollment Act of 1863, stated each citizen's obligation to defend the country and the right of the federal government to impose that obligation.[23] But the enactment of additional legislation in the veterans' behalf clarified the reciprocal nature of the obligation—the necessity for taking care of "our battered heroes…in such a way as to maintain the military spirit and the national pride…and to keep in the eye of the Nation the price of its liberties."[24]

The United States Sanitary Commission was established in 1861 by the secretary of war in response to a recommendation by the Women's Central Relief Association of New York. The association represented the joined forces of the women comprising the Women's Central Association of Relief for the Sick and Wounded of the Army, the Advisory Committee of the Boards of Physicians and Surgeons of the Hospitals of New York, and the New York Medical Association for furnishing hospital supplies in aid of the army. Pointing to "the spontaneous and earnest efforts" of women in many parts of the Union to perform volunteer service in behalf of an essentially volunteer army, the relief association called for a governmental body responsible "to keep the women of the loyal states everywhere informed how their efforts may be most wisely and economically employed."[25]

The New York association, like its counterparts in many other localities, was aware of the recent experience with sanitary science in the Crimean War, particularly as publicized through the testimony of Florence Nightingale in parliamentary hearings. The need, as set forth in an address to the secretary of war on May 18, 1861, was for preventive services, such as the supervision of the diet and hygiene of the troops, and, in addition, the furnishing of medical and nursing personnel and supplies, of financial relief, and of personal services.

The acting surgeon general of the United States acquiesced, and, on June 13, 1861, President Abraham Lincoln approved the appointment of a Commission of Inquiry and Advice in respect of the Sanitary Interests of the United States Forces.

The "voluntary" nature of the commission—its dependence upon contributions of money and labor—is reflected in its original and popular title, the People's Commission of Sanitary Inquiry and Advice.[26] Once appointed, the commission "prepared to go to work without a dollar in its treasury." Subsequently, "the irrepressible determination of the American people to manifest...their direct personal interest in the soldier" led to "countless forms of popular sympathy" demonstrated in "clamorous and persistent...offers of relief as the war went on."[27] The commission became the channel for directing this national outpouring of contributions toward the relief and comfort of the Union forces.

The nine officially appointed members of the commission were men, despite the fact that women's groups funded and implemented its programs. The work of overlooking the welfare of the military was performed in the belief that the country could "never half repay them for the sacrifices they have made or half balance our debt of gratitude."[28] From the start, these groups supported the commission's promotion of national concern for the care veterans would receive once the war was over.

On March 3, 1865, Lincoln signed an act to incorporate a national military and naval asylum for the relief of totally disabled officers and men of the voluntary forces of the United States. Subsequently, this enabling legislation was strengthened by the provision of funds to make possible the building and operation of a group of national homes, first for Union veterans suffering economic distress due to wartime disabilities and, later, for economically distressed veterans whose disabilities were not service connected. The country's view of the needy Union veteran as "worthy" was illustrated in an 1871 report of a congressional committee that had investigated the conditions of the early national homes:

> Liberal expenditures have been made to provide...facilities for recreation and for intellectual and moral culture, as well as...good quarters, food, clothing, and hospital attendance. The constant and proper aim of the management is...that the asylums were in no sense almshouses...but homes which the disabled soldiers have earned for themselves.[29]

During the Civil War and for the twenty-five years following it, the federal government liberalized the terms of entitlement to pensions and raised the level of benefits. In 1866, one year after the war's end, annual federal expenditures for Union veterans' pensions totaled $15 million; by 1882 this doubled; and by 1889, it reached $86 million.[30] In 1890, pushed by pension claims agents and the Grand Army of the Republic (GAR), and responding to the large number of disabled and destitute veterans, Congress acted to keep veterans from almshouses and from dependency on "the frigid bosom of public charity." The Dependent Pension Act of 1890 dropped the requirement that disability be service connected and instead provided pensions for veterans (and their wives) who had served at least ninety days and who were unable to earn a living by physical labor. By 1898, expenditures tripled and the number of veterans covered jumped from less than 420,000 to more than 745,000.[31]

By 1900, federal and state responsibility for the care of needy and disabled veterans and their dependents was well established. Cash payments, medical services, and domiciliary care were all parts of a system that viewed the social welfare of veterans and their families as a special obligation of the society as a whole. The

The Pension Building was constructed in the 1880s and was the home of the Bureau of Pensions until 1926. By the early twentieth century nearly a million Americans were receiving veterans' pensions because of disability, old age, or the death of a family member.
Photograph by Russell Jones. Library of Congress

obligation was being met through legislative provisions that, for their time, were generous and that were couched in language meant to protect the beneficiary's right to help and to avoid a pauper's label. New York State, for example, in 1887 went so far as to prohibit "sending indigent soldiers, sailors, and marines (or their families, or the families of those deceased), to any almshouse (or orphan asylum) without the full concurrence and consent of the commander and relief committees of the post of the Grand Army of the Republic."[32] The founding of the Grand Army of the Republic, a veterans' organization, in 1866 had provided an organized constituency able to push for progressive liberalization of benefits.

Federal largesse did not extend to Confederate veterans. In national homes established at Kecoughtan, Virginia, and Johnson City, Tennessee, only those Southerners who had served on the Union side were welcome. The Pension Act of 1890 limited benefits to veterans of the Union army. During the war and the postwar period, such benefits as did accrue to veterans of the Confederate army were provided on a local and state level. As with Northern veterans, aid for Southern soldiers and their families was outside the stigma of poor-relief laws. Families of Confederate soldiers became the "new poor" and Southern localities enacted special legislation, including special taxes, to provide emergency assistance. As the war progressed, responsibility shifted from voluntary agencies, to local government, and then to state governments and the Confederate Congress. The Confederate veteran was considered by his government and his neighbors to be as worthy as his Northern counterpart. Resources were so limited, however, that relief efforts were meager.

Social Welfare: The Rural South

During the war, the Southern states had experienced widespread destruction as well as severe curtailment of agricultural economic activity. Cessation of hostilities revealed a situation of dire need. Wounded veterans and their families, widows and orphans of slain soldiers, large numbers of freed, homeless blacks, and a civilian population were all made needy by the war itself. Near famine resulted from drought and lack of organized labor to get the economy moving. The situation was worse for lack of an extensive prewar public or private welfare system to draw upon.

In the immediate postwar period, the individual states gave first attention to the needs of veterans and their dependents for artificial limbs and cash pensions. Concern for the orphans of Confederate soldiers led to the establishment of orphanages and of apprenticeship procedures. As for the general white population, most Southern states set up central public welfare stations for the distribution of food and clothing. The states moved to deal with the freed black population through attempts to reinstitute a system of control of the labor market.

Black codes designed to regulate the lives of ex-slaves were passed in all the former Confederate states except Tennessee. The codes limited property rights, forbade working as artisans and mechanics, and otherwise specified the kinds of economic activities in which freed blacks could engage. The codes of Georgia, for example, stated that "all persons strolling about in idleness would be put in chain gangs and contracted out to employers."[33] In effect, the codes used the old Poor Law provisions in regard to vagrancy to secure state revenues while simultaneously organizing workers to be used in reconstruction and industrial pursuits. Vagrants were rounded up, labeled criminal, and subjected to leases as long as twenty years.[34]

Black children were also pushed into dependency. In 1865, for example, Mississippi declared all blacks under eighteen years who were orphans, or whose parents could not support them, available for apprenticing. Former masters were given preference. Black children were not afforded such guarantees in regard to food, clothing, and education as were written into indentureship agreements for white children. Thus, a solution to black dependency and a means for building a slavelike labor force went hand in hand.

The excesses of "white reconstruction" led Congress in March 1867 to require the Confederate states to call state conventions for the purpose of creating more representative state governments and for ratifying the Fourteenth Amendment to the Constitution as a prerequisite for readmission into the Union. By 1870, all the Southern states had complied. No redistribution of land had been required and little was achieved. There was an enlargement of the role of state government in matters of expenditures for social welfare and education for blacks and whites. A pattern of separate institutions for blacks and whites evolved. Despite much discussion of state responsibility, however, no comprehensive programs of state welfare emerged. Orphanages, mental hospitals, and almshouses were built, but each state followed its own limited design; local responsibility, especially for relief, was endemic.

All in all, the Southern social welfare scene was dominated by the federal government through the activities of the Freedmen's Bureau.[35] Even before the close of the war, it was evident that Northern effort would be required to bring the South relief from destitution. The Port Royal Experiment of 1862 represented one such effort and became precursor to the Freedmen's Bureau. When, in the face of the Union army's advance into South Carolina, whites abandoned the plantations of the Port Royal area, ten thousand slaves were left to fend for themselves. Their distress led the president to authorize (but not fund) an experimental relief and rehabilitation program. Two volunteer organizations, the National Freedmen's Relief Association of New York and the Boston Education Commission, supplied most of the funding and labor. Several hundred volunteers saw to the distribution of food and clothing and the rehabilitation of abandoned and pillaged homes. In addition, they established schools for black children and attempted to use free labor in large-scale cotton cultivation.

For all the experiment's success, the needs of the South were beyond the resources of volunteer organizations, and the Bureau of Refugees, Freedmen, and Abandoned Lands—more familiarly known as the Freedmen's Bureau—was established by Congress in March 1865, two months before the end of the war. The bureau was placed in the War Department; however, since no appropriations for relief purposes or salaries were made, the bureau was dependent upon the military for whatever was distributed in the way of food, clothing, and medical supplies. In 1866, President Johnson vetoed an extension of the life of the bureau, objecting, as had

Headquarters of the Superintendent of the Poor. During Reconstruction, the Federal government channeled resources to African Americans. This sketch shows the distribution of clothing to poor, freed men and women.

National Archives

President Pierce before him, to the federal government's assumption of responsibility for social welfare. "A system for the support of indigent persons in the United States," he wrote, "was never contemplated by the authors of the Constitution...."[36] In reasoning typical of the era, he placed responsibility for recovery from slavery on its victims. Legislation that delayed "a self-sustaining condition must have a tendency injurious alike to their character and their prospects." The veto was overridden and the life of the bureau extended by two years.

The extension was fostered by the fact that the bureau, faced with the extreme hunger and poverty of whites as well as blacks, had helped both; both protested the threatened withdrawal of relief. The 1866 act provided the first direct appropriation—$6.9 million—for the bureau's work; and in 1867, in response to the threat of famine, Congress authorized the use of funds for all destitute and helpless Southerners regardless of wartime loyalties. It set a precedent for federal participation in social welfare during emergency periods.

Originally, the bureau had been established to deal with transient, homeless blacks and with the management of abandoned and confiscated property. In time the bureau took on the task of organizing freed blacks into a labor force. In connection with the last, the bureau not only sought jobs and organized work opportunities for freed men but also drew up and supervised labor contracts for blacks in their relation with whites. General Oliver O. Howard, who carried responsibility for the operations of the bureau, saw to the adjudication of labor disputes and to the prevention of reenslavement.

The Freedman's Village, Hampton, Virginia (from Harper's Weekly, *September 30, 1865). The sketch shows a typical rebuilt Freedman's Village. The communities were generally uniform in appearance with buildings built of rough barrel staves or split boards.*
New York Historical Society, New York City

The Freedmen's Bureau was the first federal welfare agency and, between 1865 and 1869, the major source of public welfare in the South. During its existence, the bureau engaged in numerous social welfare activities. It provided transportation home for refugees and aided in reuniting families. In its first three years, it distributed 18.3 million rations, about 5.2 million of which went to whites. By the end of its fourth year of existence, it had distributed 21 million rations, about 6 million having gone to whites. In addition to distributing medical supplies, the bureau established 46 hospitals. It set up orphan asylums for children and participated in the establishment and running of 4,329 schools for black children. Among institutions of higher learning, it helped found or support Howard, Atlanta, and Fisk universities, Hampton Institute, and Talladega College.

The bureau was subject to a good deal of criticism and question. There was, of course, the basic concern about large-scale federal aid to the needy. This question was especially thorny when raised as one of redistribution of income from Northern to Southern states. Moreover, there was opposition from Southern planters and townspeople who, wanting the blacks to return to work on a more or less prewar basis, accused the bureau of fostering idleness and pauperism. Indeed, this concern about pauperizing freed blacks led General Howard to retrench on direct relief giving and to break up camps that had been organized to provide government-created jobs. The many questions addressed to the bureau's activities added to its personnel problems; a growing view that it represented a radical movement led to its demise in 1872.

Social Welfare: Urban Problems

With the demise of federal responsibility, the domination of social welfare returned to private groups in the Northeast, where urban problems were multiplying. Since the war had been fought in the South, the North was not faced with the necessity for rebuilding. Industrialization to meet the needs of the war provided it with the organization and experience for further expansion at the war's close, when the needs of the South and of the rapidly developing West for manufactured items and for markets were pressing. A high protective tariff served to prevent domestic buyers from buying foreign-made goods. Not surprisingly, the East, as the industrial center of the country, became the center for credit, the center for economic and political power, and the center of labor unrest. The Reconstruction Period was one of expanding markets and rising prices but falling real wages. The recession of 1873–1878 was a period of serious unemployment. Concern with poverty and with pauperism led to different organizational responses from labor and from philanthropic groups.

During the Civil War, the labor movement began to regain its strength as workers found that the wartime labor shortage gave them greater power. Craft unions were organized in sufficient numbers to warrant the calling of the first National Labor Congress in 1866. The power of railroads and business increased during the postwar era as corporate forms appeared and as the development of pools, legal trusts, holding companies, and consolidations was accompanied by a decline in free market competition. Numerous corporate attempts to regulate production and prices within industries, quantity discounting and rebating, wild speculation—all occurred as struggles for monopoly and control took place between larger and larger units of operation. The unhappiness of workers was aggravated by the reality of impersonal employers sufficiently powerful to lower wages. The ability of industrial giants to manipulate labor was enhanced by the presence of a large reserve labor force willing to work for lower wages.

The financial problems of working people were aggravated by the conviction among leaders of organized charities that the purpose of modern philanthropy was to suppress pauperism rather than to aid the needy. In 1895, in the midst of widespread unemployment, the New York Association for the Improvement of Conditions among the Poor railed against longshoremen striking to prevent a cut in wages:

> Every man has a right to work or not... but no man has a right to refuse to support his family and himself when he is able to do it; and no one has a right to prevent others from working, as these strikers persistently attempted to do, while they are themselves idling about the streets and wharves and corner liquor shops.[37]

It came as no surprise, then, that union members viewed supporters of benevolent societies as anti-labor.

The emergence of powerful big businesses led to some federal and state efforts to regulate interstate and intrastate commerce and to a resurgence of union activity. The Interstate Commerce Act of 1887 was an effort to limit the ability of railroads to play one section of the country against another, to their own advantage. By 1890, fourteen states and territories had antimonopoly provisions in their constitutions, and thirteen states had antitrust laws.[38] Demands for some form of federal regulation led to the passage of the Sherman Antitrust Act. It, too, was largely ineffectual, but it declared the illegality of trusts or other combinations in restraint of trade.

The problems of farmers in interstate commerce were recognized in 1889, when the Department of Agriculture was raised to the rank of an executive department and its head made a secretary with cabinet status. Federal recognition of the challenge of labor led, in 1884, to the creation of the Bureau of Labor Statistics with authority "to collect information upon the subject of labor, its relation to capital, the hours of labor, and the earnings of laboring men and women, and the means of promoting their material, social, intellectual, and moral prosperity."[39]

Public data gathering did not translate into action. Of necessity, both farmers and workers resorted to organization—farmers into granges, laborers into larger and stronger unions. By 1875, some 30,000 local granges, with a combined membership of 2.5 million, were in existence.[40] Concerned originally with securing legal protections against railroads, the granges increasingly engaged in a broad range of political activities designed to strengthen farmers in their relation to corporate enterprise. In addition, the need for low-cost loans and reduced tariffs united the Southern and Western farming communities in political movements to combat the dominance of the East.

The potential of large-scale associations of laborers to counter the power of industry and to protect workers against the risks of industrial society had led in 1878 to the organization of the International Labor Union (ILU) and to the initial attempts of the Knights of Labor to consolidate many trade unions and grades of workers. With the demise of the ILU in 1882, the Knights began to grow. In 1883, membership stood at 50,000; in 1886, the membership skyrocketed to 700,000.[41]

Despite its phenomenal growth, the Knights of Labor was torn by internal dissension. There was a fundamental difference between the leadership, which persisted in the repudiation of the strike except as a weapon of last resort, and the membership, which was finding that strikes and boycotts could secure important gains. The leadership was convinced that strikes were futile, since "a strike cannot regulate the laws of supply and demand, for if it cuts off the supply, it also cuts off the demand by throwing consumers out of work, thereby curtailing their purchasing power."[42] The decline of the Knights of Labor came swiftly. Nineteenth-century union's concern with social welfare went beyond issues of wages and control. Many unions for skilled workers—like the Knights of Labor and those in the railroad industry—connected to an older tradition of fraternal organization. These organizations often sponsored insurance and other forms of economic security for their members, a function that laid the foundation for the expansion of employee benefits during the twentieth century.

Leadership in the labor movement shifted to the American Federation of Labor, a federation of craft unions, which saw labor's advance, not in the abandonment of a capitalist mode of organization but in increasing workers' wages. By 1900, labor became increasingly militant in achieving its ends. The battle of labor was, of course, for job protection and for a share in the country's growth. It was also a battle against poverty and against the country's view of the poor. The white, male, skilled workers who made up a majority of unionized workers went to pains to differentiate "respectable" working men like themselves from the "rabble" who were dependent on relief. As long as unions discriminated against African Americans and women, they were vulnerable. The exclusion of African Americans from unions, for example, explains why they were often used as strikebreakers during this era.

There were many aspects to the intensification of problems related to the poor, including the continuing tide of immigrant workers and their threat to wage standards (already precariously low in many unorganized industries) and to the employment of the existing native labor force. Further, there was the sudden proliferation of sectarian and lay relief societies all struggling to exist as well as to meet the needs of their clientele. Finally, there was the frustration of not having been able to deal with poverty in a way consistent with what had become an American self-image, that is, with efficiency, economy, and progress. If America could make such striking progress in technology and productivity, many felt that it could eliminate poverty and social conflict as well.

In addition to machines that revolutionized industrial and agricultural activities, achievements in the realm of applied science opened new fields of communications (the telegraph and telephone), transportation (air brakes, automobiles), and business machines (typewriters, for example). Research was pursued in biology, chemistry, physics, botany, eugenics, ethnology, geology, and astronomy. The rigor of the search and success with the organization of knowledge for practical use became a "dogmatic religion...whose notaries often behaved in the manner of theologians, pretending to possess the one true key to the riddle of the universe."[43] No wonder, then, that leaders in voluntary and public social welfare should look to science and to the organization of scientific knowledge for new approaches to the alleviation of poverty.

The Charity Organization Movement

The failure of Reconstruction led many middle-class social activists to see government programs as inevitably flawed. During the late nineteenth century, these reformers led a concerted effort to wrest control of social welfare from the public sector and to establish a system that was organized and efficient. The Charity Organization movement (the first Charity Organization Society was founded in Buffalo in 1877) was modern in methods and outlook, but its view of the poor as slothful, mendacious, and treacherous looked back to an earlier era. Although the Charity Organization movement would initiate many of the practices of modern social work, including casework, educational and training programs, and the individualization of services, its ideological blinders prevented it from significantly changing the plight of the urban poor.

In large measure, the strength of the Charity Organization Movement was derived from its promise of a "scientific approach" to poverty and pauperism. The frequent communications between American and European scientists had led to widespread knowledge of Darwinian theory and of Herbert Spencer's application of that work to social theory. The new religion preached the need for a laissez-faire economy in which the fittest would become the richest. It feared that social welfare measures that supported dependency and misfits would end in the weakening of mankind. The belief in the possibility of an evolution toward a more affluent society, combined with belief in the openness of that society to individual achievement, made the acquisition of personal wealth not only a sign of fitness, but a condition of moral superiority as well. Andrew Carnegie, the capitalist, and Amos G. Warner, the economist and social welfare leader, could both agree with Russell Conwell, the educator and minister, who said:

> You ought to be rich.... When a man could have been rich just as well, and he is now weak because he is poor, he has done some great wrong; he has been untruthful to himself; he has been unkind to his fellowmen. We ought to get rich if we can by honorable and Christian methods, and these are the only methods that sweep us quickly toward the goal of riches.[44]

The Charity Organization Movement accepted social Darwinism as its theoretical underpinning for helping—or not helping—the poor and called this process "scientific charity." Thus, the belief that the times required a new orientation to social welfare matters resulted in the application of "science" to the development of a delivery system that continued to place the individual, rather than the individual's environment, at the center of the problem.

Interestingly, the stage was set for private-sector domination of social welfare in the report to the First Conference of Charities and Corrections by its Department (Committee) of Social Economy. This report of pauperism in the city of New York, written in 1874 at a time of economic depression, condemned the giving of outdoor relief, whether in the form of public funds or publicly displayed soup kitchens, as inducing many to become paupers. The report contrasted the benevolence of the business community (in spite of its own temporarily embarrassing impoverishment) with the unwillingness of the poor (having become accustomed to depending upon the bounty of others) to accept work at markedly lower wages. The fact of the depression itself, the reality of need, was all the more reason for rigidly limiting—after careful house visitation—relief and, connecting it to work. Available statistics of pauperism showed "a condition of things...less alarming than had been supposed." This did not, however, mitigate the fear of the transmittability of pauperism from adult to child and from relief recipient to worker. Concern persisted that pauperism might degenerate the individual's physical and mental powers to final extinction.[45]

The growth in numbers and power of the Charity Organization Societies in major cities ensured the continuation of an antipublic welfare stance, as well as the fear about the inheritability of pauperism. In 1890, at the seventeenth annual meeting of the National Conference of Charities and Corrections, Josephine Shaw Lowell, perhaps the leading advocate for the private sector, declared that public relief should be given only in cases of extreme distress, "when starvation is imminent." Since it is difficult to prove the imminence of starvation, conditions of deterrence must be maintained. The refuge from pauperism, according to Mrs. Lowell, was self-support or help provided by private sources presumably after investigation and determination of worthiness.[46] Even then, when contributors to the New York Charity Organization Society asked Mrs. Lowell, its president, how much of their contribution would go to the poor, she responded hopefully, "Not one cent."[47]

The harshness expressed by Mrs. Lowell must be seen in the context of contemporary beliefs about the corruptibility of human nature. This view of human nature, whose lineage extends to a doctrine of original sin, marked the religious origins as well as the sustained power of the private charity idea. If indeed human beings are flawed, they must be conscious of and guard against their potential for harm to themselves and to the species. Puritan almsgiving for the salvation of the rich was replaced by scientific charity. Now, the poor were to be helped to find social and economic salvation through work.

The sequence of events that led to the widespread institutionalization of private charity simultaneously justified the emergence of a leisure class. In a world in which the individual was seen as captain of his or her own fate, poverty and wealth were viewed as equally natural, if not equally desirable. Both the poor and the rich were threatened by the undermining, seductive influences of pauperism. The threat was to an economic system that was generally accepted as operationally and morally sound.

The optimism of the American people in accepting the economic system as structurally viable, as offering endless potential for every individual willing to work and to participate in the American dream, was rooted in some reality. Despite recessions and bitter labor disputes, the view held that, for the most part, the economy *was* working successfully. Its moments of faltering were not equated with failure, especially on the Eastern seaboard where millions of immigrants could realistically compare present living conditions with those from which they had fled. The thousands of Irish who had escaped the famine and great hunger resulting from the potato crop failures of 1845–1848 could give witness by their own changed circumstances. Immigrants from all over Europe—whose coming was slowed somewhat during the Civil War but resumed with the onset of peace—and immigrants from Asia during the last decades of the century could point to their own comparative success. Their perception was supported by a rapidly rising gross national product, by the existence of national boundaries that quite literally provided lands for cultivation, and by an element of truth in the Horatio Alger myth. The steady movement of immigrants into commercially successful ventures and into politically powerful positions confirmed the view of class mobility. And there was always the example of a Carnegie or a Rockefeller to demonstrate how far a poor boy could go if he would take advantage of the opportunities the country offered. The complement of the American faith in success was the belief that failure was attributable to individual weakness. Although poor people's failings were usually defined in moral terms, increasingly as the nineteenth century came to an end, the language of race and genetics was used to support the argument. As the century drew to a close, the fear of "feeblemindedness" led to the creation of a new class of institutions and fueled an interest in forced sterilization.

Empirical evidence was sought to sustain this position. The Reverend Oscar C. McCulloch's Report to the Fifteenth Annual Conference of Charities and Corrections on the Tribe of Ishmael, a study of 250 related families, was viewed as a frightening example of social degradation brought on by the degeneracy of the inherited influences of pauperism.[48]

No less an authority than Amos G. Warner, the general agent for the Charity Organization Society of Baltimore, stressed deterioration of character as an immediate cause of poverty. He emphasized this despite his equal awareness of the relationship of the less immediate but perhaps more important contribution of objective environmental factors to poverty. Although in his famous work of 1894, *American Charities,* Warner found unemployment and illness to be the causes of almost half of the poverty cases, he included the following in his listing of objective causes of poverty: "evil associations" and "unwise philanthropy." The latter apparently fostered such subjective causes as "indolence," "lubricity," and a variety of "unhealthy appetites."[49]

In such an atmosphere, not only did public welfare seem unnecessary, but counterproductive. The ideal of charity was service on the part of the well-to-do, service whereby the poor could learn self-respect and resolution, which would build character. This ideal was carried out by an army of "friendly visitors" recruited by the Charity Organization Societies and trained for the service.

The appeal of friendly visiting, balanced by the promise of scientific methodology in investigating the need for relief, led in some cities to turning over the responsibility for investigating applications for relief to the Charity Organization Society. In some cases, Charity Organization leaders were able to have public outdoor relief suspended and even abolished.

The overall purpose of the societies was the maintenance of virtuous families. Guidelines for establishing eligibility for relief often showed the virtue of a family to be derived from the virtue of the breadwinner. Thus, if the breadwinner were disabled or had died, then the widow and her children might be found eligible. Where poverty resulted from the breadwinner's drinking or from his having deserted his family, then the removal of the children for placement among more wholesome associates might be considered best. Unquestionably, the practice of friendly visiting was intended to make self-help the true cure for poverty.

Charity Organization leaders were, of course, not alone in their beliefs about inherited tendencies toward pauperism. Nor is it fair, with the wisdom of hindsight, to picture them as totally destructive in their work with families. Warner's statistically based delineation of objective environmental causes of poverty and the social fact finding of other welfare leaders helped foster social legislation. Such legislation impelled changes in housing, in working conditions for women, in child labor practices, in sanitation—all of which were to improve the individual's and the family's opportunity for self-betterment and success. An awakening interest in eugenics and social Darwinism provided a framework for some support of social legislation, but it carried with it the position that there was no major defect in society itself. Quite simply, the inability to take advantage of enhanced opportunity was further evidence of individual weakness.

The leaders of voluntary charity were not content with simply improving their "scientific charity," but sought to eliminate the competition posed by public sources of welfare as well. Beginning with the efforts of Brooklyn in 1879, a number of cities moved to eliminate outdoor relief so that the needy would be forced to rely on voluntary charities. Although the outdoor relief cutoff fit well into the philosophical position of the Charity Organization movement, it flowed from practical considerations as well. Democratic politicians had successfully used outdoor relief and public employment as means of assuring the loyalty of their voters.

In the end, "friendly visiting" had an unexpected impact. Initially, charity leaders had imagined that the relationship of the visitor and the client would be one-directional; the poor family would learn lessons of thrift and efficiency from the worker. Yet, over the last decades of the nineteenth century, the relationships became more complex than anticipated. In the end, the generation of middle-class women and men who were involved in charity work came away from the experience with a new appreciation of the difficulties faced by poor families. As the nineteenth century came to a close, old beliefs about the moral foundation of poverty, too, began to show their age.

Among public welfare leaders, especially, there were those ready to point out social causes of poverty and to assert society's responsibility for helping to meet individual and familial needs. At the thirteenth Conference of Charities and Corrections in 1886, Fred H. Wines questioned the use of statistics for the pseudoscientific purpose of proving individuals to be the cause of poverty and crime. He urged the conference to look at the "three or four great facts" that characterized modern social life: the invention of labor-saving machinery, the aggregation of capital in the hands of large and wealthy corporations, the aggregation of population in great centers, and the emancipation of women. Taken together, he felt these characteristics had changed the relation of people to one another and might "account in some degree for the present measure and manifestations of pauperism" and other social ills.[50]

At the seventeenth Conference of Charities and Corrections in 1890, Franklin B. Sanborn spoke more specifically about family welfare and made a strong plea for outdoor relief, which he defined as "family aid." In analyzing the purposes for which family aid was expended in Massachusetts, he pointed out that reports of outlays for aid to the poor in their own families often overstated the sum actually expended by including payments for the sick in hospitals, burials, and so on. As for the able-bodied poor in almshouses, said Sanborn, "that mythical class...are scarcely found in this country in public establishments, except for a few months in the cold season, when the number of employments... is considerably reduced by Nature herself." The statement is reminiscent of the one made by John V. N. Yates in 1824; but unlike Yates, Sanborn concluded in favor of cash payments to families in their own homes. Asking that the poor be classified according to their real character and needs and not herded together in a common "receptacle" for all forms of poverty, Sanborn pointed out that "there are persons, be the number greater or less, who need public relief at their own homes, and who can receive it there with greater advantage both to themselves and to the public than anywhere else." In a telling argument—probably embarrassing for his listeners—he pointed out that outdoor relief must continue not only because it is less costly than indoor relief but also because there would never be "almshouses, workhouses, hospitals, and other places of indoor relief in sufficient number to contain all the poor at any season, or half of them in seasons of special destitution." In a final burst, Sanborn said that one reason cash relief had been distributed, even to the point of abuse, was "the desire to prevent the breaking up of families, the corruption of the young, and the unspeakable distress of the old and the virtuous, by throwing them into forced association with the dregs of mankind, in what was ironically termed a charitable establishment."[51] It was in response to and in disagreement with Sanborn that Josephine Shaw Lowell addressed the conference on the demoralizing effects of public outdoor relief.

In time, hostility to the philosophy and methodology of Charity Organization became openly vocal and widespread. Charles D. Kellogg, chairman of the National Conference of Charities and Corrections' Committee on History of Charity Organization, reported in 1893:

> The very name of Charity Organization indicates a paramount purpose to bring about cooperation of those engaged in ministering to the poor.... Yet cooperation is one of the most difficult of attainments.... In some cities there exists a distinct hostility in the older charitable societies to Charity Organization. They resent the implication that their work may need amending....[52]

These "older charitable societies" were understandably suspicious of Charity Organization's assumed authority for standard setting in a field in which they had long been functioning. They were particularly aroused by the threat to their autonomy in being asked to "sustain [through cooperation] a society that is purely administrative,"[53] that is, a society to whom they would be accountable for their relief activities.

Charity Organization's emphasis upon the repression of fraud was taken to be the sole purpose of registering and investigating applicants for relief. Thus, charity organizers were accused of lumping the honest with the dishonest poor to the detriment of the former and the inhumane neglect of the latter.[54] In the words of a popular poem:

> The organized charity scrimped and iced
> In the name of a cautious, statistical Christ.[55]

Trade unions were particularly incensed during periods of recession and unemployment. They interpreted Charity Organization's investigatory methods and its stress upon the debilitating effects of relief as creating unnecessary suffering and as prolonging an "unfair social system as a result of which workers find themselves unemployed."[56]

Finally, the motives of the influential and wealthy leadership were suspect. Hostility toward Charity Organization Societies grew out of the view that the societies might just be "devices for saving the taxpayer, and secured for them the title 'Society for the Suppression of Benevolence.'"[57]

The Social Welfare of Women

Mrs. Lowell's prominence in the Charity Organization movement, and in social welfare generally, reflects the extent to which women had ventured into public life during the post-Civil War era. The period held enormous consequences for women—particularly, middle-class women. Expanded affluence offered independence and leisure, and women sought to establish for themselves a proper place more nearly equivalent in significance and power to that of men.

During the war, women had participated in the abolition movement, but the drive for women's rights had ceased as they became engaged in wartime tasks. As they did in the Sanitary Commission, women—in the South, as well as in the North—took on war-related services for which the government had been unprepared. Women took jobs vacated by men going off to battle. They worked in industries and businesses, on farms and plantations, and in the professions. They worked "at the bench" and loom; they taught and nursed; they organized and managed. For some, this was seen as proof of equality with men, and they were shocked by the passage and ratification of the Fourteenth Amendment, which, for the first time, explicitly defined voters as men. They felt another rebuff with the passage and ratification of the Fifteenth Amendment, which extended suffrage to include black men while excluding women.

In 1869, women in the suffrage movement split over support of the Fifteenth Amendment. The American Equal Rights Association, which had carried the fight for women's rights since 1866, was replaced by two contesting groups, the National Woman Suffrage Association, led by Susan B. Anthony and Elizabeth Cady Stanton, and the group that had supported the Fifteenth Amendment, the American Woman Suffrage Association. In 1890, they reunited as the National American Women's Suffrage Association. Yet, the women's movement purchased consensus at the price of racism. The new association asserted that women could increase the size of the "educated" voting population and reduce the influence of the "ignorant" populace. In the South, this argument for women's suffrage was coupled with efforts to curtail the political and civil rights of African Americans.[58]

For all the publicity they engendered, the number of women formally associated with the national suffrage movement was small, probably never more than 10,000.[59] Nevertheless, large numbers of women did join organizations that represented more widespread and acceptable interests. The women's auxiliaries of the Patrons of Husbandry (the Grange), the General Federation of Women's Clubs, and especially the National Women's Christian Temperance Union, for example, were organizations in which women found companionship as well as outlets for interests and energies in a limiting world.

The technological revolutions that changed the world of work changed women's domestic labor as well. Indoor plumbing, electric lighting, and household labor-saving devices, and the spread of commercial canning and baking, were examples of technological innovations that reduced the hours of labor for housekeeping. The falling birthrate among middle-class families[60] as well as the availability of inexpensive immigrant and black domestic help furthered the process by which native-born, middle-class white women were released from work at home. The founding of women's colleges offered additional opportunities. Vassar was founded in 1865; Smith, in 1871; Bryn Mawr, in 1885. Finally, in an era whose purported ideal was the married woman in the home, there was an excess of females in most of the Northeastern states, those states whose women provided leadership for the feminist movement.[61] Women's organizations and organizational activities were the result.

The National Women's Christian Temperance Union (WCTU) was formed in 1874 and constituted a nationalization of earlier local efforts to contain the manufacture and sale of alcoholic beverages. In the postwar era, the intent of the movement was abstinence and prohibition. Within twenty years, the union's membership totaled more than 200,000 women, representing "the most influential women's organization in the country."[62] Unlike the derision to which suffragists were subjected, members of the WCTU were recognized as active in a legitimate cause. Their concern about observed deleterious effects of alcoholism on the family and about the possible further deterioration of family life was considered well within the bounds of women's concerns, particularly because women were considered to possess moral superiority. The work of the WCTU was labeled "home protection"; the union's first president, Frances E. Willard, called upon all Christian women to join the crusade.[63]

Women's attraction to the temperance movement had complex social and psychological roots. On the one hand, it represented a middle-class reaction to the disorder of the early industrial city. The middle class had not yet been able to separate itself physically from other social classes. The perceived disorder and moral corruption of the working class was constantly on display. At the same time, it represented a *gendered* response to the realities of marriage in the late nineteenth century. Alcohol was at the center of the male world of leisure—dominated by taverns, clubs, and brothels—a world from which respectable women were excluded. In addition, the connection between drink and domestic violence could hardly have eluded women's sensibilities. Finally, the temperance campaign represented a cultural response of native-born Protestants to cities increasingly dominated by Catholic and Jewish ethnic groups.[64]

With moral superiority the foundation for a proper women's sphere and the home and family the appropriate locale of the operation, conflicts inevitably marked the wider women's movement. The publicness of any activity outside the home had to be rationalized. This was relatively easy in the matter of temperance. Even college education could be justified as "education for motherhood."[65] Friendly visiting for the Charity Organization Societies could be seen as instilling the virtues of independent American family life in the poor. But the right to vote, as demanded by suffragists, was another matter. The right to vote was a call for political power, and those few women who demanded it were suspect. Even when Mrs. Willard determined that the purpose of the WCTU could be achieved only by way of women's votes, her call was cloaked in the mantle of "home protection."[66] And, even then, the union's resolution, passed at its national convention in 1877, called for women's voting only in local elections and only on the question of prohibition.

For the middle class, the idea of working women represented a thorny issue. The ideal woman of the postwar era might work before marriage but not after. Thus, despite an expansion in the kinds of jobs women held,[67] many women found themselves increasingly "dependent on the money wages of their husbands or fathers, wages that they themselves did not earn."[68] The era's concept of "true womanhood" helped limit opportunities for economic and social independence.

Nevertheless, women did work. In 1890, 4 million women, fourteen years and older, were employed—18 percent of the female population, 17 percent of the civilian labor force. By 1900, 5 million women—many of them married—were working outside the home.[69] Edith Abbott, in her study of women in industry, attributed the presence of married women and of older women in the job market largely to the employment of immigrants, children of immigrants, and blacks.[70]

Whatever the middle-class ideal, foreign-born and black women, along with many American-born white women, had to work to support the family economy, which was dependent on their wages as well as those of their husbands. The double bind of lower-class women did not go unnoticed by Josephine Shaw Lowell:

> Of course there are women who can attend to home duties and also do outside work; but the average woman cannot do it; and the division of work between man and woman is discriminated by their natures,—he to do the outside work, the woman to do the inside work.... I think one of the causes of poverty is that we have adopted the theory for poor people—not for ourselves—that it is the business of women to help support the family.... When the husband dies, the double work that ought to be done by both father and mother, come to the widow.[71]

The Widow's/Mother's Pension Movement of the early decades of the twentieth century—a movement to provide cash support to widows with young children—was intended to deal with this deviation from ideal, true womanhood.

A New View of Child Welfare

By the turn of the century, the lines of disagreement between private and public welfare leaders were drawn. The private sector, despite contributions to social legislation, had opted for a professional service approach to people in need. Many in the public sector had moved away from the use of almshouses toward an income approach based upon the social necessity of giving and receiving cash relief.

The prominence of Northern social welfare leaders tended to obscure emerging efforts to meet needs in the South and West. As urban population centers grew in these areas, officials tended to follow the path of institutionalization developed fifty years earlier in the North Atlantic region. While the North argued the pros and cons of outdoor relief, the South and West started to build and expand almshouses, mental hospitals, orphan asylums, and correctional institutions. By then, however, their goal was custodial, not remedial, for by 1880 it was clear that institutions throughout the United States were not succeeding in providing an environment for the reconstruction of the lives of the residents but were offering protection for the larger society against criminals, paupers, and the insane.

Society did not, however, feel it needed protection against children. Rather, the public good required that children be rescued from a life of dependency or criminality and helped to become productive citizens. A new view of child welfare developed; child care was to be separate and special.

The legal implications of this new approach were reflected in the enactment of the first juvenile court act in 1899, "An Act to Regulate the Treatment and Control of Dependent, Neglected, and Delinquent Children."[72] This act, which established separate treatment and control for children, was of major significance because it had common-law derivations. Thus, the newly established juvenile court moved child welfare away from an orientation of statutory criminal law, which had previously governed child welfare cases.

Children were to be removed from the adult correctional system and from the general welfare system. The optimistic hopes for poorhouse care expressed by Yates in 1824 had not come to pass, and for children especially, the almshouse had come to be recognized as a disaster. New York State was the first to remove children to foster family homes and to specialized institutions, and other states followed suit.

The eighth annual report of the New York State Board of Charities (submitted January 15, 1875) contained Commissioner William F. Letchworth's study of pauper and destitute children in the state's almshouses.[73] Despite a strenuous effort at removal, in 1874 there remained 593 children in almshouses (9 percent of all inmates), nearly 300 of whom were described as intelligent children, over two years of age, who needed proper training and care to fit them for useful stations in life. The slow pace of removing children from almshouses led to the board's recommendation that "the commitment of children of intelligence over two years of age, to county poorhouses, be prohibited by statute," and on April 24, 1875, an Act to Provide for the Better Care of Pauper and Destitute Children was passed by the senate and assembly of the state of New York. It became unlawful for any child over three and under sixteen years of age to be committed to a county poorhouse "unless such child be an unteachable idiot, an epileptic or paralytic, or...otherwise defective, diseased or deformed, so as to render it unfit for family care."[74]

Much of the urgency for removing dependent and neglected children from the catchall almshouse was related to the belief in inheritable tendencies toward pauperism, tendencies that could be enhanced by children's associations during their early life, and to the fear of creating generations of dependents. Institutional care as devised during the pre-Civil War period was intended to provide for the child a model of disciplined, organized, productive life as a substitute for disorganized family living. Instead, almshouse care was found to expose children to adult paupers, frequently the child's own parents, so that the model supported the very pattern it was intended to supplant. The removal of children would break up these families, by placing the children in "good," "humble" foster homes. In these homes, according to Anne B. Richardson, reporting to the thirteenth annual Conference of Charities and Corrections (1886) on the care of dependent and delinquent children in Massachusetts, the children are restored to conditions of family life where strains produce character.[75]

Amos G. Warner, of Charity Organization, reiterated the point in 1894:

> The child who is born in an almshouse and grows up there is almost always a pauper, because his bad heredity is reinforced by such an environment.... The child that grows up in an infant asylum or orphans' home has at most an imperfect opportunity for right development, and the original possibilities of its nature are but faintly reflected by its career. With a child boarded out in a private family, or given to foster parents while still an infant, the conditions are better and more might be inferred if we could compare its characteristics with those of its parents.[76]

Pauper families, perhaps, could not be saved; but all children could.

In Pennsylvania, as in New York and Massachusetts, anxiety existed about the retention of children in almshouses. The *Report of the Commissioners of Public Charities for the Year 1882* expressed the dangers of permitting children to be in constant association with "these imbecile and debased paupers."

> It must be kept in view that they are one and all *involuntary* and *helpless* prisoners, not from any fault of their own, but too often inheriting the worst traits of a degraded parentage; and, if to this inborn nature is added the results of the society and example

of the most degraded of our race, are we to expect anything better from them than their training will promise?[77]

The commissioners recommended to the state legislature an act to prevent and forbid the detention of children between the ages of two and sixteen years in poorhouses or almshouses. The act was passed in 1883.[78]

Reports from New York, Massachusetts, and Pennsylvania showed that the removal of children already resident in almshouses was slow. Charles S. Hoyt, secretary of the New York State Board of Charities, reporting on "The Causes of Pauperism" (1877), was shrill in denouncing "the practice of receiving parents and children into poor-houses together" and of retaining them there as families. His contention that heredity entered so largely in the problem of pauperism led him to assert unequivocally that it was against sound policy to keep pauper families, whether in or out of the almshouse, together; "in fact the sooner they can be broken up the better...."[79] Certainly the fear of hereditary influences would lead to anxiety in regard to the slowness of the process of removal. At the same time, the threatened removal of children had an equally important, if less publicized, effect—that of deterring families from entering the poorhouse. Thus, poor families who required public help were doubly deterred, for if they entered almshouses they would face deplorable living conditions as well as the possibility of family breakup.

A number of reasons underlay the slowness of reducing the number of children in almshouses. Oddly enough, one reason was simply that the laws against accepting children were not always known or understood by almshouse superintendents. During the next decade, the movement to deinstitutionalize children lost ground and a concern for keeping families intact emerged. The 1883 report of the Pennsylvania Board of Commissioners of Public Charities, for example, mentioned the acceptance of families in almshouses, especially bereaved and immigrant families who must have temporary help but for whom outdoor relief was not available because of "mistaken notions of economy."[80] Such temporary use of the almshouses made it possible for families to stay together. The report urged the wider use of outdoor relief as even more efficacious in preventing the breaking up of homes.

Eventually, the momentum for removing children from almshouses accelerated. Child welfare leaders began to state a rationale for individualizing the needs of children—a parallel reaction, perhaps, to the Charity Organization emphasis upon individualizing families. In his report for 1888, Charles W. Birtwell, general agent of Boston's Children's Aid Society, described the agency's changing practices:

> The aim will be in each instance to suit action to the real need—heeding the teachings of experience, still to study the conditions with a freedom from assumptions... as complete as though the case in hand stood absolutely alone.[81]

In his report for 1893, Birtwell made the logical connection between the individualized child and the individualized family.

> These children cannot be divorced from the natural relations of family life without loss... and therefore we must humbly set ourselves to learn the ways in which family ties may be strengthened and parental responsibilities maintained....[82]

The census of 1890 showed that the number of children in the country's almshouses had decreased by 36 percent during the previous decade, from 7,770 in 1880 to 4,987 in 1890.[83] Part of the decrease could be attributed to an interesting combination of positive concern for families and for individual character leading to the removal from almshouses of entire, intact families who were then sent to the West where employment and a "proper" moral climate were both generously available. The philosophy of Charles Loring Brace was now serving a larger purpose.

The Aging: The Group That Was Left Behind

Most of the older population in the last half of the nineteenth century were not destitute. Many of the men worked. Voluntary retirement was almost unknown. Illness or disability might keep one out of the labor force, recurring economic crises might make jobs very difficult to find, but, overall, labor force participation rates were high for older men.[84] Many older men supported themselves and their spouses. In other cases, an older person often lived with an adult child. For most of the aged, most of the time, the family, be it small or extended, was the chief source of support.

It was the older person without familial aid, who could no longer work, and who had never earned enough to be able to put away a nest egg, who was most at risk of becoming a resident of the poorhouse. Women had lower incomes and fewer marketable skills, were less likely to be covered by Civil War pensions, and outlived their spouses, all factors increasing the chances of their spending their last days in an almshouse. But mothers, more than fathers, were apt to receive familial support and to live with their children. Additionally, more women than men received outdoor relief, and women were more likely than men to be placed in specialized institutions rather than in a general almshouse. Women, when they did enter the poorhouse, tended to enter at a younger age and be dependent longer than men, since they had so little means of support, but the proportion of men was considerably higher than that of women.[85]

The latter part of the nineteenth century saw efforts to remove various groups from the catchall almshouse. The deaf and dumb, the mentally ill, and children were all defined as worthy of special treatment. But the aged, especially aged men, tended to be left in poorhouses out of proportion to their presence in the poverty population. In 1855, 15 percent of the people in almshouses were aged; by 1886, that figure had reached 37 percent.[86]

The Settlement House Movement

At the end of the nineteenth century, a second major movement developed in the voluntary sector of social welfare: the Settlement House Movement. Inspired by the efforts of Canon Samuel Barnett's Toynbee Hall in London to bring the privileged and underprivileged together to overcome the effects of spiritual and social disintegration, Stanton Coit and Charles B. Stover founded the Neighborhood Guild of New York City in 1887. Their hope in opening this first American settlement house, where educated persons might live among the poor newcomers to the United States, was to bring about a sense of neighborliness that could lead to the making of good citizens. In 1889, Jane Addams established Hull House in Chicago and Vida Scudder founded the College Settlement in New York. Located in large cities, these settlement houses emphasized neighborhood services and community development. Although the Charity Organizations, in "socialized" circles at least, had captured "the family" as their area of functional expertise, settlements were no less concerned with family welfare. The groups differed, however, in their views of families, in their views of society, and, ultimately, in their views of social welfare as a helping mechanism.

Charity Organization Societies had come into being for the express purpose of organizing voluntary and public charities to direct toward worthy families the relief-giving services of others.[87] Their particular concern was with the poor, and especially with those individuals whose flawed character permitted them to sup at the public trough while contributing nothing to the public larder. Their investigations of applicants for relief—investigations that led eventually to the development of casework methodology and to the emergence of a social work profession—were meant to individualize each poor family so that particular flaws could be detected and overcome and independence could be regained. The Charity Organization Societies did make an effort to separate the "worthy" poor from the "unworthy" poor to help the former adequately, but the fear of encouraging pauperism led for the most part to a basic philosophy that deterred all from asking for help. In essence, the orientation of the Charity Organization toward relief was in line with the Poor Law tradition and led to competition with public officials for supremacy in handling relief matters. In many localities, Charity Organization Societies took on the job of investigating relief applicants for public agencies, a job they had assumed very early for private relief societies.[88]

Whereas Charity Organization Societies assumed a well-functioning society with malfunctioning families as the starting point of their operation, many social settlement workers assumed as their operational base the adequate functioning of the families they served. Much of the clientele served by settlement houses consisted of migrants and immigrants whose problems quite clearly were associated with making the transition from rural to urban living and from a known to an unknown culture. Whatever their problems with the culture or the language, clients of settlement houses were viewed as able, normal, working-class families with whom the wealthier, upper classes were joined in mutual dependence. When such families could not cope, settlement leaders assumed that society itself was at fault and this assumption led quite naturally to a drive for societal reform.[89]

The Charity Organization and Settlement House movements in the early years were quite different in goals, in techniques, and in service programs. The Charity Organization was bent upon preventing pauperism. To aid in this process of reformation, Charity Organization Societies engaged heavily in "Repressive Work," the detection of fraud through the establishment of "Confidential Exchanges," and in "Provident Work," the establishment or promotion of "various well-proved schemes for the encouragement of thrift and self help."[90] Settlement houses, on the other hand, from their inception moved toward the socialization of the normal, adequately functioning family, and their goal was reflected in the three strands of their program activities: neighborhood clubs providing recreational and educational opportunities, social research in regard to family and community needs, and, especially, social action leading to legislative and political change.

The settlement movement began with a belief in the normality of its family clientele and geared its program to an expansion of the idea of family to an ideal of communal living. When problems arose for the family unit, correction through societal change, through social reform, was sought. Jane Addams stated the difference between the Charity Organization Society and the settlement:

> The settlement does stand for something unlike that which the charity visitor stands for. You are bound, when you are doing charitable work, to lay stress upon the industrial virtues....Now the settlement...does not lay perpetual and continual stress upon them. It sees that a man may, perhaps, be a bit lazy, and still be a good man and an interesting person....It does not lay so much stress upon one set of virtues, but views the man in his social aspects....To adjust an individual to civilization as he finds it round him, to get him to the pitch which shall induce him to push up that civilization a little higher...is perhaps the chief function of a settlement.[91]

As the century drew to a close, the differences between Charity Organization and Social Settlements became less sharp. COS leaders such as Mary Richmond, who outlined the basis for casework in *Social Diagnosis,* grounded their work increasingly in observation and practice, not in sweeping moral judgments. Meanwhile, Settlement House workers soon found that good intentions and sympathy were not enough; they, too, needed to provide practical services to community residents if they were to maintain their credibility. Most importantly, workers in both areas began to see the virtue of individualization; care needed to be tailored to the specific needs of the client. By the turn of the century, the milieu that would create the social work profession was in place.

Conclusion

If Rip Van Winkle had fallen asleep during the Civil War and awakened at the end of the nineteenth century, he could hardly have been more astounded. A rural society of isolated communities had given way to a dynamic, industrial society increasingly dominated by cities.

The social welfare realities at the turn of the twentieth century, too, would have seemed new and strange. The hope in institutionalization that had animated reform before the Civil War was nearly spent by the turn of the century, even though the institutions remained, now generally warehouses for unwanted and feared populations. The dynamic public sector of the Civil War years, too, had generally disappeared. The most visible federal role in welfare at the turn of the century was the Civil War pension system, which would continue to support large numbers of older Americans for decades to come. Instead, the social welfare scene of the 1890s was dominated by voluntary social welfare organizations, often staffed and led by middle-class women.

Yet, change was in the air. The depression of the 1890s had sparked a widespread rural rebellion of smaller farmers—the Populist movement. Although Populism had fallen apart after its electoral defeat in 1896, its core message—that democracy had a role in improving the lives of ordinary citizens—was not totally lost. As the new century began, new social movements would influence the course of American history and the efforts of government and professionals to address the problems of poverty, exclusion, and disaffiliation.

Discussion Questions

1. During Reconstruction, the Federal government expanded African Americans' political and civil rights, but did little about their economic position. How might the reallocation of land to the newly freed African Americans have changed the outcome of Reconstruction?

2. By the end of the nineteenth century, class and ethnic divisions dominated American cities. The founders of the social work profession pursued charity organization and settlements as one way of addressing this division. Are there other ways that these divisions could have been addressed?

3. According to some researchers, by the end of the nineteenth century, children had gone from 'valuable' to 'priceless.' How did changing ideas about childhood influence the course of child welfare during the last four decades of the nineteenth century?

DOCUMENTS: The Civil War and After

Three documents are used to highlight the direction of social welfare developments from the close of the Civil War to the turn of the century. The documents include: the State of New York's *Act to Provide for the Relief of Indigent Soldiers, Sailors and Marines, and the Families of Deceased Military Personnel* (1887); an excerpt from Josephine Shaw Lowell's address, *The Economic and Moral Effects of Public Outdoor Relief,* delivered at the National Conference of Charities and Corrections (1890); and an *Act to Prohibit the Coming of Chinese Laborers to the United States*, September 1888, along with its October 1888 amendment. They were a follow-up to the *Chinese Exclusion Act of 1882*. The immigration legislation represents a markedly different response to perceived social problems in the post-Civil War era.

New York's legislation to provide relief for indigent servicemen and their families is an example of one state's special attention and positive response to the claims of veterans. The legislation provides state funding for relief, a shift from strict adherence to local responsibility for relief giving and from the requirement of local residence. Need was to be determined and relief was to be administered by designated relief committees in each post of the Grand Army of the Republic, a veterans' organization. Placement of indigent servicemen or their families in an almshouse without the consent of the Grand Army of the Republic was prohibited. By definition, veterans were not "paupers" and not subject to the ordinary conditions prescribed for handling the needs of "the poor."

However, other Americans in need were viewed with more caution, their worthiness not above suspicion. The excerpt from Josephine Shaw Lowell's address is significant for its demonstration of the current view of mankind and the poor. During the postwar era, an earlier view of man's perfectibility gave way to a view of the corruptibility of the individual. Social Darwinism supported a theory of social evolution that permitted the abandonment of those who could not sustain themselves or add to the resources of society. Mrs. Lowell fell short of arguing for complete abandonment, admitting that some persons do "need relief (that is, *help*) in their own homes." What she could not accept was the use of public funds for relief giving, seeing no good in such giving for the community at large. In fact, she saw an "inverse ratio between the welfare of the mass of people and the distribution of [public] relief." The moral weakening of the individual who received public relief led to a weakening of people in the larger society.

Mrs. Lowell was a leader among those who sought to apply "scientific" methodology to philanthropy. She was a major supporter of a new delivery system, the Charity Organization Society, whose original intent was to use volunteer counseling services in an attempt to avoid the necessity for cash relief.

While veterans were thought to have made their contribution to society and be entitled to aid and cash assistance when in need and other needy Americans were perhaps potentially productive and therefore to be encouraged with services and advice, Chinese workers were regarded very differently. No longer needed as workers on the railroads, they were deemed a threat to other laborers. Since they were distrusted because of their different race, religion, culture, and language, the solution was seen as avoidance. In 1882, legislation was passed that permitted no further immigration of workers from China. The legislation of 1888 went further and moved to reduce the number of Chinese in the United States.

During the eighteenth century and the first half of the nineteenth century, immigration and suffrage were largely uncontrolled by federal activity, and in practice states had considerable freedom to regulate the right to vote as well as the right to hold office. This changed after the Civil War. The federal government moved to define its control over who came to this country and who became a citizen. In this process, it established legal rights for African Americans, but it continued to deny them to Native Americans, and introduced new restrictions against immigrants. The most severe immigration and naturalization discrimination was practiced against those from Asia. The Chinese exclusion acts wanted to accomplish exactly that. Legislation was passed in 1882 and amended several times after that. The September 1888 legislation barred new laborers from arriving, although it permitted "Chinese officials, teachers, students, merchants, or travelers for pleasure or curiosity" to enter. Additionally, it prohibited any Chinese laborer in the United States from returning once having left "unless he has a lawful wife, child, or parent in the United States, or property therein of the value of one thousand dollars." One month later, it became illegal for "any Chinese laborer... who shall depart... to return."

In terms of social welfare, veterans were thought to be very worthy; they had done valued work. The American poor were somewhat worthy; they might be helped to become independent members of society. But Chinese workers were feared; they were to be excluded not only from social welfare but also from any participation in the life of the country.

LAWS OF THE STATE OF NEW YORK

ONE HUNDRED AND TENTH SESSION
January 4–May 26, 1887

Chap. 706

AN ACT to provide for the relief of indigent soldiers, sailors and marines, and the families of those deceased.

PASSED June 25, 1887; three-fifths being present.

The People of the State of New York, represented in Senate and Assembly, do enact as follows:

Town or city auditing boards may grant relief to indigent soldiers, etc.

Expenditure, how supervised.

To whom, relief may be granted.

SECTION 1. For the relief of indigent and suffering soldiers, sailors and marines, who served in the war of the rebellion, and their families, or the families of those deceased, who need assistance in any town or city in this State, the proper auditing board of such city or town may provide such sum or sums of money as may be necessary, to be drawn upon by the commander and quartermaster of any post of the Grand Army of the Republic in said city or town, upon the recommendation of the relief committee of said post, in the same manner as is now provided by law for the relief of the poor, provided said soldier, sailor and marine, or the families of those deceased, are and have been resident of the State for one year or more, and the orders of said commander and quartermaster shall be the proper vouchers for the expenditure of said sum or sums of money.

Relief committee in certain towns.

§ 2. In case there be no post of the Grand Army of the Republic in any town in which it is necessary that such relief, as provided for in section one, should be granted, the town board of said town shall accept and pay the orders drawn as hereinbefore provided, by the commander and quartermaster of any post of the Grand Army of the Republic, located in the nearest city or town, upon the recommendation of a relief committee, who shall be residents of the said town in which the relief may be furnished.

Notice to city or town clerk, of taking charge of relief.

Annual statement as to relief, etc., how filed.

§ 3. Upon the passage of this act the commander of any post of the Grand Army of the Republic, which shall undertake the relief of indigent veterans and their families, as hereinbefore provided, before the acts of said commander and quartermaster may become operative in any city or town, shall file with the city clerk of such city, or town clerk of such town, a notice that said post intends to undertake such relief as is provided by this act. Such notice shall contain the names of the relief committee of said post in such city or town, and of the commander and other officers of said post. And the commander of said post shall annually thereafter, during the month of October, file a similar notice with said city and town clerks, and also a detailed statement of the amount of relief furnished during the preceding year, with the names of all persons to whom such relief shall have been furnished, together with a brief statement in each case, from the relief committee upon whose recommendation the orders were drawn.

§ 4. The said auditing board of any city or town may require of the said commander and quartermaster of any post of the Grand Army of the Republic, undertaking such relief in said city or town, a bond with sufficient and satisfactory sureties for the faithful and honest discharge of their duties under this act. *Bond of relief committee.*

§ 5. Superintendents and overseers of the poor are hereby prohibited from sending indigent soldiers, sailors, and marines, (or their families, or the families of those deceased), to any alms-house (or orphan asylum) without the full concurrence and consent of the commander and relief committee of the post of the Grand Army of the Republic, having jurisdiction as provided in sections one and two. Indigent veterans with families, and the families of deceased veterans, shall, whenever practicable, be provided for and relieved at their homes in such city or town in which they shall have a residence, in the manner provided in sections one and two of this act. Indigent or disabled veterans of the classes specified in section one, who are not insane, and who have no families or friends with whom they may be domiciled, may be sent to any soldiers' home. Any indigent veteran of either of the classes specified in section one, or any member of the family of any living or deceased veteran of said classes, who may be insane, shall, upon recommendation of the commander and relief committee of such post of the Grand Army of the Republic, within the jurisdiction of which the case may occur, be sent to any insane asylum, and cared for as provided for indigent insane in section twenty-six of chapter one hundred and thirty-five of the laws of eighteen hundred and forty-two.

Duties of overseers and superintendents of poor, as to committals to almshouse, etc.

Outdoor or home relief, to be given when possible.

Soldiers' Home, relief at.

Care of indigent insane veterans.

§ 6. This act shall take effect immediately.

***

PROCEEDINGS OF THE NATIONAL CONFERENCE OF CHARITIES AND CORRECTIONS

1890

THE ECONOMIC AND MORAL EFFECTS OF PUBLIC OUTDOOR RELIEF.

BY MRS. CHARLES RUSSELL LOWELL, OF NEW YORK.

I have not been able to assent to the report of the Chairman of the Committee on Indoor and Outdoor Relief, only because, as it seems to me, he does not draw the distinction which is necessary between public and private relief.

I admit, of course, that there are persons who need relief (that is, *help*) in their own homes, and that both Pitt's argument and Mr. Sanborn's argument apply to such: "Great care should be taken, in relieving their distresses, not to throw them into the great class of vagrant and homeless poor." Such people, however, are, to my mind, not proper subjects for public relief at all; for what is public relief, and upon what grounds is it to be justified? Public relief is money paid by the bulk of the community (every community is of course composed mainly of those who are working hard to obtain a livelihood) to certain members of the community, not, however, paid voluntarily or spontaneously by those interested in the individuals receiving it, but paid by public officers from money raised by taxation. The only justification for the expenditure of public money (money raised by taxation) is that it is necessary for the public good. That certain persons need certain things is no reason for supplying them with those things from the public funds. Before this can be rightly done, it is necessary to prove that it is good for the community at large that it should be done. . . .

The practice of any community in this particular is a matter of great importance, for there can be no question that there is an inverse ratio between the welfare of the mass of the people and the distribution of relief. What some one has called "the fatal ease of living without work and the terrible difficulty of living by work" are closely interrelated as cause and effect; and, if you will permit me, I will try to show by a short allegory what this relation is.

Once upon a time there lived in a valley, called the Valley of Industry, a people who were happy and industrious. All the goods of this life were supplied to them by exhaustless subterranean springs of water, which they pumped up into a great reservoir on the top of a neighboring hill, the Hill of Prosperity, from which it flowed down, each man receiving what he himself pumped up, by a small pipe which led into his own house, a moderate amount of pumping on the part of every one keeping the reservoir well filled.

Finally, a few of the inhabitants of the Valley, more keen than the rest, reflected that it was unnecessary to weary themselves with pumping, so long as every one else kept at work. The Hill of Prosperity looked very attractive; and they therefore mounted to a convenient point, and put a large pipe into the reservoir, through which they drew off copious supplies of water without further trouble. The number of those who gave up pumping and withdrew to the Hill was at first so small that the loss did not add very much to the work of the mass of the people, who still kept to their pumping, and it did not occur to them to complain; but those who could followed the others up the Hill until it was all occupied, and by this time, although those who remained in the Valley did find their pumping a good deal harder than it was when all who used the water joined in the work, yet every one had become so accustomed to some people using the reservoir water without doing any pumping that it had come to be considered all right, and still there were no complaints. Meanwhile, the people on the Hill of Prosperity having nothing to do but enjoy the prospect, some of them began to explore the neighboring country, and soon discovered another valley at the foot of the Hill, running parallel with the Valley of Industry, and called the Valley of Idleness, and in it were a few people who had wandered from the former Valley (for the two were connected at the farther end), and who were living in abject misery, with no water, and apparently no means of getting any, so long as they stayed where they were. The people from the Hill of Prosperity were very much shocked at the suffering they found. "What a shame!" they cried. "The poor things have no water! We have plenty and to spare, so let us lead a pipe from the reservoir down into their Valley." No sooner said than done: the pipe was carried into the Valley of Idleness, and the people were made more comfortable. But as soon as the news was brought into the Valley of Industry, some of the pumpers who were tired or weak, and some who were only lazy, left their pumping, and hastened into the neighboring Valley, to enjoy the "free" water; but the pipe was not very large, and soon there was want and suffering again, and the people from Prosperity Hill were much disturbed, and decided to lay down another small pipe, which they did. But the result was the same, for the new supply of water attracted more people from the Valley of Industry. And so it went on, new pipe, more people, new pipe, more people, until the inhabitants of Prosperity Hill were full of distress about it, and exclaimed, "It seems a hopeless task to try to make these people happy and comfortable!" And they would have given up in despair, but a new idea occurred to them; and they said, "They do not seem to know how to take very good care of their children, and we will therefore take their children from them, and teach them to be comfortable and happy." So they built large, fine houses for the children, and they carried water in large pipes into the houses. And some of them said, "Let us put faucets, so as to teach them to turn on the water when they need it." But others said: "Oh, no! How troublesome it is to have to turn a faucet when you need water! Let them have it as we do, free." And sometimes one or other would suggest that, perhaps, after all, it was not quite right to waste so much of the water from the reservoir, and that the large pipe itself, which supplied the Hill of Prosperity, ought to have some means of checking the flow; but the answer was, "It is necessary and right that the water should be wasted; for otherwise the people in the Valley of Industry would have nothing to do, and they would starve." Usually, however, the Prosperity Hill people were too much engaged in taking care of the inhabitants of the Valley of Idleness to give much thought to those of the Valley of Industry; and their anxiety was quite justified, for they had to keep up a perpetual watchfulness, the people increasing so fast that it was necessary constantly to lay more pipe to keep them from the most abject suffering, and even this device never succeeded for very long, as I have said.

In fact, no one thought much about the Valley of Industry or its people. Those in the Valley of Idleness only thought of them long enough to reflect how silly they were to keep on pumping all the time and making their backs and arms ache, when they might have water without any exertion, by simply moving into their Valley. The children born in the Valley of Idleness did not even know there was a Valley of Industry, or any pumps, or any pumpers, or any reservoir: they thought the water grew in pipes, and ran out because it was its nature to. As for the people on the Hill of Prosperity, they were, as we have seen, rather confused in their views in this particular; and, besides thinking that their waste of the water from the reservoir was what kept the people in the Valley of Industry from starving, they used also to say sometimes: "How good it is for those people to have such nice, steady work to do! how strong it makes their backs and arms! how it hardens their muscles! What a nice, independent set of people they are! and *what* a splendid quantity of pure, life-giving water they get out of our reservoir!"

Meanwhile, you can imagine, though they could not, that it was rather hard on the men in the Valley of Industry, not only to have the water they pumped up drawn off at the top to supply two other communities, but also to have their own ranks thinned and their work increased by the loss of those who were tempted into the Valley of Idleness, to live on what the Prosperity Hill people and the Valley of Idleness people like to call euphemistically "free water," because they got it free, though actually it was not free at all; for the Valley of Industry people paid for it with their blood and muscle.

I might go on to tell you how the situation was still further complicated and made harder for them, and indeed for almost everyone, when a few of them obtained control of the inexhaustible subterranean springs; but here, I think, the allegory may end for the purposes of this Conference, and it seems to me to teach a lesson which we may well heed.

***

An Act to Prohibit the Coming of Chinese Laborers to the United States

September 13, 1888

Fiftieth Congress, Session 1

Be it enacted by the Senate and House of Representatives of the United States of America in Congress assembled, That from and after the date of the exchange of ratifications of the pending treaty between the United States of America and His Imperial Majesty the Emperor of China, signed on the twelfth day of March, anno Domini eighteen hundred and eighty-eight, it shall be unlawful for any Chinese person, whether a subject of China or of any other power, to enter the United States, except as hereinafter provided.

SEC. 2. That Chinese officials, teachers, students, merchants, or travelers for pleasure or curiosity, shall be permitted to enter the United States, but in order to

Chinese laborers. Immigration prohibited. *Post,* p. 504.

Classes permitted to enter.

entitle themselves to do so, they shall first obtain the permission of the Chinese Government, or other Government of which they may at the time be citizens or subjects. Such permission and also their personal identity shall in such case be evidenced by a certificate to be made out by the diplomatic representative of the United States in the country, or of the consular representative of the United States at the port or place from which the person named therein comes. The certificate shall contain a full description of such person, of his age, height, and general physical features, and shall state his former and present occupation or profession and place of residence, and shall be made out in duplicate. One copy shall be delivered open to the person named and described, and the other copy shall be sealed up and delivered by the diplomatic or consular officer as aforesaid to the captain of the vessel on which the person named in the certificate sets sail for the United States, together with the sealed certificate, which shall be addressed to the collector of customs at the port where such person is to land. There shall be delivered to the aforesaid captain a letter from the consular officer addressed to the collector of customs aforesaid, and stating that said consular officer has on a certain day delivered to the said captain a certificate of the right of the person named therein to enter the United States as a Chinese official, or other exempted person, as the case may be. And any captain who lands or attempts to land a Chinese person in the United States, without having in his possession a sealed certificate, as required in this section, shall be liable to the penalties prescribed in section nine of this act.

SEC. 3. That the provisions of this act shall apply to all persons of the Chinese race, whether subjects of China or other foreign power, excepting Chinese diplomatic or consular officers and their attendants; and the words "Chinese laborers," whenever used in this act, shall be construed to mean both skilled and unskilled laborers and Chinese employed in mining.

SEC. 4. That the master of any vessel arriving in the United States from any foreign port or place with any Chinese passengers on board shall, when he delivers his manifest of cargo, and if there be no cargo, when he makes legal entry of his vessel, and before landing or permitting to land any Chinese person (unless a diplomatic or consular officer, or attendant of such officer), deliver to the collector of customs of the district in which the vessel shall have arrived the sealed certificates and letters as aforesaid, and a separate list of all Chinese persons taken on board of his vessel at any foreign port or place, and of all such persons on board at the time of arrival as aforesaid. Such list shall show the names of such persons and other particulars as shown by their open certificates, or other evidences required by this act, and such list shall be sworn to by the master in the manner required by law in relation to the manifest of the cargo.

The master of any vessel as aforesaid shall not permit any Chinese diplomatic or consular officer or attendant of such officer to land without having first been informed by the collector of customs of the official character of such officer or attendant. Any refusal or willful neglect of the master of any vessel to comply with the provisions of this section shall incur the same penalties and forfeitures as are provided for a refusal or neglect to report and deliver a manifest of the cargo.

SEC. 5. That from and after the passage of this act, no Chinese laborer in the United States shall be permitted, after having left, to return thereto, except under the conditions stated in the following sections.

SEC. 6. That no Chinese laborer within the purview of the preceding section shall be permitted to return to the United States unless he has a lawful wife, child, or

---

Sidenotes (left margin):

Certificates to be obtained.

Penalty for violation.

Scope of act.

Master to deliver certificates, etc., on arrival in United States.

List to be delivered.

Contents of list.

Diplomatic and consular officers.

Penalty.

Return of laborers prohibited. Conditions for permission to return.

parent in the United States, or property therein of the value of one thousand dollars, or debts of like amount due him and pending settlement. The marriage to such wife must have taken place at least a year prior to the application of the laborer for a permit to return to the United States, and must have been followed by the continuous cohabitation of the parties as man and wife.

If the right to return be claimed on the ground of property or of debts, it must appear that the property is bona fide and not colorably acquired for the purpose of evading this act, or that the debts are unascertained and unsettled, and not promissory notes or other similar acknowledgments of ascertained liability.

Sec. 7. That a Chinese person claiming the right to be permitted to leave the United States and return thereto on any of the grounds stated in the foregoing section, shall apply to the collector of customs of the district from which he wishes to depart at least a month prior to the time of his departure, and shall make on oath before the said collector a full statement descriptive of his family, or property, or debts, as the case may be, and shall furnish to said collector such proofs of the facts entitling him to return as shall be required by the rules and regulations prescribed from time to time by the Secretary of the Treasury, and for any false swearing in relation thereto he shall incur the penalties of perjury. He shall also permit the collector to take a full description of his person, which description the collector shall retain and mark with a number. And if the collector, after hearing the proofs and investigating all the circumstances of the case, shall decide to issue a certificate of return, he shall at such time and place as he may designate, sign and give to the person applying a certificate containing the number of the description last aforesaid, which shall be the sole evidence given to such person of his right to return. If this last named certificate be transferred, it shall become void, and the person to whom it was given shall forfeit his right to return to the United States. The right to return under the said certificate shall be limited to one year; but it may be extended for an additional period, not to exceed a year, in cases where, by reason of sickness or other cause of disability beyond his control, the holder thereof shall be rendered unable sooner to return, which facts shall be fully reported to and investigated by the consular representative of the United States at the port or place from which such laborer departs for the United States, and certified by such representative of the United States to the satisfaction of the collector of customs at the port where such Chinese person shall seek to land in the United States, such certificate to be delivered by said representative to the master of the vessel on which he departs for the United States. And no Chinese laborer shall be permitted to re-enter the United States without producing to the proper officer of the customs at the port of such entry the return certificate herein required. A Chinese laborer possessing a certificate under this section shall be admitted to the United States only at the port from which he departed therefrom, and no Chinese person, except Chinese diplomatic or consular officers, and their attendants, shall be permitted to enter the United States except at the ports of San Francisco, Portland, Oregon, Boston, New York, New Orleans, Port Townsend, or such other ports as may be designated by the Secretary of the Treasury.

Sec. 8. That the Secretary of the Treasury shall be, and he hereby is, authorized and empowered to make and prescribe, and from time to time to change and amend such rules and regulations, not in conflict with this act, as he may deem necessary and proper to conveniently secure to such Chinese persons as are provided for in articles second and third of the said treaty between the United States and the Empire of China, the rights therein mentioned, and such as shall also protect the United

Marginal notes:
- Property requisites.
- Identification of Chinese wishing to return.
- Certificate.
- Transfer void.
- Extension of period.
- No entry without certificate.
- Chinese permitted to land only at certain ports.
- Secretary of the Treasury to prescribe regulations, etc.

States against the coming and transit of persons not entitled to the benefit of the provisions of said articles. And he is hereby further authorized and empowered to prescribe the form and substance of certificates to be issued to Chinese laborers under and in pursuance of the provisions of said articles, and prescribe the form of the record of such certificate and of the proceedings for issuing the same, and he may require the deposit, as a part of such record, of the photograph of the party to whom any such certificate shall be issued.

SEC. 9. That the master of any vessel who shall knowingly bring within the United States on such vessel, and land, or attempt to land, or permit to be landed any Chinese laborer or other Chinese person, in contravention of the provisions of this act, shall be deemed guilty of a misdemeanor and, on conviction thereof, shall be punished with a fine of not less than five hundred dollars nor more than one thousand dollars, in the discretion of the court, for every Chinese laborer or other Chinese person so brought, and may also be imprisoned for a term of not less than one year, nor more than five years, in the discretion of the court.

SEC. 10. That the foregoing section shall not apply to the case of any master whose vessel shall come within the jurisdiction of the United States in distress or under stress of weather, or touching at any port of the United States on its voyage to any foreign port or place. But Chinese laborers or persons on such vessel shall not be permitted to land, except in case of necessity, and must depart with the vessel on leaving port.

SEC. 11. That any person who shall knowingly and falsely alter or substitute any name for the name written in any certificate herein required, or forge such certificate, or knowingly utter any forged or fraudulent certificate, or falsely personate any person named in any such certificate, and any person other than the one to whom a certificate was issued who shall falsely present any such certificate, shall be deemed guilty of a misdemeanor, and upon conviction thereof shall be fined in a sum not exceeding one thousand dollars, and imprisoned in a penitentiary for a term of not more than five years.

SEC. 12. That before any Chinese passengers are landed from any such vessel, the collector, or his deputy, shall proceed to examine such passengers, comparing the certificates with the list and with the passengers; and no passenger shall be allowed to land in the United States from such vessel in violation of law; and the collector shall in person decide all questions in dispute with regard to the right of any Chinese passenger to enter the United States, and his decision shall be subject to review by the Secretary of the Treasury, and not otherwise.

SEC. 13. That any Chinese person, or person of Chinese descent, found unlawfully in the United States, or its Territories, may be arrested upon a warrant issued upon a complaint, under oath, filed by any party on behalf of the United States, by any justice, judge, or commissioner of any United States court, returnable before any justice, judge, or commissioner of a United States court, or before any United States court, and when convicted, upon a hearing, and found and adjudged to be one not lawfully entitled to be or remain in the United States, such person shall be removed from the United States to the country whence he came. But any such Chinese person convicted before a commissioner of a United States court may, within ten days from such conviction, appeal to the judge of the district court for the district. A certified copy of the judgment shall be the process upon which said removal shall be made, and it may be executed by the marshal of the district, or any officer having authority of a marshal under the provisions of this section. And in all such cases the person who

Form of certificate, etc.

Punishment to master of vessel unlawfully bringing Chinamen.

Vessels in distress.

Punishment for counterfeiting certificate, etc.

Landing passengers.

Arrest of Chinese unlawfully in the United States.

Appeal.

brought or aided in bringing such person into the United States shall be liable to the Government of the United States for all necessary expenses incurred in such investigation and removal: and all peace officers of the several States and Territories of the United States are hereby invested with the same authority in reference to carrying out the provisions of this act, as a marshal or deputy marshal of the United States, and shall be entitled to like compensation, to be audited and paid by the same officers.

SEC. 14. That the preceding sections shall not apply to Chinese diplomatic or consular officers or their attendants, who shall be admitted to the United States under special instructions of the Treasury Department, without production of other evidence than that of personal identity.

SEC. 15. That the act entitled "An act to execute certain treaty stipulations relating to Chinese," approved May sixth, eighteen hundred and eighty-two, and an act to amend said act approved July fifth, eighteen hundred and eighty-four, are hereby repealed to take effect upon the ratification of the pending treaty as provided in section one of this act.

Approved, September 13, 1888.

***

An Act, a Supplement . . .

October 1, 1888

Fiftieth Congress, Session 1

CHAP. 1064.—An act, a supplement to an act entitled "An act to execute certain treaty stipulations relating to Chinese," approved the sixth day of May eighteen hundred and eighty-two.

Be it enacted by the Senate and House of Representatives of the United States of America in Congress assembled, That from and after the passage of this act, it shall be unlawful for any Chinese laborer who shall at any time heretofore have been, or who may now or hereafter be, a resident within the United States, and who shall have departed, or shall depart, therefrom, and shall not have returned before the passage of this act, to return to, or remain in, the United States.

SEC. 2. That no certificates of identity provided for in the fourth and fifth sections of the act to which this is a supplement shall hereafter be issued; and every certificate heretofore issued in pursuance thereof, is hereby declared void and of no effect, and the Chinese laborer claiming admission by virtue thereof shall not be permitted to enter the United States.

SEC. 3. That all the duties prescribed, liabilities penalties and forfeitures imposed, and the powers conferred by the second, tenth, eleventh, and twelfth, sections of the act to which this is a supplement are hereby extended and made applicable to the provisions of this act.

SEC. 4. That all such part or parts of the act to which this is a supplement as are inconsistent herewith are hereby repealed.

Approved, October 1, 1888.

Margin notes:

Punishment of person aiding.

Diplomatic and consular officers.

Prior acts to be repealed.
Vol. 22, p. 58.
Vol. 23, p. 115.

October 1, 1888.

Exclusion of Chinese laborers.
Vol. 22, p. 59.
Ante, p. 476.

No certificates for return to be issued.

Penalties.

Repeal provisions.

Notes

1. U.S. Department of Commerce, Bureau of the Census, *Historical Statistics of the United States: Colonial Times to 1957* (Washington, D.C.: Government Printing Office, 1960), pp. 7, 143 (hereafter cited as *Historical Statistics*).
2. S. E. Forman, *The Rise of American Commerce and Industry* (New York: Century, 1927), p. 317.
3. *Historical Statistics*, p. 7.
4. An excellent overview of this process is presented in the video production series *500 Nations* by Jack Leustig (Burbank, Calif.: TIG Productions, 1994), Vol. 8, "The Attack on Culture."
5. Quoted in John Rhea Dulles, *The United States Since 1865* (Ann Arbor: University of Michigan Press, 1971), p. 41.
6. *Historical Statistics*, pp. 56–57.
7. Roger Daniels, *Coming to America: A History of Immigration and Ethnicity in American Life* (New York: HarperCollins, 1990), pp. 265–284.
8. Theodore Hershberg, "Free Blacks in Antebellum Philadelphia: A Study of Ex-Slaves, Freeborn, and Socio-economic Decline," *Journal of Social History* 5 (Winter 1971–1972): 190.
9. Ibid., pp. 238–250.
10. Walter W. Jennings, *A History of Economic Progress in the United States* (New York: Thomas Y. Crowell, 1926), p. 380; *Historical Statistics*, p. 8.
11. Forman, op. cit., p. 471.
12. *Historical Statistics*, p. 14.
13. Jennings, op. cit., p. 409.
14. Ibid., p. 412.
15. *Historical Statistics*, p. 302.
16. Ibid., p. 297.
17. Ibid., p. 546.
18. Ibid., p. 139.
19. Forman, op. cit., p. 481.
20. *Historical Statistics*, p. 139.
21. Jennings, op. cit., p. 447.
22. U.S. Congress, House Committee Print No. 4, *Medical Care of Veterans*, 90th Cong., 1st sess., April 17, 1967, p. 49. Printed for the use of the Committee on Veterans' Affairs.
23. Ibid., p. 52.
24. U.S. Sanitary Commission, Document No. 49, October 1862.
25. Charles J. Stille, *History of the United States Sanitary Commission* (Philadelphia: Lippincott, 1866), p. 524.
26. U.S. Sanitary Commission, *The Sanitary Commission of the United States Army: A Succinct Narrative of the Works and Purposes* (New York: Published for the benefit of the Commission), 1864.
27. Stille, op. cit., p. 82.
28. U.S. Sanitary Commission, Document 4042, May 1865.
29. U.S. Congress, House of Representatives, Report No. 45, 41st Cong., 3rd sess., 1871.
30. Knowlton Durham, *Billions for Veterans* (New York: Brewer, Warren and Putnam, 1932), pp. 25–26.
31. The President's Commission on Veterans' Pensions, *The Historical Development of Veterans' Benefits in the United States*, A Report on Veterans' Benefits in the United States, 84th Cong., 2nd sess., House Committee Print No. 244, May 9, 1956, pp. 17–18.
32. Laws of the State of New York, An act to provide for the relief of indigent soldiers, sailors and marines, and the families of those deceased, June 25, 1887.
33. William Miller, *A New History of the United States* (New York: Braziller, 1958), p. 219.
34. Elizabeth Wisner, *Social Welfare in the South* (Baton Rouge: Louisiana State University Press, 1970), p. 107.

35. George R. Bentley, *A History of the Freedmen's Bureau* (New York: Octagon, 1970).
36. President Andrew Johnson, *Veto Message, the Freedmen's Bureau*, in *The Congressional Globe*, "The Debates and Proceedings of the First Session," 39th Cong., 1866.
37. New York Association for Improving the Condition of the Poor, *Thirty-Second Annual Report 1875* (New York, 1875), p. 367. Also to be found in Albert Deutsch, "American Labor and Social Work," *Science and Society*, Vol. 8 (Fall 1944), p. 294.
38. Jeannette P. Nichols and Roy F. Nichols, *The Growth of American Democracy* (New York: Appleton-Century, 1939), p. 450.
39. Ewan Clague, *The Bureau of Labor Statistics* (New York: Praeger, 1968), p. 8.
40. Forman, op. cit., p. 292.
41. Ibid., p. 337.
42. Terence V. Powderly, *Proceedings of the General Assembly, 1882*, p. 278. Quoted in Philip S. Foner, *History of the Labor Movement in the United States* (New York: International Publishers, 1947), 1:508.
43. Charles A. Beard and Mary R. Beard, *The Rise of American Civilization* (New York: Macmillan, 1930), 2:416.
44. Russell H. Conwell, *Acres of Diamonds* (Philadelphia: Temple University Press, n.d.), pp. 18, 19.
45. "Pauperism in the City of New York," A Report from the Department of Social Economy, *Proceedings, NCCC: 1874*, pp. 18–28.
46. Mrs. Charles Russell Lowell, "The Economic and Moral Effects of Public Outdoor Relief," *Proceedings, NCCC: 1890*, pp. 81–91.
47. Community Service Society of New York, *Frontiers in Human Welfare: The Story of a Hundred Years of Service to the Community of New York, 1848–1948* (New York, 1948), p. 35.
48. The Reverend Oscar C. McCulloch, "The Tribe of Ishmael, A Study in Social Degradation," *Proceedings, NCCC: 1888*, pp. 154–159.
49. Amos Griswold Warner, *American Charities* (New York: Thomas Y. Crowell, 1894), pp. 36–63.
50. Fred H. Wines, "Causes of Pauperism and Crime," *Proceedings, NCCC: 1886*, pp. 207–214.
51. Franklin B. Sanborn, "Indoor and Outdoor Relief," *Proceedings, NCCC: 1890*, pp. 73–80.
52. Charles D. Kellogg, "Charity Organization in the United States: A Report of the Committee on History of Charity Organization," *Proceedings, NCCC: 1893*, p. 72.
53. Ibid., p. 82.
54. Ibid., p. 93.
55. John Boyle O'Reilly, "In Bohemia" (1886), quoted in Jane Addams et al., *Philanthropy and Social Progress* (New York: T.Y. Crowell, 1893), p. 135.
56. Leah Hanna Feder, *Unemployment Relief in Periods of Depression* (New York: Russell Sage Foundation, 1936), p. 133. See also, Charles D. Kellogg, "The Situation in New York City during the Winter of 1893–1894," *Proceedings, NCCC: 1894*, p. 24. Kellogg ascribes to organized labor the belief that charitable agencies are "an aristocratic concession to poverty."
57. Frank D. Watson, *The Charity Organization Movement in the United States* (New York: Macmillan, 1922), pp. 215, 225–226.
58. See letter "To the Editor of the Times-Democrat" of New Orleans, March 18, 1903. The letter is signed by NAWSA's officers, including Susan B. Anthony and Carrie Chapman Catt. Reprinted in Judith Papachristou, *Women Together, A Ms. Book* (New York: Knopf, 1976), pp. 143–144.
59. Andrew Sinclair, *The Better Half: The Emancipation of the American Woman* (New York: Harper & Row, 1965), p. 194.
60. *Historical Statistics*, p. 49.
61. Ibid., p. 22. Also: Ernest R. Groves, *The American Woman: The Feminine Side of a Masculine Civilization* (New York: Arno Press, 1972), p. 112.
62. Papachristou, op. cit., p. 90.
63. Frances E. Willard, *Woman and Temperance, or Work of the Women's Christian Temperance Union* (Hartford: Park, 1884), pp. 457–459.
64. Ibid.

65. For an interesting review of higher education for women during the post-Civil War and Progressive eras, see Sheila M. Rothman, *Woman's Proper Place* (New York: Basic Books, 1978), pp. 26–42, 97–132.

66. Willard, op. cit. For a discussion of the connection between the temperance and suffrage movements, see Papachristou, op. cit., pp. 88–97.

67. U.S. Labor Commissioner Wright reported "that by 1890 only nine out of 360 general groups to which the country's industries had been assigned did not employ women." Sharlene J. Hesse, *Working Women and Families* (Beverly Hills: Sage, 1979), p. 42.

68. Joan D. Mandle, *Women and Social Change in America* (Princeton: Princeton Book Company, Publishers, 1979), p. 23.

69. U.S. Department of Labor, Women's Bureau, *1969 Handbook on Women Workers*, Bulletin No. 294 (Washington, D.C.: Government Printing Office, 1969); and *Historical Statistics*, pp. 132–133.

70. Edith Abbott, *Women in Industry: A Study in American Economic History* (New York: D. Appleton, 1909), p. 123.

71. "Discussion on Charity Organization," *Proceedings, NCCC: 1888*, p. 420.

72. Laws of the State of Illinois, 1899, An Act to Regulate the Treatment and Control of Dependent, Neglected, and Delinquent Children.

73. State Board of Charities of the State of New York, *Eighth Annual Report*, 1875.

74. Laws of the State of New York, An Act to Provide Better Care of Pauper and Destitute Children, April 24, 1875.

75. Anne B. Richardson, "Massachusetts Institutions: Supplementary Work in the Care of Dependent and Delinquent Children," *Proceedings, NCCC: 1886*, pp. 131–138.

76. Warner, op. cit., p. 99.

77. Commonwealth of Pennsylvania, *Report of the Commissioners of Public Charities for the Year 1882*, Legislative Document No. 5.

78. Welfare Laws of the State of Pennsylvania, 1883 Laws, p. 1074, sec. 904.

79. Charles S. Hoyt, "The Causes of Pauperism," *Tenth Annual Report of the New York State Board of Charities*, 1877, pp. 97–292.

80. Board of Commissioners of Public Charities of the State of Pennsylvania, *Fourteenth Annual Report*, 1883, p. 2.

81. *Twenty-fourth Annual Report* (Boston: Boston Children's Aid Society, 1888), p. 16. The report is quoted extensively in Henry W. Thurston, *The Dependent Child* (New York: Columbia University Press, 1930).

82. *Twenty-eighth and Twenty-ninth Annual Reports* (Boston: Boston Children's Aid Society, 1893), p. 10. This two-year report is quoted extensively in Thurston, op. cit., pp. 191–192.

83. Homer Folks, *The Care of Destitute, Neglected and Delinquent Children* (New York: Macmillan, 1911), p. 80.

84. Brian Gratton, "The New History of the Aged: A Critique," in David van Tassel and Peter N. Stearns, eds., *Old Age in a Bureaucratic Society* (Westport, Conn.: Greenwood Press, 1986), p. 17.

85. Michael B. Katz, *Poverty and Policy in American History* (New York: Academic Press, 1983), p. 76; Seamus p. Metress, "The History of Irish-American Care of the Aged," *Social Service Review*, March 1985, p. 24.

86. Michael B. Katz, *In the Shadow of the Poorhouse* (New York: Basic Books, 1986), p. 87.

87. Zilpha D. Smith, "Report of the Committee on the Organization of Charity," *Proceedings, NCCC: 1888*, pp. 120–130.

88. Charles D. Kellogg, "Report of the Committee on History of Charity Organization," *Proceedings NCCC: 1893*, pp. 52–93.

89. Allen F. Davis, *Spearheads for Reform: The Social Settlements and the Progressive Movement, 1890–1914* (New York: Oxford University Press, 1967).

90. Humphreys S. Gurteen, *A Handbook of Charity Organization* (Buffalo: Courier, 1882), pp. 120–123.

91. Jane Addams, "Social Settlements," *Proceedings, NCCC: 1897*, p. 339.

5

Progress and Reform: 1900–1930

The rapid social and economic changes of the late nineteenth century had caught many Americans by surprise. As the new century dawned, many felt like strangers in their own land. In the countryside, the creation of a global market for agricultural goods meant that the price of wheat in Kansas was tied not only to the success of the year's harvest, but how well farmers in Canada and Australia did as well. In the cities, a predominantly native-born, white middle class and a foreign-born working class studied one another across barriers of social class, language, and culture. But the striking economic reality of the era was the emergence of economic giants: "trusts," monopolies, and corporations.

Over the first thirty years of the twentieth century, Americans from all walks of life tried to come to terms with these changes and their implications for their welfare. It was an era of experimentation and innovation, but ultimately, most of the reform efforts of the era fell short of their goals. Although the motivation for reform was in abundant supply, Progressive reforms lacked two critical ingredients for success: ideas and institutions.

Intellectually, Americans lacked a set of coherent ideas for changing the economic and social structure. Many of their ideas looked to the past, to returning to a society dominated by small-town values. Others, like the creation of a socialist commonwealth that would eliminate capitalism, never received serious consideration by most Americans.

The institutional realities of the early twentieth century, too, could not support serious reform. The forces that were reshaping economic and social life were national and international in scope. Yet, most Americans owed their allegiance to social institutions that were local or sectarian. Fraternal organizations, political parties, and labor unions—even if they were affiliated with national federations—were effective only in addressing local issues.

If reform were to succeed, it would need to reach across the rigid cultural barriers that dominated American society in the early twentieth century: the lines between the countryside and the city, between workers and the middle class, between foreigners and native-born, and between men and women.

The Progressives made a start at building the ideas and institutions that could ultimately reform American society, but it was only a start. Ironically, many of its gains occurred after the end of the "Progressive Era" with America's entry into World War I. After the War, the dominant political climate turned more conservative as the culture sought "100 percent Americanism" and "normalcy."[1] Yet, below the surface, many reform movements would continue to grow, although their success would have to wait.

By the 1920s, the United States had become the richest country on earth—a world leader in farm and manufacturing output. By 1925, it was producing 55 percent of the world's iron ore, 66 percent of the steel, 62 percent of the petroleum, 52 percent of the timber, 60 percent of the cotton, 80 percent of the sulfur, and 95 percent of the automobiles.[2] Solutions to all economic problems seemed within the reach of rational individuals.

Revolutions in technology and communication began to knit America into a single country. The American frontier had only disappeared in the last decade of the nineteenth century. By the turn of the twentieth century, train lines connected cities and regions. In American cities, trolley lines and commuter trains made it possible for people to live in one section of town and work or shop in another. Before the 1920s had ended, the automobile and the airplane were becoming increasingly common forms of transportation.

The telephone had an equally dramatic impact on communications. In 1890, only about 2 percent of American homes had a telephone. By 1930, 40 percent did. No longer did it take days or hours to get word across town or across the nation. During the first three decades of the twentieth century, motion pictures and radio improved people's access to information and culture from across the world.

Twentieth-century inventions and innovative managerial skills revolutionized industry and agriculture. Between 1899 and 1929, the total output of manufacturing increased 273 percent.[3] Growth occurred throughout the period but was particularly stimulated by the war, when new industries were developed to replace the previously imported German dyes, chemicals, and optical instruments. When European industries were left devastated by World War I, the United States became the leading world supplier of both manufactured and agricultural products.

The period from the turn of the century to the depression of the 1930s saw the development of new power supplies, greater mechanization, and the spread of "scientific management." Whereas in 1913 it had taken 14 hours to assemble a car, in 1914 the job was done in 93 minutes. By 1925, Henry Ford was able to produce an automobile every 10 seconds.

In agriculture, too, mechanization and new sources of power joined with improved transportation to increase productivity. The value of agricultural output rose steadily, due almost entirely to the increase in crop yields per acre. As farming became mechanized, labor was freed to move into manufacturing. By the end of the period, although the United States had only 4 percent of the world's farmers and farm laborers, it was producing nearly 70 percent of the world's tobacco, 25 percent of the oats and hay, 20 percent of the wheat, 13 percent of the barley, and 7 percent of the potatoes.[4]

Technological progress and relatively steady employment levels resulted in a climbing gross national product (GNP), despite brief recessions. GNP stood at about $17 billion in 1900 and $104 billion in 1929. Per capita GNP rose by 73 percent in the first thirty years of the century.[5]

The increase in GNP was based on the ability of the agricultural sector to support a larger and larger urban, industrial population. Between 1900 and 1930, the population of the United States increased by 46.8 million to reach 123 million. During those same years, the total number of persons living in urban areas increased by 38 million to a total of 69 million. Forty percent of the population lived in urban areas in 1900; this rose to 51 percent in 1920 and to 56 percent in 1930.[6] Much of the shift from an agricultural to a predominantly urban society was achieved by a steady migration to the cities. This was true for both the black and white populations. For the United States as a whole, 27 percent of the black population and 49 percent of the white population lived in urban areas in 1910; in 1930, 44 percent of the black population and 58 percent of the white population lived in urban areas.[7] Although the Southern African American population remained predominantly rural, in the Northern and Western parts of the country, blacks concentrated in urban areas. After 1915, as blacks were forced off the farms, they moved increasingly into the cities of both the North and the South.

A measure of the economy's strength was its ability to absorb the almost 20 million immigrants who entered the country. Most of this immigration occurred during the first fifteen years of the century, when 14.5 million people came, many from southern and eastern Europe. The anti-Chinese legislation of the 1880s was followed by restrictions on Japanese immigration early in the twentieth century and then by anti-Filipino legislation. Eventually, nativist sentiment prevailed completely and general restriction of immigration became the policy of the United States in 1924. The National Origins Act of 1924 set up a complicated system of quotas for immigration, with each country allotted a quota related to the proportion of nationals already present in the United States. Reflecting anti-Catholic and anti-Jewish sentiments of the era, it was intended to slow the increase in southern and eastern Europeans and to limit the total number of foreigners admitted.

However, despite the constraints of World War I and the legislative restrictions of the 1920s, the number of foreign-born as a percentage of the total population stayed at 13 to 14 percent—one of seven people were immigrants. An even larger number of people had at least one foreign-born parent. The immigrants and their children accounted for more than one-third of the population. Most—about 75 percent—lived in cities, where rapid population growth meant a period of booming construction.[8]

Between 1920 and 1930, some 6 million people moved from farms to cities, resulting for the first time in a net loss—of 1.2 million—in farm population. As cities grew, they became increasingly commercial and industrial in character. The number of such urban centers with populations of at least 100,000 grew from 38 in 1900 to 83 in 1930.[9] The growth was haphazard, causing crowded, unsanitary, tenement living. Families, both from abroad and from rural areas, were unfamiliar with urban living. Their social and economic vulnerability made them subject to political exploitation and corruption. Political leaders manipulated the processes of democratic

government, while the pressing need for housing, sanitation, fire protection, polic-
ing, traffic regulation, and educational facilities often went unheeded.

Growth and change occurred in the organization of industry, as well as in its
output. In 1897, about a dozen corporations other than railroads were capitalized at
$10 million. By 1903, the number of such corporations had risen to 300, of which
about 50 were capitalized at more than $50 million; 17 were capitalized at more than
$100 million; and one, U.S. Steel became the first billion-dollar corporation. These
were the years in which some of the largest trusts in America were formed: Standard
Oil, Consolidated Tobacco, and American Smelting, in addition to U.S. Steel. The
efforts of the federal government to enforce antitrust laws were largely ineffective.
Nevertheless, by 1914, large corporations dominated anthracite coal, agricultural machinery, sugar, telephone and telegraph, and public utilities in addition to iron and
steel, railroads, oil, tobacco, and copper. Control of American industry had shifted
from individual owners to a professional managerial class responsible to a board of directors often controlled by a small and powerful group of investment bankers.[10]

Paralleling the concentration of corporate power was a concentration of wealth
and income. As the nation prospered, the growth at the top far exceeded that of
either the middle class or the working class. It was the era of the multimillionaire.
Andrew Carnegie, for example, was said to have had an average annual income of
more than $10 million—not subject to any income tax—at the turn of the century. In
1899, the richest 1.6 percent of the population had received 10.8 percent of national
income. By 1910, this had jumped to 19 percent. Rising wages and relatively steady
employment meant that working-class incomes rose, too, but at a much slower rate.
A 1915 report by the Commission on Industrial Relations took the critical question
of the era to be: "Have workers received a fair share of the enormous increase in
wealth which has taken place in this country during the period, as a result largely of
their labor?" Its response: "The answer is emphatically—No!"[11]

Poverty and the Working Class

The commission's report pointed out that during the period 1890–1912, personal
wealth had increased 188 percent; but the aggregate income of wage earners in manufacturing, mining, and transportation had risen only 95 percent. The wage earner's
share of the net product in manufacturing had actually declined. The commission estimated that to achieve a minimum decency level, an average family of 5.6 members required an annual income of $700. Since 79 percent of the country's fathers earned less
than $700 a year, earnings from other family members were necessary to sustain the
family. And, indeed, the Census Bureau reported that 1,750,000 children between ten
and fifteen years of age were gainfully employed in 1900; by 1910, this number had
dropped to 1,600,000. In 1930, however, the figure still stood at 667,000.[12]

The report of the Commission on Industrial Relations concluded that, despite
the labor of wives and children, and the widespread practice of taking in boarders
and lodgers, 50 to 66 percent of working-class families were poor and that a third
lived in "abject poverty." Other estimates confirmed the judgment of poverty and risk.

Robert Hunter, a social worker, writing in 1904, estimated the poverty population at 10 million.[13] Father John A. Ryan, ethical theorist and economist, writing in 1906, found that the average family needed an annual income of at least $600 and that 60 percent of all wage earners received less.[14] Within the ranks of the working class, as the American Federation of Labor (AFL) succeeded in unionizing some crafts, dissatisfaction was further aggravated by the notable difference in payments to skilled and unskilled workers. Each recession (1910–1911, 1914–1915, 1920–1921) meant increased unemployment and lowered wages, especially for unskilled workers—largely ex-farmhands, African Americans, and immigrants. Indeed, by 1928–1929 social welfare agencies were reporting increased caseloads. Between the newly rich, with their extreme wealth, and the working class, with its extreme poverty, lay the large middle class—a group with adequate income but little to spare, a group that was dissatisfied because it could not keep pace with the rapidly rising standard of living of those at the top.

By the 1920s, the farm economy had slipped into depression. The pre-World War I period was one of prosperity marked by rising farm income. The closing of the frontier, however, meant rising land prices. This, combined with rising costs of mechanization, made easy access to low-cost credit to buy land and machinery a major issue for most farmers. For the marginal farmer, land became more and more difficult to acquire. As the average size of farms started to grow, farm tenancy, already prevalent in the South, began to spread to the Midwest. In 1900, 35 percent of the nation's farms were tenant operated; by 1930, this had risen to 42 percent. For black farmers in the South, the figure reached 79 percent in 1930. The demands of World War I had led to an overextension of agriculture; in 1920, an agricultural depression occurred, and it continued intermittently throughout the decade. Between 1919 and 1929, the number of farms actually declined.[15]

The well-being of African Americans in the early twentieth century was worse than at any time since the end of slavery. With the end of Reconstruction, the African Americans had lost any real political power; they had been abandoned to the "oppression of those who had formerly exercised unlimited domination" over them.[16] They still retained most of the political and civil rights they had won after the Civil War.

The Populist revolt of the 1890s created fear among the white elite, however, that an alliance of poor whites and blacks might challenge their power. In the early years of the twentieth century, Southern states moved to pass "Jim Crow" laws that excluded African Americans from voting or serving on juries, segregated schools and public accommodations, and provided economic elites with even more power with which to control black workers.[17]

Collusion in the segregation and suppression of blacks was given judicial respectability by the Supreme Court's approval in 1896 of the "separate but equal" doctrine.[18] Northern rationalization of the necessity for segregation and suppression was epitomized by the widespread acceptance of D. W. Griffith's 1915 film *Birth of a Nation*, in which freed blacks were stereotyped as cruel, vengeful rulers over starving, helpless whites and as "racially incapable of understanding, sharing, or contributing to Americanism."[19] In this atmosphere, Booker T. Washington's espousal of progress by separate evolution for his people found support among whites, who gained comfort and conviction from the seeming acquiescence of the country's outstanding Negro leader—the founder of Tuskegee Institute—in policies of social segregation and political cooperation. Washington wrote:

> The wisest among my race understand that the agitation of questions of social equality is the extremest folly, and that progress in the enjoyment of all the privileges that will come to us must be the result of severe and constant struggle rather than of artificial forcing. No race that has anything to contribute to the markets of the world is long in any degree ostracized. It is important and right that all privileges of the law be ours, but it is vastly more important that we be prepared for the exercise of these privileges.[20]

Thus, the Progressive Era was not one of progress for African Americans. Sunk in the tenancy-mortgage morass of the sharecropper and crop-lien systems and subjected to the lynchings and harassments of Klansmen, the black population began to migrate to urban areas. In 1900, there were only 2 million blacks living in cities. The largest single group was in Washington, D.C.. Baltimore, New Orleans, Philadelphia, and New York each had more than 60,000 black residents.[21] Net migration of blacks to Northern states amounted to only 426,000 between 1910 and 1920, but it jumped to 713,000 during the next decade.[22]

The beginning of the flight from the South coincided with a period of dramatically increased labor productivity, as mass production techniques and assembly lines were introduced. From 1919 to 1929, manufacturing output increased by 53 percent, while the number of wage earners in manufacturing remained stable.[23] Annual real earnings rose and the length of the workweek fell, so that for those employed it was a prosperous period. But for blacks forced off the farms and trying to gain entry into the labor market, times were always hard. Although there were not enough black migrants in the cities for them to have political or economic clout, their numbers were sufficient to foster white hostility, both because of competition with whites for jobs and because of their use, along with immigrants, as strikebreakers in labor disputes. Discrimination dominated white–black relations, and blacks were successfully excluded from the ranks of organized labor. Indeed, African Americans were even excluded from unskilled factory jobs in most cities, even though these jobs were near the bottom of the occupational ladder (Figure 5.1).

The black population was generally unaffected by reform activities and the social welfare benefits that resulted from them. In an era marked by economic progress and social mobility, this group remained poor and powerless. More social legislation aiding and protecting the working class was passed during the Progressive Era than had been passed in any previous century. For the most part, however, legislation affecting the labor of women and children, workmen's compensation, regulation of hours and wages, and industrial safety all applied to industries in which black participation was minimal. This fact eluded social welfare reformers who tended to view the problems of all minorities as coextensive with the problems of immigrants. Despite periodic race riots, the relatively small number of blacks in the cities of the North (where most agitation for social reform was concentrated) and their segregation

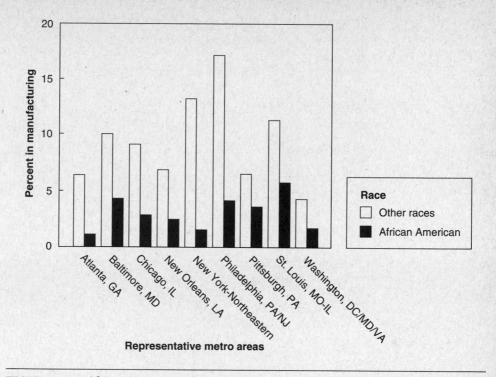

FIGURE 5.1 *African Americans migrated from rural to urban areas during the early years of the twentieth century; yet, they continued to face severe discrimination. In most cities, even factory employment was closed to them.*

Source: U. S. Census 1910, author's calculation

from the mainstream of economic, political, and social life made it possible to ignore their special problems.

For Native Americans, too, conditions improved very slowly. They were poor, largely uneducated, and deprived of citizenship and suffrage. Of those living on reservations, almost three-quarters of the children received no schooling. Much of the education that occurred was in boarding schools, which alienated the children and left them prepared for very little. Not until 1928 were federal funds increased, and it was to be the mid-1930s before states received special funds to provide public education for Native Americans.[24]

Before the Civil War, Native Americans had been declared aliens. Their tribes were domestic dependent nations. As aliens, they were not citizens; they could not be naturalized. After the Civil War, some Native Americans, off reservations, were enfranchised. After World War I, those who were veterans were granted citizenship. Finally in 1924 most Native Americans were recognized as citizens of the United States of America.[25]

"Breaker Boys," Working in Ewen Breaker, Pittstown, Pennsylvania
The National Archives

Coalitions for Reform

Progressivism grew out of middle-class concerns that the battle between big business and labor would engulf American society. It was the first attempt to fashion a "third way" between unregulated capitalism and a more radical alternative. Reformers, however, found themselves pulled in two directions. Culturally, they had much in common with the social and economic elite whose actions they attacked. Although many reformers had sympathy for the plight of workers, they were suspicious of the political and labor leaders who were their representatives. Although many Progressives worked hard to forge new coalitions for reform, their contradictory impulses often undermined their effectiveness.

The industrial collapse of 1893 produced hardships for 4 million unemployed and for small businessmen, farmers, and investors. Many demanded a change in power relationships and the development of a more equitable system of distribution of wealth and income. The march of "General" Jacob Coxey's army of the unemployed on Washington, D.C. in 1894, the increased prevalence of strikes and industrial violence, the growth of union membership (particularly in the Western Federation of Miners and the United Mine Workers), and the strength of the Populist Movement were part of an agrarian/working-class coalition for reform.

In the early years of the twentieth century, the reform movement shifted toward the center. The American Federation of Labor (AFL), representing more highly paid craft workers than the older, industrial unions, became the dominant force in the labor movement. Writers and educators undertook an exposé of the "robber barons"; new political leadership took on the task of city and state reforms; social workers worked on behalf of the poor segregated into urban slums. Social protest became the property of intellectuals and professionals.

It became clear to more and more Americans that laissez-faire and small business no longer characterized their economy. The era of small business firms engaged in competition had supported a model of individual achievement, but the emergence of large corporations or trusts engaged in monopolistic market control increasingly made this model appear irrelevant. In a competitive, individualistic society, the dominant social theorists had argued for social reform based on individual reformation; the corporate universe of the twentieth century seemed to require a reform of institutions.

During most of the nineteenth century, it had been liberal dogma that the limited government action was good for the economy and society. In the early twentieth century, more Americans were willing to ask if government had a role in creating a more just social order. A "new liberalism" based on a belief in positive government action provided the ideological basis for many Progressives. Research would provide knowledge of social and political problems; extension of democratic institutions in government would lead to enactment of the appropriate legislation. In retrospect, it was a romantic and an optimistic belief in rational, peaceful, and democratic processes.

Characteristic of the reform activity of the Progressive Era was its emphasis upon sympathy for the underdog. Change in social conditions through the provision, improvement, or regulation of government programs and services was meant to facilitate the individual's chance for assimilation into the mainstream of society, as well as to enhance the potential for successful living. For immigrants, this constituted an especially important opportunity to become like "us"—that is, like the dominant Anglo-Saxon members of the society.

Progressives wanted to maintain the cultural values of an earlier time—individuals, opportunity, "lifting one's self by one's bootstraps"—even as the social order that supported those values disappeared. This contradiction limited the effectiveness of many reform efforts.

The reform activities of the Progressive Era were spearheaded by many groups, some working independently, some working cooperatively as particular issues warranted cooperation, some working for individual aggrandizement, and some working altruistically for the larger society. One group was composed of small businessmen who were anxious to control and stop the domination of trusts and banking establishments. They were joined by writers and social workers, as well as by lawyers and clergymen, two professional groups for whom the rise of big business had meant a loss of status. Lawyers had lost status by a shift from being independent professionals to employed representatives of nouveau riche industrialists; the clergy had lost status by the secular, impersonal thrust of the process of industrialization and the wholesale abandonment of the church by the working class. Farmers, in search of easy credit, also became a part of the struggle against the domination of "organized money."

The growth of the Socialist Party in the early years of the century strengthened the hand of reformers by raising the specter of more radical alternatives to Progressive reform. Starting with a membership of less than 5,000 in 1900, it enrolled 118,000 members by 1912, including many of the nation's leading intellectuals— John Dewey, Stuart Chase, Paul Douglas, Jack London, Walter Lippmann, and Alexander Meikeljohn. Eugene Debs, running for president as the Socialist candidate, polled 6 percent of the popular vote in 1912. More important perhaps was the Socialists' success that same year in electing more than 1,000 members to various public offices. Socialist doctrines were widely reviewed, discussed, and quoted. Socialists were sometimes allied in specific causes with other reform groups. The growth of the Socialist party and its increased visibility served as a threat and catalyst for more moderate reform groups seeking regulation of industry.[26]

In 1902, President Roosevelt instructed the attorney general to bring suit under the Sherman Antitrust Act against the Northern Securities Company, a consolidation of railways including the Northern Pacific, the Great Northern, and the Chicago, Burlington, and Quincy systems. The Supreme Court sustained the government's appeal and effectively frustrated the plan of E. H. Harriman to bring all the important railways in the country under his control. In 1906, Congress passed the Hepburn Act, which permitted the Interstate Commerce Commission (ICC) to fix the rates of railroads, of storage, refrigeration, and terminal facilities, and of sleeping car, express, and pipeline companies. In 1910, authority was extended to the ICC to regulate telephone and telegraph companies.

Economic and regulatory reforms took various shapes. As a result of Upton Sinclair's *The Jungle* and of other exposés of the food and pharmaceutical industries, editors of popular journals and the American Medical Association, among others, formed a coalition to secure passage of the Food and Drug Act in 1906. In 1909, the Sixteenth Amendment, which established a federal income tax, was introduced in Congress by Cordell Hull. By 1913, it had been ratified by the required number of states and became law. During this same year, Congress created the Federal Reserve System, bringing about major reforms in banking.

Labor's cause and the frequency with which the lower courts had found against that cause were increasingly arousing sympathy. In 1914, the enactment of the Clayton Antitrust Act represented a culmination of the struggle between labor and small business, on the one hand, and big business on the other. Passage of this act, then, was an indication of labor sympathy and strength and of the success of the reform coalition. The Supreme Court had already begun to reverse the antilabor decisions of lower courts. Now an act of Congress laid the foundation for further restricting corporate monopolies, while simultaneously exempting labor unions from much of the antitrust legislation. The Clayton Act was supplemented by the Federal Trade Commission Act, establishing a commission whose purpose was to bring to bear the knowledge and advice of a group of economic experts on "unfair" methods of competition and alleged infractions of antitrust laws.

The "democratic" thrust of the Progressive Era made political reform a partner of economic reform. Just as muckraking publications had reported lurid instances of fraud and graft and of monopolistic control in industry, in railroading, and in public utilities,[27] they detailed corruption in state and local governments, in the courts, and in the U.S. Senate.[28] A veritable avalanche of widely read, eagerly awaited exposés of the "shame of the cities," of "treason in the Senate" led the way to political change. The effort was twofold: to provide for greater citizen participation in political affairs and to increase governmental responsiveness and honesty. The first strengthened the movement for women's suffrage, the secret ballot, direct primaries, direct election of senators, initiative, referendum, recall, and municipal home rule. The second led to demands for civil service reform, the short ballot, regulation of campaign expenditures, accountability and leadership on the part of elected officials, and the commission and city manager plans of municipal government. A few highlights suggest the thrust of the changes.

Middle- and upper-class white women, including the founders of social work, exercised unprecedented political influence during these years. Although the search for gender equality motivated many of them, their broadest influence was tied to their traditional roles as mothers and wives. *Maternalism*—an ideology based on the moral authority associated with women's traditional role—provided a means of uniting women whatever their position on equality. A variety of reforms, including mother's pensions, the creation of the Children's Bureau, child and women labor legislation, and efforts to improve maternal and child health were tied to the rise of maternalism.

On the federal level, Congress, in 1907, banned political contributions by corporations. In 1913, the Seventeenth Amendment to the Constitution provided for direct election of senators. In 1919, the Nineteenth Amendment, providing for women's suffrage, was passed. It was ratified by the required thirty-six states just one year later, bringing victory to this cause after almost seventy-five years of campaigning.

On a state and local level, twenty states introduced the initiative (making it possible for the citizenry to propose legislation) and the referendum (making it possible for voters to pass on measures introduced in legislative bodies). By 1915, direct primary and presidential preference laws were on the books of two-thirds of the states, thus giving a blow to the power of political bosses. The drive for efficiency, economy, and honesty in the administration of local governments began in Galveston, Texas, in 1900, when the entire political machinery of mayor, council, and bureaus was abolished and replaced by a board of commissioners. Thereafter, the commission form of government spread rapidly, especially in smaller cities, where its structure— generally five commissioners elected at large and each responsible for a particular department—was most appropriate. Starting with Dayton, Ohio, in 1914, the city manager type of government—a government run by an appointed expert in city administration—also found widespread acceptance.

In public welfare administration, change resulted in an initial shift of responsibility from local overseers of the poor to local or county departments of welfare. Kansas City, Missouri, established a city department of welfare in 1910, with authority to provide for the relief of the poor and the care of delinquents, the unemployed, and other needy groups. St. Joseph, Missouri, established a county–city department of public welfare, and Chicago set up the Cook County Bureau of Public Welfare, both in 1913.

The rise of "public welfare" marked a dramatic break with late nineteenth century thought about poverty. In place of a voluntary movement to limit "excessive almsgiving," philanthropic leaders called for government action to reduce the distress of the poor. Increasingly, Progressives came to see that poverty was primarily an economic, not a moral, condition.

Nor did the country's entry into World War I completely stop local governmental restructuring. Westchester County, New York, established a department of welfare in 1916. In 1917, an important reorganization of the Illinois state government occurred with the passage of the Civil Administrative Code, which provided for the grouping of all state functions and activities into nine departments, each with its own director. Among the nine was a Department of Welfare with its director of public welfare responsible for administering the state's assistance, services, and institutional programs. The Illinois code was emulated by other states and was the start of a new era in public administration. In many states, for example, public welfare services were consolidated into statewide systems administered by appointed heads of state departments of welfare. Both in the statewide scope of the organizations and in the removal of department executives "from current political responsibility, except through [the ultimate political responsibility of] the governor,"[29] the trend foreshadowed the requirements of the Social Security Act of 1935.

No reform activities were more representative of the Progressive Era than those that occurred in the arena of social welfare. The aura of justice, of social consciousness, of morality and ethics, most logically reposed here. The reform movement responded to and fostered the new profession of social work. Individual social workers, through research, persistence, and expertise, moved to the forefront of advocacy for social legislation. Theodore Roosevelt himself, acting on the commonly held conviction that all were personally responsible for the current state of affairs depicted so graphically in muckraking literature, called upon each citizen to contribute to "reform through social work."[30] Social work, acting on society's will for social change, carried that projection in two sometimes converging but basically different operations—the Charity Organization and Settlement House movements.

Those who labored for social reform were primarily concerned, as a matter of social justice, "to bring the power of the state and national governments into the economic struggle on the side of women, children, and other unprotected groups."[31] Whether prompted by the Charity Organization hope to sustain and strengthen individuals in their own efforts to cope, or by the Settlement House conviction that any intervention short of intrinsic societal restructuring must be considered only "a down payment toward justice,"[32] social workers could find common ground for the work that needed doing.

At the height of the reform movement, between 1905 and the beginning of World War I, leaders of the Charity Organization and Settlement House movements came together in behalf of social reform activity. The participation of Charity Organizations in reform was impelled by their changing view of the family. In 1900, Charles Faulkner's presidential address at the National Conference of Charities and Corrections had labeled the family "the unit of social order" and laid out a program of education in the home and in the school for the moral improvement of individuals. His Darwinian bent took him from a concern for the maintenance of "the blessings and protection of society through its family life" to call for avoiding "unrestrained comingling of . . . defectives with the people. . . ."[33] By 1908, however, Mary Richmond was arguing for the protection of family life against the onslaughts of a hostile environment.

Miss Richmond referred to the family as "the great social unit, the fundamental social fact." She demanded changes in agency practices, action in regard to child labor laws, industrial safety regulations, and protection of working women, as well as administrative changes in industrial operations to strengthen family life. She challenged the members of her social work audience to ask themselves: "Have we at least set plans in motion that will make the children better heads of families than their parents have been?"[34] Miss Richmond's challenge was based on a new recognition of "the overwhelming force of heredity *plus* the environment that we inherit." Social workers and their allies strove for legislation to regulate tenement and factory construction; to prevent and compensate for industrial accidents and diseases; to prohibit child labor and provide for compulsory education; to improve sanitary and health conditions; to provide social insurance as security against unemployment, retirement, or death of the breadwinner; and to protect workers—especially women—in regard to minimum wages and working hours.

Improvement in housing conditions had been a concern of social workers at least since 1882, when the Boston Associated Charities appointed a Committee on Dwellings of the Poor. In the same year, the New York and Buffalo Charity Organization Societies combined to get a tenement housing bill through the state legislature. During the next decade, they allied themselves with settlement residents and others to investigate and publicize the housing conditions of the poor. The New York City Tenement House Law was passed in 1901. Aimed at preventing the construction of lightless, airless tenements, the law became a model to follow. Similar legislation was passed for Chicago in 1902; by 1910, most large cities had inaugurated some housing reform.

Social Reform: Working Conditions

Child labor and women's working hours were matters of great concern for Progressives. In 1900, nearly 2 million children aged ten to fifteen and almost 5 million women over fifteen were in a labor force totaling about 29 million.[35] Twenty-eight states had already adopted some legal protections for children. By 1914, as a result of the continued assault by the National Child Labor Committee, the National Consumer's League, the General Federation of Women's Clubs, and others, almost all the states had laws covering hours and conditions of child labor in factories, mills, and workshops and setting minimum ages for leaving school.[36]

But the laws were weak and inadequate. Owen R. Lovejoy, secretary of the National Child Labor Committee and chairman of the Committee on Standards of Living and Labor of the National Conference of Charities and Corrections, reported the following:

No state has made any adequate plan to protect its children to sixteen years from bare-handed contact with the red hot tools of our industrial competition. Nearly half the states have no effective way of protecting children even to the fourteenth birthday. Several permit their employment at twelve or even younger.[37]

Much of the problem occurred in industries engaged in interstate commerce, and, therefore, federal intervention seemed necessary. The first formal attempts to bring child labor under federal control were made in 1906, when bills were introduced in Congress to prohibit the interstate shipment of articles produced in factories or mines employing children. The bills were not passed. A few years later, President Theodore Roosevelt directed the secretary of labor to investigate the situation. In 1912, the Children's Bureau was created to report, among other things, on "dangerous occupations, accidents and diseases of children, employment legislation affecting children."[38] The bureau's investigations bolstered the report of the secretary of labor as to the need for child protections, and further efforts to obtain federal regulation of child welfare followed. The Keating-Owen bill was passed by Congress in 1916, but it was found unconstitutional two years later on the grounds that it transcended "the authority delegated to Congress over commerce."[39] Subsequent improvements in child labor legislation remained with the states; by 1930, all of the states and the District of Columbia had taken legal measures to safeguard the employment and working conditions of children. In many instances, old provisions had been strengthened.[40]

In the country as a whole, child labor had steadily declined so that by 1930 less than 5 percent of the children between ten and fifteen years of age were employed, compared to 18 percent in 1900. Even in the South, which had lagged in regulatory legislation, the ratio of children employed in its newly developing textile industry was no higher than in its Northern counterpart. These advances were chronicled in the census of 1930. Despite within-industry equivalency, however, there were wide interindustry distinctions, reflecting geographic and racial differences. For example, only 3 percent of children between ten and fifteen years were at work in industrial Rhode Island, whereas 24 percent were at work in Mississippi, where child welfare laws were loosely enforced and the cheap farm labor of black children was deemed necessary. Nor did the census takers secure information concerning the paid employment of children under ten.[41] One can only surmise what that meant for black children, especially in those Southern states where legislation provided minimal protection.

Efforts to effect child labor legislation were paralleled by efforts to regulate conditions and hours of female workers, who constituted 20 percent of the labor force. The coalition of groups working to obtain legislation for each was largely the same.

The Consumer's League, under the leadership of its executive, Florence Kelley, was particularly active in regard to legal protections for working women. Under the aegis of the league, Mrs. Kelley and Josephine Goldmark, a social worker, completed research that was successfully used by Louis Brandeis in arguing the constitutionality of Oregon's law limiting working hours for women to ten hours per day. When, in 1908, the Supreme Court upheld the constitutionality of the law, the right of states to protect women from excessive hours of labor was established, and virtually all the states moved to enact laws in this field. By 1912, the year in which the Committee on Standards of Living and Labor of the National Conference of Charities and Corrections made its report, the battle was for such specific protections as the eight-hour day and the six-day workweek. The committee predicted: "The day will come—come tripping on the heels of social regulation—when our manufacturers and merchants will be able to distribute . . . [their products] without compelling the sacrifice of the health of our mothers or burning out the eyes of our little children who now bend over their work . . . at all hours of the night."[42]

The average workday at the close of the Civil War remained at eleven hours,[43] and organized labor began to campaign for an eight-hour day. The eight-hour movement, such as it was, collapsed in 1886, when the violence and aftermath of Chicago's Haymarket Square riot proved disastrous to the Knights of Labor. In 1900, according to an estimate based on information of the Bureau of Labor Statistics, the average standard workweek was still more than fifty-seven hours, having declined very little during the previous decade.[44] For industry as a whole, there was wide variation, so that unorganized workers, such as those in the blast furnaces of steel mills, ordinarily worked a twelve-hour day and eighty-four-hour week, whereas organized workers in the building trades had achieved a forty-eight-hour week, working eight hours a day, six days a week.[45]

After 1900, reduction in working hours might not have occurred without organization on the part of workers, who were panicked by the threat of unemployment posed by technological advance. The eight-hour day was seen, in effect, as "job making," a method of spreading available employment among the greatest number of workers. At the same time, the demand for fewer working hours coincided with higher labor-hour productivity and with increased sales from lowered prices. Differentials in work hours between unionized and nonunionized industries indicate the significance of unionization for reduced work hours. Average weekly hours in 1900 for unionized manufacturing industries were fifty-three, compared to sixty-two for nonunion manufacturing. By 1920, unionized manufacturing hours had declined to forty-six per week and nonunion manufacturing to fifty-four. Unionized manufacturing had achieved the eight-hour day and nonunion manufacturing had made significant gains. The gap between organized and unorganized labor narrowed.[46]

In response to the increased militancy of labor following World War I, major corporations pursued the "American plan" during the 1920s. This combined "welfare capitalism"—the expansion of programs to employees, including unemployment and pension benefits—with an aggressive anti-union campaign. Companies like the Ford Motor Company employed "social secretaries" to provide social services to workers. Yet, without a fully developed set of professional ethics, these social workers often reported "undesirable" behavior to employers, including labor union membership and drinking. Although welfare capitalism died during the Great Depression, the idea that employers would provide significant social welfare benefits to their employees became one of the defining features of American social welfare.

Social Reform: Women, Work, and Suffrage

In 1900, the National American Women's Suffrage Association (NAWSA), representing the joining of the two earlier rivals in the women's suffrage movement, was still unclear as to directions for achieving votes for women. The association's flirtation with "educated suffrage," offering to counter the votes of lower-class blacks and immigrants with those of middle-class women, contributed to a separation of white women from black women, middle-class women from lower-class women, nonworking women from working women, and native-born women from immigrant women. There were seemingly irreparable divisions.

In the Progressive Era, racism and nativism, as integral parts of the suffrage movement, began to subside. Josephine Shaw Lowell's statement of 1888, pointing up the discrepancy between middle-class rhetoric and lower-class reality in the matter of working mothers, signified a beginning shift in her own stance toward people in need.[47] The NAWSA moved away from a position that not only failed but that was generally untenable in the climate of the times. In addition, the limiting nature of a single-issue organization became apparent as other women's groups moved to the fore. These new organizations—for example, the National Consumers' League, the National Women's Trade Union League, and the Young Women's Christian Association—were at once concerned with matters affecting women as women and with the potential of the vote for righting wrongs. The NAWSA broadened its view. Its publication, *The Woman's Journal*, supported the garment workers' strike of 1909 and 1910 and reported the tragic Triangle Shirt-Waist Company fire of 1911 as demonstrating the need for women's votes to ensure "more effective factory legislation and a larger number of [factory] inspectors."[48] This broadened view resulted in increased membership. By 1910, the official numbers in NAWSA had risen to 100,000; in 1917, the membership stood at 2 million.

Part of the reality of the Progressive Era was the increasing participation of women in the labor force. In 1900, there were more than 5 million gainfully employed female workers. Most worked as unskilled factory hands or as domestics; most were foreign born or black; some were married. The number of female workers increased rapidly to meet the demands of this generally prosperous era—later, the added demands of a Europe at war, and finally, in 1917, the demands of the United States itself as its own male workers, drafted for wartime service, had to be replaced. By 1910, the number of gainfully employed women had risen to 8 million. With the war over, labor force adjustments resulted from the return of soldiers to the workforce and of many women to working solely in the home. Nevertheless, by 1920, the number of gainfully employed women had risen to more than 8 1/2 million.[49] The formation of the National Women's Trade Union League and its activities in supporting existing unions of women wage earners and of assisting in the formation of new women's unions attest to the increase in the numbers of women workers, their beginning entrance in skilled positions, and their increasing political consciousness.

Progress toward the unionization of women was nevertheless slow and fraught with difficulty. Much of the history was characterized by spontaneous work stoppage and strikes against low wages and torturous working conditions. These strikes resulted in efforts to organize; but even when success in gaining demands followed, unionization tended to fall apart. In skilled industry, the responsibility for this can be traced to the overall antagonism of male workers, who accused women of scabbing during strike actions on the part of male-dominated unions, of taking men's jobs, and of lowering wage rates. These antagonisms carried over in the halfhearted attempts by the AFL, an organization of craft unions made up of skilled workers, to organize women's unions or to admit women into existing organizations. The AFL, like its constituents, was suspicious of women's commitment to work, of their staying power during strikes, and of their effect upon wages. The AFL's lack of interest was encouraged by the fact that by far the largest number of women continued to work in unskilled jobs—in textiles, in garments, shirt, and waist making, in laundries, and in domestic service. Among these unskilled workers, foreign-born and black women predominated. Black women particularly suffered exclusion from unionizing efforts, even from the efforts of other unskilled workers.

The task of bringing together the work-related and suffrage-related concerns of women was not easy. Concern for their physical, moral, and emotional well-being sprang from the conviction that "the prime function of woman must ever be the perpetuating of the race. . . . The woman is worth more to society . . . as the mother of healthy children than as the swiftest labeler of cans."[50] The result was a great deal of effort to estimate "a living wage" for women and to clarify the special needs of women in regard to working hours and working conditions. Although similar concerns were being explored in connection with all workers, very special legislative protection was sought for the unique circumstances of women.[51] The culmination of these concerns for women, reflecting the additional burdens they had assumed during World War I, came with the establishment by Congress in 1920 of the Women's Bureau within the Department of Labor.

By the time of the armistice in 1918, women's groups had become accustomed to cooperation. This unity of action comprised a powerful political force. Under the direction of Carrie Chapman Catt, who had been reelected its president in 1915, the NAWSA was revitalized and led the final march toward victory. Mrs. Catt was able to gain President Wilson's support. Not the least of that support derived from the contribution of women and of women's organizations to the war effort. The Nineteenth Amendment to the Constitution was approved by Congress on June 4, 1919. The amendment was ratified by the required number of states on August 26, 1920. The NAWSA went out of existence but was revived as the League of Women Voters.

The end of World War I also brought success to another women-led movement, the drive for prohibition. In fact, the strength of the National Women's Christian Temperance Union combined with the government's wartime conservation efforts—that is, the need to limit the use of grain for the production of liquors—to win congressional approval for prohibition sooner than woman's suffrage. The Eighteenth Amendment to the Constitution prohibiting the manufacture, sale, and import or export of liquor was ratified in 1919. The disastrous results of attempts to enforce its provisions led to its being rescinded in 1933 by the Twenty-First Amendment.

With the passage of the Eighteenth and Nineteenth Amendments to the Constitution the women's movement went into an eclipse, a part of the decline in all reform activity suffered in the aftermath of World War I. The women's movement was not to revive until the 1960s.

Social Reform: Income Security

Social welfare legislation was additionally sought to protect against loss of income from the major hazards of an industrial society—accident, illness, death of the breadwinner, old age and retirement, and unemployment. Industrialization and urbanization required enormous change on the part of the family. Economic survival required mobility, freedom to move from farms to industrial sites where jobs existed. The mobile family was almost by definition a small family. Having moved to the cities, the families were then trapped by low wages and a lack of resources and industrial skills. Most family members had to stand ready to work to meet the costs of urban living. The family became increasingly dependent for income on factory owners, who themselves felt no responsibility for their workers' welfare, and on nonfamily members for services previously performed internally—child care for working mothers, for example. The family of the Progressive Era was a unit caught in the stress of a period of social change, a unit socially and economically insecure in its day-to-day living and vulnerable to anxieties about an unknown future.

The changes forced upon the family by industrial society, coupled with the dependence upon others for the means of production and for money payments, led to a sharp decline in the economic independence of the family unit. Thus, there was a need for safeguards to alleviate economic insecurity.

Workmen's compensation for injuries resulting from industrial accidents was first discussed at the American Sociological Conference of 1902. During this same year, when the National Conference of Charities and Corrections appointed a committee to investigate the topic, Maryland's Workmen's Compensation Act was declared illegal. The fact that no one could be found to appeal this decision of the lower court did not impede growing national enthusiasm for such a measure. Action was spurred by the realization that "the industries of our country every year claim an army of 15,000 men killed, and some half a million injured."[52] President Roosevelt's enthusiastic support of Senate action resulted in the Federal Employee's Act of 1906.

In 1904, a Massachusetts commission and, in 1907, an Illinois commission each recommended industrial insurance to their respective states. The recommendations went unheeded; nevertheless, agitation continued. Discussion of workmen's compensation occurred again at the annual meetings of the National Conference of Charities and Corrections in 1905 and 1906; a National Conference on Workmen's Compensation was held in 1909. By 1910, the year of the second National Conference on Workmen's Compensation, a groundswell of support had developed. The American Association for Labor Legislation, the National Civic Federation, the American Federation of Labor, the American Economic Association, and, though reluctantly, the National Association of Manufacturers were all encouraging the enactment of industrial insurance. During 1911, the year regarded "as the beginning of an intelligent grappling with the problem," ten states enacted workmen's compensation laws.[53]

The issue of old age security was raised for discussion in the United States in the decade before World War I. The number of older people in the population had risen as birth rates fell, and, at the same time, industrialization increased the likelihood of dependency in old age. The more advanced European industrial nations,

France, Germany, and England, had already instituted old age support systems. Both the National Conference of Charities and Corrections and the Progressive party endorsed the principles of social insurance as a response to economic need from unemployment, illness, and old age in 1912. Case studies documented the inability of individuals to save for their own old age, the inadequacy of private charity, and the inability or unwillingness of industry to provide private pensions. Nonetheless, attempts to provide income in old age either through public or private pensions failed. At the outbreak of World War I, only Arizona and Alaska had even limited pension plans, and less than 1 percent of American workers were covered by private insurance. The economic status of the elderly declined and their dependence on public welfare rose steadily.

In the years immediately following World War I, reform groups, especially the National Consumers' League, the American Association for Labor Legislation, and the Women's Trade Union League, gave health insurance their first priority, and the impetus toward old age pensions came to a standstill.

The old age pension movement began to gather support once more in the 1920s as the needs of older people became more acute. But this time the research and leadership of social reformers, economists, and social scientists had a new political base of support. The Fraternal Order of Eagles, a broad-based popular group, began to organize community pension clubs and lobby for state pension bills. Three states—Montana, Nevada, and Pennsylvania—passed voluntary, limited pension bills in 1923. Most other states followed suit in the next few years. By 1927, the American Association for Old Age Security, headed by Abraham Epstein, was created to work for an income support program for the elderly. Together with the American Association for Labor Legislation, they lobbied for old age assistance pensions and laid the groundwork for the enactment of social security.[54]

By 1929, however, they had achieved little success. In all, eleven states had pensions for the aging, and reached one thousand people with total benefits of $222,000.52. The first mandatory system was legislated in California where the percentage of people over 65 was twice the national average and unemployment among the aged, high. In every state that had pensions, the payments were far too low and the coverage woefully inadequate, but a precedent of state responsibility for old age security had been set.

Social Reform: Family Welfare

Legislation to regulate the working conditions of women and children and to insure against loss of income due to industrially caused illness and accident was the first part of a package that might loosely be identified with family welfare. Additional elements of the package were those that dealt with the development of juvenile courts and widows' pensions. The juvenile court movement was an expression of a growing consensus as to the importance of differentiating the needs of children. The first juvenile court law, An Act to Regulate the Treatment and Control of Dependent, Neglected, and Delinquent Children, had been enacted in 1899 by Illinois, where the Illinois

Sanitation Parade, Philadelphia, 1911. Social reform measures of the Progressive Era placed emphasis upon sanitation as an area of environmental change designed to enhance the social well-being of the entire citizenry.

City of Philadelphia, Department of Records

State Conference of Charities had taken responsibility for having the act drafted. The law applied to children under sixteen years of age and provided for a special juvenile courtroom and record-keeping system and for probation officers "to take charge of any child before and after trial as may be directed by the court."[55] Within ten years, similar laws had been passed in twenty-two states. By 1919, all the states except Connecticut, Maine, and Wyoming had enacted juvenile court laws emphasizing the "principle of separate treatment of juvenile delinquents and . . . cure rather than punishment. . . ."[56] Once again Illinois set the character of juvenile probation services, when several agencies assigned social workers to the court in the hope of making the state's new juvenile court law operate effectively by providing casework services.

As professional services developed, social research became a tool for advancing social legislation. Social work's contribution to social reform during the Progressive Era was in large measure derived from its introduction of systematic social surveys to the study of social problems. This was best illustrated by the Pittsburgh Survey of 1907–1908, directed by Paul Kellogg, a social worker and assistant editor of *Charities and the Commons*, the national journal published under the auspices of the New York Charity Organization Society. An article in the March 1906 issue of *Charities and the Commons*, "Neglected Neighborhoods in the Alleys, Shacks and Tenements of the National Capitol," led to the suggestion by the chief probation officer of the Allegheny County (Pennsylvania) Juvenile Court that a similar investigation be made in the Pittsburgh area. The suggestion was favorably received by the Publications Committee of the Charity Organization Society and an advisory committee was formed. Among the members of the committee, in addition to Kellogg, were William H. Matthews, head worker at Kingsley House in Pittsburgh; Robert A. Woods, another leading settlement house worker and former Pittsburgh resident; Florence Kelley, director of the National Consumers' League; and John R. Commons, a well-known economist. Funding was secured from a number of sources but primarily from the Russell Sage Foundation, which used the survey as its initial large investment in social research.

The Pittsburgh Survey was "the first major attempt to survey in depth the entire life of a single community,"[57] and for this purpose Kellogg pulled together a study team of workers and students of social welfare and the social sciences. The findings, published serially in *Charities and the Commons* and later in book form, covered "wages, hours, conditions of labor, housing, schooling, health, taxation, fire and police protection, recreation [and] land values."[58] They became widely known not only through their publication in professional literature but also through their being brought to the public's attention in such popular periodicals as *Collier's Weekly*. The result was a factual base for use in social action.

Similarly, social research was a major weapon of the National Child Labor Committee, whose primary interest was child labor legislation. The officers of the National Child Labor Committee included persons who were active on the many fronts of the social reform movement. Edgar Gardner Murphy had seen to the formation of the committee. Also on the committee were Jane Addams, founder of Hull House; Florence Kelley; Felix Adler, of Columbia University and longtime crusader for tenement housing reform; Lillian Wald, founder of the Henry Street Settlement House; and Edward T. Devine and Robert W. DeForest, executive and president, respectively, of the New York Charity Organization Society. An awareness of the value of coalitions for achieving social welfare goals was demonstrated when the committee set up headquarters in Chicago's United Charities Building, which also sheltered the Association for the Improvement of the Conditions of the Poor, the Charity Organization Society, the Children's Aid Society, and the National Consumer's League.

As early as 1906, the National Child Labor Committee was able to have introduced in Congress a bill for the establishment of a children's bureau. As part of a campaign to have the bill passed, the committee was successful in influencing President Roosevelt to call the 1909 White House Conference on Child Dependency. The president established the theme of the conference by extolling the virtues of home life and by urging that children "not be deprived of it except for urgent and compelling reasons."[59] The conference went on record as favoring home care for children—care in their own home as well as foster home care—and recommended the creation of a publicly financed bureau to collect and disseminate information affecting the welfare of children and a national voluntary organization to establish and publicize standards of child care. The first, the Children's Bureau, was created in 1912; the Child Welfare League of America followed in 1921. Equally important was the establishment of the principle of federal interest in child welfare, a principle that has resulted in the reconvening of the conference at ten-year intervals.

Even after World War I, reformers continued to have limited successes. Thanks to the advocacy of social workers in the Children's Bureau, Congress passed the Act for the Promotion of the Welfare and Hygiene of Maternity and Infancy, better known as the Sheppard–Towner Act.

Annual appropriations for five years were made to states designating a state child hygiene or child welfare division to carry responsibility for the local administration of the act's provisions. The general purpose of the act was educational, and instruction in maternal and infant care was conducted by nurses and physicians either through itinerant conferences held in homes or at established health centers. Instruction in maternal and infant care was also offered to professionals involved in teaching or caring for mothers and young children. The life of the Sheppard–Towner Act was extended for two years in 1927, with the understanding that the act would lapse after June 30, 1929. At the time of its expiration, forty-five states and Hawaii were cooperating. Although organized opposition by physicians led to Sheppard–Towner's demise, the programs it established were ultimately incorporated into the Social Security Act in 1935.

The recommendation of the White House conference that children not be deprived of home care except for "urgent and compelling reasons" stimulated controversy. On one side were those social workers who supported the conference's position that private—not public—funds be used to prevent the removal of children from their own homes. On the other were such prominent juvenile court judges as Ben Lindsey and Merritt Pinckney, whose daily practice required the institutionalization of children of poor (though competent) mothers. There was an underlying conflict, too, posed by the question of whether mothers should work at all. Before the enactment of the first mother's pension in 1911, while the possibility of such pensions was still being explored, the question of balance between pension and earnings was major. A speaker at the National Conference of Charities and Corrections in 1910 stated the problem:

> The first question to consider, after regular relief on a pension basis has been decided upon, is whether it should be a full pension or whether the widow should be encouraged to earn. At a recent meeting of the Secretaries of the Boston Associated Charities . . . most . . . felt that a day or two of work a week outside was really better for the mother than to keep her always at home, for life can be too dull some times. . . .[60]

The emergence of mother's pensions represented changes in the ideas and institutions that guided social welfare in the early twentieth century. Although leaders in the Charity Organization movement still held to their belief in strict investigation and limited aid, front-line social workers had come to learn that the inadequacy of aid to widows with children had caused irreversible harm to these families. The old tenants of voluntary charity were supplanted by a maternalist belief that women's role as mothers provided the surest compass for social welfare policy. Although often embraced by women who had chosen to remain unmarried and childless, maternalism provided a means for broadening public support for reform, because it did not threaten traditional ideas about a woman's sphere. As a result, mother's pensions were embraced by the General Federation of Women's Clubs and the National

Congress of Mothers (predecessor to the Parent–Teachers Associations), support that was critical to their passage.

The first mother's pension law was passed by Missouri in April 1911. The law had been enacted at the behest of a single county and its provisions left the decision to provide assistance to the individual counties. The first statewide mandatory law, the Funds to Parents Act, was passed by the General Assembly of Illinois in June 1911. With the sudden adoption of laws providing public funds for the aid of dependent children in their own homes, many social workers were shocked. Mary Richmond's outcry that the Funds to Parents Act had been "drafted and passed without consulting a single social worker" expressed the view of an older generation of charity workers for which the expansion of public welfare was anathema. Yet, a younger generation of social workers—the first products of professional social work schools and training programs—embraced the idea that public welfare was critical to improving the condition of the poor.[61]

After the passage of the act, social workers did rally to help establish the program and to survey its operation. But Mary Richmond, for all her concern with the burdens that society placed on family life, maintained that families pensioned under the system were without the competent supervision of social workers to ensure that "the children of the widow are in school, that they are morally protected, that their health is safeguarded, that they have a good chance to grow up right."[62] Frederic Almy, secretary of the Buffalo Charity Organization Society, was more willing to permit experiments in public relief giving. Nevertheless, he viewed private charity as safer. He warned that "to the imagination of the poor the public treasury is inexhaustible and their right, and that they drop upon it without thrift, as they dare not do on private charity."[63] Almy stressed the importance of professional casework help in investigating the need for relief and for redeeming recipient families. And since such help was not characteristic of public relief giving, he favored having public relief funds administered by voluntary agencies. He objected to relief being dispensed without professional help, for "like undoctored drugs, untrained relief is poisonous to the poor. . . . Poor charity is worse than none."[64]

The number of states with Mother's Assistance programs increased rapidly. Within two years of the passage of the Illinois Funds to Parents Act, twenty states had provided cash relief programs for widows with children, and within ten years, forty states had done the same.[65] The Children's Bureau's study of Mother's Assistance, conducted in ten representative localities during the period October 1923 to April 1924, reported that "the principle of home care for dependent children as a public function is generally accepted in this country."[66] The bureau also reported generally good relationships between voluntary agencies and the public agencies studied and, of most importance, that families were functioning with the help of Mother's Assistance "on a par with . . . self-supporting families."[67] By the 1920s, then, both the ideas and institutions of 'scientific philanthropy' had come to a dead end. Even before the Great Depression caused political upheaval, the public sector had established itself as the innovator in addressing poverty and need.

The policy intent that widowed mothers were not to be expected to work was clear, but the reality was that the policy was being undermined by inadequate funding of budgets. Emma O. Lundberg, director of the Children's Bureau, and

C. C. Carstens, executive of the Child Welfare League of America, made this clear when they addressed the national conference in 1921. Carstens said this:

> The granting of this aid [mother's pensions] was intended to meet the needs of the budget. . . . In theory this was a clearly established policy . . . but in practice . . . in many of the states the mother is expected to earn a very large share of the budget and much more than it is best that she should earn in view of her own needs and those of her children.[68]

A Children's Bureau report of a study of the administration of mother's pensions suggests the latent intent of inadequate budgets.

> It was the testimony of the workers in the field and of the executives that the aid did not tend to develop a spirit of dependency but on the contrary developed self-confidence, initiative, and generally a desire for economic independence as at early a date as possible.[69]

The example of someone in the family working was important. To be expected then was the failure of another intent of the various state mother's and widow's pensions—that is, the education of women, particularly immigrant women, for American motherhood:

> The degree to which mothers receiving aid were encouraged to join clubs and classes of an educational character varied greatly. . . . In some communities the grants were too small to permit the mothers to give their time to anything more than housekeeping and gainful employment.[70]

The inability of the mother's pension movement to fulfill its intent because of inherent conflicting values need not detract from its contribution to redefining the plight of women in the American economic structure. Despite reform efforts, however, it was not until the Great Depression that there were any federal programs to maintain female-headed families. After World War I, federal programs were restricted to insuring federal employees against a loss of income due to retirement or disability and to insuring the families of veterans against the loss of the breadwinner's life. Insurance programs operated or required by the states were few, scattered, and inadequate. In the private sector—notably in the railroad industry—pension systems were started and then collapsed.[71] For the most part, then, the responsibility for resolving family economic problems continued to fall on local public welfare departments or on private agencies. The sparseness of the public effort is shown in the data on public welfare expenditures at federal, state, and local levels. In 1913, they totaled only $57 million—1 percent of total government expenditures and only 0.1 percent of the gross national product.[72]

Social Work and the Black Population

Neither the public nor the private sector was responsive to the needs of black families. The overall indifference of white social welfare workers to black problems was demonstrated by the thrust of interests of the Charity Organization and Settlement

House movements, those movements that had taken the lead in social welfare. In 1905, the year in which W. E. B. Du Bois and his followers met at Niagara Falls to consider legal solutions to Negro problems, an entire issue of *Charities and the Commons* was devoted to "The Negroes in the Cities of the North."[73] In 1909 and in 1910, *The Survey* gave the news of the first and second national Negro conferences, at which the National Association for the Advancement of Colored People was organized.[74] In 1913, *The Survey* carried a special collection of articles on the status of Negroes.[75]

The primary interest of Charity Organization Societies, however, was not in African Americans, not in their deprivation or segregation as factors requiring broad social reform. Nonetheless, their emphasis on character reform might have helped fuel public discussions of blacks' ability to function in a civilized society. In the 1905 examination of blacks in the cities of the North, for example, the famous anthropologist Franz Boas said:

> There is every reason to believe that the Negro when given facility and opportunity will be perfectly able to fill the duties of citizenship as well as his white neighbor. It may be that he will not produce as many great men as the white race and that his average achievement will not quite reach the level of the average achievement of the white race, but there will be endless numbers who will be able to outrun their white competitors, and who will do better than the defectives whom we permit to drag down and to retard the healthy children of our public schools.[76]

Such interest in the plight of blacks as might have developed from direct contact was constrained by the relatively few blacks in the caseloads of Charity Organization Societies. Many agencies enforced a "color line" and refused to serve African Americans, a reflection of discrimination and the small number of African Americans living in cities. In Chicago in 1900, for example, blacks numbered 108,000 in a total population of 1,698,000. They ranked tenth among the city's ethnic groups.[77] The black population did, of course, have major social welfare problems, and in 1910, the National Urban League was established to help with those problems, as well as to promote interracial cooperation.

Settlement House workers were more geared to social change, but they, too, tended to lump the problems of blacks with those of immigrant groups and then to expend their energies on the latter. Among the leaders and allies of the settlement house movement, however, were those who recognized the problem as a prohibition of common rights to a particular group of Americans. Louise de Koven Bowen, Sophonisba Breckenridge, and others spoke out in opposition to discrimination and prejudice that held minorities responsible for the economic and social inferiority to which they had been condemned. Florence Kelley and Lillian H. Wald were among those who gathered for the first meeting of the National Committee on the Negro held in New York on May 31, 1909. Jane Addams was among a group of distinguished white reformers who joined Du Bois and the Niagara group in founding the National Association for the Advancement of Colored People. When antiblack discrimination surfaced at the Progressive party's presidential convention of 1912, Miss Addams debated leaving. Her decision to remain suggests again the tenor of the times. The party's nominee, Theodore Roosevelt, eventually lost the election, partly because his having entertained Booker T. Washington at the White House dashed any hope of gaining votes in the solid South.

The limited government programs for blacks and for whites and the overall absence of a sense of responsibility for helping families meet the risks of industrial life demonstrate how little acceptance there was of social determinant of family problems. Indeed, in official circles the nineteenth-century belief still held. Family problems were indicative of the deviant family, the family that was unable and unwilling to make use of its own potential for taking advantage of opportunities offered so abundantly by society. Unquestionably, a great deal had been accomplished as America's attention shifted to the war in Europe. Nevertheless, the amount of reform activity should not obscure the fact that basic inequities remained intact and basic needs unmet.

The End of Reform

The end of World War I did not see a return to reform activity. The years between the close of the war and the Depression of the 1930s were a time of peace during which many Americans achieved individual prosperity. They found it through credit and installment buying and through participation in the glittering promises of speculation. They did not concern themselves with the problems of those brushed aside by society's advances or with the obvious abuse of power and influence by those who led the way in speculative activity. Despite the recession of 1921, urban standards of living improved. Booming profits, high levels of employment, and rising real wages meant that Americans felt able to purchase and enjoy a flood of new products—cars, radios, home electricity, motion pictures, silk stockings. There was new life in the doctrine of laissez-faire and a renewed belief that what was good for business was good for the nation. The solution to poverty did not lie in corporate regulation, minimum wages, social insurance, or public welfare, but rather in providing an atmosphere that was encouraging to business.

Americans were determined to believe assurances offered by President Herbert Hoover in his inaugural address:

> We in America today are nearer to the final triumph over poverty than ever before in the history of any land. The poorhouse is vanishing among us. We have not yet reached the goal, but given a chance . . . we shall soon with the help of God be in sight of the day when poverty will be banished from this nation.[78]

At the close of the war, the era of the reform coalition had come to an end, and a new era of professionalization of social work had begun. The change seems attributable to a number of factors. The war itself had wrought havoc among social work leaders who, prior to the events leading to the country's involvement, had in the main counted themselves pacifists. Jane Addams was a leader in pacifist causes. Her membership on the Platform Committee of the Progressive party in 1912 was an effort to further specific social goals despite her disagreement with the party's stand in regard to war and defense.[79] World War I split those who could not abandon a lifetime's philosophical stance from those who supported the war and saw this support as serving their country in a time of crisis. The Russian Revolution further split the reform spirit of social workers. Some moved closer to revolutionary positions; some moved further away from an interest in social action. All were subject to the threatening atmosphere created by the investigations and raids of U.S. Attorney General Mitchell Palmer. The wartime and postwar fear of subversive activity, sparking a demand for law and order, led to severe political repression, to expulsion of radical aliens, and, in turn, to hostility toward expressions of need for political change or political redress. Even modest efforts at community revitalization, like the pioneering Social Unit Plan in Cincinnati, were labeled "socialistic" and saw their funding cut off. Emphasis shifted to personality reform, as psychoanalysis—the work of Sigmund Freud—offered a new professional direction for social workers and social work education.

The push for social reform was further dissipated by the stemming of the flow of immigrants. The increase in immigration during the early years of the twentieth century, with masses of immigrants coming from eastern Europe at a time of anarchy and revolution there and of labor unrest and wartime preparation here, had stimulated efforts for social reform and socialization. Severe legal restrictions caused the numbers to drop dramatically and almost disappear during the late 1920s. As immigration declined, ethnic communities were increasingly dominated by a second generation more oriented to life in the United States.

While the impetus toward social reform had waned, the Progressive Era was one of major and lasting importance. The first Mother's Pension law was enacted in 1911 and established the principle that single mothers of young children should receive support to stay at home as parents. It was the beginning of a safety net that was to prevail for eighty-five years.

The prosperity of the 1920s—with its surge of economic growth and affluence accompanied by the hope for the imminent disappearance of poverty—came on top of the seeming achievement of many of the goals of the reform movement and decreased the pressure for further social legislation. In actuality, the reform spirit of the agencies regulating business was often reversed by administrative practices; new political bosses arose to negotiate the ballot reforms, and much of the social legislation passed by the states was thrown out by the courts. The moral fervor that pervaded the Progressive movement shifted to the drive against alcoholic beverages. The success of Prohibition became a crowning moral victory.

With social reform abandoned, character reform was revived as an orientation toward people in need. Emil Frankel's *Poor Relief in Pennsylvania*, a statewide survey published in 1925, demonstrated the persistent suspicion of public relief and of relief recipients. In a report that generally attacked historic fears of public welfare, Frankel supported the significance of professional social work service, if only to allay the fear that public aid would be considered a right. Frankel wrote:

> Outdoor relief without constructive service can lead only to increasing dependency because while a certain portion of the families receiving relief may pull themselves out of a rut with the aid of the grants, a good many will not. . . .

A good many have the feeling that inasmuch as the poor fund is raised through public taxation they have a right to demand relief and are entitled to it as a matter of course. And a good many families feel that although they may not be in need of relief they can see no reason why they should not get it when other families do.[80]

Public and voluntary orientations toward relief giving—especially toward public relief—seemed to have changed little since the inception of the Charity Organization in 1877. The views and foreboding of Frankel, a public official, were not unlike those of Josephine Shaw Lowell, who had argued in 1890 that public relief should be given only in cases of extreme distress, "when starvation is imminent." The refuge from pauperism, according to Mrs. Lowell, was self-support or help provided by private sources.[81] The similarity in their views is probably not surprising when one considers the 1918 appeal of Francis McLean, director of the American Association for Organizing Charities, that member agencies aid "in the socialization [i.e., professionalization] of both staff and methods of work of . . . public family social work agencies."[82] Not until 1921 was membership in the association extended to public agencies.

The Social Welfare of Veterans

Social welfare in the early twentieth century was strongly influenced by the veterans of two wars. Most men who had fought in the Civil War had reached retirement age by the early years of the century, and their economic needs were a major domestic policy issue during these years. As the Civil War generation aged, America's entry into World War I created a new generation of veterans. The entitlements of World War I veterans influenced politics during the 1920s and dramatized the nation's problems during the early years of the Great Depression.

In the late nineteenth century, the federal government had enacted generous pensions for Union veterans with disabilities and the dependents of soldiers who died in the Civil War. These pensions had become important in competition between Republicans and Democrats during many elections. Yet, in the first decade of the twentieth century, a much larger number of veterans reached old age. As their ability to support themselves declined, they too turned to the federal government for support.

As in other periods of American history, poor veterans avoided the strict use of eligibility rules used to deny aid to the needy. Indeed, in the early years of the century, eligibility for pensions was liberalized by classifying old age alone as qualifying a veteran for pension and by easing the length of service and the supporting documentation that were necessary to qualify for a pension.

As a result, the number of veterans receiving pensions and their cost increased during the first twenty years of the twentieth century. By some estimates, nearly half of all native-born elderly men living in the North at the turn of the century received pensions. The number of pensioners peaked at around a million in the first decade of the century, but disbursements for pensions increased until 1912 when it reached $170 million. Armed forces participants in World War I numbered 4,744,000.[83] The war brought about an enormous expansion of benefits and services, first to attract enlistees, later to compensate veterans and their families for services rendered.

On September 2, 1914, only one month after the declaration of war in Europe, Congress passed the War Risk Insurance Act, insuring enlistees in the merchant marines against the hazards of submarine warfare. In 1917, President Wilson appointed a Council of National Defense to review and make recommendations in regard to veterans' benefits. The council's report, incorporated shortly after into law, introduced a new concept: the offer of readjustment and rehabilitation services, along with monetary benefits. The new package of benefits and services included the following:

1. Compulsory allotments and allowances to families of soldiers, paid for by the soldiers themselves and by the government
2. A system of voluntary insurance against death and total disability
3. Medical and surgical hospital treatment, as well as prosthetic appliances for those injured in the line of duty
4. Vocational rehabilitation services for injured veterans who could not resume prewar occupations

The close of the war, on November 11, 1918, compelled further consideration of veterans' benefits. Not only had an enormous number of Americans served in the armed forces, but a large number—116,000—had died and an even greater number—204,000—had been wounded. By mid-1920, the Public Health Service had increased its total available beds to 11,639 in 52 hospitals. A year later the use of available beds in army and navy hospitals and in National Homes for Disabled Volunteer Soldiers was also authorized. The necessarily rapid expansion of in-hospital services to meet the needs of wounded veterans helped clarify the returning veterans' need for outpatient and nonmedical services. The urgency of the need also pointed up the extent to which veterans' benefits were fragmented by the historical delegation of responsibility for benefits among the Bureau of War Risk Insurance, the Rehabilitation Division of the Federal Board for Vocational Education, the Public Health Service, and the armed services themselves.

Early in 1921, President Warren G. Harding appointed the Dawes Commission to devise a program for the immediate and future needs of ex-servicemen "to the end that the intention of Congress to give the full measure of justice to ex-servicemen may be adequately, promptly, and generously met." The commission's report concluded that "no emergency of war itself is greater than is the emergency which confronts the Nation in its duty to care for those disabled in its service and now neglected."

The new Congress, which convened on April 11, 1921, took up consideration of the commission's report and incorporated most of its recommendations in Public Law No. 47, passed on August 9, 1921. The commission's most important recommendation, the creation of a single entity to administer veterans' affairs, resulted in the establishment of the Veterans' Bureau. The bureau brought together most veterans' benefits, including medical care, insurance payments, and vocational rehabilitation services.

A still further expansion of benefits for veterans occurred in 1924, when Congress made hospital services available for honorably discharged veterans with nonservice-connected disabilities. The recommendation for this particular benefit had been submitted jointly by the director of the Veterans' Bureau, the American Legion, the Disabled American Veterans, and the Veterans of Foreign Wars to the House Committee on World War Veterans' Legislation. The enactment of this law highlighted the continuing, enlarging interest that Congress had in providing special consideration for the needs of veterans. Additionally, the 1924 enactment demonstrated the strength of the constituencies organized to advance and to protect the social welfare rights of this particularly "worthy" group of Americans.

The Professionalization of Social Work

The professionalization of social work had begun with the formation of voluntary charitable associations after the Civil War. It expanded with the growth of reform organizations. For a time during the Progressive Era, charity organizations and settlements worked together for social reform, but eventually their different ideologies drove them away from each other and toward their separate professionalization, rather than social change.

No such constituencies as supported veterans' rights—neither the Charity Organization nor the Settlement House movement—stood ready to support public relief giving as a major requirement for the maintenance of family welfare. In voluntary social welfare as well as in corporate management, the 1920s were years of bureaucratization and professionalization. For Charity Organization Societies and for settlements, "scientific philanthropy" had led to internal organizational changes paralleling the managerial changes of corporate enterprise. The developing of supervision, of supervisors accountable for the successful operation of professional workers, was a further example of internal adherence to structural authority. Beyond that, Charity Organization Societies were largely responsible for the formation of Councils of Social Agencies accountable for social welfare planning and of Federated Funds that undertook "effective economy" in funding the social welfare establishment.[84]

The definition of "scientific philanthropy" was broadened to encompass developments in helping methodology. The failure of friendly visiting, the hiring of paid agents, and, finally, the emergence of social workers were sequential steps in the search for techniques to deal with the variety of situations uncovered by individualized investigations of families. The body of techniques that were codified in Mary Richmond's *Social Diagnosis*, published in 1917, further explicated in *What Is Social Casework?*, published in 1922 and enriched by the newly discovered psychological theories of Freud, established casework as a major methodology of social work. Casework represented a therapeutic model of professional service. In addition, the development of casework from friendly visiting, at a time when these Charity Organization Societies were relinquishing responsibility for social reform, not only reawakened an old image of the rich helping the poor but also strengthened the view of individual and family responsibility for social and economic problems.

The overriding interest of Charity Organization Societies in relief, their longtime charity organizing purposes, and their slowness in moving toward an explicit family welfare stance are demonstrated in the successive names given the societies' national association:

1911: National Association of Societies for Organizing Charity
1912: American Association of Societies for Organizing Charity
1917: American Association for Organizing Charity
1919: American Association for Organizing Family Social Work
1930: Family Welfare Association of America
1946: Family Service Association of America

Not until 1919, when the era of professionalization had begun to take hold, did the association's name include the word "family": American Association for Organizing Family Social Work. Not until 1930, with the adoption of Family Welfare Association of America as its name, did the title suggest an aggressive force for the welfare of families. This slow evolution of purpose from charity organization to social work organization to family welfare can be traced through a relatively cursory perusal of the *Proceedings of the National Conference of Charities and Corrections* (1880–1929) for the contributions of Charity Organization leaders. Particularly striking in the *Proceedings* is the extreme fragmentation of topics discussed. There is limited concern with the family as a unit or with the interaction between family life and social institutions.

The settlement movement shifted to its own brand of professionalism. Social reform activity diminished as an area of functional responsibility and "social group work," a methodological approach to helping through recreational and educational activities, became the core of settlement house programming. The extent of the shift was indicated by George Bellamy of Cleveland's Hiram House in 1914, when he addressed the National Conference on the use of recreational programs by neighborhood centers to help neighborhood residents maintain community control and strengthen family life. "It is far better," he said, "for the city to throw the responsibility of self-support and self-improvement upon the people themselves than to hire at great expense . . . others to entertain the community. We need a recreation by the people, not, for the people."[85] In 1926, Mary K. Simkhovitch addressed the National Federation of Settlements on settlement goals for the "next third of a century." She argued that settlements had "turned the social welfare corner" and were "launched on the larger task of social education" in an effort to democratize and civilize industrial society by popularizing art and developing the creative instinct.[86] A far cry from social reform!

The definitive statement on the professionalization of social work was made by Porter R. Lee in his presidential address at the National Conference in 1929. Lee traced the development of social work as "a movement directed toward the elimination of an entrenched evil" and its culmination as a profession with a professional responsibility for operating "a methodical, organized effort . . . to make enduring the achievement of the cause."

> In the last analysis I am not sure that the greatest service of social work as a cause is contributed through those whose genius it is to light and hand on the torch. I am inclined to think that in the capacity of the social worker, whatever his rank, to administer a routine functional responsibility in the spirit of the servant in a cause is the explanation of the great service of social work.[87]

Amazingly rapid development occurred in social work during the period 1900–1929. The organization and professionalization of social work was carried out by the Charity Organization and Settlement House movements. Both movements claimed a concern with the family as the core unit of society, and each, to its own lights, developed its program so as to try to bring stability and fulfillment to family living. While the economy appeared to prosper, social work turned to family dynamics and individual personality development. Therapy had become the door to social well-being.[88]

Discussion Questions

1. By accepting motherhood as the most important social role for women, maternalist reformers were able to broaden their political appeal and win important victories. Would it have been better to focus on equal rights even if it limited their political appeal?

2. Professionalization can be defined in a number of ways: a unique body of skill, control of jobs in the occupation, the emergence of a unique subculture. How has social work defined itself as a profession and what strengths and weaknesses are associated with this definition?

3. In 1911, mother's pensions were seen as a major innovation in social welfare. By 1996, Americans saw these programs—now called welfare—as a major part of the problem of poor women and their families. What changed during the century to cause this change in perspective?

DOCUMENTS: Progress and Reform

The three documents that follow, Florence Kelley's statement on *The Family and the Woman's Wage* (1909), the text of the first Funds to Parents Act (1911), and the National Conference of Charities and Corrections discussions of *Public Pensions to Widows* (1912), highlight major conflicts in social welfare during the Progressive Era.

Florence Kelley, both as an individual and in her position as secretary of the National Consumer's League, was in the forefront of social welfare reform activity during the Progressive Era. Her close personal connections with leaders in the Settlement House movement and the coalitions they formed with other groups on behalf of an array of social welfare measures make her utterances a reflection of the settlement view. She pictured the family and family members as needing economic and legal protections against industrial and political hindrances that prevented their full democratic participation in society. Mrs. Kelley's special interest was in wages and working hours and their meaning for family welfare. In *The Family and the Woman's Wage,* she challenges the depth of the value placed on the home as "the fundamental thing in our national life." Her point is that truly valuing the home and the family would require legislation to regulate the conditions and places of employment of children—in this instance, girls—and the working hours and wages of women. She is convinced of the importance of home life for children and, therefore, of the necessity for making it financially possible for mothers and children to remain in the home. Her outcry against the economic exploitation of women and children is, therefore, not only a demand for higher wages but also a condemnation of conditions that make it necessary for them to work at all. The necessity to work, she believed, distracted the mother from the care of children: "if one really thought about the family and the home . . . one should have none of that work today."

One result of the kind of agitation for reform encouraged by Mrs. Kelley was the Funds to Parents Act, passed by the state of Illinois in June 1911. The act provided public funds for the care of dependent and neglected children, making it unnecessary to remove them from their own homes when parents were otherwise adequate. The significance of the act resides in its being the first demonstration of public responsibility for supporting the care of children at home. The act is, therefore, the predecessor of the Aid to Dependent Children program included in the Social Security Act in 1935.

The discussions of Frederic Almy, Mary Richmond, Homer Folks, and Merritt Pinckney of "public pensions to widows" indicate the controversy resulting from the passage of the Funds to Parents Act. Supporting widows and dependent children in their own homes was still a controversial issue for workers in charities and corrections, despite the recommendation of the first White House Conference on Children. By 1912, however, the discussants of public pensions no longer addressed themselves to this particular question. Their arguments centered on the use of public, rather than private, funds and on the necessity for social work professionals to oversee the use of funds.

Frederic Almy, secretary of the Buffalo Charity Organization Society, wavers in his opinion. He is not entirely afraid of public funds—"neglect is the great pauperizer, not relief"—but he is afraid of relief that is not professionally dispensed: "untrained relief is poisonous to the poor." Mary Richmond, a most eminent figure in social work, is also fearful of the possible lack of supervision over the use of funds by recipients. For her, the question is twofold. First, there is the issue of money versus service as a key to helping. Second, there is the fear that increases in public funding will dry up sources of private funding—that bad money will drive out good money—and that private agencies might themselves become pauperized through dependence on government grants. Homer Folks, secretary of New York's State Charities Aid Association, also argues for private funds and private agency control. He concludes, however, "If we do not secure from private sources sufficient funds, then, without hesitation we ought to have a system of public relief for widows." As might be expected, Judge Pinckney, who spearheaded the drive to make public funds available for the care of dependent children, disagrees with opponents of public funding. Speaking from experience, he insists that his court is "doing something toward administering this law efficiently, intelligently, and honestly, too, and through public channels."

PROCEEDINGS OF THE
NATIONAL CONFERENCE OF CHARITIES
AND CORRECTIONS

1909

THE FAMILY AND THE WOMAN'S WAGE
BY MRS. FLORENCE KELLEY, SECRETARY OF THE NATIONAL
CONSUMER'S LEAGUE

There is no subject concerning which we more persistently live in a fool's paradise than this of woman's wage. We say on all occasions that we consider the home the fundamental thing in our national life. If we really valued the home, such things could not happen as I saw last Thursday in the night court in the city of New York. A girl, seventeen years of age, was taken away by a policeman from her two-year-old, fatherless boy to spend three years in a prison which, with the bitterest irony, we call a house of mercy. No charge has been proved against her. As a little cash girl, at fourteen years, in the enlightened city of New York, she went out from her home and worked under the temptations of a great department store. Before her fifteenth birthday her little fatherless boy was born, because of the conditions under which our laws allowed her to work. Her mother thought that the home needed the little girl's wages more than the little girl needed protection. When she was seventeen years old she had been working nearly a year, every night, in a telephone exchange, and she could bear it no longer. She was so weary that she could not even endure being with her little boy during the day. Finally she left her work, which meant taking six dollars a week out of her mother's family budget. She took her child and went away to look for other work, for her mother refused to keep the child unless the six dollars a week were paid. After a week she confessed herself beaten and sent the little boy back through a neighbor to his grandmother, with word that she believed she would have work in a few days and could take care of him. This mother sent her daughter to prison for three years under no other charge than that, for less than a week, the girl had not been able to maintain herself and her little boy and was therefore "a wayward girl."

That girl, after she comes out of prison, will never make a home for her little boy. Her heart is effectively broken; three years hence it will be effectively hardened. There are thousands of little cash girls working in our stores, and thousands of young girls never before did in the history of the world, because there never were telephone exchanges to be served in the dead of night.

If we valued home life as we hypocritically say that we do, there would not be one of these young girls away from the family home in the dead of night serving the public, not because they serve it better than men would do, but because they are cheaper and because the interest of the stockholders and the bondholders of the corporation is of greater importance than the sacrifice of these young girls. Now every man and woman of us who passively consent, as we do, to be served by telephone exchanges which employ these young victims in the night, everyone of us who is not striving to get legislation, and protesting as only subscribers can protest, is *particeps criminis* with these employers and stockholders. If there be a telephone exchange in this country which is served at night exclusively by men over twenty-one years of age, I beg that its patrons stand up now. I have never been able to hear of one in any city.

Lest anyone should believe that the young girls in New York City are less cherished in this service than those of other cities, I know of a city not far from Buffalo, where, within a month, a factory inspector took out of a leading hotel a girl under sixteen years of age who worked regularly until three o'clock in the morning serving a telephone exchange in that lobby, subject to the insults of passing travelers. But on her sixteenth birthday there will be no legal offense if her cruel father sends her back insisting, like the mother of the telephone girl, upon having six dollars a week.

The telephone exchange commands girls chiefly because there they are paid fifty-two weeks in the year, while the rest of our industries are so ill-organized that very few of them offer steady work throughout the year.

It may be said that I have spoken unjustly of the store where the first little girl was working. It is true that many young girls go as cash girls into stores and advance until they become clerks, and come out unhurt, so far as one can see, from that experience. It is also true that some of our boys came home sound in mind and limb from the Cuban war. Some children do not take scarlet fever, although exposed to it. Some unvaccinated people never take smallpox. But the risk is not greater which the families took who sent their sons to the Cuban war, than the risk these parents take who send their little girls into department stores. The protest cannot be made too strong, to those who believe that they value the home, against sending future mothers and makers of homes out of the schools knowing nothing of that which they should know when they shall have homes of their own, into institutions, commercial and otherwise, which, as Mr. Lee has said, "diseducate" the children and unfit them for life in the home.

It is not only the earnings which the future mothers bring into the homes that are earned at a frightful social price. The widows of working men, cleaning the filthy floors of railway stations, and hotels, and stores, and offices on their knees, after inhaling first the dust from the dry broom—is there any greater exposure to tuberculosis conceivable than that of the weary mother of little children doing such work at night? A friend of mine has conceived the monstrous idea of having a night nursery to which women so employed might send their children. And this idea was seriously described in so modern a publication as Charities and the Commons "before it changed its name" without a word of editorial denunciation. The mothers of young children cannot be sent away from their homes to do such work without the gravest social injury, any more than daughters can be sent away so young and untrained as they are sent in this country today. The proper place for a workingman's widow who has young children is in her home taking care of those children, unless she is a bad woman or a drunkard, or so ill that her proximity is a menace to the health of her children. But assuming that the mother is bad or ill, there is nothing gained by sending the children away for a few hours a day to a nursery. If she is infectious she would infect the children in their close sleeping quarters.

There is no subject concerning which we are more foolish than this of the wages of women in their homes, this idea of establishing institutions to take little children away from good mothers during their working hours, insisting that widowed mothers shall perform the tasks of fathers while some hired person pretends to be mother to their little ones.

There are conditions under which the day nursery is acceptable. For instance, where the mother is temporarily in the hospital for treatment from which her convalescence may be reasonably prompt; or, if there is illness in a home and the mother ought to be relieved temporarily of the care of the children. But when Americans boast of a national, or state, or city society of day nurseries (instead of humbly apologizing that we need more than one in Greater New York) we show how little we value the presence of the mother in her home. The day nursery which encourages the mother to go out to work, leaving the larger children to spend their day on the street and to buy penny lunches, is an argument for school luncheons for the larger children. No money earned in the United States costs so dear, dollar for dollar, as the money earned by the mothers of young children.

When we permit mothers to work in the homes industrially, on a large scale, as is the case in New York, we have the degradation of the home by industry, and the mother distracted from the care of the children through the invasion of the home. If we really thought about the family and the home as we say we do, we should have none of that work today.

***

LAWS
of the
STATE of ILLINOIS

Enacted by the
FORTY-SEVENTH GENERAL ASSEMBLY
at the
REGULAR BIENNIAL SESSION

BEGUN AND HELD AT THE CAPITOL, IN THE CITY OF
SPRINGFIELD, ON THE FOURTH DAY OF JANUARY
A.D. 1911, AND ADJOURNED SINE DIE ON THE
FIRST DAY OF JUNE, A.D. 1911.

Printed by authority of the General Assembly
of the State of Illinois.

Juvenile Courts—Funds to Parents

1. Amends section 7, Act of 1907. 7. As amended, provides for funds to parent or parents.

(Senate Bill No. 403. Approved June 5, 1911.)

AN Act to amend an Act entitled, "An Act relating to children who are now or may hereafter become dependent, neglected or delinquent, to define these terms, and to provide for the treatment, control, maintenance, adoption and guardianship of the person of such children," approved June 4, 1907.

Section 1. Be it enacted by the People of the State of Illinois, represented in the General Assembly: That section 7 of the Act entitled "An Act relating to children who are now or may hereafter become dependent, neglected or delinquent, to define these terms and to provide for the treatment, control, maintenance, adoption and guardianship of the person of such children," approved June 4, 1907, be and the same is hereby amended so as to read as follows:

7. If the court shall find any male child under the age of seventeen years or any female child under the age of eighteen years to be dependent or neglected within the meaning of this Act, the court may allow such child to remain at its own home subject to the friendly visitation of a probation officer, and if the parent, parents, guardian or custodian consent thereto, or if the court shall further find that the parent, parents, guardian or custodian of such child are unfit or improper guardians or are unable or unwilling to care for, protect, train, educate or discipline such child, and that it is for the interest of such child and the people of this State that such child be taken from the custody of its parents, custodian or guardian, the court may make an order appointing as guardian of the person of such child, some reputable citizen of good moral character and order such guardian to place such child in some suitable family home or other suitable place, which such guardian may provide for such child or the court may enter an order committing such child to some suitable State institution, organized for the care of dependent or neglected children, or to some training school or industrial school or to some association embracing in its objects the purpose of caring for or obtaining homes for neglected or dependent children, which association shall have been accredited as hereinafter provided.

If the parent or parents of such dependent or neglected child are poor and unable to properly care for the said child, but are otherwise proper guardians and it is for the welfare of such child to remain at home, the court may enter an order finding such facts and fixing the amount of money necessary to enable the parent or parents to properly care for such child, and thereupon it shall be the duty of the county board, through its county agent or otherwise, to pay to such parent or parents, at such times as said order may designate the amount so specified for the care of such dependent or neglected child until the further order of the court.

APPROVED June 5, 1911.

***

PROCEEDINGS OF THE
NATIONAL CONFERENCE OF CHARITIES
AND CORRECTIONS

1912

PUBLIC PENSIONS TO WIDOWS
EXPERIENCES AND OBSERVATIONS WHICH LEAD ME TO
OPPOSE SUCH A LAW.

By Frederic Almy, Secretary Buffalo Charity Organization Society.

This paper will not discuss the recent laws giving pensions to widows in Illinois, Missouri, California, Michigan and Oklahoma, or the bills now pending in New York and Ohio, or the State Commission studying this subject in Massachusetts, or the efforts in Colorado, but will discuss general principles. I find I am scheduled to oppose such laws, though for over a year in the SURVEY and elsewhere I am on record as well disposed towards them, though of the opinion that private charity is, for the present, safer.

Widowhood is a most innocent cause of poverty, especially pitiful because of its pain and waste, and very costly to society because the poverty is apt to increase in geometrical progression, two-fold, four-fold, or even more in each generation, as the neglected children mature. Sickness is also usually an innocent cause of poverty, though there are sexual diseases of appetite. The poverty of a family is still greater when the husband is not dead but is a living cost and danger. In such cases, the children have a father's counsel but less food than if they had none.

Neglected childhood is, in all the world, the very most innocent, appealing and frequent cause of poverty and crime. Poverty is often chosen, but the pauper child never chooses his poverty and his curses punish the society which has so foolishly neglected him. The cry of the children has been heard; street children are gone, factory children are going and the institution child must go. Home made children give the best results and even the foster home must go, unless the parents of the child are unfit.

A stupid fear of spending on the part of the Philistines of charity, who do not comprehend it, and a fear of pauperizing on the part of the Pharisees of charity, who have made a creed of it has made us penny wise and pound foolish. Neglect is the great pauperizer, not relief. The devil of pauperizing has been made a bogy of. That devil has his claws cut long ago by organized charity; but organized charity hates to give, and in some cities gives only in secret. When organized charity learns to be generous, without blushing, it will come into its own, and the widowhood of poverty will then get as liberal indemnity as the widowhood of industrial disaster. Such widowhood is just as innocent; and it is just as dangerous to society if not relieved.

I should like to see in every city a survey of all the children who are in institutions and in foster homes, and then a statement of the cost of maintenance of those children among them whose own homes are more fit except for poverty. I have always favored private out-door relief, but it is inadequate, and to-day all over the country, except in a few cities, families of widows are being ruthlessly scattered for lack of charity. Will public out-door relief be more adequate or better? Students of public out-door relief know well how it increases pauperism, but does not neglected childhood increase pauperism even more?

For nearly twenty years I have been a charity organization secretary and a special student and opponent of public out-door relief. In Charities for 1899, I had elaborate articles on the public and private out-door relief of forty cities. I know the dangers of relief, but last year at Boston I said, with Devine, "Our resources for relief are woefully inadequate. Our use of relief has been most sparing and timid. I am inclined to believe that we have caused more pauperism by our failure to provide for the necessities of life, for the education and training of children, and for the care and convalescence of the sick, than we have by excessive relief, even if we include indiscriminate alms." Can we harness public relief as we have harnessed steam and electricity through skillful engineers, so that we can have its power without its danger?

Why am I opposed to this plan of public pensions for widows? My opposition is not academic. I do not care whether the relief is a public or a private function, or whether it is given by the poor master, or by the Juvenile Court as in Chicago, or by children's guardians, or by a board of home assistance as proposed in New York. I think much, very much, of Thomas Mackay's classic argument that to the imagination of the poor the public treasury is inexhaustible and their right, and that they drop upon it without thrift, as they dare not do on private charity, and this argument is one that cannot be met by any excellence of administration; but I remember too that pauperizing by alms is no worse than pauperizing by neglect. Moreover, Mackay's argument applies mainly to indolence and improvidence, which are voluntary. The poverty of widowhood is not usually due to lack of thrift, and what widow ever became a widow because aid was public rather than private?

The crux of my opposition to public pensions today is that the public does not stand for fit salaries for relief. I am an advocate of more adequate relief, but I am an advocate first of more adequate brains and work for the poor. Relief without brains is as bad as medicine without doctors. I would much rather see doctors without medicine, or salaries without relief, as is the practice of some of the best of our charity organization societies. Like undoctored drugs, untrained relief is poisonous to the poor. Good charity is expensive, and poor charity is worse than none, yet what city would support adequate case work for its public aid?

In Buffalo where we have had organized charity for thirty-five years and for five years much talk and less practice of adequate relief, public opinion supports adequate salaries for a large staff in the charity organization society. Nevertheless, the city poor office has but five investigators, while we have fourteen, of better ability. Moreover, the city investigators merely investigate, while we make plans, find friends and find money from natural sources. Last month the money found by our paid visitors from relatives, employers and friends nearly equalled the total of their salaries, and if we add the wages for work found by them it would have exceeded their salaries. Of course these visitors gave the poor also a service which is worth ten times more than the money they get for them; but I find that the monthly statement of this money got by them for their poor, does much to justify the salaries in the eyes of the public.

Will the voters stand in any city for the salaries without which charity is a pest and curse? Even in Chicago where a bad law in a good cause is redeemed by a good judge, I do not find any indication of adequate case work. Judge Pinckney has voluntarily associated with himself a salaries case committee, paid for by private charities and not from the public treasury; but the record stories, which I have glanced at in the few days since I undertook this paper, would not pass muster for case work in some cities. They show good diagnosis and study of temperament, but I have not noticed in them search for relatives who can give, or attempts to find work or to find better paid work, or official records of the school attendance of children as a condition of aid, or constructive plans for removing poverty. A pension committee needs all of these things for its action. Even under Judge Pinckney, the Chicago relief looks like mere relief, which keeps the family from deteriorating after the bread-winner has gone. Indemnity relief may have no higher function than to prevent deterioration, but charity relief aims to redeem the family. It is not too much to ask that the tax payers' money should be educational and constructive.

How does the adequacy of Judge Pinckney's relief compare with private charity relief? I have only Buffalo to compare with. Judge Pinckney has pretty nearly carte blanche; his work has been splendidly guarded and intelligent and is the high-water mark of what can be expected today of public charity. In eleven months (to June 1, 1912) 316 families had an average of $262.00 each per year. In Buffalo, which is above the average in private relief, 707 widows applied last year, of whom 230 had money aid, averaging $35.00 a year each. This means nothing, however, for the figures include old widows without children, widows who had one month's casual aid, etc., twenty-four widows, who had our aid for twelve consecutive months, averaged $152.00 per annum from us or with city aid included, $180.00 per annum, which is 70 per cent of the Chicago aid. The Buffalo families have earnings, however, and aid from relatives, as the Chicago families must have had also. The only fair comparison would be the budgets rather than the pensions, and these I have not on tap for Buffalo, though I have been given the Chicago figures. The maximum C. O. S. pensions in Buffalo were $301.00 and $307.00 per year. An adequate family budget for the poor is not less than $700.00 a year.

A fact of the very first importance in this connection was stated last year in my Boston paper at this Conference that out of 2,240 families treated in that year by the Buffalo Society only seven were found to be absolutely dependent for as much as even six months with no income at all from earnings, relatives, lodgers, or any source except charity. This shows clearly both the danger of exaggeration and the need of investigation.

Salaries are usually far more adequate with private charity than with public. Money relief is inadequate with either, but bad, very bad, as the relief given by private charity has been in many cities it has not been so bad or so niggardly with individual families as public outdoor relief. We still find doles with either public or private charity, though $2.00 a week orders to widows every one, two, or three weeks (with $2.00 weekly or $104.00 a year as a maximum for the family) is still typical with public charity, but the rare exception with private. The private charity which has not the energy to find adequate relief will not be likely to have the wisdom to use it wisely when found. The valuable pension system of private charity is not half developed as a money raiser. It is my belief that modern organized charity is the most liberal as well as the most tender, personal and effective charity that the world has ever known. Politics exist with either public or private charity, but more with public charity. Fit men are more often found by private charity than by public where the tail of a long ticket is often designated by party managers with little public attention. The valuable co-operation of volunteers through case committees is a splendid part of the Chicago plan and exists with Boston out-door relief but is as exceptional with public charity as it is universal with private charity.

Will public relief check the giving of private relief as suggested in Chalmers "seven fountains" so that nothing will be gained because private givers will leave it all to the public treasury? My elaborate study in Charities, in 1899 seemed to show that just this happened, and that private giving was trifling in cities where public aid was given. Dr. Devine thinks this and said at the last New York State Conference of Charities at Watertown that public out-door relief would require at least a million dollars a year in New York City and that he firmly believed from ample experience in Berlin, Paris, and this country, that with it there would be more neglected poverty and distress than without it. Dr. Devine thinks private relief most inadequate, however, and so do Alexander Johnson, Folks, Hebberd, Tucker, Kingsley and many others who differ as to public pensions.

The question is active in New York State where the report of the congestion commission February 28, 1911, which was reviewed at length in the Survey for March 11, 18, and 25, 1911, was followed by the report to the New York City Conference of Charities and Correction rendered last May after a year's consideration. This report advocated public pensions to widows. Both this report and the New York bill recognize the danger of public administration as inadequate and provide that the public money shall go through private charities. If this is a return to public subsidies to private charities it seems to me indescribably bad, for such subsidies lead to sectarian appeals, to lobbying and to a scrambling at the public trough for patronage.

I have the detail of many of the state bills and laws, but they cannot be described in a paper so short as this must be if there is to be time for discussion.

It is no light thing to reverse a policy of many years in regard to public out-door relief. It was abolished in New York and Brooklyn thirty years ago, and in many of our chief cities and it was thought to be a dead issue in this Conference. Times change, however, and I am not willing to believe that in this day public out-door relief cannot be successful. It weighs with me that the equally delicate work of child placing is successfully done by public charity, though the arguments against it would be similar. Over and over private charity has blazed the way for what became public safety after standards had been developed and established, and this process I believe in. The curse of the old name of city out-door relief is something and the new and better associations will make it easier to keep up the new and better standards.

I am myself still opposed to public pensions, though with their aims I am so much in sympathy that I shall welcome experiments, in states not my own which may demonstrate whether they will succeed. Even if in the beginning such public relief does not reach the best standards of private relief I shall be willing to wait before judging if it improves steadily. Universal suffrage does not give immediate good government.

This paper has been prepared under extreme pressure as a basis for discussion. It is not a straddle, but voices the doubts which I have been expressing publicly for some time. I am here to learn.

DISCUSSION

MR. HOMER FOLKS—It seemed to me I could best make my thoughts on this matter clear by asking a few questions in serial order and then answering them as best I could. So far as I deal with facts I have in mind entirely the facts in New York City.

The first question is this: Is it desirable that children of widows of good character and efficiency be kept with their mothers? Is poverty alone a sufficient cause for breaking up families?

I think that all of us here probably without exception would answer this first question in the affirmative. There are those who would answer it in the negative, but they don't come to conferences, and we have to deal with them when we get home. I think we can assume that substantially all those present would agree with the conclusion of the White House Conference in that regard. I, at least, stand without qualification on the answer as stated in those conclusions.

Again, if such families should be kept together, should the relief come preferably from private sources?

I take it that there is difference of opinion. A very considerable, and perhaps an increasing number, probably, would say that they would have no special preference, or even prefer public relief. Personally, I take the other side. Under present circumstances I decidedly prefer the relief of such families from private sources for these three reasons:

First, it is desirable to develop and maintain private relief giving, and that this offers a clear and easy division of the field—the public authorities to maintain the public institutions and the private societies to give the family relief.

Second, the administration of public family relief is perhaps admitted by all to be decidedly difficult. I do not agree with Mr. Almy that the difficulty lies in getting adequate salaries for relief officers. I think it is the rule that public work pays better salaries than private work. Charity may be the one exception, but if it is, I believe we can change that particular exception, and that adequate money for adequate salaries for an adequate number of officers, could be had.

But the more difficult point is the clumsiness of the machinery by which public employees are selected. It is still difficult, to be sure, by any process that we now know of to get competent people at a given time for a given job in the public service.

But the most serious objection of the three is, that I think there is a subtle psychological, but very important difference between the feeling of reliance upon private relief and the feeling of reliance upon public charity claimed as a matter of right. I am not so sure, in the case of widows, that it is not a matter of right. A feeling of reliance upon a steady and regular income wisely adapted to the family needs and the family budget, ought to be a good thing. I am not so sure that it is not a desirable thing in the home of the widow or where the totally disabled wage earner is concerned, but certainly it is a very dangerous thing in other households where there is a wage earner, able-bodied, but disposed to shirk his responsibility.

If it is preferable that relief come from private sources, is sufficient relief now given from private sources to such families? Speaking as to New York: I doubt if any person would have the hardihood to say that such is the case at the present time and for one, I have to state most emphatically, that it is not sufficient, and that families of that character are not kept together and that considerable numbers of children of widows who should be kept at home are committed, and that the process which Judge Pinckney described of the tearing apart of children from their mothers for poverty alone, occurs from time to time in every borough of the City of New York.

Third. If it is desirable that such families should be kept together and if the relief should come preferably from private sources, and if sufficient relief does not come now, is it, after all, a very serious thing to break up such families and send the children to institutions? I doubt whether any person present would answer that question thus put, in the negative, and yet some of our best friends do by their actions, answer it in the negative, because, while this breaking up of families goes on admittedly and openly, they do not actually do anything in a large way to stop it.

It is suggested sometimes that the proper course is to relieve in the best and finest and most constructive and up-to-date method such families as can be aided by existing resources. As to what is to happen to the other families not so aided, no particular reply is made.

What should we think of a city which had a thousand destitute aged persons and which was about to construct a new almshouse, and which proposed plans for an entirely modern building to accommodate two hundred persons, and pointed with pride to its sanitary arrangements, its bath rooms and cottage plan, and spoke of this as a model provision for the aged poor, but refused to answer the question as to what is to happen to the other eight hundred? What would the people of the city think of that sort of a municipal policy? But in my judgment that would be far more defensive, far less serious than to provide adequately for a few families leaving others to the tender resources of nothing.

Now, if it is desirable that these families be kept together, and if the relief should come preferably from private sources, and if it is really a very serious matter, is it possible to find from private sources sufficient relief? Some say yes and some say no, and I say that I do not think any of us know, for the reason that in New York it has never been intelligently tried.

We have possibly between six and seven thousand children of widows in institutions in New York City. Not all of them should be at home. Is it possible to secure from private sources sufficient additional funds to provide for them? I am not sure, and I hope the relief societies will make one more combined serious, final effort to secure such funds. But I think they should distinctly realize that this is the last call for dinner, and if they don't get together and secure such funds they will be provided from some other source in some other way.

Now, just one question more: If it develops that sufficient private resources are not to be had, is the evil of breaking up families as we are now doing, a lesser evil than public relief to widows? A good many say yes. My opinion is distinctly not; and that if we do not secure from private sources sufficient funds, then, without hesitation we ought to have a system of public relief for widows.

HON. MERRITT W. PINCKNEY—I am not convinced, notwithstanding what I have heard, against the "Funds to Parents" law—no, I am not convinced. I have listened with great interest to a very able and intelligent paper read by Mr. Almy. Anybody who knows him, knows of his ability to grasp this subject, must treat what he says with the highest consideration, and I do. If I had known him as well and liked him as well as I do now, before I came to Cleveland, I don't know whether I would have taken the opposite side of any question that he was to discuss. He certainly looks to me as though he was by experience authorized to speak, and I want to thank him personally, too, for the way he treated the subject. He didn't shut the door in our faces and say, "Stay outside." He didn't say to us, "The honest and judicious administration of the law of the Funds to Parents Act is impossible, go away and don't bother me." He left the door open, as I always believe he has left his mind open, for honest, intelligent thought, regardless of what his years of experience have been, and regardless of what his thought was on any particular subject, and I want to thank him for that consideration.

It comes to me now that someone of the speakers said it will cost a million dollars to try this out in the City of New York. I have read with interest the report of the State Board of Charities for the State of New York for the year 1911, and I recognize Mr. Hebberd as the Secretary of that Board. I assume that those gentlemen in their experience and grasp of this subject, and in their study of it, in their service to the State of New York, have made investigation and inquiry and have consulted with the various organizations, private and otherwise, through the State of New York, and therefore, when I read in their report that it is confessedly admitted by the private charities in the City of New York that they have not the adequate means to meet the needs of the dependents in that city, that it stands for something; and when I see in that report that thirty-four thousand five hundred and thirty children were in dependent institutions at the close of the fiscal year ending September 30, 1910, that it must take three hundred and fifty thousand dollars of New York's money to take care of those children for one month and that it must take for the year something over four million of dollars. I say, when these gentlemen, after their investigation, tell us these things and report that many of the children could have been taken care of at home in the normal condition of family life, that it means something, and I say it would pay the City of New York, as an experiment, to keep some of those children at home with their mothers instead of sending them away to institutions, even if it did cost one million dollars.

I want to say to Judge Baker from Boston, when you say that the administration of this relief ought not to be left to the Juvenile Court of Chicago, or to any Juvenile Court, I say, Amen! but I do say it is possible to so frame a law that public officials will be able to administer this relief.

Now, Mr. Persons, I want to say to you that it is probably due to the short time allowed me that I did not explain about these eight hundred and fifty families who were refused relief. I have the figures here on those families and I think there must be three hundred and fifty of them who were, through undisclosed property interests, money or funds of some kind, amply able to take care of themselves. That shows, if it shows anything, that we have a committee that is doing its work of investigation and inquiry well.

So, out of eight hundred and fifty families, three hundred and fifty were able to take care of themselves, and naturally, under the law, we couldn't give them relief. And of the other five hundred there are various reasons set down for refusing them relief. They were turned over to other agencies to be taken care of. Under the law, we say that these families, for reasons set down by the conference group after consultation with the Court, are not entitled to relief, but they are taken care of wherever it is necessary to take care of them.

Now, with reference to supervision, I wish to say to Miss Richmond that she is mistaken when she says that there is no supervision in Chicago. I will admit, ladies and gentlemen, after eleven months, under a law that is too brief, and into which we have had to read certain essentials before we undertook to administer it—I will admit that the law is not complete. I will admit that we are in the beginning of the dawn, but I say we are doing something toward administering this law efficiently, intelligently and honestly, too, and through public channels.

Don't let us be satisfied with what is partial, but let us ask for all. Why, we have been working for years now, for what? For compulsory insurance against accident, sickness, old age and invalidity.

Let us nail our colors to the mast and insist on what we have been asking for these many years, the full program; insurance against industrial accident, insurance against sickness, insurance against old age, insurance against invalidity, and compulsory insurance against all these four items in every State of the Union.

MISS M. E. RICHMOND—Mr. Senior has struck the keynote, I think. We must not attempt to meet our present difficulties, serious though they be, in such a bungling way as to put up permanent barriers against their solution. So far from being a forward step, "funds to parents" is a backward one—public funds not to widows only, mark you, but to private families, funds to the families of those who have deserted and are going to desert!

The breaking up of homes through poverty alone is, as I have said, a serious evil, but its prevention demands elements that this Chicago experiment, so carefully watched and safeguarded by some of the best known social workers in the country, conspicuously lacks. Even here, with their hearty good will and earnest co-operation, and with a judge willing to aid them, there has been practically no competent supervision of the pensioned families; there has been, in some cases, less adequate relief than private charity was giving, and far less supervision. If this has been the case in Chicago, what may we expect, at this stage of social service development, from experiments less co-operative and under administrations less able to withstand undue influence?

Another point in my too brief four minutes: This Illinois bill was drafted and passed without consulting a single social worker, and then they had to ask the social workers to come to their rescue in order that the worst might not happen. Watch your Legislatures carefully, when you go back to your several states, and see that the social workers are consulted in time.

Miss Lathrop has said that the private charities have been "pauperized" in Chicago by the new law, and are turning their cases over to the court. There is another aspect of that. No private fund for relief can successfully compete very long with a public fund, whether the latter is adequate or not. Inevitably the sources of private charitable relief dry up. A greater danger threatens in the state of New York, where it is actually proposed publicly to pay private charities for the relief of widows one hundred cents for every fifty that they spend in relief from their own funds—a two for a cent plan that will be an admirable way of hammering down our standards of adequate treatment in such cases. If we spend any of the fifty cents in seeing that the children of the widow are in school, that they are morally protected, that their health is safeguarded, that they have a good chance to grow up right, we are to get less than a dollar for the family; but if we, or our colleagues, spend all of the fifty cents on material relief, we get a dollar. The methods of public pensioning so far proposed are full of such incongruities as I have pointed out.

When a widow is granted relief under the law, the last thing that is said to her in court by myself, is to explain to her the necessity of accounting to a regular probation officer as to how she spends her money. And she is cautioned to keep her receipts, and that probation officer's duty is to visit that family regularly, and report on that family, giving it such supervision as it is possible for him or her to give. I don't say that this is enough, but I say that somewhere along the line, when we have had the experience and we get right down to what is possible to do under public administration, that we can rightly supervise and investigate and control this situation.

Now, I noticed in Mr. Almy's paper, the argument which he read, that to the imagination of the poor the public treasury is inexhaustible, and they drop on it without thrift—that is a forceful statement, that is true, but which is the worse, the pauperizing by alms or by neglect? For my part, I would rather have a pauper with a well-filled stomach than a pauper who is starving to death.

Notes

1. Herbert Hoover, *The New Day* (Stanford, Calif.: Stanford University Press, 1928), p.16.
2. S. E. Forman, *The Rise of American Commerce and Industry* (New York: Century, 1927), p. 369.
3. U.S. Department of Commerce, Bureau of the Census, *Historical Statistics of the United States: Colonial Times to 1957* (Washington, D.C.: Government Printing Office, 1960), p. 414 (hereafter cited as *Historical Statistics*).

4. Forman, op. cit., p. 442.

5. *Historical Statistics*, p. 139.

6. Ibid., p. 14.

7. U.S. Bureau of the Census, *Fourteenth Census of the United States: 1920*, Vol. 3, p. 15, and *Fifteenth Census of the United States: 1930*, Vol. 2, p. 27.

8. An excellent history of immigration policy in the United States may be found in Roger Daniels, *Coming to America: A History of Immigration and Ethnicity in American Life* (New York: Harper Collins, 1990).

9. *Historical Statistics*, p. 14.

10. An excellent survey and analysis of the growth of concentration in American industry may be found in Arthur R. Burns, *The Decline of Competition* (New York: McGraw-Hill, 1936).

11. U.S. Commission on Industrial Relations, *Final Report* (Washington, D.C.: Government Printing Office, 1915), p. 8.

12. U.S. Bureau of the Census, *Sixteenth Census of the United States: 1940, Comparative Occupation Statistics for the United States, 1870 to 1940*, p. 93.

13. Robert Hunter, *Poverty* (New York: Grossett & Dunlap, 1904), pp. 2–7, 56–65, 76–88, 96–97, 350–351. Reprinted in Roy Lubove, ed., *Poverty and Social Welfare in the United States* (New York: Holt, Rinehart & Winston, 1972), pp. 7–18.

14. John A. Ryan, *A Living Wage: Its Ethical and Economic Aspects* (New York: Macmillan, 1910), pp. 123–177. Father Ryan estimated the minimum "living wage" at more than $900 for the large eastern cities.

15. *Historical Statistics*, p. 278.

16. Slaughterhouse Cases, 16 Wallace 36, 1873. Opinion of Justice Samuel Miller, U.S. Supreme Court.

17. C. Vann Woodward, *The Strange Career of Jim Crow* (New York, Oxford University Press, 1957).

18. *Plessy v. Ferguson*, 163 U.S. 537 (1896).

19. Imperial Wizard Hiram W. Evans, "The Klan of Tomorrow." Quoted in William Miller, *A New History of the United States* (New York: Braziller, 1958), pp. 355–356.

20. Booker T. Washington, "The Atlanta Cotton Exposition Address of 1895." Quoted in *Up From Slavery*, in *The Booker T. Washington Papers*, ed. Louis R. Harlan (Urbana: University of Illinois Press, 1972), 1:333.

21. Lillian Brandt, "The Make-up of Negro City Groups," *Charities and the Commons* 15 (October 7, 1905): 7.

22. *Historical Statistics*, p. 46. New York, Pennsylvania, Ohio, Illinois, and Michigan accounted for 78 percent of this.

23. Ibid., pp. 409, 73.

24. Phyllis J. Day, *A New History of Social Welfare* (Englewood Cliffs, N.J.: Prentice Hall, 1989), p. 247.

25. Daniels, op. cit., p.114.

26. Sidney Lens, *Poverty: America's Enduring Paradox* (New York: Thomas Y. Crowell, 1969), pp. 209–210.

27. See, for example, Ida M. Tarbell, *The History of the Standard Oil Company* (New York: McClure, Phillips, 1904); Ray Stannard Baker, "The Right to Work," *McClure's Magazine* 20 (January 1903): 323–326; Samuel Hopkins Adams, "Fraud Medicines Own Up," *Collier's* 48 (January 20, 1912): 11–12, 26–27.

28. See, for example, Lincoln Steffens, *The Shame of the Cities* (New York: McClure, Phillips, 1904); David Graham Phillips, "The Treason of the Senate," *Cosmopolitan* 40 (March 1906): 603–610.

29. Arthur P. Miles, *An Introduction to Public Welfare* (Washington, D.C.: Heath, 1947), p. 124.

30. Theodore Roosevelt, "Reform Through Social Work," *McClure's Magazine* 26 (March 1901): 448–454.

31. Arthur S. Link, *American Epoch: A History of the United States Since the 1890's* (New York: Knopf, 1955), p. 68.

32. Lens, op. cit., p. 212.

33. Charles Faulkner, "Twentieth Century Alignments for the Promotion of Social Order," *Proceedings, NCCC: 1900*, pp. 2–6.

34. Mary E. Richmond, "The Family and the Social Worker," *Proceedings, NCCC: 1908*, pp. 76–79.

35. *Sixteenth Census: 1940*, pp. 93, 100.

36. *The Child Labor Bulletin*, Vol. 3, No. 1, May 1914 (New York: National Child Labor Committee).

37. Owen R. Lovejoy, "Report of the Committee on Standards of Living and Labor," *Proceedings, NCCC: 1912*, p. 386.

38. U.S. 37 stat. 79, The act establishing the Children's Bureau, approved April 7, 1912.

39. *Hammer* v. *Dagenhart* 247 U.S. Reports 251, 268 (June 1918). To be found in Grace Abbott, *The Child and the State* (Chicago: University of Chicago Press, 1938), pp. 495–506.

40. "State Child-Labor Standards, January 1, 1930," a chart prepared by the U.S. Department of Labor, Children's Bureau, and reprinted by permission of the Federal Board for Vocational Education (Washington, D.C.: Government Printing Office, 1930), chart no. 2.

41. *Fifteenth Census: 1930*, Vol. 2, pp. 1180–1196.

42. Lovejoy, op. cit., p. 383.

43. Edward C. Kirkland, *A History of American Economic Life* (New York: Appleton-Century-Crofts, 1969), p. 409.

44. Paul H. Douglas, *Real Wages in the United States, 1890–1926* (Boston: Houghton Mifflin, 1930), p. 208.

45. George Soule, *American Economic History* (New York: Dryden Press, 1957), p. 277.

46. Douglas, op. cit., pp. 112, 114.

47. "Discussion on Charity Organization," *Proceedings, NCCC: 1888*, p. 420.

48. Alice Stone Blackwell, "Editorial," *The Woman's Journal*, April 11, 1911.

49. U.S. Department of Labor, Women's Bureau, *Handbook on Women Workers*, Bulletin No. 294 (Washington, D.C.: Government Printing Office, 1969); and *Historical Statistics*, pp. 132–133.

50. Annie Marion MacLean, *Wage-Earning Women* (New York: Macmillan, 1919), p. 178.

51. Even a small number of references to the literature of the Progressive Era confirm the nature of special concern for women. See John A. Ryan, "A Minimum Wage and Minimum Wage Boards: With Special Reference to Immigrant Labor and Woman Labor," *Proceedings, NCCC: 1910*, pp. 457–475; Ann Garton Spencer, "What Machine Dominated Industry Means in Relation to Woman's Work: The Need for New Training and Apprenticeship for Girls," *Proceedings, NCCC: 1910*, pp. 202–211; Florence Kelley, "The Family and the Woman's Wage," *Proceedings, NCCC: 1909*, pp. 118–121; Mary Anderson, "Women's Work and Wages: The Women's Bureau and Standards of Work," *Proceedings, NCCC: 1921*, pp. 285–287.

52. Douglas, op. cit., p. 384.

53. Ibid.

54. An excellent review of this history may be found in Clarke A. Chambers, *Seedtime of Reform* (Minneapolis: University of Minnesota Press, 1963), pp. 151–182.

55. Abbott, op. cit., Vol. 2, p. 395.

56. Ibid., Vol. 2, p. 332.

57. Clarke A. Chambers, *Paul U. Kellogg and the Survey* (Minneapolis: University of Minnesota Press, 1971), p. 36.

58. Ibid.

59. Special message by the president of the United States to the Senate and House of Representatives at the conclusion of the White House Conference Meeting of 1909. Reprinted in *Dependent and Neglected Children*, Report of the Committee on Socially Handicapped—Dependency and Neglect—of the White House Conference on Child Health and Protection (New York: Appleton-Century, 1933), p. 56.

60. Alice Higgins, "Helping Widows to Bring Up Citizens," *Proceedings, NCCC: 1910*, p. 140.

61. Mary E. Richmond, "Public Pensions to Widows—Discussion," *Proceedings, NCCC: 1912*, pp. 492–493.

62. Ibid.
63. Frederic Almy, "Public Pensions to Widows: Experiences and Observations which Lead Me to Oppose Such a Law," *Proceedings, NCCC: 1912*, p. 482.
64. Ibid.
65. Abbott, op. cit., Vol. 2, p. 229.
66. U.S. Department of Labor, Children's Bureau, *Administration of Mother's Aid in Ten Localities*, prepared by Mary F. Bogue in Children's Bureau Publication No. 184 (Washington, D.C.: Government Printing Office, 1928), p. 4.
67. Ibid., pp. 25–26.
68. C. C. Carstens, "Discussion" of Emma O. Lundberg's "The Present Status of Mother's Pension Administration," *Proceedings, NCSW: 1921*, pp. 230–240. Carsten's remarks are to be found on p. 240.
69. Mary F. Bogue, *Administration of Mother's Aid in Ten Localities: With Special Reference to Health, Housing, Education and Recreation.* Children's Bureau Publication No. 184 (Washington, D.C.: Government Printing Office, 1928), p. 5.
70. Ibid., p. 20.
71. J. S. Parker, *Social Security Reserves* (Washington, D.C.: American Council on Public Affairs, 1942).
72. *Historical Statistics*, pp. 139, 723.
73. "The Negroes in the Cities of the North," *Charities and the Commons* 15 (October 7, 1905).
74. W. E. Burghardt Du Bois, "National Committee on the Negro," *The Survey* 22 (June 12, 1909): 407–408, and "National Negro Conference," *The Survey* 24 (April 23, 1910): 124.
75. *The Survey* 29 (February 1, 1913): 567–581.
76. Franz Boas, "The Negro and the Demands of Modern Life: Ethnic and Anatomical Considerations," *Charities and the Commons* 15 (October 7, 1905): 2.
77. Steven Diner, "Chicago Social Workers and Blacks in the Progressive Era," *Social Service Review* 44 (December 1970): 393–410.
78. Hoover, op. cit., p. 16.
79. Jane Addams, *The Second Twenty Years at Hull House* (New York: Macmillan, 1930), pp. 10–48.
80. Emil Frankel, *Poor Relief in Pennsylvania: A State-Wide Survey of Pennsylvania* (Commonwealth of Pennsylvania: By the Public Board of Welfare, 1925), pp. 65–66.
81. Josephine Shaw Lowell, "The Economic and Moral Effects of Public Outdoor Relief," *Proceedings, NCCC: 1890*, p. 82.
82. Margaret E. Rich, *A Belief in People: A History of Family Social Work* (New York: Family Service Association of America, 1956), p. 74.
83. All material dealing with the expansion of benefits to veterans in the Progressive and predepression eras is based on information to be found in U.S. Congress, House Committee Print No. 4, *Medical Care of Veterans*, 90th Cong., 1st sess., April 17, 1967. Printed for the use of the Committee on Veterans' Affairs.
84. Roy Lubove, *The Professional Altruist: The Emergence of Social Work as a Career, 1880–1930* (New York: Atheneum, 1969).
85. George A. Bellamy, "The Culture of the Family from the Standpoint of Recreation," *Proceedings, NCCC: 1914*, pp. 104–105.
86. Arthur Kennedy, ed., *Settlement Goals for the Next Third of a Century: A Symposium* (Boston: National Federation of Settlements, 1926), p. 45.
87. Porter R. Lee, "Social Work: Cause and Function," *Proceedings, NCSW: 1929*, p. 20.
88. An interesting analysis of the development of social work may be found in Stanley Wenocur and Michael Reisch, *From Charity to Enterprise* (Urbana and Chicago: University of Illinois Press, 1989).

6

The Depression and the New Deal: 1930–1940

The economic prosperity of the 1920s was both real and imaginary. Factory workers and second-generation ethnics experienced better economic times than during any previous era of American history. Like the "e-commerce bubble" of the 1990s, however, much of the economic growth of the 1920s was fueled by speculation and plain fraud. Thanks to the availability of consumer credit, working families no longer had to save patiently for years to purchase an icebox or a radio; for a few dollars down and a few more every month, they could bring these new consumer products home. Again like the 1990s, some economists and politicians believed that depression was a thing of the past.

The rudeness of the stock market crash of October 24, 1929, the near collapse of the whole credit structure of the American economy, and the spiral of falling sales, rising unemployment, declining income, further production cuts, and more unemployment touched all and shattered the confidence that had recently heralded the approaching "triumph over poverty."

The crisis that descended upon the country had not come without forewarning. In addition to the large-scale bull market speculation and the credit-buying rampage, several other factors indicated the precariousness of the "permanent" prosperity that preceded the crash. A study by the Brookings Institution analyzed the income and savings of families in our richest year, 1929, and found that almost 6 million families, 21 percent of the population, had annual incomes of less than $1,000. These families of necessity spent more than they earned—$2.1 billion more. The next income group, the 5.8 million families with incomes between $1,000 and $1,500, had very slight savings—less than $200 million. Thus, 40 percent of the population had no reserves to fall back on when the Depression set in. The fact was that 30 percent of American families had incomes under $3,100 and had saved only 2 percent of all that families had saved during 1929. And could it have been any different? The Brookings study had declared that $2,000 in 1929 prices was sufficient to supply a family with only basic necessities. An annual income of $2,500 was a very moderate one. Nevertheless, 60 percent of all families had incomes below $2,000, and 71 percent of all families had incomes below $2,500.[1] Despite the talk of prosperity, low incomes were the reality for the vast majority of American families before the Depression hit.

Equally clear is the reason for the cessation of purchasing once the unsoundness of the economic situation became evident and the fear of its consequences took hold. The country beat a hasty retreat, with consequent increased unemployment, from "overproduction of capital; overambitious expansion of business concerns; overproduction of commodities . . . the maintenance of an artificial price level for many commodities. . . . "[2] The gross national product (GNP) dropped yearly from an all-time high of $103.1 billion in 1929 to reach $55.6 billion in 1933. GNP started upward in 1934, reached $90.4 billion in 1937 but fell back to $84.7 billion the following year. Not until 1941 did national income reach precrisis levels.[3]

Other economic indicators followed the same pattern. Unemployment, which had averaged about 4 percent of the civilian labor force in the 1920s, rose by 4 million, or about 9 percent during 1930. In 1933, the year that marked the depth of the Depression, an average of 13 million persons, some 25 percent of the civilian labor force, were unemployed, and many more could find only part-time employment. Despite recovery programs, 14 percent of the American workforce was still jobless in 1937; and by 1938 that figure was up again to 19 percent.[4] The crash of 1929 was the start of a twelve-year period of deprivation.

In a situation in which earnings for most workers were near poverty level, security was necessarily measured in terms of steady employment. Unemployment of a breadwinner was obviously disastrous for a family. The finding of the Relief Census conducted by the Federal Emergency Relief Administration during October 1933 that 3 million families, consisting of more than 12.5 million persons (about 10 percent of the population), were dependent upon unemployment relief suggests the scope of the disaster that had befallen the country. A new view of poverty and of the poor was in order.

Despite earlier economic crises, Americans had remained convinced that the United States was the land of opportunity and that anyone who really wanted to work could find a job. That some people could not manage—that some apparently able-bodied individuals could be classed as permanently poor—had been observed, of course. In 1924, a century after the Yates report had provided a rationale for using the almshouse as a means of motivating the poor to work harder and become self-reliant, the New York Association for Improving the Conditions of the Poor released a study that argued that assistance levels were too low and that raising them might enable recipients to break the "vicious circle of poverty."[5] The Depression demonstrated that one could be poor and unemployed as a result of the malfunctioning of society. The temporary relief programs developed to meet the exigencies of the Depression acknowledged the existence of this kind of poverty and of a "new poor." The later permanent programs of the Social Security Act recognized the possibility of inherent societal malfunctioning. Thus, for the time being, the "old poor" were caught up in a larger whole and were included in programs originating in the economic crisis.

There was, of course, dissent from the dominant view of poverty as a self-induced condition. The emergence of a distinctive subculture among professional social workers was one contributor to this alternative view of need and deprivation. Illustrative and factual support for such dissent began to appear in the publications of the Family Welfare Association of America (FWA) and of the National Federation of Settlements. The FWA journal, *The Family*, reported a study of breakdown in family income during 1928. One thousand cases, including 3,996 individuals known to three Boston family-relief agencies, were analyzed for factors associated with dependency. Of the total 1,000 cases, 41 percent showed that "some form of physical incapacity made charitable aid necessary."[6] Although the report, as part of letting the facts speak for themselves, made no comment about 30 percent of the cases in which dependency was associated with unemployment or underemployment.

Still, this new recognition that unemployment was a structural risk of an industrial society sat uncomfortably with older characterizations of the poor. Thus, the Boston agencies still concluded that 7 percent of their clients were dependent because they had "bad character." This was in sharp contrast with the results of Amos Warner's classic study, *American Charities*, of 1892, which found intemperance to be the cause of dependency in one-fifth of the cases studied. The principal researcher of the later study hoped that the analysis would contribute to an understanding of "the inevitable economic maladjustments in a society which distributes its wealth to individuals capable of earning it . . . and assumes that the family system of consumption surviving from an earlier economic organization will have its needs supplied."[7]

In 1931, the Unemployment Committee of the National Federation of Settlements sponsored *Case Studies of Unemployment*, an account of 150 cases offering "cross-sections of human experience where unemployment is due to industrial rather than individual causes."[8] The volume was distributed widely and the impact of its illustrations from life contributed not only to the eventual acceptance of federal participation in emergency relief measures but also to the recognition of the need for permanent insurance against the risks of the industrial society. Looking beyond the immediate crisis, the National Federation declared:

> Experience has taught us to recognize broken work not merely as a symptom of financial crises, but as a recurring fault of modern production. We are confronted by unemployment, not as a single episode in the history of a household, but as something that may come again and again, impeding and stopping the normal development of the family.[9]

The Hoover Response to Crisis

The years that elapsed between the early recognition by social workers of rising unemployment and the beginning of federal involvement in the financing and administration of direct relief underlined the unwillingness of the federal government to recognize the depth of the crisis. Hoover, in fact, had been seen as a "Progressive" during the 1920s because of his leadership of the effort to feed a hungry Europe after

World War I. He believed that government's proper role was to encourage voluntary action, a conviction that was woefully inadequate to cope with the magnitude of the economic emergency of the Great Depression. During 1930, President Herbert Hoover engaged in a major campaign of optimistic rhetoric and a minor campaign of public works that failed to stop the precipitous economic decline. This refusal to depart from traditional political and ideological thinking imposed serious restraints on responses considered appropriate to deal with the event. Trapped by the hope of his own prediction of an early return to economic normalcy and by his belief in balanced budgets, laissez-faire, and states' rights, Hoover was reluctant to have the federal government assume new responsibilities and powers. This was especially true in matters of social welfare, long considered a province for state and local activity as well as the special domain of private voluntary activity. Not until 1932 did Congress charter the Reconstruction Finance Corporation (RFC) "to provide emergency financing facilities for financial institutions to aid in financing agriculture, commerce and industry, and for other purposes."[10]

During the Hoover administration, the RFC's ability to stimulate economic recovery was stymied by its being restricted largely to making loans to help maintain the stability of financial, industrial, and agricultural institutions. In effect, the RFC became federally mandated aid for businessmen, while individuals and families were left to the mercy of inadequate state and local treasuries. Later, in 1932, the powers of the RFC were extended to permit federal loans to states "for relief and work relief to needy and distressed people and in relieving the hardship resulting from unemployment."[11] But even then the need for direct relief, as indicated by the findings of the National Federation of Settlements' case studies of unemployed families, generally went unheeded:

> Neither savings in cash, nor in homes, furniture, or personal keepsakes, neither charity nor getting into debt to butcher and baker, neither moving to cheaper quarters nor scrimping on food, nor the enforced labor of mothers and children gave adequate assurance of livelihood. . . . All combined, these makeshifts did not offer a reasonable solution of their predicament nor one which we should tolerate as part of our going life.[12]

The platform statements of the Republican and Democratic parties demonstrated the essential conservatism of both parties as they entered the presidential campaign of 1932. Ironically, the Republican platform gave more explicit recognition to the human suffering occasioned by the widespread economic depression and to the need "to bring encouragement and relief to the thousands of American families that are sorely afflicted."[13] The Democratic platform did not use the word "depression" at all; and although it did mention the "unprecedented economic and social distress of the times,"[14] it did not refer to the personal consequences of this distress. Nevertheless, the Democratic platform, called for public works and unemployment and old age insurance. The Republican platform "true to American traditions and principles of government . . . [confirmed] the relief problem as one of State and local responsibility"[15]—and voluntary action.

FDR and the New Deal

During the 1932 presidential campaign, the Democratic nominee, Franklin D. Roosevelt, moved somewhat unevenly toward a more open position as he pledged a New Deal for the American people. On the one hand, he advocated increased spending for the unemployed and more public works; on the other hand, he advocated a 25 percent cut in federal expenditures.[16] Roosevelt's original program did not see social welfare programs as central to economic recovery. He hoped that restricting competititon through programs like the National Recovery Act and the Agricultural Adjustment Act would increase corporate profits and revive the economy. Welfare payments were a short-term emergency measure that Roosevelt hoped to end as soon as possible. During his first term, however, political and economic dynamics served to make social welfare measures more central to New Deal economic policy. It slowly dawned on government officials that increasing the purchasing power of the ordinary people was more important than business profits in stimulating economic growth.

The effects of the crisis were visible for all to see. In addition to the inability of the stock market to sustain a rally, banks were closing, industries were failing, and farms were going into bankruptcy. Corporate profits, farm income, and wage earnings all fell, and the need for money brought the meaning of economic collapse into every home. By the time that Roosevelt came into office in March 1933, governmental intervention in social and economic affairs was expected and accepted—particularly on the federal level. As one contemporary commentator noted:

> There is a country-wide dumping of responsibility on the Federal Government. If Mr. Roosevelt goes on collecting mandates, one after another, until their sum is startling, it is because all the other powers—industry, commerce, finance, labor, farmer and householder, state and city—virtually abdicate in his favor. America today literally asks for orders. . . .
>
> Among all the phenomena on the landscape, viewed from any angle, none is more striking than the reversal of the traditional relation between the country and the capital; for once Washington is the center of activity and the states beyond are passive, waiting for direction. Here is the stage, scene of a performance partly rehearsed, partly prompted by events; the nation is like a vast audience, hanging on to their seats to see what happens.[17]

New Deal policy contained a combination of three contradictory strategies in economic policy. First, there was a basic belief in the efficacy of the market system as a tool of economic "control," if only prices could be pushed upward. Second, there was the traditional view of the importance of a balanced budget; whenever possible, the Roosevelt administration moved to cut expenditures and reduce deficits. Finally, and often in conflict with what was seen as "sound" fiscal policy, there was the Keynesian theory of "effective demand," which saw the key to recovery in increased spending—government programs to increase purchasing power and direct spending for public works to increase employment. The regulated economy and the free market economy, compensatory finance and debt reduction, all played their parts in New Deal programs.

The early responses of the New Deal were, despite the rhetoric of change, conservative. Roosevelt's initial emphasis was to try generally to instill confidence and specifically to induce inflation in the expectation that a price rise would increase profits and thus stimulate output. A variety of measures were instituted to this end.

The banking crisis required immediate attention. There were 4,400 bank failures between 1930 and the end of 1932, and by January 1933 panic was widespread. Runs and heavy withdrawals led one state after another to declare "bank holidays." When Roosevelt took office on March 4, 1933, banks were either closed or severely curtailed in forty-seven states. Within two days, on March 6, FDR had declared a bank holiday, forbidden all gold payments and exports, and instituted new penalties for hoarding gold. Three days later Congress met in special session, the start of the "Congress of the Hundred Days," and passed an emergency Banking Bill. The emergency legislation that supervised the reopening of the banks and the more permanent banking reforms instituted within the next few years demonstrated the determination of the Roosevelt administration to maintain and preserve the American enterprise system. Banking was not nationalized. Instead, the federal government, through the Federal Reserve banks, the Reconstruction Finance Corporation, and the Treasury Department, was to aid and regulate the banking industry so as to permit the emergence of a strengthened system of private financial institutions. In order to extend the system of control and to offer increased security to investors as well as depositors, there was legislation regulating stock exchanges and the financial operations of holding companies.

In housing, too, the New Deal moved to preserve the concept of private property. The one thousand homeowners threatened with foreclosure each month in 1933 were helped to refinance their mortgages through the Home Owners Loan Corporation, established in June 1933. The home construction industry, almost at a standstill in 1933, was revived through the Federal Housing Administration, which insured loans for home repairs and mortgages for new houses.

Roosevelt hoped to induce inflation through experimental monetary policy measures. There was a retreat from the gold standard, forced devaluation of the dollar, and a program of gold and silver purchases. He expected currency manipulation, support and regulation of credit institutions, along with rising prices, to increase business investment.

Despite the talk and promise of inflation, prices did not rise. In part this was due to the reluctance of the Federal Reserve to expand the money supply and in part to the deflationary impact of fiscal policy. The Economy Act of March 11, 1933, called for major cuts in government spending in an effort to balance the budget. Although Congress restored the cuts, political leaders were slow to understand that government spending was the key to stimulating the economy. Budget deficits were kept small, seen as a problem more than a solution; and, in fact, when production started to show real signs of recovery in 1937, government spending was cut and taxes increased. As a result, production, which in 1937 finally reached 1929 levels for the first time since the stock market crash, dropped precipitously in 1938 and unemployment rose again.[18]

The conflicting thrusts of New Deal policies were particularly dramatic in the development of agricultural and land policy. Native Americans saw some relief from their difficulties in land ownership during the period. The Dawes Act of 1887 had divided their land. But, in too many cases, Native American land was allotted to white people. In 1934, the Indian Reorganization Act helped end this practice. Additionally, Congress gave the tribes more than a million acres of new land, permitted more autonomy in local government, improved health services and education, and supplied credit for agricultural development and industrial projects. Native Americans were given preferential hiring in the Bureau of Indian Affairs, and the development of native crafts was encouraged. The secretary of the interior still exercised political control, regulated land management, and supervised expenditures. Nonetheless, there was some encouragement of the expression of indigenous cultures and pride.[19]

For farmers, generally, the horrors of the Depression of the 1930s seemed an extension and deepening of a crisis that had descended during the 1920s with the collapse of domestic and European demand for farm commodities. At first the problem seemed part of the general economic recession that plagued the country during 1920 and 1921; but subsequent improvements, during the twenties, in the overall situation did not bring full recovery to farmers. Thus, whereas the share of agriculture in the national product had been 13 percent in 1919, its share was only 10 percent in 1929.[20] The situation became desperate during the thirties. The ratio of prices for commodities sold by farmers to prices paid for purchases—using 1909–1914 as the base period—fell from 92 percent in 1929 to 58 percent in 1932.[21] Total farm income dropped to $2.5 billion in 1932, less than one-half of total farm income in 1919.[22] Individual farm income dropped from $945 per farm in 1929 to $379 per farm in 1933.[23] Ironically, farm production fell by less than 5 percent, dashing hopes for an increase in prices of farm commodities. Farm debt soared as the value of farm property declined sharply. Farmers organized, demonstrated, and threatened a nationwide strike.

Despite agricultural difficulties, the Depression brought about a brief reversal of the long-term trend in the decline in the farm population. In 1929, 30.6 million persons—25 percent of the total population—lived on farms; by 1933 the farm population had risen to 32.4 million—26 percent of the total population. After 1933, the number of persons living on farms resumed its downward trend.[24] Disenchantment with the realities of farm living had set in, industrial production had started a slow recovery, and, perhaps most important, relief, when needed, was more readily available in the cities. As with farm population, the number of farms rose during the early Depression years and then began to fall.

The Roosevelt administration's New Deal package responded to the farmers' plight and unrest with legislation and administrative regulations designed to ease credit and to raise commodity prices through restricting output. In particular, the Agricultural Adjustment Act, approved by Congress on May 10, 1933, authorized the imposition of production controls to achieve a balance between production and consumption of farm commodities at the index parity level of farm income enjoyed during the 1909–1914 period.

The restriction of output contributed to a decline in the number of farms during the Depression years. By 1940, the number of farms stood at 6,097,000, representing a ten-year loss of almost 200,000 farms.[25] Since the number of farms owned or operated by whites remained essentially unchanged, the loss was almost entirely among black farms—down from 15 percent of the total number of farms in 1930 to 12 percent in 1940.[26] This rapid decline testifies to the precarious position of black farmers in the Southern agricultural economy. As farm prices fell, black tenant farmers were more likely to face eviction. At the same time, many African Americans were evicted because of their involvement with the Southern Tenant Farm Union that attempted to negotiate fairer conditions for poor black and white farms. These efforts to push poor African Americans off rural farms contributed to the rapid black migration to Northern cities over the next three decades.

As the Depression progressed, the percentage of fully owned farms increased as the total number of farms fell. This was true for black-owned as well as white-owned farms. The percentage of fully owned farms rose from 46 in 1930 to 51 in 1940; the percentage of black farms that were fully owned rose from 17 to 23 in the same period.[27] Farm ownership was accompanied by a steady increase in farm size—from an average of 150.7 acres in 1930 to an average of 167.1 acres in 1940.[28] Growth in farm ownership and in the average size of farms was stimulated directly and indirectly by New Deal policies.

Following his inauguration, President Roosevelt consolidated all federal agricultural credit agencies into the Farm Credit Administration. Congress authorized loans to save farmers from the immediate danger of foreclosures, to underwrite production costs, and to regain lost property on easy credit terms. The result of this package of New Deal farm legislation, including the Agricultural Adjustment Act (AAA), was to raise net farm income from $2.5 billion in 1932 to more than $5.9 billion in 1935.[29] Additionally, the $9.6 billion farm mortgage debt load of 1930 was reduced to $7.6 billion in 1935 and to $6.6 billion in 1940.[30]

The success of early New Deal legislation, designed to help farmers through easy credit, supported not only farm ownership but also the introduction of farm machinery, which, in turn, encouraged the development of larger farms. The Farm Security Administration had authority to lend money to make it possible, among other things, for farmers to become landowners and to refinance and rehabilitate their lands. The withdrawal of submarginal land was encouraged.

In its early years, New Deal legislation spelled disaster for the most marginal group of farmers—tenants. In general, government support was for large farmers, with little assistance going to the small farmer. Not until 1935 was a tenant clause added to the AAA requiring farmers to keep the same number of tenants they had when they joined the program. Thus, between 1930 and 1940, while the number of full-farm owners increased by 172,000, the number of tenants decreased by 303,000. All of the decrease was accounted for by changes occurring in the South where the number of white tenant farmers dropped by 149,289 and the number of black tenants by 192,291. Blacks accounted for 56 percent of the total decrease in the number of tenant farmers. In terms of total numbers of tenant farmers, the loss represented a 28 percent decrease in the total number of black tenant farmers and a 14 percent decrease in the total number of white tenant farmers.[31] As the most marginal part of the farm population, tenant farmers and sharecroppers bore the heaviest burden of the agricultural depression. Homeless, they joined the other jobless and dispossessed who wandered the country.

Sharecropper Families Evicted from the Dibble Plantation near Parkin, Arkansas, January 1936. These evictions followed charges that the sharecroppers, by membership in the Southern Tenant Farmers' Union, were engaging in a conspiracy to retain their homes. This contention was granted by the court. The evictions, though at the point of a gun, were considered legal. The picture was taken just after the eviction near Parkin, Cross County, Arkansas, before the sharecroppers were moved into a tent colony.
Photography by J. Vachon, reproduced from the collection of the Library of Congress

In industry, as in agriculture, New Deal policy sought to regulate prices and output. Large firms tended to dominate policy. The major legislation aimed at bringing about a manufacturing revival was the National Industrial Recovery Act (NIRA) presented to Congress on May 15, 1933. The NIRA was designed to meet labor's demand for limited hours of work in order to spread employment and business's demand for the relaxation of antitrust laws in order to stabilize output and raise prices.

Title I of the NIRA established a set of industry codes that would end "cutthroat" competition, raise prices, limit output, and provide for workers a reasonable workweek at a reasonable wage. Each industry was, in theory, to be regulated by a tripartite committee representing management, labor, and the public. FDR signed the bill on June 16, 1933. An interim, blanket code was established with the Blue Eagle, as posted by business, as its symbol of acceptance. Within a few weeks, almost 2.5 million employers, with 16 million workers, had signed codes. By September, within three months of the inception of the codes, the ten largest industries were brought under the National Recovery Administration (NRA). All the codes contained minimum wage and maximum hour scales; all contained provisions for collective bargaining. In practice, however, the industry codes reflected the price and output policies of the dominant firms in each industry, and competition restraint operated to the serious disadvantage of small businessmen. When the NRA was declared unconstitutional by the Supreme Court in May 1935, it was already under severe attack.

How successful was this organization of industry for recovery? During its two years of operation, employment rose by 2 million, industrial production rose from 62 percent to 79 percent of the 1929 level of output, and GNP increased from $55.6 billion to $72.2 billion.[32] But 20 percent of the labor force was still unemployed, industrial output was 21 percentage points less than before the crash, and GNP was still far below the level of prosperity. Paralleling the irony of the AAA's curtailment of food production and destruction of livestock when people were starving, the NRA limited competition and output when what was needed for prosperity was an expansion of industry.

Title II of the NIRA provided for a Public Works Administration (PWA) and allocated $3.3 billion for this program. Had this money been used speedily to increase employment and purchasing power, it might have been an extremely helpful stimulant. PWA was intended, however, for capital investment and pump priming. Under the cautious direction of Harold Ickes, its immediate expansionary potential was never exercised.

Labor and Social Welfare

Perhaps the most significant and long-lasting result of the experiment in industrial control was its impact on organized labor and the precedent for social legislation it established. As the United States entered the decade of the 1930s and economic depression, labor was largely unorganized. Union gains made during World War I were lost in a postwar environment of generally steady employment, increasing real wages, and political repression. Furthermore, the AFL, representing skilled labor, tended to cooperate with management in a "welfare capitalism" effort. Ignored by that effort was the great mass of workers, generally unskilled, in the basic industries. Trade union membership declined from 5 million in 1920 to 3.4 million in 1930; membership in the AFL declined from 4.1 million in 1920 to 3 million in 1930.[33] The violent and largely unsuccessful strikes led by the United Mine Workers in 1921 and 1922 and by the United Textile Workers in 1929 further weakened organized labor as the Depression settled in.

The fortunes of labor began to turn in 1932 with the passage of the Norris–LaGuardia Act, which restricted the right of the federal courts to issue injunctions against unions engaged in peaceful strikes and to enforce "yellow dog" contracts. In 1933, the newly formulated codes of the NRA reaffirmed the right of collective bargaining in covered industries, established the forty-four–hour week, outlawed child labor, and set minimum wages ranging from thirty to forty cents an hour. The underlying motive was to maintain wages at the same time that the elimination of child labor and the reduction in working hours spread jobs among a larger number of adult workers. Falling wages stimulated workers to organize and unions to recruit membership. By 1935, union membership had grown to 3.7 million.[34]

Labor's success was not easily attained. Its efforts to organize and to force concessions were matched by management's determination to prevent unionization and to preserve the open shop. In August 1933, President Roosevelt established the

National Labor Board to mediate labor disputes. When it failed for lack of authority to enforce decisions, it was replaced by the National Labor Relations Board. The new board, authorized to hold elections to determine the right of unions to conduct collective bargaining, but lacking authority to prevent unfair management practices, was equally unsuccessful in preventing and settling labor disputes. By May 1935, when the NRA was declared unconstitutional, business had generally revolted against the labor provisions of the codes; labor believed itself betrayed.

The National Labor Relations Act—the Wagner Act—was signed into law on July 5, 1935. The new law contained all that had been foreshadowed in the Norris–LaGuardia and National Industrial Recovery acts. In addition, it outlawed company-dominated unions and gave the new National Labor Relations Board authority to supervise elections and determine the appropriate bargaining unit, to hear complaints of unfair labor practices, and, when necessary, to petition the courts for enforcement of its orders. The legal authorization of collective bargaining led to the unionization of large numbers of unskilled workers in basic industries. By 1937, the new industrial unions, organized into the Congress of Industrial Organizations (CIO), had achieved major victories in the automobile and steel industries, initially, and most significantly with United States Steel and General Motors.

A report of the La Follette Civil Liberties Committee, the first part of which was made public in December 1937, strengthened the hand of the National Labor Relations Board and ultimately ensured the passage of the Fair Labor Standards Act of June 1938. The report publicized in detail industry's disregard for labor's legal rights. Not the least of its revelations was the fact that a selected list of companies had spent a total of $9.4 million for labor spies, strikebreakers, and munitions between 1933 and 1936.[35] The disclosures were important in moving management toward collective bargaining. As the decade of the thirties ended, organized labor could boast a total membership of 10.6 million. Of the total, 5 million workers belonged to the CIO and 4.6 million belonged to the AFL.[36]

The Fair Labor Standards Act legislatively retrieved those provisions of the NRA that had dealt with work hours, minimum wages, and child labor. The act established a minimum wage of twenty-five cents an hour (rising to forty cents an hour in seven years), a forty-four–hour week to be reduced to forty hours in three years, and sixteen years as the age below which a child could not work in industries whose products entered interstate commerce.[37] The act's provisions were, for the most part, already a reality for much of organized labor, so those largely affected were nonunionized, unprotected workers—women, minors, and minority group members, the rank and file of the unskilled. As a result, the hourly pay of 300,000 workers was immediately raised and the workweek was shortened for 2,382,000 people.[38]

The success of the CIO in its efforts to organize the mass industries was enormously significant for unskilled workers. Such workers were frequently members of minority groups, women, and children, and their status was easily exploited in times of labor strife or economic recession. In the strikes of 1921 and 1922, unorganized blacks had been extensively used as strikebreakers. Blacks were often the first to feel the crush of the Depression of the 1930s as social discrimination played its role in decisions to release workers. A National Urban League survey of 106 cities disclosed that 20 to 30 percent of the black population was unemployed in 1931.[39] As the economic situation worsened, many industries replaced men with women at cheaper rates; many replaced men and women with children. In other situations, "desperate heads of families took women's jobs at women's wages, Negro jobs at Negro wages, leaving the minority groups without means of support."[40]

The size of the labor force increased between 1930 and 1940. This was true for both male and female workers.[41] As with blacks, the severity of the unemployment situation aggravated long-established patterns of prejudice and discrimination against women. The notion of women's "proper place" was enhanced by the urgency of a drive to "get the men back to work." The country as a whole was convinced that employment for men was the priority, and this was the view of many social workers and social scientists, as well as the official position of unions and government. Congresswoman Florence Kahn said: "Woman's place is not out in the business world competing with men who have families to support."[42] In 1932, Congress established a "married persons' clause" for all federal and service employees, whereby the first employees to be considered redundant when reductions in personnel were necessary were those whose spouses were also federal employees.[43] For the most part, this meant that women were dismissed.

Actually, the get-the-men-back-to-work slogan was aimed at all women; and single women seem to have suffered even greater discrimination than married women. Nevertheless the percentage of married female workers rose. In 1920, married women comprised 23 percent of female workers; by 1930, one of the earlier years of the Depression, the percentage had risen to 28.9; and in 1940, married women represented 36.7 percent of women in the labor force.[44] Married or single, the fact was that employers found in women a pool of workers suitable for employment at low wages.

Veterans and the Bonus

The Depression years were years of distress for veterans as for others, but the difference was that their visibility as veterans and as a strongly organized constituency meant a continuing ability to elicit special consideration. Almost immediately after World War I, veterans began pushing for a bonus that would provide an economic redress to balance the wartime earnings of workers in industry. A bill making such provisions in the form of "adjustment compensation certificates" was passed over President Calvin Coolidge's veto in 1924. Payments were to come due in 1945. By 1930, with unemployment mounting, demands for immediate payment began to be made. The demand culminated in June 1932 in the "bonus march" on Washington, D.C., of some 15,000 to 20,000 veterans, many accompanied by their families. The march ended a month later when, on the order of President Hoover, army troops were dispatched to clear the veterans from their Washington campsites. Despite Hoover's objections, however, and over his veto, Congress passed a bill allowing veterans to obtain, in cash, half the value of the certificates.

Smaller bonus marches were attempted in 1933 and 1934, but with little immediate success. Payment of the bonus was made in 1937, the year of a disastrous reversal

Bonus Army, 1932. Shacks put up by the Bonus Army on the Anacostia flats in Washington, D.C., burning after the battle with the military. The Capitol is in the background.
Photograph by U.S. Signal Corps, in the National Archives

of the long climb out of the Depression. The bonus succeeded in putting almost $3.5 billion into the hands of veterans and, eventually, into the nation's economy.

The bonus marches of 1933 and 1934 were triggered by the Economy Act of March 1933, the same act that had cut congressional salaries and reduced federal expenditures. The act also cut the amount of veteran's benefits, and the number of eligible recipients. Especially hard-hit were thousands of veterans who needed care for non–service-connected conditions and who were unemployed because of the Depression. The resulting outcry was such that in 1934, Congress passed new legislation in effect rescinding the Economy Act. The liberality of newly enacted monetary, medical, and hospital benefits brought about a presidential veto, which also was overridden. In connection with the provisions for money payments, the new legislation stressed the word "compensation" to define the uniqueness of such payments to veterans.

Veterans were given special attention in the matter of job opportunities, too. From the bonus armies of 1933 and 1934, more than 10,000 veterans—transients stranded in Washington—were enrolled in the Civilian Conservation Corps (CCC) and assigned to work camps. Additional camps were established by the Federal Emergency Relief Administration (FERA) for veterans whose physical condition made them ineligible for CCC camps. Still other veterans were assigned to Works Progress Administration (WPA) projects. In all, some 17,000 veterans were certified by the Veterans Administration for CCC, FERA, or WPA employment between

1933 and 1935.[45] The bonus payment of 1937 was, of course, of much greater significance because of the number of individuals reached and the dollar amount of benefits received. The bonus concept, joined to the benefit structure of the veterans' legislation of 1934, set a pattern that would influence veterans' legislation during and after World War II.

Public Money for Relief

One of the most urgent and immediate problems of Roosevelt's first year in office was certainly the problem of relief. In response he proposed three types of remedial legislation: (1) grants to states for direct relief, (2) public works programs to stimulate investment, and (3) immediate public employment programs.

A commonly held belief had been that anyone who really wanted to work could find a job. This particular myth had been shattered by every household's firsthand experience, by newly developed systems of statistical fact-finding in regard to unemployment, and by social agency revelations of the causes and effects of dependency. More difficult to dispel were the myths that the chief burden of relief was being carried by privately supported agencies and that, in any case, relief was a local responsibility. The development of a powerful, voluntary family welfare movement and the existence of local public welfare departments that were "stereotyped, inarticulate, politics-ridden, and generally of lower standards"[46] had obscured the shift to public relief that had already occurred in 1929.

The larger part of relief was being paid with public funds, although it was generally administered by voluntary family agencies directly or by family agency workers on loan to public agencies. This realization stimulated a reconsideration of alignments between voluntary family and public welfare agencies. In effect, the Depression had created a functional crisis for family agencies. These agencies had historically opposed the giving of public relief and the development of public welfare agencies, arguing that they themselves were best equipped to handle relief problems. Now, with the coming of the Depression, they could not meet the financial demands no matter how much they wanted to help. Furthermore, mushrooming caseloads of "new poor" families whose only need was money distracted attention from families requiring professional casework services. Necessity was forcing the separation of professional service from the provision of financial help.

Noting that the four large family agencies of Manhattan had had, during November 1930, 5,739 applications for "material need" and only 669 other types of applications, social worker Gordon Hamilton admitted that voluntary agencies had "attempted to carry . . . many types of problems which should be carried under public auspices."[47] She suggested the appropriateness of a public family agency geared primarily to offering financial help but also offering casework help when requested by the family. In such a realignment of public–private welfare relationships, "the contribution of private social work to welfare administration is chiefly through urging a professional rather than political considerations in the selection of personnel, the idea of budgeted rather than fixed relief, and the attempt to offer trained casework service to those who desired it."[48]

Soup Kitchen, 1931. Unemployed men queued outside a Depression soup kitchen opened in Chicago by Al Capone, who is standing at the far left. The storefront sign reads, "Free Soup Coffee & Doughnuts for the Unemployed."

Photograph by U.S. Information Agency, in the National Archives

Hamilton's presentation of the situation in New York was borne out by information derived from fifty-one agencies reporting to the Russell Sage Foundation for the period between March 1929 and March 1931. As might be expected, all the agencies had been confronted with the necessity of dealing with enormously increased numbers of families. They had met the emergency by classifying the unemployment cases as a separate and distinct group, by using volunteers and "junior" workers for routine duties, and by protecting the intensive treatment of "regular run" cases from being swamped.[49] Overall, the fifty-one reporting agencies had emphasized "the urgent need for giving individualized treatments so far as possible, and . . . stood out against such mass methods of treatment as bread lines and soup kitchens, with the result that these primitive, inadequate, and demoralizing devices for giving large scale relief . . . [had] been used but very little"[50] with families.

A compilation of the Department of Statistics of the Russell Sage Foundation of relief expenditures of eighty-one American cities showed that 74 percent of such expenditures ($31 million) had come from public funds during 1929. Expenditures in 1930 for relief were about double those of 1929. Seventy-five percent of relief expenditures ($51 million) had come from public funds. An emergency appeal for private funds reduced the share of public relief expenditures to 66 percent during 1931, but

*View of Squatter Shacks under the D Street Bridge, Marysville, Yuba County, California,
February 1940.*

Photograph by Dorothea Lange Taylor, in the National Archives

public relief expenditures had, nevertheless, increased to $54 million.[51] Obviously,
voluntary giving could not meet the demand.

By 1931, it was clear, too, that local units of government could not keep pace
with the need for public funding. Municipal welfare payments, where they existed,
were painfully small. As the Depression deepened, the need for relief increased, and
it became less and less possible for cities to meet that need.

New York—with its Temporary Relief Administration set up in 1931—was the
first state to appropriate funds to be disbursed to cities and counties for home-relief and
work-relief programs. Other states followed suit so that by the close of 1931, New Jersey, Rhode Island, Illinois, Wisconsin, Ohio, and Pennsylvania had joined New York in
making relief funds available to localities. Efforts to obtain federal participation in relief
funding also occurred during 1931 but were defeated by presidential veto. Be that as it
may, New York, in setting up its Temporary Relief Administration to administer that
state's relief appropriations, provided the prototype for the federal program to come.

Federal Emergency Relief Administration

On May 12, 1933, acting on the overwhelming need of states for money for relief,
Congress established the Federal Emergency Relief Administration (FERA) to channel a half billion dollars in relief money through state and local welfare agencies. That

same month the Public Works Administration (PWA) was established as a stimulant to business investment. In November 1933, recognizing the urgent need for jobs, and interpreting flexibly the provisions of the National Industrial Recovery Act, President Roosevelt established the Civil Works Administration (CWA) and made $400 million of PWA money available to finance programs of "civil works." Both FERA and CWA came under the direction of Harry Hopkins. When CWA proved too expensive a means of job creation, the Emergency Work Relief Program was established within FERA. Subsequent "temporary" measures to deal directly with unemployment and the needs of the unemployed led to the creation of the Federal Surplus Commodities Corporation, the Civilian Conservation Corps, and finally, when direct federal relief was phased out, to the Works Progress Administration. From the beginning of the New Deal, a threefold approach to income maintenance was envisioned: cash relief, short-term work relief, and the expansion of employment through the pump-priming effects of public works.

The major direct relief effort of the federal government was FERA. It was established "to provide for cooperation by the Federal government with the several States and Territories and the District of Columbia in relieving the hardship and suffering caused by unemployment and for other purposes." Half of the appropriation was to be made available to the states on a matching basis—$1 of federal money for every $3 of state and local expenditures; the other $250 million was to be distributed to the states on the basis of need without matching funds.[52] In authorizing direct grants to states for relief, the legislation set a major precedent for a new fiscal relationship between the federal government and the states and for a new interpretation of the responsibility of the federal government for social welfare.

Of more immediate importance, however, was the speedy flow of cash to the needy. Grants for seven states were approved one day after Harry Hopkins took office in May 1933; and by the end of the next month, $51 million had been paid out to 45 states, the District of Columbia, and the territory of Hawaii. During the last half of 1933, about 3.5 million people were supported; and by the end of December 1933, $324.5 million had been distributed—with all states and territories participating. In the three years of its existence, FERA spent more than $3 billion. Despite some tendency of state and local governments to substitute federal money for local effort, the states also increased their relief expenditures during this period. In all, something over $4 billion was distributed in cash and work relief by federal and state governments.[53]

Relief money was not always distributed fairly. Racial discrimination in the administration of funds was a major problem. As with other New Deal programs, particularly in Southern rural areas, the black population found it difficult to get on relief rolls. For example, the Civilian Conservation Corps had racial quotas, the Agricultural Adjustment Act distributed funds based in part on race, and the codes for pay rates of the National Labor Administration discriminated against people of color. Blacks were more apt to receive relief in Northern cities. Overall they suffered much higher rates of unemployment and poverty and this was reflected in the relief rolls. In 1933, nearly 18 percent of all black family heads were certified for relief and about 15 percent in 1935—about twice the rate for white breadwinners.[54] For all, black and white, grants were pitifully low throughout the period.

In part, the shortfalls of the relief effort reflect the speed with which the federal government tried to establish a federal–state public welfare program. The need was widespread and immediate, and the administrators of FERA tried to provide cash to meet that need as quickly as possible. The difficulties arose, too, from a conflict between ideology and necessity. The philosophy of the New Deal was relief for the unemployed through the provision of jobs. Direct relief was to be a temporary, necessary expedient until those who were employable could be employed. For the moment, in the emergency, "employables" and "unemployables" were brought together in one program; but direct relief for the able-bodied was only a stopgap measure.

Harry Hopkins, the president's mentor on welfare matters, had indicated as much in his clarification of the purpose of the Federal Emergency Relief Act. Addressing the National Conference of Social Workers, Hopkins had said:

> The intent of this act is that relief should be given to the heads of families who are out of work and whose dependency arises from the fact that they are out of work, and to transient families, as well as the transient men and women roaming about the country. . . .
>   Our job is to see that the unemployed get relief, not to develop a great social work organization throughout the United States.[55]

FDR's distaste for relief can be measured by his statement two years after assuming office:

> The Federal Government must and shall quit this business of relief.
>   I am not willing that the vitality of our people be further sapped. . . . We must preserve not only the bodies of the unemployed from destitution but also their self-respect, their self-reliance and courage and determination.[56]

This fear of relief, the "subtle destroyer of the human spirit,"[57] and the threat to old values posed by a citizenry awakened to the hazards of unrestricted private enterprise had already led to the appointment by executive order of a Committee on Economic Security to develop a plan of income security for individuals and families. The committee's recommendations were to echo the president's concern that the productivity of American workers be secured at the same time that their loyalty to the American "free" market system be assured.

In his congressional message of January 4, 1935, President Roosevelt had separated the productive from the nonproductive poor, accepting primary responsibility for the former, the group that was "the victim of a nation-wide depression caused by conditions which were not local but national."[58] Approximately 5 million families and single people were then on the relief rolls. FERA estimated that 3.5 million of these recipients were employable, and FDR was determined to give them employment "pending their absorption in a rising tide of private employment."[59] Although not abandoning the additional 1.5 million people remaining on the relief rolls, he nevertheless stated his intention that those who in the past had been "dependent upon local efforts" be maintained again "by State, by counties, by towns, by cities, by churches, and by private welfare agencies."[60]

The fact that excessive unemployment continued year after year and gave rise to the specter of a huge demoralized and unproductive class dependent upon a public dole required not only insurance against future industrial hazards but also an immediate new approach to unemployment relief. With a program of work-related social insurance already in the making by the Committee on Economic Security, the president's interim solution was the establishment of the Works Progress Administration to "supersede the Federal Emergency Relief Administration with a coordinated authority . . . charged with the orderly liquidation of our present relief activities and the substitution of a national chart for the giving of work."[61] As for those who could not work, said the president, "I stand ready through my personal efforts, and through the public influence of the office that I hold, to help these local agencies to get the means necessary to assume this burden."[62]

The WPA, funded in 1935 at $4.9 billion, actually spent more than twice that amount in its lifetime. Eventually it provided jobs for 8 million Americans in a wide range of activities, from heavy construction to the painting of murals in local libraries and orchestral performances in the schools. For those for whom jobs were provided, life was much improved. Wages were higher than relief payments, and there was no deterrent income eligibility test. But work projects got under way slowly and many "employables" never found work at all.

The federal government did not immediately substitute the proposed program of work relief for all direct relief. Congress did not pass the Emergency Appropriation Act until April 1935 and included requested funds to cover a period of transition from home relief to work relief. The work was constituted by executive order in May, and Harry Hopkins was appointed its administrator. Actual liquidation of FERA was not begun until the closing months of the year, and the final emergency relief grants went out to the states in December 1935.

By the end of 1935, with the phasing out of federal participation in direct relief under way, with the inability or unwillingness of many states to replace the lost funds, and with the transfer of employables to WPA projects slower than had been contemplated, the transition period became a "bitter one for families on relief in many parts of the country."[63] The problem was exacerbated by the slowness with which the public assistance programs of the Social Security Act—programs designed to help some categories of unemployables—were being put into operation among the states.

Social workers were wary of the phasing out of federal funding for direct relief. Some had been catalysts for the organization of client groups of which they were themselves members. Many had a personal and professional intimacy with problems resulting from unemployment and a new understanding of poverty and the poor.[64]

Private agencies were not able to pick up the slack even as much as they had prior to 1933 because the events of the Depression had begun to define a new role for them. Harry Hopkins's administration of FERA had formalized the changed relationship between public and voluntary family agencies. Regulation No. 1 of the *Rules and Regulations* promulgated by FERA required that public relief funds be administered by public agencies. Recognition was given to the thousands of private family and child welfare agency workers who had helped with the administration of public funds, but Regulation No. 1 required that they be designated as public officials working under the control of public authority.[65] The process by which private family agencies had already begun to delineate the uniqueness of their service was now accelerated and suddenly required consideration not only of alignments with public agencies but also with private child welfare agencies.

FERA's Regulation No. 3 clarified further the separation of public and private agencies in regard to administering public relief funds. At the same time, the regulation revealed the extent to which public officials were influenced by private agency experience. Regulation No. 3 required the investigation and the demonstration of need on the part of the individual family. Means testing and budgeting to ensure that "no relief is given to persons unless they are actually in need and that such relief . . . is adjusted to . . . actual needs"[66] was the outcome. The use of trained and experienced investigators, at least in supervisory positions, regular home visiting, and attention to state relative responsibility laws were required.

FERA's *Rules and Regulations* represented an advance in standard-setting over pre-Depression approaches to public giving. They also established certain operating principles that were to have negative consequences in later years: administrative discretion, rather than legal definitions, for establishing eligibility for aid; a professional casework service orientation toward relief giving; and a subtly pervading, if unnoted, reservation that relief was somehow a necessary evil. For the moment, however, people were helped and their need was of primary importance. Harry Hopkins stated:

> We are now dealing with people of all classes. It is no longer a matter of unemployables and chronic dependents, but of your friends and mine who are involved in this. Everyone of us knows some family of our friends which is or should be getting relief.[67]

Hopkins's statement, his administration of FERA, and his realization that "however well this thing is administered, this enormous relief business can never be anything more than a makeshift"[68] set the stage for a major shift in the federal approach to income maintenance. The change had several facets. For the short run, there had been a switch in the allocation of federal funds to employment—work relief—programs and a return to the states of responsibility for the direct relief of "unemployables." For the long run, there were to be permanent social security programs.

The shift in approach to income maintenance must be considered in a context of the essential conservatism of President Roosevelt and of most Americans, a conservatism hard pressed by the realities of the Depression and by the appeal of radical solutions. In his 1932 speech accepting the presidential nomination, Roosevelt had stated:

> The great social phenomenon of this depression, unlike others before it, is that it has produced but a few of the disorderly manifestations that too often attend upon such times.
>
> Wild radicalism has made few converts, and the greatest tribute that I can pay to my countrymen is that in these days of crushing want there persists an orderly and hopeful spirit on the part of the millions of our people who have suffered so much.[69]

The inspirational wording of the speech, the eloquence of its delivery, and the breaking of tradition that brought the presidential nominee to the convention could not mask the traditionalism of the proposed program for recovery: economy in government, shorter working hours, public works financed and self-sustained by the issuance of government bonds, protective tariffs for industry and agriculture, and increased prices for industrial and farm products. The pledge of assistance with "distress relief" seemed almost an afterthought.

The Social Security Act

The Social Security Act, signed into law by President Roosevelt on August 15, 1935, was the major legislative achievement of the New Deal. It was a landmark in American political and social history, reflecting a public commitment to the economic rights of people and, consequently, extending federal responsibility for social welfare. The act, from the point of view of program provisions, administrative structuring, and federal–state fiscal arrangements, represented a watershed for the mingling of old and new orientations toward people as social and economic beings.

During the early decades of the twentieth century, Congress considered, but did not accept, plans to provide old age and unemployment insurance. By 1935, however, demographic, economic, and political pressures for federal action were overwhelming.

The aged as a percentage of the population were increasing at twice the rate of general population growth as life expectancy rose and birthrates fell. They suffered severe unemployment and for the most part had little in the way of savings to fall back upon. Existing state pensions reached only 5 percent of the aged and in any case were unable to provide anywhere near adequate support. Private pensions were virtually nonexistent. The elderly and their adult children were faced with an "unbearable" burden. Roosevelt's Advisory Council on Economic Security noted that:

> Many children who previously supported their parents have been compelled to cease doing so, and the great majority will probably never resume this load. . . . The Depression has deprived millions of workers past middle life of their jobs. . . . Regardless of what may be done to improve their condition, this cost of supporting the aged will continue to increase. In another generation it will be at least double the present total.[70]

There was strong political pressure for the federal government to act to provide old age insurance. In California, the Townsend movement, a major lobby for aged pensions under the direction of Francis E. Townsend, gained enormous support with its demand for a $200-a-month pension for all over the age of 60, provided that they left the labor market and that they spent the money. There were many other popular schemes. The Old Folks Picnic Association, End Poverty in California (EPIC), the Ham and Eggs movement, and many others suggested a variety of plans for helping the aging that ranged from free fishing licenses to monthly payments of $400. The proposal of Senator Huey Long of Louisiana to "Share Our Wealth" and provide a minimum income of $5,000 a year for all was receiving enthusiastic support around the nation. Overall, popular pressure pushed the Roosevelt administration to adopt a moderate pension plan for the aged.[71]

The Social Security Act evolved from the work of the Committee on Economic Security, which submitted its report to the president on January 15, 1935. The report was accompanied by drafts of bills representing an expedient "piecemeal approach" whose primary aim was "the assurance of an adequate income to each human being in childhood, youth, middle age, or old age in sickness or in health."[72] Within an overall recommendation that the federal government assume responsibility for employment assurance, the committee made specific recommendations in regard to security against the risks of unemployment, retirement in old age, and ill health. Additional recommendations provided for the current security of old people and children through the provision of federally aided, state-administered "pensions." Finally, the committee recommended an array of employment, health, educational, and rehabilitative services. Many of these were to be administered by the states, with standard setting to be stimulated by the federal government through the offer of financial and other types of assistance.

Having made sweeping recommendations in regard to federal involvement in a program of assurances against the hazards of life, the committee recognized the need for residual relief for "genuine unemployables—or near unemployables." The committee commended the care and guidance of this group to the states—and to social workers:

> With the Federal Government carrying so much burden for pure unemployment, the State and local governments. . . should resume responsibility for relief. The families that have always been partially or wholly dependent on others for support can best be assisted through the tried procedures of social casework, with its individualized treatment.[73]

President Roosevelt recommended the committee's report to Congress in January 1935 as the basis for legislation. His message emphasized the soundness of the committee's proposals and the caution with which they should be considered.

> The detailed report of the Committee sets forth a series of proposals that will appeal to the sound sense of the American people. It has not attempted the impossible nor has it failed to exercise sound caution and consideration of all the factors concerned: the national credit, the rights and responsibilities of States, the capacity of industry to assume financial responsibilities and the fundamental necessity of proceeding in a manner that will merit enthusiastic support of citizens of all sorts.[74]

The president's sense of fiscal and political realities led him to specifying legislative principles that necessarily ordained a modest beginning program of social assurances: no health insurance, no federal administration of relief programs and only fiscal administration of unemployment insurance, and no use of the general revenues for old age insurance. Not unexpectedly, then, the Social Security laws, when enacted, were more conservative than the recommendations of the Committee on Economic Security.

The policy of the United States in regard to permanent programs of income maintenance was stated in the preamble to Public Law No. 271:

> An Act to provide for the general welfare by establishing a system of Federal old-age benefits, and by enabling the several States to make more adequate provision for aged persons, blind persons, dependent and crippled children, maternal and child welfare, public health, and the administration of their unemployment compensation laws. . . . [75]

The law's program provisions covered loss of income due to temporary loss of job (Unemployment Compensation), inability to participate in the labor force due to age or disability (Federal Old Age Insurance, Old Age Assistance, Aid to the Blind, Aid to Dependent Children), the promotion of the welfare of mothers and children (Maternal and Child Health Services, Services for Crippled Children, Child Welfare Services), and the encouragement of adequate state and local public health services. Provisions for the extension and improvement of maternal and child health services offered by local health authorities restored programs that had languished or collapsed when the Sheppard–Towner Act had been permitted to expire in 1929. Nonetheless, the decision against legislating health insurance at that time effectively stopped the movement toward the development of a health insurance mechanism. Not until thirty years later did the movement again become viable. The decision was especially constraining because the overall thrust of the Social Security Act toward cash payments as opposed to in-kind services simultaneously limited federal contributions toward the development of a comprehensive health care delivery system.

Social Insurance

The enactment of Federal Old Age Insurance and Grants to States for Unemployment Compensation recognized flaws in the country's private enterprise market system and the need for institutional change to mitigate unavoidable economic and social distress. Insurance against the hazards of unemployment and of retirement in old age bolstered the security of beneficiaries and of the private enterprise system itself because these institutional reforms, aimed at meeting universal needs, guaranteed permanent economic stabilizers for both. Thus, social insurance benefits, based on a joint employee–employer contributory scheme, ensured an income for individuals who had worked steadily but could not necessarily be expected to maintain the burden of self-support in retirement or unemployment. The structure of social security was meant to fit the demographic and market structure of most families: one wage earner, working full-time for a full year with just a few employers during a working life. It was a model for an industrial economy. The social insurance approach assumed the essential viability of the market system while acknowledging the need to support the public's purchasing power. This assumption by the federal government of responsibility for the worker's income security suggested that the flaws in society were, after all, correctable.

Social insurance started out closely modeled on private insurance with benefits tightly tied to contributions. The insurance emphasis on individual equity was one thrust. Concern for the poverty of the aged was another. The intent was to have characteristics of both insurance and social welfare. An insurance model would make benefits closely dependent on contributions. A social model would show concern for the poorest of the aged and feature redistribution from the wealthy to lower income groups so that lower income workers would receive more in return for their contributions than would high-income workers. The emphasis in 1935 on equity—an insurance approach—outweighed concerns for adequacy—a social welfare approach.

Although the 1935 law was conservative, the 1939 amendments added benefits for the spouses and children of deceased workers and expanded the number of workers covered by old age insurance. The formula for calculating benefits was adjusted to become more redistributive in its structure. Benefits were expanded between 1939 and 1974, which retained the connection between contributions and benefits, but loosened it to permit large families to receive more than small families, and low wage earners to receive a higher proportion of their contributions than highly paid earners. Workers who earned low wages would still receive pensions that were smaller than those of better-off workers, but the difference in pensions was smaller than that in their wages. As a result, the income distribution of older Americans became more equal over the next five decades. Many of the controversies during these years flowed from efforts to maintain the delicate balance between adequate benefits for all recipients and the link between wage history and benefits.

The desire to model social insurance after private insurance programs was reflected in the concept of a reserve fund to hold the assets of the program. A trust fund is essentially a bookkeeping mechanism for specifying that particular revenues be related to specific programs. The original concept in 1935 was to establish a fund in accordance with accepted actuarial principles: at any time, the fund should be large enough to pay off all future obligations. But by 1939, Congress began to worry that the assets might grow too large. The law required Social Security assets to be invested exclusively in special issues of U.S government bonds. The fear was that there would not be enough government debt for appropriate investment. The Social Security Board was required to report to Congress whenever the assets of the trusts reached three times the size of benefit payments and thus became so large that they would absorb too much of the government debt. After 1939, the trustees abandoned a full actuarial reserve to a partial or contingency reserve fund which would build assets to meet needs for a limited period of time.

The 1935 Social Security Act and its 1939 amendments had many flaws. Many workers, including domestic workers and farm laborers, were excluded from coverage. In addition, other common sources of poverty, including disability and the desertion of one's spouse, were ignored by its insurance provisions. In addition, for those groups it did cover, the programs needed time to build up funds from which benefits might be dispensed. These factors meant that programs of temporary assistance were required. Categorical programs that made federal grants-in-aid available to the states were designed to assist the destitute aged, the blind, and dependent children.

Although it was hard to see at the time, the greatest flaw of the Social Security Act was its construction of a two-class social welfare system. Workers who were regularly employed in established industries were protected against the major risks of an industrial society—old age, unemployment, and (eventually) disability. Workers with less stable industries would continue to rely on the old poor law system for aid. The decisions of Congress to exclude the major industries that employed African Americans—domestic and farm labor—quickly imposed a racial division on this class structure.

Public Assistance

The Social Security Act established a dual system for federally supported income maintenance. The result for the country was a tripartite approach to public relief. The act provided for federally administered insurance programs and federally aided, state-administered assistance programs for selected groups. The grant-in-aid, state-administered financial assistance programs served to separate again the old poor from the new. The new poor, the unemployed, were covered by social insurance; the old "worthy" poor, by categorical public assistance. Left to the states was the third group, the "unworthy poor," for whom states and localities were to develop programs without federal aid.

The creation of federally aided categories of assistance evolved from longtime state efforts to help certain classes of the poor whose circumstances could not readily be attributed to personal inadequacy and who, therefore, were not to be stigmatized as recipients of the dole. State provisions of aid for the aged, the blind, and the widowed were generally viewed as pensions without stigma. By 1935, aid to the blind was available in twenty-four states; aid to the aged, in thirty-four states; and aid to mothers, in all states and jurisdictions except Alabama, Georgia, and South Carolina. The decision of Congress to lend federal support for the beneficiaries of these programs acknowledged the legitimacy of their claim. Besides, it was believed that the necessity for such programs would recede as federal measures for social insurance, maternal and child welfare, and public health work took hold.

The provision of public assistance on the basis of requirements in addition to need and the decision for state, rather than federal, administration indicated continuing ambivalence about all non–work-related relief. Continuing reliance on local surveillance of recipients persisted. Categorization separated out those who could not work and for whom public benefits were acceptable and relatively uncontroversial. At the same time, the system tried to meet the service needs of these exceptional groups and to ensure the proper use of income benefits. Be that as it may, the federal categories, as designed in 1935, were no return to traditional, almshouse-oriented relief programs. The popularity of the old age pension movement, the past success with wholly state-financed categorical programs, and the new understanding of the causes of poverty would not permit this. The federal public assistance categories were community oriented in that they required that recipients be living in their own homes. Furthermore, the Social Security Act defined assistance as "money payments," requiring that grants be made in cash. Finally, the act mandated the opportunity for a fair hearing for any individual whose "claim" for assistance was denied. These particular provisions, plus the fact that they legislatively joined insurance and assistance programs, gave some support to the concept of the "right to assistance" for eligible recipients.

Additional factors contributed to the standard-setting character of the Social Security Act. The act required that participating states submit plans making assistance programs mandatory in all political subdivisions, appointing a single state agency responsible for administering or supervising the state's assistance program, ensuring the efficiency of state program administration, and guaranteeing compliance with the Social Security Board's regulations and reporting requirements. Of equal standard-setting significance was the act's rejection of unusual and deterring residence requirements. For all the differences still possible under its essentially permissive requirements, the act did succeed in bringing the federally funded public assistance programs to all the states and in giving the various programs an identifiable common base.

The Social Security Act had profound significance for family welfare generally, and for the roles of family members in particular. For women, the addition to Old Age Insurance of dependents' benefits in 1939 reinforced their roles as wives and homemakers. Despite the increase in the labor force participation of women, the act did not cover many traditionally female jobs. It penalized heavily for interrupted employment, and compensated inadequately for pay discrimination. Thus, over the years, many women workers have found it more advantageous to draw benefits as dependents than to draw them on the basis of their own labor force participation.

For the larger society, Old Age Insurance and Old Age Assistance meant that a major portion of the financial burden of caring for aged parents was lifted from adult children. The money thus freed could be shifted to the care of minor children. The adequacy of Aid to Dependent Children (ADC) benefits was questionable from the start.

The Committee on Economic Security had described mothers' pensions as "defensive measures for children."

> They are designed to release from the wage-earning role the person whose natural function is to give her children the physical and affectionate guardianship necessary not alone to keep them from falling into social misfortune, but more affirmatively to rear them into citizens capable of contributing to society.[76]

Despite the committee's encouragement and the seeming popularity of Mother's Aid among the states, limited professional social work attention was given to ADC during congressional hearings. Leaving aside the testimony of Katherine Lenroot, chief of the Children's Bureau,[77] and Jacob Kepecs, president of the Child Welfare League of America,[78] little interest was demonstrated. Edwin Witte, executive for the committee, stated after the passage of the Social Security Act that the poor outcome of provisions for dependent children, as compared to provisions for other needy groups, was mainly due to this lack of interest.[79]

The inattention to provisions for dependent children resulted, first, in the administration of ADC along with the adult categories of assistance. The original intent that the program be under the jurisdiction of the Children's Bureau was thus ignored. Second, the phrase "aid to dependent children" did not include caretakers. Third, the grant-in-aid formula limited federal payments to one-third of a total of $18 per month per family provided for one dependent and to one-third of $12 per month provided for additional dependent children. The formula contrasted sharply with that used for Old Age Assistance. In the latter instance, the federal government offered payment monthly of one-half of $30 for each eligible person. ADC obviously provided less than the "defense measures" envisioned by the Committee on Economic Security. In fact, there was such contrast between the provisions for dependent children and for the aged and the blind that one might wonder whether aiding such children was still subject to suspicion despite the widespread adoption of mothers' pensions by the states.

One basis perhaps for the suspicion and distrust of the new ADC program was uncertainty about who was to be helped by it. The older, states' Mothers' Aid programs, for the most part, did not provide for payments for children born out of wedlock; they were widows' pensions. Many social workers felt either unprepared to accept these clients or unprepared to fight for them in nonaccepting communities. By June 1938, 604,142 children in forty states were being helped by ADC. It is estimated that less than 4 percent of these were children who lived with unmarried mothers. Sixteen percent of the reporting states had not accepted any children of unwed mothers.

The low coverage rate reflects the unwillingness to move from the old Mothers' Aid to the less restrictive coverage. While neither the Social Security Act nor the Social Security Board regulations restrict coverage to children of unmarried mothers, scarcity often left distribution of funds to the interpretation of local boards and workers. What is a suitable home? Between states and within states definitions of suitability varied:

> There is surprising little of a censorious attitude towards girls with limited opportunities in our mountain counties. . . . Give aid to dependent children . . . to an unmarried mother from an undesirable home but . . . consider . . . the unmarried from a good family with good background has committed an inexcusable act.
>
> Any mother is considered fit to care for her child unless she is so unfit that a petition for neglect should be filed.
>
> If all the children in a family were illegitimate the commission would decide this was not a fit mother. If only one or two were illegitimate it might be overlooked or forgiven.
>
> It is a matter of state policy that the parent must not have had an out-of-wedlock child within a year.[80]

There was even more variation in the treatment of children of color than of white children, and in most communities it was difficult for black mothers to receive help. As one field supervisor put it: "Communities . . . see no reason why the employable Negro mother should not continue her usually sketchy seasonal labor or indefinite domestic service rather than receive a public-assistance grant."[81] From its start, the economics of the marketplace, concepts of morality and appropriate sexual behavior, and racism combined to limit the scope and the effectiveness of this program. The Social Security Act of 1935 put federal social welfare policy on its trajectory for the remainder of the twentieth century. The division between insurance programs that were "earned" and assistance programs that were not grew stronger during the next fifty years. The groups that received insurance coverage, including people with disabilities who were added to the program in 1956, saw their poverty rates decline steadily between 1940 and 2000. Over the same years, poor mothers and their children were left behind, their proportion of all poor people increased steadily in subsequent decades.

Family Life and Social Workers

A summary of staff reports prepared for the Committee on Economic Security declared that "the chief aim of social security is protection of the family life of wage earners, and the prime factor in family life is the protection and development of children."[82] As the Depression deepened, social workers became increasingly insistent that the economic base of the family be strengthened and that the federal government share in the cost.

Changes in the family were particularly evident in the move of women to occupations outside the home. The number of wage-earning women sixteen years of age and over increased from 1,701,000 in 1870, when the Bureau of the Census first collected such data, to 10,546,000 in 1930.[83] During the 1920s, the increase in female employment was 29 percent, while the increase of the female population was 22 percent.[84] The number of employed married women had reached 3,071,000 in 1930, a nearly 300 percent increase over the 769,000 employed at the beginning of the century.[85] Were it not "for the retardation of business activity which was well under way at the time of the 1930 census, probably even more women would have reported themselves as occupied."[86] As it was, 33 percent of those who worked were in domestic and personal services, 18 percent were in manufacturing and mechanical industries, 19 percent were in clerical occupations, and 12 percent were in trade and transportation. The vast majority were in semiskilled or unskilled positions.[87]

The unemployment crisis of the 1930s of necessity affected family life. The formation of new families—getting married and having children—was delayed. The marriage rate per 1,000 unmarried women declined from 92 percent in 1920 to 68 percent in 1930.[88] In 1933, the birthrate was 18.4 per 1,000 of population, down from 27.7 per 1,000 of population in 1920 and from 21.3 in 1930.[89] The psychological climate, as well as economic reality, was one of depression for families already formed. Unemployment struck women as well as men, with discrimination falling heavily upon the former as jobs became scarcer and men displaced women. At the same time, the well-paid industrial and construction work performed by most men was more liable to lay offs than the lower-paid, unskilled work performed by most women. One result was role reversal, wherein wives worked and supported families while husbands were confined to the home. Although the divorce rate showed no appreciable change between 1920 and 1940—actually the rate for 1930 (7.5 per 1,000) married women was slightly lower than the 1920 rate (8.0 per 1,000)[90]—family instability was evidenced by a sharp increase in suicide and desertions.[91] And the plight of older people forced permanently out of the labor force by the Depression was frightening to contemplate.

Thus the attitude of the social work and social welfare community toward the Social Security Act as a family welfare measure is worth exploring. The act itself had been approved on August 15, 1935, but federal funds did not become available until

February 1936. Beyond that, the process of having states submit plans for the administration of public assistance and of having those plans approved by the newly created Public Assistance Board proved slow. By mid-November 1936, forty-two states had finally received grants for Old Age Assistance. Only twenty-six states had received grants for Aid to Dependent Children, bearing out the lack of concern for this group of recipients. The states, in their reluctance to move into this category of assistance, reflected the attitude of the federal government in its differential treatment of children.

All in all, social workers were alarmed by the course of events, and the delegate conference of the American Association of Social Workers, held in Washington, D.C., February 14–16, 1936, considered carefully "this business of relief." The delegates gave public hearing to a number of convictions and concerns.[92]

1. That the factors that made relief necessary were demoralizing, not the act of receiving relief itself
2. That the work provided by WPA should be productive in itself and not just a technique for avoiding idleness
3. That need should be the criterion for federal assistance and that separating employables from unemployables left the matter to the uncertain mercies of states and localities
4. That there was a residual relief problem caused by the fact that WPA work relief payments were inadequate to cover the needs of large families and by the fact that some groups were not covered by the federally aided public assistance categories at all
5. That permissive requirements for state participation in federally aided public assistance programs threatened irresponsibility

The dissatisfaction expressed at the delegate conference did not alter the course of events. The collapse of social work's pressure for a return to a federal program geared primarily to direct relief seems first of all due to the political unreality of such a return but also to a conflict among social workers as to their professional view of the poor and of the needs of the poor.

Aubrey Williams, deputy administrator for the WPA, expressed his bewilderment and concern at the "growing disposition on the part of social workers to advocate the return of the federal government to direct relief." He implied that this pressure resulted from the tendency on their part to see caseworkers as necessary to the poor and casework as a necessary adjunct to poor relief. "To put caseworkers into the old poor relief system," Williams argued, "is to put new wine into old bottles that will crack." He warned that the demolition of the WPA would give social workers "3.5 million people on direct relief and nothing else" and, in a final thrust, said that "the sooner social work as a profession can turn its back on direct relief as a valid form of social treatment, the better off will be the nation and the higher the standing of social work."[93] Like Harry Hopkins back in 1933, Williams seemed to be saying that federal programs should not be used "to develop a great social work organization throughout the United States." Those who led the attack against the WPA could not easily dismiss the accusation.

Having been admonished by Williams to think of new approaches to unemployment and income security, the delegates were also treated to Ewan Clague's description of the potentialities of the provisions of the Social Security Act.[94] Perhaps because it did join, no matter how uneasily, new social insurance and old public relief measures, the act offered some satisfaction to those social workers who had urged social reform through social insurance and to those who urged reform through the professionalization of relief giving.

Many social workers—especially those working for public agencies—demanded more sweeping action to address the Depression which put them to the left of the New Deal and their professional organizations. The Rank-and-File movement and its publication *Social Work Today* became the voice of this concern. At its peak, the Rank-and-File movement claimed 15,000 members. The Rank-and-File movement represented an attempt to redefine social workers as *both* professionals and as workers, workers with the right and need to organize into labor unions. The idea of social workers' unions outlived the demise of the movement in 1942.

The early years of the Depression were ones during which social workers clarified their own views about relief and about people who needed financial help. The professional literature between 1930 and 1935 abounds with discussion and controversy. One issue, federal versus state and local responsibility for relief, was settled quite easily. State and local coffers were empty. The issue of public versus private responsibility for relief was similarly resolved. A third issue was that of cash versus in kind. In 1933, Dorothy Kahn, director of the Philadelphia County Relief Board and soon to become chairman of the American Association of Social Workers, made "an ardent appeal for one form [of relief giving], namely, cash."[95] As demonstrated by the categorical programs of the Social Security Act, the proponents of cash payments won the day. The literature would suggest that social workers believed the issue of right versus privilege as a basis for financial aid to have been settled in favor of the right to assistance. Certainly this was true for the social insurances whose benefits were related to worker contributions. As for the categorical programs, the Social Security Act's use of the word "claim" in connection with the receipt of benefits distributed in cash and the right to a fair hearing both indicated an entitlement to public assistance, no matter how conditioned that entitlement might be. Harry Hopkins thought the federal administering agency, along with state and local boards, would pass benefits on "as a pension without stigma."[96]

Perhaps most important to an understanding of the fate of Aid to Dependent Children was the issue of social insurance versus public assistance. Although both types of programs were included in the Social Security Act, the reality was that the social insurance mechanism was favored as an approach to income security. The strengthening of the work ethic by relating premiums and benefits to earnings and the attempted simulation of actuarial, private insurance soundness (with almost no contribution from the general revenue) was designed to ensure the political attractiveness of social insurance.

Of course, the current unemployment crisis required public relief programs; but whatever fears remained about supporting public, non–work-related programs could be allayed with the belief that such programs would wither away. The need for

Old Age Assistance would disappear as Old Age Insurance matured and covered an increasing number of workers. Of importance, too, was the fact that survivors of workers, although not sufficiently provided for, had not been entirely forgotten. The Committee on Economic Security had recommended that a death benefit be paid to a worker's surviving dependents should the worker die before the age of 65 or before the amount of his own contributions had been paid to him as an annuity.[97] The committee had also given consideration to the future when "families and widows would be given primary consideration in broad plans for survivors' insurance or insurance for widows and orphans."[98] The Social Security Act did in fact provide for a lump sum benefit to survivors as recommended by the Committee on Economic Security. There was reason to believe that insurance coverage eventually would be extended to widows and orphans and that Aid to Dependent Children, like Old Age Assistance, would fade in significance. Perhaps that is one reason why the Senate and House committees heard only perfunctory social work support for Aid to Dependent Children and only perfunctory social work criticism of its deficiencies as a program.

New Alignments in Social Welfare

An exploration of social work's attitude toward Aid to Dependent Children must take into account that the Depression required social workers to clarify not only their views about relief and relief recipients but also alignments between public and private social welfare. Inevitably this meant a reconsideration of the functions of professional social work. Regulation No. 1 had begun the reversal of a tradition whereby voluntary agencies shaped the contribution of public agencies to social welfare. The enactment of the Social Security Act furthered the process and established the dominance of public welfare. The impact on voluntary agencies—on voluntary family agencies, in particular—was enormous. Voluntary family agencies and family agency personnel had impeded the development of public welfare prior to the Depression. And despite their beginning development of casework as a professional methodology and of family counseling as a professional function, they had remained absorbed with problems of relief giving. With the onset of the Depression, they became involved in cooperative efforts to help families needing relief because of the unemployment crisis, and their day-to-day practice consisted chiefly of relief-related activities. The Family Welfare Association of America described the extent of its member agencies' involvement:

> Every good public program owes something to the pioneer work of private agencies. . . . Private agencies have readily loaned or released trained persons for service in public agencies, often at a great cost to their own programs. Supervisory and advisory aid have been accorded continuously by many private agencies to public agencies. In addition . . . private agencies have also engaged actively in obtaining general support of public welfare programs.[99]

Now, with the passage of the Social Security Act, family agencies seemed devoid of a viable social welfare function. Family agency workers, who in large measure carried the professional status for social work, seemed similarly affected. Both agencies and workers needed to find a raison d'être; and it was perhaps the knowledge of this, as much as anything else, that underlay the heated discussions of public welfare at the February 1936 delegate conference of the American Association of Social Workers. The apparent collapse of organized social work support for unemployment relief suggests a perception that professional social work practice and relief giving were separate entities, however overlapping their concerns.

This recognition was confirmed in March 1936, when the Family Welfare Association of America (FWAA) published a report of responses by member agencies to questions related to "the crisis in community programs."[100] Of the total of ninety-three agencies responding, eighty-nine agreed that "it would be folly for private agencies . . . to attempt to meet any appreciable part of the unemployment relief burden . . . being abandoned by the Federal Government." They agreed that it was essential "to hold firmly to the principle that intensive casework treatment is the primary function of a family service organization." Nevertheless, when asked to list developments of new or more clearly defined channels of services to the community, the agencies gave "a great variety of answers which constitute[d] a confusing picture." Many listed their emphasis on "intensive casework" as a new development.

The extent to which voluntary agencies were threatened by the Social Security Act's establishment of a permanent public welfare structure and by the vacuum created by the loss of a primary relief-giving responsibility can also be discerned from FWAA's report of responses to its questionnaire. When asked what they were doing to rally community support for public welfare, one-third of the respondents expressed interest in helping but were inactive; another one-third were indifferent.[101] Perhaps they felt all the more upset by the fact that the problem was again largely of their own making. If earlier they had impeded the development of an adequate public sector of social welfare, now they must share responsibility for the existence of a permanent, powerful establishment they could not control. Furthermore, the existence of such an establishment required change at the core of the voluntary agency.

Despite the frequent reference in the social work literature to a "right to assistance," this view was inconsistent with the philosophy that had impelled the development of voluntary social welfare. The latter had begun with an assumption of a character flaw for which—as with man's original fall—man was himself responsible. This view of human nature as essentially evil and of society as the blameless victim of human frailty led to religious, eventually voluntary, social welfare efforts to change the human being. The Protestant ethic was particularly concerned with work, thrift, and financial independence. When voluntary social welfare secularized this ethic, the family agency tied social work practice and relief giving into a single package. In a situation where societal, public responsibility was not admitted, there was no need for public welfare.

The Depression of the 1930s revolutionized conventional thinking about social need. The discovery that people could be unemployed and in need through no fault of their own led, first, to an admission of fault in the economic and social system and, second, to a conception of the individual-at-risk in the system. Society, therefore, had an obligation to help. In such a circumstance, financial need was truly secularized— one might say, publicized—and the need for public welfare was inherent. Furthermore, the acceptance of societal responsibility for financial need led quite naturally to the depersonalization of relief giving. Relief recipients needed money, not service. They did not require the skill of professional service and could best be helped by government aid administered objectively. Federal and state aid represented the elimination of the control of individuals by local communities and was all to the good.

Voluntary social agencies renewed efforts to define a unique professional service function. The widespread dissemination of Freudian theory demonstrating the significance of parent–child relationships brought home the psychological underpinnings of family survival. Having moved away from providing relief for families, voluntary family agencies moved to the further development of highly skilled "casework treatment to assist individuals in removing their own handicaps."[102] The Freudian symbiotic tie of parent to child suggested family, rather than individual, treatment; and attention was focused on the relationship between voluntary family and children's agencies and on the possibility of their merging.

In November 1937, the Family Welfare Association of America distributed an outline of points discussed in meetings of its Committee on Relationship between Family and Children's Work in a meeting of that Committee with a similar committee of the Child Welfare League (CWL) of America.

> In considering the relationship between family and children's case work . . . it is evident that they have the same roots in social case work, as far as the basic knowledge and equipment of the case worker are concerned. . . .
>
> Any family case work agency is also a children's case work agency, in the sense that it has the same obligation for skilled treatment of the problems of children in families as it does for meeting the needs of adults. Any children's case work agency, dealing with children in their own homes or in foster homes, is or should be a family case work agency, in so far as it attempts to treat children's needs in relation to the family setting, or to deal with those difficulties in family relationships that affect the child.[103]

Relationships between voluntary family and children's agencies were to be the subject of controversy throughout the 1940s and 1950s; but already in 1937, mergers between family and children's agencies were being considered. The reasons were: (1) the similarity of casework base, (2) the development of cooperative structures between agencies offering family and children's services, and (3) the development of children's services within family agencies and vice versa. In the *Social Work Year Book, 1951*, Frank J. Hertel reported the following:

> Figures available to FSAA [Family Service Association of America] over the past eight years show that the number of its member agencies engaging in this multiple service [family and child welfare services] increased from 46 in 1942 to 82 (33 percent of the member agencies) by the close of 1949. Of these, 42 had expanded their services to include child placement, whereas 40 represented the merging of two or more agencies . . . to provide the services formerly considered special to each.[104]

By 1960, the number of merged family and children's agencies holding common membership in FSAA and CWL had risen to sixty. In 1974, FSAA and CWL were themselves considering a merger, which they finally rejected.

At the same time that there was a strong trend toward the merging of concerns of family and child welfare agencies, specialized services for each appeared in response to the strains the Depression put on family life. Marital counseling emerged as a particular concern and the first marriage clinic opened in 1930. A variety of family support programs—visiting housekeepers and parent education programs to name just two—developed and the number of child guidance clinics increased.[105]

Conclusion

The Depression of the 1930s left an indelible mark on the United States and on a generation of Americans. Despite the effort expended in the attempt to wrest the country out of the crisis, neither Franklin Roosevelt nor the New Deal programs achieved success until World War II boosted the economy to full employment. Nevertheless, the president had been able to invest the people with psychological endurance and, in the face of severe challenges from the political right and the left, to preserve the basic economic system of private property.

The essential conservatism of the New Deal, however, does not negate the fact that the federal government had emerged as the prime promoter of social welfare. Voluntary welfare as well as state and local governments had been tried and found wanting. The extent to which a new realism had taken hold was exhibited in the Supreme Court opinion delivered by Justice Benjamin Cardozo upholding the constitutionality of the Social Security Act:

> The concept of the general welfare is not static. Needs that were narrow or parochial a century ago may be interwoven in our day with the welfare of the nation. What is critical or urgent changes with the times.[106]

The United States emerged from the Depression aware of the hazards of the industrial society and having accomplished a major structural change in its income transfer system. The provision of social insurance—and, for the moment, public assistance too—represented aggressive federal responsibility for guaranteeing minimum financial security as a matter of right.

Unquestionably, the Social Security Act was the major legislative accomplishment of the New Deal. The act declared the birth of the welfare state and established a direction for its growth and development. As a start, the necessity for opening up jobs for young adults (which required that the elderly be retired from the labor market) and the political clout of older people meant that the welfare measures of the Act were geared primarily to persons over age 65. The risks suffered by children and young adults were given short shrift, a situation not really repaired by the minimum wage and hour or child labor provisions of the Fair Labor Standards Act of 1938. For the most part, the Fair Labor Standards Act did little more than give federal sanction to provisions that already existed in many of the states. Nevertheless, precedent for societal protection for all had been established and would serve as a base for substantial expansion of old programs and the creation of new ones.

For social work, the return to prosperity meant a return to a period of further introspection and professionalization. In the early years of the New Deal many social workers had been active social reformers and community organizers. In 1934, the general sessions and section meetings of the National Conference of Social Work strongly emphasized unemployment, health, and justice as social welfare policy concerns and social legislation as the route to social change. By 1936, the meetings emphasized social work methodology, social agency administration, and social work education.[107]

Discussion Questions

1. In what ways were the social welfare ideas of the New Deal consistent with earlier periods of American history? In what ways did they depart from older ideas?
2. What ideas about family life lay behind the New Deal welfare state? How do these compare with family realities both during and after the New Deal?
3. Was social work as a profession more concerned with maintaining the status quo or pushing the country toward more sweeping reforms during the 1930s? How did this influence the history of the profession?

DOCUMENTS: The Depression and the New Deal

The documents used to demonstrate social welfare issues during the Depression of the 1930s are excerpts from the *Monthly Reports of the Federal Emergency Relief Administration* (1933) and from the Social Security Act (1935) as originally passed by Congress. The two documents illustrate continuity and change in social policy.

The monthly reports of the FERA set forth the famous *Rules and Regulations,* which not only governed the administration of developing public welfare programs but also revolutionized the relationship between the public and private sectors of social welfare. The most famous of these regulations, Regulation No. 1, ordered that relief funds be administered by public agencies. This new principle—"public funds in public hands"—removed voluntary agencies from the business of relief. Taking into account the enormous significance of cash relief for social welfare during the Depression, the dominance of the public sector was immediately established.

Nevertheless, the influence of voluntary agency experience and tradition can be detected. Regulation No. 3 requires that need be determined on the basis of individual budgeting and that a variety of individual and family resources be taken into account in establishing the final amount of the relief grant. The requirements for individualized budgeting and resource determination led directly to the investigations of applications and the use of trained investigators at least in supervisory positions.

The Social Security Act was the most important piece of social welfare legislation of the Depression era. It substituted a group of permanent programs for the temporary programs of FERA and, in so doing, acknowledged long-term federal responsibility for social welfare. This new thrust did not, however, make a total break with the past. In fact, a major characteristic of the act is its dual nature, its putting together of old and new orientations.

On the one hand, the Social Security Act establishes a number of social insurance programs to meet the hazards of old age and unemployment. The insurance programs are meant to cover those with former or current workforce connections. They are financed through payroll-tax deductions. Simultaneously, the act provides for a group of categorical non–work-related programs of assistance for the elderly, the blind, and dependent children. These programs are funded through a grant-in-aid formula providing a joint federal–state funding device. They are to be administered by states and provide an income safety net for this population.

The social insurance and public assistance programs differ markedly in their orientation to people in need. The former, perhaps because of the direct taxation involved, makes carefully spelled-out benefits available to claimants as a matter of right. The public assistance categories, because they are based on a "demonstrated need" approach, continue the practice of investigation and individualized budgeting.

The delineation of categories of public assistance recipients indicates the extent to which need per se as a determinant for helping was compromised. Nevertheless, the new public assistance programs were also a break with the past. The Social Security Act requires that each participating state develop a state plan for public assistance and that the plan meet certain requirements. In this regard, the act is standard setting. In addition, the act requires that grants be made in cash and to people living in their own homes, marking the end of institutional almshouse care for the poor. Finally, the act provides for a "fair hearing" for those applicants who believe they have been unfairly treated. The changes are such that social welfare workers began to talk of a "right to assistance."

MONTHLY REPORT

OF

THE FEDERAL EMERGENCY RELIEF ADMINISTRATION

LETTER OF TRANSMITTAL

JULY 1, 1933

SIR: Pursuant to subsection (d) of section 3 of the Federal Emergency Relief Act of 1933, the Federal Emergency Relief Administration has the honor to submit this report of its activities from May 22, 1933, to June 30, 1933, inclusive. . . .

RULES AND REGULATIONS

Rules and Regulations Nos. 1, 2, and 3 were promulgated by the Federal Emergency Relief Administrator, and were printed and distributed to the governors and State Emergency Relief Administrators. They read as follows:

No. 1

(a) Grants of Federal emergency relief funds are to be administered by public agencies after August 1, 1933.

Just as all State commissions responsible for the distribution of Federal and State funds to local communities are public bodies, so in turn should those local units be public agencies responsible for the expenditure of public funds in the same manner as any other municipal or county department.

This policy obviously must be interpreted on a realistic basis in various parts of the United States. Hundreds of private agencies scattered throughout the land have freely and generously offered their services in the administration of public funds. It would be a serious handicap to relief work if the abilities and interests of these individuals were lost. But these individuals should be made public officials, working under the control of public authority. Thousands of these workers are serving and will continue to serve without pay, but if paid, they should be compensated in the same manner as any other public servant.

It is not the intention of this regulation to instruct the several States to make hasty changes in agreements which the State administration may have made with the private agencies. Adjustment, however, to this policy is to be made no later than August 1, 1933.

This ruling prohibits the turning over of Federal emergency-relief funds to a private agency. The unemployed must apply to a public agency for relief, and this relief must be furnished direct to the applicant by a public agent.

(b) Grants made to the States from Federal funds under the Federal Emergency Relief Act of 1933 may be used for the payment of medical attendance and medical supplies for those families that are receiving relief.

(c) These funds may also be used to pay the cost of shelter for the needy unemployed.

(d) These funds may not be used for the payment of hospital bills or for the boarding out of children, either in institutions or in private homes, or for providing general institutional care. These necessary services to the destitute should be made available through State or local funds.

(e) The personnel employed on work relief projects by the States or their subdivisions are not Federal employees and must not be considered as such; therefore, premiums for accident insurance in connection with work relief programs may not be paid from Federal funds, but should be paid out of State or local moneys.

No. 2

Grants of Federal relief funds cannot be made on the basis of expenditures for rental of buildings used for relief operation; salaries of regularly employed public employees other than those employed full time in connection with emergency unemployment relief and under the supervision of the unemployment relief authority; salaries of relief workers not working directly under the supervision of the unemployment relief authority; and the purchase of automobiles and other equipment used in connection with relief administration.

No. 3

SUPPLEMENT TO RULES AND REGULATIONS NO. 1

Rule No. 1 stated: "Grants of Federal emergency relief funds are to be administered by public agencies after August 1, 1933." The rule further stated, "This ruling prohibits the turning over of Federal Emergency Relief funds to a private agency. The unemployed must apply to a public agency for relief and this relief must be furnished directly to the applicant by a public agent."

Three points need to be clarified:

(*a*) Public agency.

(*b*) Public agent or public official.

(*c*) Use of private agency personnel.

(*a*) Public agency.—A public welfare department, supported by tax funds and controlled by local government, if approved by the State emergency relief administration to administer unemployment relief, is a "public agency." Where a public welfare department does not exist and a local unemployment relief administration is responsible for unemployment relief this local unemployment relief administration, in order to be recognized as a "public agency" in the meaning of that term as used in Rules and Regulations No. 1, must have the following factors:

(1) It must have the full sanction and recognition of the State emergency relief administration.

(2) It must be vested with full authority and control in the expenditure of State and Federal public funds appropriated for local relief purposes.

(3) It must conform to the rulings of the State emergency relief administration.

(4) It must keep such records and forms as are required by the State emergency relief administration.

NOTE.—This interpretation recognizes as a "public agency," an agency created and sustained by Executive action in the absence of creative local legislation.

(*b*) *Public official or public agent.*—"Public official" or "public agent" in the meaning of the term as used in Rules and Regulations No. 1, includes every person who is engaged in carrying out the purposes of the public agency, and so must be:

(1) A member of the official staff of the public agency responsible to the chief executive employed by the public agency to administer the entire organization of unemployment relief. This relationship must be made official by definite appointment and acceptance of such appointment.

(2) The compensation of the "public official" or "public agent" may or may not be paid from public funds. Such official may be loaned by a private agency, but when so loaned must become a member of the official staff of the public agency.

(*c*) *Use of personnel loaned by private agency.*—The public agency may make use of personnel of private agencies provided—

(1) Where such personnel is used for the giving of unemployment relief it becomes for the time being an integral part of the public agency. The public agency must assume full responsibility over personnel loaned by the private agency.

(2) That visible evidence of the integration into the public agency is provided as follows:

a. The name of the public agency clearly set out on the office door so that clients may know that they are applying to a public agency for relief.

b. All order forms must be those of the public agency; receipts must be made out to the public agency; identification cards of relief workers must be as staff members of the public agency and relief workers at all times in handling unemployment relief clients must report themselves as public agents or officials.

c. All bills for direct relief, wages for work relief, service or administration costs must be paid directly by the public agency; e.g., when grocery orders are issued by the relief worker the bills must be paid by the public agency directly to the grocer and not through a private agency.

d. It is expected that on other matters than the determination of relief there will be cooperative relationships established between public agencies and private agencies, but the public agency shall not pay for supplemental services so rendered by private agencies.

ADEQUACY OF RELIEF

(Either work relief or direct relief)

Relief shall be given as provided in this act to all needy unemployed persons and/or their dependents. Those whose employment or available resources are inadequate to provide the necessities of life for themselves and/or their dependents are included.

This imposes an obligation on the State emergency relief administration and on all the political subdivisions of the States administering relief, insofar as lies in their power, to see to it that all such needy unemployed persons and/or their dependents shall receive sufficient relief to prevent physical suffering and to maintain minimum living standards.

It also imposes an obligation on the part of the State emergency relief administration and the local relief administration to see that no relief is given to persons unless they are actually in need, and that such relief as is allowed is adjusted to the actual needs of each individual or family.

At the same time the obligation exists to develop maximum efficiency and economy in the furnishing of relief, with a minimum of delay in providing relief to those in distress.

The amount of relief to be given must be based on the following:

(1) An estimate of the weekly needs of the individual or family including an allowance for food sufficient to maintain physical well-being, for shelter, the provision of fuel for cooking and for warmth when necessary, medical care and other necessities. Taxes may be allowed in lieu of allowances for shelter, and not to exceed the normal rent allowance providing such tax allowance is necessary in order to maintain the shelter or home of the relief recipient.

(2) An estimate of the weekly income of the family, including wages or other cash income, produce of farm or garden, and all other resources.

(3) The relief granted should be sufficient to provide the estimated weekly needs to the extent that the family is unable to do so from its own resources.

Any or all of the following types of relief may be allowed under direct relief or under work relief:

(1) Food, and/or food orders or allowance, determined by the number, ages, and needs of the individual members of the family in general accordance with standard food schedules.

(2) Orders or allowances for the provision of shelter, or its equivalent, where necessary.

(3) Orders or allowances for light, gas, fuel, and water for current needs.

(4) Orders or allowances for necessary household supplies.

(5) Clothing or orders or allowances for clothing sufficient for emergency needs.

(6) Orders or allowances for medicine, medical supplies, and/or medical attendance to be furnished in the home.

See further interpretation under *"Direct relief."*

INVESTIGATION AND SERVICE

(Work relief and direct relief)

To carry out the purposes of the Federal Emergency Relief Act of 1933 the investigation of all applications for direct and/or work relief is required. The following rules are hereby established:

(1) Each local relief administration should have at least one trained and experienced investigator on its staff; if additional investigators are to be employed to meet this emergency, the first one employed should have had training and experience. In the larger public welfare districts, where there are a number of investigators, there should be not less than 1 supervisor, trained and experienced in the essential elements of family case work and relief administration, to supervise the work of not more than 20 investigating staff workers.

(2) Registration records of all local applications for relief should be kept at a central office. Where no such central registration index now exists, one should be established by the local relief administration. This is absolutely necessary if duplication is to be avoided where there is more than one agency, either public or private, administering relief.

(3) The minimum investigation shall include a prompt visit to the home; inquiry as to real property, bank accounts, and other financial resources of the family; an interview with at least one recent employer; and determination of the ability and agreement of family, relatives, friends, and churches and other organizations to assist; also the liability under public welfare laws of the several States, of members of a family, or relatives, to assume such support in order to prevent such member becoming a public charge.

(4) Investigation shall be made, not only of persons applying directly to the office but also of those reported to it. In this emergency, it is the duty of those responsible for the administration of unemployment relief to seek out persons in need, and to secure the cooperation of clergymen, school teachers, nurses, and organizations that might assist.

(5) There must be contact with each family through visits at least once a month, or oftener if necessary. The local field worker should be in sufficiently close touch with the family situation to avoid the necessity of applicants reapplying to the office for each individual order.

(6) Investigators should not be overloaded with cases. While no exact standard is being set as to the number of cases per worker, State emergency relief administrators should see to it that a sufficient number of workers are utilized in each local relief district to insure reasonable investigation procedure.

(7) Relief should be given only to persons in need of relief, and on the basis of budgetary deficiency established after careful investigation.

(8) Duplication of relief must be avoided, and every precaution should be taken to prevent overlapping of relief agencies, both public and private.

(9) Frequent and careful reinvestigation should be undertaken at regular intervals in order to establish the continued need of those who are receiving relief in order to determine whether or not some member of the family may have obtained part or full-time work, which would indicate the necessity for cutting down or cutting off on relief. Where adequate staff for investigation is provided, under able direction and supervision, these reinvestigations may be carried out automatically and the relief rolls kept clear of those who do not qualify.

DIRECT RELIEF

Such relief shall be in the form of food, shelter, clothing, light, fuel, necessary household supplies, medicine, medical supplies, and medical attendance, or the cash equivalent of these to the person in his own home.

Direct relief does not include relief—where provision is already made under existing laws—for widows or their dependents, and/or aged persons. There is further disallowed the payment of hospital bills or institutional care, and the costs of the boarding out of children.

Any or all of the following types of relief may be granted:

(1) Food, in the form of food orders, determined by the number, ages, and needs of the individual members of the family in general accordance with standard food schedules.

(2) Orders for the payment of current rent, or its equivalent, where necessary.

(3) Orders for light, gas, fuel, and water for current needs.

(4) Necessary household supplies.

(5) Clothing or orders for clothing sufficient for emergency needs.

(6) Orders for medicine, medical supplies, and/or medical attendance to be furnished in the home.

A broad interpretation of direct relief may be followed by the State relief administration where such is called for in meeting the immediate needs of individuals or families, or in aiding such needy persons in providing the necessities of life for themselves and/or their dependents.

Feed for livestock cannot be allowed as a relief expenditure except feed for domestic livestock may be allowed as a relief expenditure where such allowance makes it possible for the distressed family to produce additional food for the immediate family need.

Seed for gardens under the same reasoning may likewise be allowed as a relief measure.

Tax or mortgage interest payments on real property (home and land) may be allowed in lieu of rent as a relief measure where such allowance is no greater than the normal minimum relief rent allowance and when such payment of tax or mortgage interest is vitally necessary in preventing the loss of the home and the eviction of the owner.

A liberal interpretation of direct relief as above indicated must be controlled by the rule of reason and public policy. Under no circumstances shall an allowance be made which makes provision for other than the emergency needs of the immediate family. State relief administrations are not authorized to make allowances for feed or seed to such an extent that provision is made possible for more than the individual family requirements. Likewise, tax or mortgage interest payments in lieu of rent shall be allowed only on properties occupied and held title to by relief recipients. In no event shall a relief grant be made which directly or indirectly makes possible an increased capital investment in private properties.

WORK RELIEF

(Work relief wages and projects)

Work relief wages in cash or in kind are to be interpreted as follows:

(1) All work relief wages shall be based upon the relief need of the individual and/or his dependents.[1]

(2) The rate of wages should be a fair rate of pay for the work performed. Total compensation should meet the budgetary requirement of the relief recipient.

(3) Payment shall be by check, in cash, or in kind.

(4) Allowance should be on the basis of days' wages, or the equivalent, for the hours worked.

(5) Work relief should be allowed only to those who are employable.

(6) There shall be no discrimination because of race, religion, color, noncitizenship, political affiliation, or because of membership in any special or selected group.

(7) Where skilled personnel is required, skilled wages for skilled work must be paid. Such personnel taken from the work relief lists should be staggered. Where such skilled personnel is required full time, it should be provided otherwise than on a work relief basis.

(8) Work relief projects must be projects undertaken on Federal, State, or local public properties. Work projects for private institutions or agencies, nonprofit or otherwise, are therefore prohibited except

[1]See further interpretation under "Direct relief" and "Adequacy." Allowances on work relief may be made to cover food, shelter, clothing, light, fuel, necessary household supplies, medicine, supplies, and medical attendance.

as such projects, undertaken by governmental units, may benefit the public health or welfare as, for example, the prosecution of a drainage project which may benefit private interests but is withal of definite benefit to the public health of the community.

It therefore follows that work relief may not be used in the improvement of hospitals, libraries, churches, parks, cemeteries, etc., which are privately owned or incorporated, except that if State or local public moneys are regularly contributed to the support of such institutions, and such public support creates a quasi-public institution which may receive the benefit of work relief.

(9) Work relief projects under this act must be for work undertaken by a State or local relief administration independent of work under a contract or for which an annual appropriation has been made. It must be, in general, apart from normal governmental enterprises and not such as would have been carried out in due course regardless of an emergency.

The construction, as a work relief project, of public buildings, such as schools, firehouses, garages, etc., would in general not be acceptable as a proper work relief project, such construction falling within the usual contract work which would provide labor for those unemployed at large.

(10) Persons employed on work relief projects are not Federal employees and the premiums for their compensation or accident insurance may not be paid from Federal funds. If such insurance is provided, it therefore must be carried by State or local moneys.

Persons employed on work-relief projects by the States and their subdivisions ought to be covered by compensation or accident insurance.

(11) All local work relief projects must be submitted for approval to the State emergency relief administration.

***

THE SOCIAL SECURITY ACT

Approved, August 14, 1935

[PUBLIC—NO. 271—74TH CONGRESS]

[II. R. 7260]

AN ACT

To provide for the general welfare by establishing a system of Federal old-age benefits, and by enabling the several States to make more adequate provision for aged persons, blind persons, dependent and crippled children, maternal and child welfare, public health, and the administration of their unemployment compensation laws; to establish a Social Security Board; to raise revenue; and for other purposes.

Be it enacted by the Senate and House of Representatives of the United States of America in Congress assembled,

TITLE I—GRANTS TO STATES FOR OLD-AGE ASSISTANCE

APPROPRIATION

SECTION 1. For the purpose of enabling each State to furnish financial assistance, as far as practicable under the conditions in such State, to aged needy individuals, there is hereby authorized to be appropriated for the fiscal year ending June 30, 1936, the sum of $49,750,000, and there is hereby authorized to be appropriated for each fiscal year thereafter a sum sufficient to carry out the purposes of this title. The sums made available under this section shall be used for making payments to States which have submitted, and had approved by the Social Security Board established by Title VII (hereinafter referred to as the "Board"), State plans for old-age assistance.

STATE OLD-AGE ASSISTANCE PLANS

SEC. 2 (a) A State plan for old-age assistance must (1) provide that it shall be in effect in all political subdivisions of the State, and, if administered by them, be mandatory upon them; (2) provide for financial participation by the State; (3) either provide for the establishment or designation of a single State agency to administer the plan, or provide for the establishment or designation of a single State agency to supervise the administration of the plan; (4) provide for granting to any individual, whose claim for old-age assistance is denied, an opportunity for a fair hearing before such State agency; (5) provide such methods of administration (other than those relating to selection, tenure of office, and compensation of personnel) as are found by the Board to be necessary for the efficient operation of the plan; (6) provide that the State agency will make such reports, in such form and containing such information, as the Board may from time to time find necessary to assure the correctness and verification of such reports; and (7) provide that, if the State or any of its political subdivisions collects from the estate of any recipient of old-age assistance any amount with respect to old-age assistance furnished him under the plan, one-half of the net amount so collected shall be promptly paid to the United States. Any payment so made shall be deposited in the Treasury to the credit of the appropriation for the purposes of this title.

(b) The Board shall approve any plan which fulfills the conditions specified in subsection (a), except that it shall not approve any plan which imposes, as a condition of eligibility for old-age assistance under the plan—

(1) An age requirement of more than sixty-five years, except that the plan may impose, effective until January 1, 1940, an age requirement of as much as seventy years; or

(2) Any residence requirement which excludes any resident of the State who has resided therein five years during the nine years immediately preceding the application for old-age assistance and has resided therein continuously for one year immediately preceding the application; or

(3) Any citizenship requirement which excludes any citizen of the United States.

PAYMENT TO STATES

SEC. 3. (a) From the sums appropriated therefore, the Secretary of the Treasury shall pay to each State which has an approved plan for old-age assistance, for each quarter, beginning with the quarter commencing July 1, 1935, (1) an amount, which shall be used exclusively as old-age assistance, equal to one-half of the total of the sums expended during such quarter as old-age assistance under the State plan with respect to each individual who at the time of such expenditure is sixty-five years of age or older and is not an inmate of a public institution, not counting so much of such expenditure with respect to any individual for any month as exceeds $30 and (2) 5 per centum of such amount, which shall be used for paying the costs of administering the State plan or for old-age assistance, or both, and for no other purpose: Provided, That the State plan, in order to be approved by the Board, need not provide for financial participation before July 1, 1937 by the State, in the case of any State which the Board, upon application by the State and after reasonable notice and opportunity for hearing to the State, finds is prevented by its constitution from providing such financial participation. . . .

DEFINITION

SEC. 6. When used in this title the term "old-age assistance" means money payments to aged individuals.

TITLE II—FEDERAL OLD-AGE BENEFITS

OLD-AGE RESERVE ACCOUNT

SECTION 201. (a) There is hereby created an account in the Treasury of the United States to be known as the "Old-Age Reserve Account" hereinafter in this title called the "Account." There is hereby authorized to be appropriated to the Account for each fiscal year, beginning with the fiscal year ending June 30, 1937, an amount sufficient as an annual premium to provide for the payments required under this title, such amount to be determined on a reserve basis in accordance with accepted actuarial principles, and based upon such tables of mortality as the Secretary of the Treasury shall from time to time adopt, and upon an interest rate of 3 per centum per annum compounded annually. The Secretary of the Treasury shall submit annually to the Bureau of the Budget an estimate of the appropriations to be made to the Account. . . .

OLD-AGE BENEFIT PAYMENTS

SEC. 202. (a) Every qualified individual (as defined in section 210) shall be entitled to receive, with respect to the period beginning on the date he attains the age of sixty-five, or on January 1, 1942, whichever is the later, and ending on the date of his death, an old-age benefit (payable as nearly as practicable in equal monthly installments) as follows:

(1) If the total wages (as defined in section 210) determined by the Board to have been paid to him, with respect to employment (as defined in section 210) after December 31, 1936, and before he attained the age of sixty-five, were not more than $3,000, the old-age benefit shall be at a monthly rate of one-half of 1 per centum of such total wages;

(2) If such total wages were more than $3,000, the old-age benefit shall be at a monthly rate equal to the sum of the following:

(A) One-half of 1 per centum of $3,000; plus

(B) One-twelfth of 1 per centum of the amount by which such total wages exceeded $3,000 and did not exceed $45,000; plus

(C) One-twenty-fourth of 1 per centum of the amount by which such total wages exceeded $45,000.

(b) In no case shall the monthly rate computed under subsection (a) exceed $85.

(c) If the Board finds at any time that more or less than the correct amount has theretofore been paid to any individual under this section, then, under regulations made by the Board, proper adjustments shall be made in connection with subsequent payments under this section to the same individual.

(d) Whenever the Board finds that any qualified individual has received wages with respect to regular employment after he attained the age of sixty-five, the old-age benefit payable to such individual shall be reduced, for each calendar month in any part of which such regular employment occurred, by an amount equal to one month's benefit. Such reduction shall be made, under regulations prescribed by the Board, by deductions from one or more payments of old-age benefit to such individual.

PAYMENTS UPON DEATH

SEC. 203. (a) If any individual dies before attaining the age of sixty-five, there shall be paid to his estate an amount equal to 3 1/2 per centum of the total wages determined by the Board to have been paid to him, with respect to employment after December 31, 1936.

(b) If the Board finds that the correct amount of the old-age benefit payable to a qualified individual during his life under section 202 was less than 3 1/2 per centum of the total wages by which such old-age benefit was measurable, then there shall be paid to his estate a sum equal to the amount, if any, by which such 3 1/2 per centum exceeds the amount (whether more or less than the correct amount) paid to him during his life as old-age benefit.

(c) If the Board finds that the total amount paid to a qualified individual under an old-age benefit during his life was less than the correct amount to which he was entitled under section 202, and that the correct amount of such old-age benefit was 3 1/2 per centum or more of the total wages by which such old-age benefit was measurable, then there shall be paid to his estate a sum equal to the amount, if any, by which the correct amount of the old-age benefit exceeds the amount which was so paid to him during his life.

PAYMENTS TO AGED INDIVIDUALS NOT QUALIFIED FOR BENEFITS

SEC. 204. (a) There shall be paid in a lump sum to any individual who, upon attaining the age of sixty-five, is not a qualified individual, an amount equal to 3 1/2 per centum of the total wages determined by the Board to have been paid to him, with respect to employment after December 31, 1936, and before he attained the age of sixty-five.

(b) After any individual becomes entitled to any payment under subsection (a), no other payment shall be made under this title in any manner measured by wages paid to him, except that any part of any payment under subsection (a) which is not paid to him before his death shall be paid to his estate. . . .

OVERPAYMENTS DURING LIFE

SEC. 206. If the Board finds that the total amount paid to a qualified individual under an old-age benefit during his life was more than the correct amount to which he was entitled under section 202, and was 3 1/2 per centum or more of the total wages by which such old-age benefit was measurable, then upon his death there shall be repaid to the United States by his estate the amount, if any, by which such total amount paid to him during his life exceeds whichever of the following is the greater: (1) Such 3 1/2 per centum, or (2) the correct amount to which he was entitled under section 202. . . .

DEFINITIONS

SEC. 210. When used in this title—

(a) The term "wages" means all remuneration for employment, including the cash value of all remuneration paid in any medium other than cash; except that such term shall not include that part of the remuneration which, after remuneration equal to $3,000 has been paid to an individual by an employer with respect to employment during any calendar year, is paid to such individual by such employer with respect to employment during such calendar year.

(b) The term "employment" means any service, of whatever nature, performed within the United States by an employee for his employer, except—

(1) Agricultural labor;

(2) Domestic service in a private home;

(3) Casual labor not in the course of the employer's trade or business;

(4) Service performed as an officer or member of the crew of a vessel documented under the laws of the United States or of any foreign country;

(5) Service performed in the employ of the United States Government or of an instrumentality of the United States;

(6) Service performed in the employ of a State, a political subdivision thereof, or an instrumentality of one or more States or political subdivisions;

(7) Services performed in the employ of a corporation, community chest, fund, or foundation, organized and operated exclusively for religious, charitable, scientific, literary, or educational purposes, or for the

prevention of cruelty to children or animals, no part of the net earnings of which inures to the benefit of any private shareholder or individual.

(c) The term "qualified individual" means any individual with respect to whom it appears to the satisfaction of the Board that—

(1) He is at least sixty-five years of age; and

(2) The total amount of wages paid to him, with respect to employment after December 31, 1936, and before he attained the age of sixty-five, was not less than $2,000; and

(3) Wages were paid to him, with respect to employment on some five days after December 31, 1936, and before he attained the age of sixty-five, each day being in a different calendar year.

TITLE III—GRANTS TO STATES FOR UNEMPLOYMENT COMPENSATION ADMINISTRATION

APPROPRIATION

SECTION 301. For the purpose of assisting the States in the administration of their unemployment compensation laws, there is hereby authorized to be appropriated, for the fiscal year ending June 30, 1936, the sum of $4,000,000, and for each fiscal year thereafter the sum of $49,000,000, to be used as hereinafter provided.

PAYMENTS TO STATES

SEC. 302. (a) The Board shall from time to time certify to the Secretary of the Treasury for payment to each State which has an unemployment compensation law approved by the Board under Title IX, such amounts as the Board determines to be necessary for the proper administration of such law during the fiscal year in which such payment is to be made. The board's determination shall be based on (1) the population of the State; (2) an estimate of the number of persons covered by the State law and of the cost of proper administration of such law; and (3) such other factors as the Board finds relevant. The Board shall not certify for payment under this section in any fiscal year a total amount in excess of the amount appropriated therefor for such fiscal year.

(b) Out of the sums appropriated therefor, the Secretary of the Treasury shall, upon receiving a certification under subsection (a), pay, through the Division of Disbursement of the Treasury Department and prior to audit or settlement by the General Accounting Office, to the State agency charged with the administration of such law the amount so certified.

PROVISIONS OF STATE LAWS

SEC. 303. (a) The Board shall make no certification for payment to any State unless it finds that the law of such State, approved by the Board under Title IX, includes provisions for—

(1) Such methods of administration (other than those relating to selection, tenure of office, and compensation of personnel) as are found by the Board to be reasonably calculated to insure full payment of unemployment compensation when due; and

(2) Payment of unemployment compensation solely through public employment offices in the State or such other agencies as the Board may approve; and

(3) Opportunity for a fair hearing, before an impartial tribunal, for all individuals whose claims for unemployment compensation are denied; and

(4) The payment of all money received in the unemployment fund of such State, immediately upon such receipt, to the Secretary of the Treasury to the credit of the Unemployment Trust Fund established by section 904; and

(5) Expenditure of all money requisitioned by the State agency from the Unemployment Trust Fund, in the payment of unemployment compensation, exclusive of expenses of administration; and

(6) The making of such reports, in such form and containing such information, as the Board may from time to time require, and compliance with such provisions as the Board may from time to time find necessary to assure the correctness and verification of such reports; and

(7) Making available upon request to any agency of the United States charged with the administration of public works or assistance through public employment, the name, address, ordinary occupation and employment status of each recipient of unemployment compensation, and a statement of such recipient's rights to further compensation under such law.

(b) Whenever the Board, after reasonable notice and opportunity for hearing to the State agency charged with the administration of the State law, finds that in the administration of the law there is—

(1) a denial, in a substantial number of cases, of unemployment compensation to individuals entitled thereto under such law; or

(2) a failure to comply substantially with any provision specified in subsection (a); the Board shall notify such State agency that further payments will not be made to the State until the Board is satisfied that there is no longer any such denial or failure to comply. Until it is so satisfied, it shall make no further certification to the Secretary of the Treasury with respect to such State.

TITLE IV—GRANTS TO STATES FOR AID TO DEPENDENT CHILDREN

APPROPRIATION

SECTION 401. For the purpose of enabling each State to furnish financial assistance, as far as practicable under the conditions in such State, to needy dependent children, there is hereby authorized to be appropriated for the fiscal year ending June 30, 1936, the sum of $24,750,000, and there is hereby authorized to be appropriated for each fiscal year thereafter a sum sufficient to carry out the purposes of this title. The sums made available under this section shall be used for making payments to States which have submitted, and had approved by the Board, State plans for aid to dependent children.

STATE PLANS FOR AID TO DEPENDENT CHILDREN

SEC. 402. (a) A State plan for aid to dependent children must (1) provide that it shall be in effect in all political subdivisions of the State, and, if administered by them, be mandatory upon them; (2) provide for financial participation by the State; (3) either provide for the establishment or designation of a single State agency to administer the plan, or provide for the establishment or designation of a single State agency to supervise the administration of the plan; (4) provide for granting to any individual, whose claim with respect to aid to a dependent child is denied, an opportunity for a fair hearing before such State agency; (5) provide such methods of administration (other than those relating to selection, tenure of office, and compensation of personnel) as are found by the Board to be necessary for the efficient operation of the plan; and (6) provide that the State agency will make such reports, in such form and containing such information, as the Board may from time to time require, and comply with such provisions as the Board may from time to time find necessary to assure the correctness and verification of such reports.

(b) The Board shall approve any plan which fulfills the conditions specified in subsection (a), except that it shall not approve any plan which imposes as a condition of eligibility for aid to dependent children, a residence requirement which denies aid with respect to any child residing in the State (1) who has resided in the State for one year immediately preceding the application for such aid, or (2) who was born within the State within one year immediately preceding the application, if its mother has resided in the State for one year immediately preceding the birth.

PAYMENT TO STATES

SEC. 403. (a) From the sums appropriated therefor, the Secretary of the Treasury shall pay to each State which has an approved plan for aid to dependent children, for each quarter, beginning with the quarter commencing July 1, 1935, an amount, which shall be used exclusively for carrying out the State plan, equal to one-third of the total of the sums expended during such quarter under such plan, not counting so much of such expenditure with respect to any dependent child for any month as exceeds $18, or if there is more than one dependent child in the same home, as exceeds $18 for any month with respect to one such dependent child and $12 for such month with respect to each of the other dependent children. . . .

DEFINITIONS

SEC. 406. When used in this title—
(a) The term "dependent child" means a child under the age of sixteen who has been deprived of parental support or care by reason of the death, continued absence from the home, or physical or mental incapacity of a parent, and who is living with his father, mother, grandfather, grandmother, brother, sister, stepfather, stepmother, stepbrother, stepsister, uncle, or aunt, in a place of residence maintained by one or more of such relatives as his or their own home;
(b) The term "aid to dependent children" means money payments with respect to a dependent child or dependent children.

TITLE V—GRANTS TO STATES FOR MATERNAL AND CHILD WELFARE

PART 1—MATERNAL AND CHILD HEALTH SERVICES

APPROPRIATION

SECTION 501. For the purpose of enabling each State to extend and improve, as far as practicable under the conditions in such State, services for promoting the health of mothers and children, especially in rural areas and in areas suffering from severe economic distress, there is hereby authorized to be appropriated for each fiscal year, beginning with the fiscal year ending June 30, 1936, the sum of $3,800,000. The sums made available under this section shall be used for making payments to States which have submitted, and had approved by the Chief of the Children's Bureau, State plans for such services.

ALLOTMENTS TO STATES

SEC. 502. (a) Out of the sums appropriated pursuant to section 501 for each fiscal year the Secretary of Labor shall allot to each State $20,000, and such part of $1,800,000 as he finds that the number of live births in such State bore to the total number of live births in the United States, in the latest calendar year for which the Bureau of the Census has available statistics.
(b) Out of the sums appropriated pursuant to section 501 for each fiscal year the Secretary of Labor shall allot to the States $980,000 in addition to the allotments made under subsection (a), according to the

financial need of each State for assistance in carrying out its State plan, as determined by him after taking into consideration the number of live births in such State.

(c) The amount of any allotment to a State under subsection (a) for any fiscal year remaining unpaid to such State at the end of such fiscal year shall be available for payment to such State under section 504 until the end of the second succeeding fiscal year. No payment to a State under section 504 shall be made out of its allotment for any fiscal year until its allotment for the preceding fiscal year has been exhausted or has ceased to be available.

APROVAL OF STATE PLANS

SEC. 503. (a) A State plan for maternal and child-health services must (1) provide for financial participation by the State; (2) provide for the administration of the plan by the State health agency or the supervision of the administration of the plan by the State health agency; (3) provide such methods of administration (other than those relating to selection, tenure of office, and compensation of personnel) as are necessary for the efficient operation of the plan; (4) provide that the State health agency will make such reports, in such form and containing such information, as the Secretary of Labor may from time to time find necessary to assure the correctness and verification of such reports; (5) provide for the extension and improvement of local maternal and child-health services administered by local child-health units; (6) provide for cooperation with medical, nursing, and welfare groups and organization; and (7) provide for the development of demonstration services in needy areas and among groups in special need.

(b) The Chief of the Children's Bureau shall approve any plan which fulfills the conditions specified in subsection (a) and shall thereupon notify the Secretary of Labor and the State health agency of his approval. . . .

PART 2—SERVICES FOR CRIPPLED CHILDREN

APPROPRIATION

SEC. 511. For the purpose of enabling each State to extend and improve (especially in rural areas and in areas suffering from severe economic distress), as far as practicable under the conditions in such State, services for locating crippled children, and for providing medical, surgical, corrective, and other services and care, and facilities for diagnosis, hospitalization, and aftercare, for children who are crippled or who are suffering from conditions which lead to crippling, there is hereby authorized to be appropriated for each fiscal year, beginning with the fiscal year ending June 30, 1936, the sum of $2,850,000. The sums made available under this section shall be used for making payments to States which have submitted, and had approved by the Chief of the Children's Bureau, State plans for such services.

ALLOTMENTS TO STATES

SEC. 512. (a) Out of the sums appropriated pursuant to section 511 for each fiscal year the Secretary of Labor shall allot to each State $20,000, and the remainder to the States according to the need of each State as determined by him after taking into consideration the number of crippled children in such State in need of the services referred to in section 511 and the cost of furnishing such services to them.

(b) The amount of any allotment to a State under subsection (a) for any fiscal year remaining unpaid to such State at the end of such fiscal year shall be available for payment to such State under section 514 until the end of the second succeeding fiscal year. No payment to a State under section 514 shall be made out of its allotment for any fiscal year until its allotment for the preceding fiscal year has been exhausted or has ceased to be available.

APPROVAL OF STATE PLANS

SEC. 513. (a) A State plan for services for crippled children must (1) provide for financial participation by the State; (2) provide for the administration of the plan by a State agency or the supervision of the administration of the plan by a State agency; (3) provide such methods of administration (other than those relating to selection, tenure of office, and compensation of personnel) as are necessary for the efficient operation of the plan; (4) provide that the State agency will make such reports, in such form and containing such information, as the Secretary of Labor may from time to time require, and comply with such provisions as he may from time to time find necessary to assure the correctness and verification of such reports; (5) provide for carrying out the purposes specified in section 511; and (6) provide for cooperation with medical, health, nursing, and welfare groups and organizations and with any agency in such State charged with administering State laws providing for vocational rehabilitation of physically handicapped children.

(b) The Chief of the Children's Bureau shall approve any plan which fulfills the conditions specified in subsection (a) and shall thereupon notify the Secretary of Labor and the State health agency of his approval. . . .

PART 3—CHILD-WELFARE SERVICES

SEC. 521. (a) For the purpose of enabling the United States, through the Children's Bureau, to cooperate with State public-welfare agencies in establishing, extending, and strengthening, especially in predominantly rural areas, public-welfare services (hereinafter in this section referred to as "child-welfare services") for the protection and care of homeless, dependent, and neglected children, and children in danger of becoming delinquent, there is hereby authorized to be appropriated for each fiscal year, beginning with the fiscal year ending June 30, 1936, the sum of $1,500,000. Such amount shall be allotted by the Secretary of Labor for use by cooperating State public-welfare agencies on the basis of plans developed jointly by the State agency and the Children's Bureau, to each State, $10,000, and the remainder to each State on the basis of such plans, not to exceed such part of the remainder as the rural population of such State bears to the total rural population of the United States. The amount so allotted shall be expended for payment of part of the cost of district, county or other local child-welfare services in areas predominantly rural, and for developing State services for the encouragement and assistance of adequate methods of community child-welfare organization in areas predominantly rural and other areas of special need. The amount of any allotment to a State under this section for any fiscal year remaining unpaid to such State at the end of such fiscal year shall be available for payment to such State under this section until the end of the second succeeding fiscal year. No payment to a State under this section shall be made out of its allotment for any fiscal year until its allotment for the preceding fiscal year has been exhausted or has ceased to be available. . . .

PART 4—VOCATIONAL REHABILITATION

SEC. 531. (a) In order to enable the United States to cooperate with the States and Hawaii in extending and strengthening their programs of vocational rehabilitation of the physically disabled, and to continue to carry out the provisions and purposes of the Act entitled "An Act to provide for the promotion of vocational rehabilitation of persons disabled in industry or otherwise and their return to civil employment," approved June 2, 1920, as amended (U.S.C., title 29, ch. 4; U.S.C., Supp. VII, title 29, secs. 31, 32, 34, 35, 37, 39, and 40), there is hereby authorized to be appropriated for the fiscal years ending June 30, 1936, and June 30, 1937, the sum of $841,000 for each fiscal year in addition to the amount of the existing authorization, and for each fiscal year thereafter the sum of $1,938,000. Of the sums appropriated pursuant to such authorization for each fiscal year, $5,000 shall be apportioned to the Territory of Hawaii and the remainder shall be apportioned among the several States in the manner provided in such Act of June 2, 1920, unamended. . . .

PART 5—ADMINISTRATION

SEC. 541. (a) There is hereby authorized to be appropriated for the fiscal year ending June 30, 1936, the sum of $425,000, for all necessary expenses of the Children's Bureau in administering the provisions of this title, except section 531.

(b) The Children's Bureau shall make such studies and investigations as will promote the efficient administration of this title, except section 531.

(c) The Secretary of Labor shall include in his annual report to Congress a full account of the administration of this title, except section 531. . . .

TITLE X—GRANTS TO STATES FOR AID TO THE BLIND

APPROPRIATION

SECTION 1001. For the purpose of enabling each State to furnish financial assistance, as far as practicable under the conditions in such State, to needy individuals who are blind, there is hereby authorized to be appropriated for the fiscal year ending June 30, 1936, the sum of $3,000,000, and there is hereby authorized to be appropriated for each fiscal year thereafter a sum sufficient to carry out the purposes of this title. The sums made available under this section shall be used for making payments to States which have submitted, and had approved by the Social Security Board, State plans for aid to the blind.

STATE PLANS FOR AID TO THE BLIND

SEC. 1002. (a) A State plan for aid to the blind must (1) provide that it shall be in effect in all political subdivisions of the State, and if administered by them, be mandatory upon them; (2) provide for financial participation by the State; (3) either provide for the establishment or designation of a single State agency to administer the plan, or provide for the establishment or designation of a single State agency to supervise the administration of the plan; (4) provide for granting to any individual, whose claim for aid is denied, an opportunity for a fair hearing before such State agency; (5) provide such methods of administration (other than those relating to selection, tenure of office, and compensation of personnel) as are found by the Board to be necessary for the efficient operation of the plan; (6) provide that the State agency will make such reports, in such form and containing such information, as the Board may from time to time require, and comply with such provisions as the Board may from time to time find necessary to assure the correctness and verification of such reports; and (7) provide that no aid will be furnished any individual under the plan with respect to which he is receiving old-age assistance under the State plan approved under section 2 of this Act.

(b) The Board shall approve any plan which fulfills the conditions specified in subsection (a), except that it shall not approve any plan which imposes, as a condition of eligibility for aid to the blind under the plan—

(1) Any residence requirement which excludes any resident of the State who has resided therein five years during the nine years immediately preceding the application for aid and has resided therein continuously for one year immediately preceding the application; or

(2) Any citizenship requirement which excludes any citizen of the United States.

PAYMENT TO STATES

SEC. 1003. (a) From the sums appropriated therefor, the Secretary of the Treasury shall pay to each State which has an approved plan for aid to the blind, for each quarter, beginning with the quarter commencing July 1, 1935, (1) an amount, which shall be used exclusively as aid to the blind, equal to one-half of the total of the sums expended during such quarter as aid to the blind under the State plan with respect to each individual who is blind and is not an inmate of a public institution, not counting so much of such expenditure with respect to any individual for any month as exceeds $30, and (2) 5 per centum of such amount, which shall be used for paying the costs of administering the State plan or for aid to the blind, or both, and for no other purpose. . . .

SHORT TITLE

SEC. 1105. This Act may be cited as the "Social Security Act."
Approved, August 14, 1935.

Notes

1. Maurice Leven, Harold G. Moulton, and Clark Warburton, *America's Capacity to Consume* (Washington, D.C.: The Brookings Institution, 1934).
2. Frederick Lewis Allen, *Only Yesterday* (New York: Bantam, 1959), p. 241.
3. U.S. Department of Commerce, Office of Business Economics, *The National Income and Product Accounts of the United States, 1929–1965—Statistical Tables* (Washington, D.C.: Government Printing Office, 1966).
4. U.S. Department of Commerce, Bureau of the Census, *Historical Statistics of the United States: Colonial Times to 1957* (Washington, D.C.: Government Printing Office, 1960), p. 73 (hereafter cited as *Historical Statistics*).
5. William H. Matthews, "Breaking the Poverty Circle," *Survey* 52 (April 15, 1924): 96–98.
6. Lucille Eaves, "Studies of Breakdowns in Family Income," *The Family* 10 (December 1929): 228.
7. Ibid., p. 227.
8. Marion Elderton, ed., *Case Studies of Unemployment* (Philadelphia: University of Pennsylvania Press, 1931), p. xxiv.
9. Ibid., pp. xxiii–xxiv.
10. U.S. 72nd Cong., 1st sess., Public Law No. 2, January 22, 1932.
11. 47 Stat. 1932, p. 709.
12. Elderton, op. cit., p. xlix.
13. U.S. Congress, House, *Platforms of the Two Great Political Parties, 1932* (Washington, D.C.: Government Printing Office, 1945), p. 340.
14. Ibid., p. 335.
15. Ibid., p. 343.
16. Franklin D. Roosevelt, speeches at Sioux City, Iowa, September 1932, and Pittsburgh, Pennsylvania, October 1932. Quoted in William Leuchtenberg, *Franklin D. Roosevelt & the New Deal* (New York: Harper & Row, 1963), p. 11.
17. Anne O'Hare McCormick, "Vast Tides That Stir the Capital," *New York Times Magazine*, May 7, 1933. Also to be found in Frank Freidel, ed., *The New Deal and the American People* (Englewood Cliffs, N.J.: Prentice Hall, 1964), p. 5.
18. *Historical Statistics*, pp. 409, 473.
19. Phyllis J. Day, *A New History of Social Welfare* (Englewood Cliffs, N.J.: Prentice Hall, 1989), p. 300.
20. Historical Statistics, p. 141.
21. Ibid., p. 283.
22. Ibid.
23. U.S. Department of Agriculture, Economic Research Service, *The Farm Income Situation*, July 1958.
24. *Historical Statistics*, p. 7, 47.
25. Ibid., p. 278.

26. Ibid.

27. Ibid.

28. U.S. Department of Commerce, Bureau of the Census, *Statistical Abstract of the United States* (Washington, D.C.: Government Printing Office, 1969), Table 892, p. 590.

29. *Historical Statistics*, p. 283.

30. Ibid., p. 286.

31. Ibid., p. 278.

32. Ibid., pp. 73, 409; and *The National Income and Product Accounts*, op. cit.

33. Arthur S. Link, *American Epoch: A History of the United States Since the 1890s* (New York: Knopf, 1935), p. 347.

34. Ibid., p. 395.

35. U.S. Congress, Senate, Committee on Education and Labor, 74th Cong., 1st sess., *Hearings on Senate Resolution 266;* and 75th Cong., 1st sess., *Hearings on Senate Resolution 60.*

36. Link, op. cit., pp. 431–432.

37. Public Law 718, 75th Cong.

38. Dixon Wecter, *The Age of the Great Depression: 1929–1941*, Vol. 13 of Arthur M. Schlesinger and Dixon Ryan Fox, eds., *A History of American Life* (New York: Macmillan, 1948), pp. 119–120.

39. National Urban League, "The Negro in the Industrial Depression: Negroes Out of Work," *Nation* (April 22, 1931): 441–442.

40. Bruce Minton and John Stuart, *Men Who Lead Labor* (New York: Modern Age, 1937), p. 167.

41. *Historical Statistics*, p. 71.

42. Quoted in William H. Chafe, *The American Woman* (New York: Oxford University Press, 1972), p. 107.

43. The National Economy Act, 1932, Sec. 213. For extensive documentation in regard to federal and state restrictions on the employment of married women, see Chafe, op. cit., p. 283.

44. *Historical Statistics*, p. 72.

45. U.S. Congress, House Committee Print No. 4, *Medical Care of Veterans*, 90th Cong., 1st sess., April 17, 1967, pp. 154–155. Printed for use of the Committee on Veterans' Affairs.

46. Joanna C. Colcord, "The Challenge of the Continuing Depression," *The Annals* 176 (November 1934): 17.

47. Gordon Hamilton, "Refocusing Family Casework," *Proceedings: NCSW, 1931*, p. 176.

48. Ibid., p. 178.

49. Wendell F. Johnson, "How Caseworking Agencies Have Met Unemployment," *Proceedings: NCSW, 1931*, pp. 189–200.

50. Ibid., p. 197.

51. Joanna C. Colcord, "Unemployment Relief, 1929–32," *The Family* 13 (December 1932): 270–274.

52. U.S. Federal Emergency Relief Administration, *Monthly Report*, May 22–June 30, 1933, pp. 1–2.

53. U.S. Federal Emergency Relief Administration, *Final Statistical Report* (Washington, D.C.: Government Printing Office, 1942).

54. A. F. Kifer, "The Negro Under the New Deal: 1933–1941" (Ph.D. diss., University of Wisconsin, 1961).

55. Harry L. Hopkins, "The Developing National Program of Relief," *Proceedings: NCSW, 1933*, pp. 65–67, 71.

56. President Franklin D. Roosevelt, "Annual Message to Congress," January 4, 1935. *Public Papers and Addresses of Franklin D. Roosevelt* (New York: Random House, 1938), Vol. 4, 15–25.

57. President Franklin D. Roosevelt, "Message of the President Recommending Legislation on Economic Security," January 17, 1935, op. cit., 43–46.

58. President Franklin D. Roosevelt, "Annual Message to Congress," January 4, 1935, op. cit., 15–25.

59. Ibid.

60. Ibid.

61. Ibid.

62. Ibid.

63. William Hodson, "Unemployment Relief," *Social Work Year Book: 1937* (New York: Russell Sage Foundation, 1937), p. 522. A good review of WPA may be found in Wecter, op. cit.

64. Helen Seymour, *When Clients Organize* (Chicago: American Public Welfare Association, 1937), pp. 16–17.

65. U.S. Federal Emergency Relief Administration, *Monthly Report*, May 22–June 30, 1933, *Rules and Regulations*, p. 7.

66. Ibid., p. 10.

67. Hopkins, op. cit., p. 68.

68. Ibid., p. 69.

69. President Franklin D. Roosevelt, "Acceptance of the Nomination for the Presidency," Chicago, Illinois, July 2, 1932, op. cit., 647–659.

70. Ibid., p. 3.

71. D. H. Fischer, *Growing Old in America* (New York: Oxford University Press, 1978).

72. *The Report of the Committee on Economic Security* (Washington, D.C.: January 15, 1935), p. 25.

73. Ibid., p. 44.

74. President Franklin D. Roosevelt, "Message of the President Recommending Legislation on Economic Security," January 17, 1935, op. cit., 43–46.

75. U.S. 74th Cong., 1st sess., Public Law No. 271.

76. *The Report of the Committee on Economic Security*, op. cit., p. 36.

77. U.S. Congress, Senate, Committee on Finance, Statement of Miss Katherine F. Lenroot, *Hearings on S. 1130, The Economic Security Act, January 22 to February 20, 1935*, revised, pp. 337–341.

78. U.S. Congress, House, Committee on Ways and Means, statement of Mr. Jacob Kepecs, *Hearings on H.R. 4120, The Economic Security Act*, January 1935, pp. 500–503.

79. Edwin Witte, *The Development of the Social Security Act, A Memorandum on the History of the Committee on Economic Security and Drafting and Legislative History of the Social Security Act* (Madison: University of Wisconsin Press, 1962), p. 164.

80. Mary S. Labaree, "Unmarried Parenthood under the Social Security Act," *Proceedings: NCSW*, June 1939, pp. 470–454. Reprinted in *Journal of Progressive Human Services*, 6:2, November 2, 1995, pp. 73–76.

81. Ibid., p. 78.

82. Committee on Economic Security, *Social Security in America, The Factual Background of the Social Act as Summarized from Staff Reports for the Committee* (Washington, D.C.: Government Printing Office, 1937), p. 229.

83. S. P. Breckinridge, "The Activities of Women Outside the Home," *Recent Social Trends in the United States, Report of the President's Research Committee on Social Trends* (New York: McGraw-Hill, 1933), 1:711.

84. Ibid., p. 712.

85. Ibid., p. 715.

86. Ibid., p. 712.

87. Ibid., p. 717.

88. *Historical Statistics*, p. 30.

89. Ibid., p. 23.

90. Ibid., p. 30.

91. Caroline Bird, *The Invisible Scar* (New York: David McKay, 1966), pp. 41–70.

92. American Association of Social Workers, *This Business of Relief*, Proceedings of the Delegate Conference, Washington, D.C., February 14–16, 1936 (New York: AASW, 1936).

93. Aubrey Williams, "The Works Progress Administration," AASW Proceedings, 1936, pp. 128, 137.

94. Ewan Clague, "The Social Security Act as a Relief Measure," AASW Proceedings, 1936, pp. 78–82.

95. Dorothy C. Kahn, "The Use of Cash, Orders for Goods, or Relief in Kind, in a Mass Program," *Proceedings: NCSW, 1933*, p. 273.

96. Harry L. Hopkins, *Spending to Save* (New York: W. W. Norton, 1936), p. 81.

97. *The Report of the Committee on Economic Security*, op. cit., p. 30.

98. Committee on Economic Security, *Social Security in America*, op. cit., p. 239.

99. Family Welfare Association of America, *The Crisis in Community Programs*, March 1936. Multigraph.

100. Ibid.

101. Ibid.

102. Ibid.

103. Family Welfare Association of America, Committee on Relationship between Family and Children's Work, *Preliminary Report*, November 1937. Multigraph.

104. Frank J. Hertel, "Family Social Work," *Social Work Year Book, 1951* (New York: American Association of Social Workers, 1951), p. 187.

105. Mimi Abramovitz, *Regulating the Lives of Women: Social Welfare Policy from Colonial Times to the Present* (Boston: South End Press, 1988), p. 226.

106. *Helvering v. Davis*, 301 U.S. 619 (1937).

107. National Conference on Social Welfare, *Proceedings, 1934*, and *Proceedings, 1936* (Chicago: University of Chicago Press, 1934 and 1936, respectively), tables of contents.

7

War and Prosperity: 1940–1968

The period from 1940 to 1968 was one of contradiction—of growth and of conflict, of affluence and of the rediscovery of poverty. First in Europe and the Pacific, later in Indochina, the United States was involved in war. The military mobilization and wartime production of World War II led initially to economic recovery and subsequently to a "revolution of rising expectations" at home. The 1950s and 1960s were decades of internal as well as external conflict, of battles at home against discrimination on the basis of race, ethnicity, and gender and against poverty, while abroad we waged war in Korea and Vietnam.

Supported by military and civilian demand, the years from 1940 to 1968 were prosperous ones that marked a transition from the consumer demand deficiency of the Depression to the threat of inflation of the 1970s, from the problems of mass unemployment to the problems of spiraling inflation. The gross national product (GNP) had managed to climb to almost $100 billion by 1940 as a result of efforts to rearm and to supply future allies. By 1970, the GNP had soared almost tenfold to $976 billion. Corrected for inflation GNP had tripled.[1] Real disposable personal income—that is, purchasing power available to consumers—had more than doubled by 1970; and per capita consumer expenditures and savings had risen dramatically.[2] Family income, and therefore family welfare measured in money terms, showed significant improvement.

All income groups of the population shared in the prosperity, as did most racial and ethnic groups. Median family income grew for whites and nonwhites. Nonwhite families had a median income of $1,614 in 1947, 51 percent of white family median income. In 1950, nonwhite family income was 54 percent of white; in 1960, 55 percent; and in 1970, 61 percent. This was an improvement in one sense, but the actual dollar gap between white and nonwhite families widened as all incomes grew: The gap went from $1,543 in 1947, to $1,576 in 1950, to $2,602 in 1960, and to $3,957 in 1970.[3]

The same mixed picture of prosperity is demonstrated through the use of the poverty index developed by the Social Security Administration (SSA) to measure the minimum income needed for purchasing a subsistence level of goods and services. In 1960, a nonfarm family of four required $3,022 to escape poverty as defined by SSA.

In that year, almost 40 million individuals were counted poor, 22.4 percent of the population. Ten years later, in 1970, the poverty index for a nonfarm family of four had risen to $3,968. The number of individuals counted poor had dropped to 25.4 million, 12.6 percent of the population. But again, there was a difference between the progress of whites and nonwhites. The 17.5 million whites counted poor in 1970 represented 10 percent of all whites in the population; the 8 million nonwhites counted poor represented 32 percent of all nonwhites. The poverty rate for blacks was more than three times that for whites.[4] Conditions were particularly harsh for those in the South and Southwest. Mexican Americans and Native Americans as well as African Americans experienced very high poverty rates and severe discrimination.

The increase in income was in part a result of the expansion of the labor force. The civilian labor force grew from 55.6 million in 1940 to 82.7 million in 1970. The expansion was due partially to population growth and partially to a longtime secular increase in labor force participation rates from 56 percent in 1940 to 61 percent of the population in 1970.[5] The trend was accelerated by World War II when there was a major infusion of women into the labor force. In 1940, 24 percent of all women of working age were in the labor force; by 1970, the figure had risen to more than 43 percent. In 1970, as in 1940, economic necessity made for a higher labor force participation rate among black women—49 percent as against 42 percent for white women—but the gap had closed appreciably.[6]

The strength of the economy was demonstrated by its ability to resist major recessions at the same time that it absorbed an ever-expanding labor force. In 1940, the unemployment rate stood at 14.6 percent. In 1943, with war production in full swing, the unemployment rate dipped as low as 1.2 percent. Unemployment averaged 4.5 percent during the 1950s, 5.7 percent between 1960 and 1965, and 3.8 percent between 1965 and 1970. The apparent strength of the economy at first obscured, but then increasingly made visible, the extent to which unemployment struck disproportionately at certain groups. In 1960, when white unemployment averaged 4.9 percent, the rate for nonwhites was 10.2 percent. For teenagers it stood at 14.7 percent. Structural imbalance persisted throughout the era. The rates averaged 4.5 percent and 8.2 percent for whites and nonwhites, respectively, in 1970.[7]

Satisfaction with the state of the economy, and with the social and economic choices it made possible, tended to suppress recognition of the factors that contributed to the decreases in poverty. An increase in wages and earnings was one factor, but income transfers in the form of veterans' benefits, unemployment insurance, social security, and to a lesser extent Aid to Dependent Children also played a part in the improved well-being of families. Even more important in the rapid exit out of poverty of male-headed families was the entrance of wives in such families into the labor force. For well over half of households in which the man was not earning enough for a living wage, the labor force participation of the wife and the availability of a second income became the route out of poverty.[8] There was even slower recognition of the discriminatory differential between male and female earnings. By the close of the 1960s, women's wages averaged only 59 percent of wages and salaries received by male workers.[9] And beyond reluctance to recognize the contribution to familial economic well-being attributable to increased labor participation by women was the slowness in coming to grips with the significance of their working. Their growing financial independence had implications for the development of new family forms, for changes in the roles of family members, and for new child care arrangements.

Population Shifts

The military and social eruptions of the 1940–1970 period were accompanied by enormous changes in population size and distribution. Total U.S. population grew from 132.1 million in 1940 to 204.8 million in 1970. Congressional action during the 1920s had slowed immigration to a trickle. In 1924, there were 707,000 immigrants and 77,000 emigrants, for a net inward flow of 630,000. Five years later, the restrictions drove immigration down to 280,000; there were 69,000 emigrants and a net growth in population of 210,000. By 1932, the Depression and legislation combined to slow immigration to less than 36,000; emigration was more than 103,000 for a loss of 68,000 people. The war and the U.S. refugee policy kept immigration low, and not until the Immigration Act of 1965 lowered the barriers did the number of new entrants rise significantly. Immigration in the decade from 1961–1970 reached 3,300,000 people.[10]

Immigration policy changed slowly during the postwar years, reflecting the general biases of the American electorate. During the depression years, immigration was low—in part because of the lack of job opportunities and in part because of the stricter enforcement of the "likely to become a public charge" (LPC) rule, which was used to reinforce defensive and nativist feelings. Emigration was large, primarily for economic reasons. Many returned to their home countries. In particular, many destitute Mexicans and Mexican Americans went back to Mexico where they had families and significant support networks.

After the forced deportation of Mexican Americans during the Great Depression, immigration from Mexico increased in response to the labor force demands of World War II. Increased demand for manual labor, particularly in the fields and on the railroads of the Southwest, meant a growth in the presence of Mexican immigrants. There were 80,000 immigrants in the 1940s, 275,000 in the 1950s, and more than 440,000 in the 1960s—a third of all legal immigrants. There is no agreement about the number of illegal entrants; estimates range widely—varying from 1 million to 8 million at any one time.[11]

When Franklin D. Roosevelt became president, he continued the restrictive immigration policies of the thirty years preceding him. No open door was extended to the refugees from Hitler's Germany. Despite the clear evidence that Roosevelt knew of the events in Germany and the desperate situation of its Jewish population, he did not intervene for their admission nor did he interfere with the antirefugee position of the State Department. To the contrary; Jewish refugees were systematically denied admission. The quotas that had been established for Germany and Italy were not increased. In fact, only 48 percent of the existing quota was used in 1941.[12] During the war years, an array of bureaucratic hurdles was used to prevent the admission of Jews into the country.[13]

*The attack on Pearl Harbor set off a wave of anti-Japanese fervor in
1941–42. By executive order, 120,000 Japanese Americans, many of them
American citizens, were ordered to leave their homes and businesses and sent to
internment camps.*

Photograph by Russell Lee. Library of Congress

That the country was still anti-Asian as well as anti-Semitic can be seen in the treatment of unnaturalized Germans and Italians in the United States as compared to Japanese aliens. Early in the war, 120,000 Japanese residents were removed from their homes on the West Coast to internment camps in the Western deserts and the swampland of Arkansas. A change in policy was put in place, however, for the Chinese. China was an ally. In 1943, Congress repealed the Chinese Exclusion Act of 1882 (and its subsequent additions and amendments), established a small, token quota for Chinese immigration, and made Chinese immigrants eligible for naturalization. Even more important to the Chinese community, the War Brides Act of

1946 expedited the entry of Chinese wives and children of members of the armed forces. During the period from 1945 to 1952, 11,000 Chinese people emigrated to the United States, 10,000 of whom—91 percent—were nonquota wives.

The 1946 War Brides Act eased the entry of wives, husbands, and children of servicemen and women. For this group, it waived visa requirements, ignored racial and ethnic restraints, and eliminated prohibitions based on physical and mental handicaps. It was the beginning of a shift in policy from an emphasis on national origins to an emphasis on family affiliation.

Refugee policy changed as well. After World War II, the gates began to open for European refugees. The first Displaced Persons Act was passed in 1948. It admitted victims of fascism and also many who were fleeing communist regimes.

The shift was slow and incomplete. In 1952, as part of the severe anticommunist spirit of the period, strict anticommunist screening and deportation were introduced. The same act did, however, eliminate all exclusion of entrants on the basis of race or ethnicity. In addition, it laid the basis for emergency, nonquota, admission of those fleeing communism or experiencing emergency hardship. Future legislation allowed for refugees from many parts of the world, including Hungary, Cuba, Tibet, and Vietnam. Not incidentally, the flow of new refugees meant new social welfare needs that, increasingly, were met by voluntary agencies.

The 1965 Immigration Act (Hart–Celler Act) formalized the new criteria for entry into the United States. Race, national origin, and ancestry quotas were replaced by admission standards of family relationship, occupation, and skill. The new preference system exempted spouses and minor children of U.S. citizens from all quotas and gave spouses and children of resident aliens high priority. Married children and siblings also received preferential treatment. Thus, once immigration was opened to Latin Americans and Asians, their numbers increased rapidly.

But most of the population expansion from 1940 to 1970 was due to changes in birth and death rates. By the middle of the 1930s, decisions to delay marriage and childbearing had lowered the birthrate to about 17 per 1,000 persons in the population. As the Depression ended at the beginning of World War II and as young people faced the initial prospect of separation, the birthrate briefly increased—and then fell again. Immediately after the war, however, the birthrate soared, reaching a high of 26.6 per 1,000 persons in 1947 and remaining high until the mid-1960s.[14]

The increased birthrate was accompanied by an increase in life expectancy and a decline in the death rate. In 1940, the estimated average length of life in the United States was 62.9 years. Thirty years later, it stood at 70.8 years. During this same period, the estimated average life expectancy among nonwhites rose from 82.7 percent to 90 percent of estimated average life expectancy among whites. Simultaneously, death rates declined for the total population from 10.8 per 1,000 individuals in the population in 1940 to 9.4 in 1970. Most significantly, the death rate among nonwhites declined from 13.8 in 1940 to approximate the national average at 9.5 in 1970.[15] Native Americans also shared in the general decline in mortality rates and rise in life expectancy. But despite improvements in infant and maternal death rates and from some infectious diseases, Native Americans continued to have the lowest life expectancy of any ethnic group in the United States.[16]

The changes in life expectancy reflected better nutrition as incomes rose and sulfa and penicillin and new medical and surgical procedures became widely available. The visibility of actual and potential results from improved medical and health care sustained an increased vigorous concern for further progress. The demand, too, was for assured availability of care to the general public.

Changing birth and death rates produced changing demographic patterns. Over the years, the country's population grew both younger and older. The percentage of those under 19 years grew from 34.2 percent of the total population in 1940 to 37.9 percent of the population in 1970. The percentage of the population over 65 years grew from 6.8 percent to 10.2 percent in the same time. Clearly, a declining percentage of "productive" individuals was being called upon to support a growing percentage of the "nonproductive." Added to this was the nonproductivity of groups who wanted jobs but could not find them. In this regard, the effect of racial discrimination upon employment opportunities for blacks intensified as the percentage of blacks in the total population grew.[17]

Population growth was accompanied by population shifts and dislocations. World War II accelerated the historical process of industrialization and mechanization. The wartime necessity for spreading industry, shipping, and the training of service personnel across the country to engage in a war being fought on two fronts reinforced the continuous westward movement of the center of population. Rapid development of the Pacific states ensued. Equally important was the movement of the population from rural to urban areas. The pull of jobs in urban centers and the push of technical advances making small marginal farms obsolete and therefore unprofitable impelled the move of 20 million people from rural to urban areas between 1940 and 1970. Of the total, about 16 million were white and about 4 million were black.[18] By 1950, 64 percent of the country's total population lived in urban areas—64 percent of the white population and 62 percent of the nonwhite population—and the rest lived in rural areas. By 1970, 72 percent of the white population and 81 percent of the nonwhite population lived in urban areas.[19]

Yet, the long movement of Americans to metropolitan areas took a decisive turn during the 1940s and 1950s. Many central cities, like Philadelphia and St. Loius, attained their highest population during the early 1950s and began a steady decline. Between World War II and 1970, the United States became a suburban nation. In 1940, two out of three metropolitan residents lived in a central city. By 1960, three in five lived in a suburb. Yet, the growth of suburbs was sharply defined by race. As suburbs grew, their population was overwhelmingly white. Blacks, migrating from the South, moved into the older city neighborhoods. By 1960s, cities with large black populations surrounded by white suburbs were common throughout the nation.

In the search for factory employment, large numbers of blacks had left the South. The percentage of the black population residing in the South dropped from 77 percent in 1940 to 52 percent in 1970. Despite a continuous migration to

Northeastern and North Central states, however, a heavy concentration of blacks continued to live in the South.

Perhaps of more importance than place of residence was the fact of black urbanization itself, a response to changes in agriculture. For the country as a whole, the relative share of employment in agriculture fell from 15 percent of the civilian labor force in 1940 to 4 percent in 1970.[20] At the same time, mechanization increased the real value of farm output by $6.4 billion between those same years.[21] Technological developments—increased mechanization that had led to increased productivity—had necessitated the development of larger farms to ensure adequate monetary returns. Average farm size increased from 167 acres in 1940 to 373 acres in 1970. The size of farms owned by whites more than doubled; but the size of farms owned by blacks grew only 20 percent.[22] Since average black-owned and -operated farm holdings had historically been small and only marginally profitable, black families and farm workers suffered disproportionate dislocation. Black migration was inherent in the changed economic situation.

The black migration of the early 1940s was caught up and hidden in the general necessity for wartime mobility. More than 16 million men were transported for military reasons; women, wives, and families followed. An additional 16 million men and women moved for job-related reasons. The general wartime atmosphere was characterized by migration and mobility. Family life and the family unit were severely challenged. Between 1940 and 1946, the number of divorces increased from 264,000 to 610,000 annually.[23] The divorce rate had shot from 2.0 to 4.3 per 1,000 of population. Between 1940 and 1950, the number of illegitimate births per 1,000 unmarried women, 15 to 44 years of age, increased from 3.6 to 6.1 for white women and from 35.6 to 71.2 for nonwhite women.[24] Many high school students left school to take jobs, so that as early as September 1942, the National Child Labor Committee reported that of the 4 million juveniles who had been employed in industry and agriculture during the preceding summer months, 3 million were still employed as the new school term began. About 75,000 were under age 16.[25] During the midst of the war, J. Edgar Hoover, head of the Federal Bureau of Investigation, reported "an alarming" increase in juvenile delinquency.[26]

The postwar years aggravated, even institutionalized, the trend toward mobility and its concomitant social risks. The creation of a "mobile attitude," with its seeming homogenization of values, was sustained by the increased ease of transportation and communication. Moving was no longer unusual or frightening in a world made familiar by commercial civilian flying and by television. And as automobile ownership mushroomed and discontent with city dwelling surfaced, suburbanization followed upon urbanization. As families moved from their home base, they moved too from the support and help of relatives and longtime friends.

Technology, Productivity, and Economic Insecurity

The key to postwar affluence, consumerism, and leisure was increased output per man-hour. A continuous development of new materials, new products, and new industries called forth an evolution of new processes involving greater efficiency in harnessing the uses of energy. The building of specialized, labor-saving machinery, the increasing attention to standardization and use of interchangeable machinery parts, and the extension of mass production techniques further increased productivity. These new processes were enhanced by the development of computer technology, advanced information systems, and systems engineering. World War II had given a big boost to the chemical and airplane industries, to the development and exploitation of synthetics such as nylon and metals such as aluminum, and to the expansion of the importance of electricity. The postwar period saw the continuation of the preeminence of the automobile industry but saw, too, the emergence of major new industries—television, space technology, commercial aviation, and others. Industrial and technological advances were reflected in worker productivity and work hours. Between 1950 and 1970, the real GNP per capita rose 50 percent while average annual working hours per worker dropped 8.5 percent.[27]

The impact of industrial and technological change on worker output was reflected not only in a reduction in average work hours but also in the occupational distribution of employees. After 1950, the proportion of employment in manufacturing began to decline, falling to 25 percent by 1970.

At the same time, growing wealth and increasing societal complexity led to rapid expansion in service industries—health, recreation, and so on—and in government. By 1970, employment in services had risen to 17 percent and in government to 18 percent of the total employment picture.[28]

The postwar era also included a public acceptance of the expansion of governmental activities into new areas of public life. The Employment Act of 1946 had set "maximum employment, production and purchasing power" as goals of governmental policy. The act's creation of the Council of Economic Advisors led to the conscious use of fiscal and monetary policy and of the federal budget as tools to control employment, production, and price levels—that is, to plan economic stability. In a related area, there was continued and growing acceptance of the responsibility of government for the income security of those with lifetime attachments to the labor force. The government's program of Old Age and Survivors Insurance was expanded first to disability and then to health insurance for the aged; with little opposition, payroll taxes were increased from 2 percent of the first $3,000 of income in 1940 to 9.6 percent of $7,800 in 1970. The popularity of Social Security showed little sign of abating.

Public attitudes did not change appreciably toward the acceptance of an expanded governmental role in regard to direct relief for the nonworking poor. Categorical public assistance programs had been included in the Social Security Act and were accepted as temporary programs. To the extent that minor program expansions did not challenge the belief that the need for relief would "wither away," little opposition appeared. When, however, it became clear that the public assistance programs—particularly Aid to Dependent Children (ADC)—were expanding, not withering away, resistance developed. The discovery that poverty in America included a substantial group of working poor at the same time that ADC was becoming identified as a "black program" almost guaranteed hostility and opposition. Beyond that, however, was the vigor of renewed confidence in the work ethic and in economic growth as a way out of poverty.

The Depression had shaken the confidence of Americans in the ability of society to control economic fluctuations. It introduced fears of a permanent "mature" economy that would stagnate. The events of World War II and the postwar period seemed to most Americans to demonstrate the ability of government to develop control mechanisms to moderate the ups and downs of business cycles and the continued vigor of the economy. A renewed faith in the productive process took hold. The final reality was that organized labor, that segment of society that might have been expected to become allied with the poor, had itself become part of the establishment. Beginning with the New Deal, government had legalized almost all of labor's demands: the right to organize and bargain collectively, workmen's compensation, minimum wages, old age insurance and unemployment insurance, limitations on hours, and the prohibition of injunctions. Through the process of collective bargaining, labor had not only been able to raise and even control its wage position relative to prices, but it had also been able to have a whole series of fringe benefits instituted comprising a private health and welfare security system. Membership in unions rose to 20 million by 1970.[29] Organized labor increasingly identified itself with the status quo and separated itself from the poor.

World War II

The most dramatic changes of the thirty-year period from 1940 to 1970 occurred during World War II. The upheaval of war brought full employment and rising incomes. For oppressed groups, particularly blacks and women, the period offered increased opportunity for economic, educational, and social equality and laid the groundwork for the civil rights and feminist movements of the 1950s and 1960s.

Indicators of change between 1940 and 1945 abound. The GNP, for example, rose from $99.7 billion in 1940 to $211.9 billion in 1945; and although this was a period of rapidly advancing prices, GNP rose 56 percent in "real" terms—that is, in constant dollars.[30] Furthermore, full employment and progressive taxation brought about basic changes in income distribution—changes that the New Deal had hoped, but failed, to achieve.

In 1940, the total noninstitutional population of the United States was 100.4 million. Of this total, 56 million were in the labor force, including 540,000 in the armed services. Civilian employment stood at 47.5 million. By 1945, the population had risen to 105.5 million. The total labor force had increased to 65.3 million, including the 11 million men and women in the armed forces. This increase in the number of armed forces personnel took these people out of the civilian work force. Nevertheless, total civilian employment rose by 5 million, or 11.1 percent. The increase was made possible by the sharp decline in unemployment and the expansion of the labor force as women, retirees, and children went to work. By 1945, civilian employment had reached 52.8 million. Between 1940 and 1945, unemployment declined from 8 million to 1 million.

Whereas income redistribution during the 1930s had benefited middle income groups, redistribution during the World War II period favored the lowest income groups. Real income rose for families in all income ranges between 1941 and 1947, but it rose proportionately more for poor families than for rich ones. The average increase in real income of families in the lowest fifth of family income rankings was 41.6 percent; the average increase for families in the highest fifth was 18.3 percent.[31]

In spite of continued economic growth, poverty remained a common feature of American life. A third of Americans still lived on incomes below minimum adequacy in 1949. Even among workers employed full-time for the full year, poverty was common. In 1949, more than 20 percent of workers who were fully employed still did not earn enough to pull their families out of poverty. Still, the expansion of the economy during and after World War II did equalize incomes. Between 1941 and 1947, the share of income that went to the richest 5 percent of households fell from 23 to 17 percent.[32] Within these limits, therefore, democratization of income had occurred. A combination of factors—decrease in unemployment, an increase in the number of multiearner families, the opening up of job opportunities for minority groups, and the expansion of government welfare benefits—was responsible. Of major consequence for income redistribution was the influx of women into the labor force and the shift of blacks from farm to higher paying factory jobs.

Rising incomes combined with restrictions on the availability of civilian goods increased personal savings. During the worst of the Depression in 1933, savings were negative; almost $1 billion of dissaving occurred. In 1940, personal savings totaled $3.8 billion. It climbed throughout the war, reaching a peak of $37.3 billion in 1944.[33] Thus during the war years a huge backlog of savings developed—about 24 percent of annual disposable income, as compared to 3.4 percent of disposable income in prewar years and 6 to 7 percent in postwar years.

The wartime redistribution of jobs and income was not achieved easily. Tremendous resistance to the employment of blacks in defense industries was encountered, and race riots occurred in 1940 and 1941. A march on Washington, D.C., by 50,000 to 100,000 blacks to highlight the demand for jobs was threatened by A. Philip Randolph, president of the Brotherhood of Sleeping Car Porters. The march, planned for July 1941, was canceled when the March on Washington Movement, under Randolph's leadership, was able to negotiate the establishment of the Fair Employment Practices Committee (FEPC).

FEPC was established by Executive Order 8802 on June 25, 1941, and promised "no discrimination in the employment of workers in defense industries or Government because of race, creed, color, or national origin . . . [and] the full and equitable participation of all workers in defense industries, without discrimination."[34] Widespread defiance of the committee's recommendations, the lack of power to punish offenders, and reluctance to have war contracts and the manufacturing of war equipment canceled rendered FEPC ineffectual.

The response of the black community to the failure of FEPC was strong and immediate, as several factors came together. First, of course, was the fact that blacks had been migrating to urban industrial centers, where their congregating under conditions of segregation lent strength for joint action. Second, a significant number of blacks had been educationally prepared and were ready for greater participation in the work opportunities opened up by the war. Experience on WPA projects, vocational training received by way of the National Youth Administration's vocational

Racial segregation in education, employment—even drinking fountains—was part of everyday life in the South before the 1950s. Halifax, North Carolina

Photo by John Vachon. Library of Congress

work program, defense training financed through programs sponsored by the U.S. Office of Education, all pointed up a source of untapped and underutilized labor. The training was in itself a promise of opportunity that remained unfulfilled, joining other promises to a string of disappointments. The National Defense Advisory Committee's statement against discriminatory hiring practices in defense plants and President Roosevelt's inclusion of a similar statement in a message to Congress, both in 1940, failed to change the situation. The efforts of the Office of Production Management's Negro Employment and Training Branch to facilitate the hiring of blacks in defense industries were unsuccessful. Finally, the ineffectiveness of FEPC was demonstrated when its scheduled public hearings into discrimination on railroads were canceled by the War Manpower Commission despite widespread support by the black press and civil rights leaders. This particular affront loosened the cap that Executive Order 8802 had placed on a well of discontent.

To white Americans, the civil rights movement seemed to appear from nowhere, but it was based on years of institutional and intellectual effort by blacks and whites who were committed to equality and justice. Within the black community, the commitment to pursuing integration by legal and political means grew out of organizations like the NAACP Legal Defense Fund that systematically attacked the constitutional basis of segregation. In addition, African American churches, which for decades had accepted segregation, became central institutions for organizing the black community. Churches and labor unions were among the few places in the United States where black and white Americans could come together as equals. Randolph's Brotherhood of Sleeping Car Porters worked with other unions to put pressure on politicians to support change and to spread methods to mobilize resistance to segregation. In addition, there was the evolution of an influential African American press—Baltimore's Afro-American, Harlem's Amsterdam Star News, the Chicago Defender, the Houston Informer, and so on—which pushed editorially for black rights and simultaneously encouraged blacks to make their own demands.

Discrimination and resistance to discrimination in defense employment and in the armed forces resulted in a series of racial clashes in Newark, New Jersey; Philadelphia, Pennsylvania; Centreville, Mississippi; and Mobile, Alabama. A particularly severe outbreak in Detroit left 35 dead, 700 wounded, and 1,300 under arrest. Riots occurred in Texas, Massachusetts, New York, and California. In the latter instance, the rioters were largely Mexican Americans.

The growing militancy of minority groups resulted in the creation of a second FEPC in May 1943, and greater headway against discriminatory employment practices was achieved. By 1943, black workers held 1 million factory jobs, though largely as unskilled laborers. Black union membership had increased to 500,000. The number of blacks in government rose from 50,000 in 1939 to 200,000 in 1944. Resistance to the induction of blacks under the provisions of the Selective Service Act of 1940 yielded, so that by the end of the war, about 1 million black men and women had served in the armed forces—a remarkable achievement considering that only about 2,000 were drafted during the first year of the act's operation. The war had brought about gains for blacks as a response to economic pressures and to the successful mobilization of protest.[35]

Other people of color benefited as well. The military draft reduced the supply of workers while the production needs of the war increased the demand for factory labor. Employment opportunities for minority groups expanded. In addition to women and young adults, African Americans, Native Americans, Mexicans and Mexican Americans, and Puerto Ricans found new opportunities in the busy factories.

During World War II, nearly half a million Native Americans left reservations to work in war industries, and about 25,000 served in the armed forces. When they returned as veterans, they were entitled to job preferences, housing, and the GI Bill for education. They became part of the leadership of the Native American protest movement of the 1960s and 1970s.[36]

Wartime Economic and Social Advances

As incomes rose during World War II, the nation's health improved as well. Concern about physical and mental health developed as armed services induction procedures revealed serious deficiencies; the inability of large numbers of young people to meet induction standards caused a startling rejection rate. A shift toward improved health conditions occurred for the civilian and noncivilian populations. Routine health care, including dental care, was provided for servicemen and their families. In 1943, Congress appropriated special funds for the Emergency Maternity and Infant Care Program. This program, which was administered by the Children's Bureau through state health departments, provided regular health care for the wives and children of servicemen in the lower pay grades of the armed services. More than 1.2 million women and 230,000 infants were given care during the war years.[37] For servicemen themselves, the armed services offered both corrective and preventive care through regular physical and dental examinations and emergency clinic care for minor illnesses. Beyond that, "military medicine" fostered improvements in standards of physical fitness through balanced diets, better clothing, and "more and better hospitals completely staffed."[38]

Rising incomes made for better, healthier living conditions for the civilian population. In addition, rising incomes made it possible for the civilian population to take advantage of the discovery and development of new drugs and new medical and surgical procedures. Attention to health needs and health care as matters of daily living was demonstrated in new practices such as the stepping up of various inoculation programs. Increased labor participation by women led to improved safety conditions in factories. The National Mental Health Act of 1946 provided new funding for research and training programs, as well as the establishment of community mental health services. In 1948, President Harry Truman proposed a national health insurance scheme. The National Mental Health Act was not funded until 1948; the proposal for national health insurance was defeated after a gigantic attack by the American Medical Association. Delays aside, however, events of the future had begun to take shape.

The passage of the Emergency Maternal and Infant Care Act serves to point out the extent to which wartime improvements in economic and social well-being flowed from exigencies of the war rather than from social welfare concerns per se. At the beginning of the war, even as large-scale unemployment continued, pressure began to mount for phasing out the many New Deal social welfare programs. During the war, very little explicit social legislation was passed. The Civilian Conservation Corps was abolished in 1941, and WPA in 1943. Expenditures for work relief declined from $1.9 billion in 1940 to less than $5 million by the end of the war.[39] The National Youth Administration survived as a mechanism for administering vocational training for recruits to war industries.

The social legislation of the time was related primarily to the needs of communities disrupted by army camps and war plants and to the needs of families dislocated by the absence of husbands and fathers as they left for the armed forces or for war industries and by the absence of mothers as women took jobs. Housing, day care, education, health, recreation, and transportation needs as they affected "home front" preparations became the focus of concern.

In November 1940, President Roosevelt named the administrator of the Federal Security Agency as coordinator of the Office of Health, Welfare, and Related Defense Activities with special responsibility for providing service in defense communities and communities near training camps. In May 1941, the Office of Civilian Defense was created in the Office of War Management for the purpose of integrating the provision of health, welfare, and recreation services with other defense activities. The two departments underwent considerable reorganization as experience demonstrated conflicting areas of jurisdiction and the need for clarifying their relationships with a variety of national and local public and voluntary social welfare organizations. By 1943, the government had organized the Office of Community War Services under the Federal Security Agency to take responsibility for coordinating state and local efforts to provide health, welfare, recreation, family, and community services for members of the armed forces and for the civilian population. The Community Facilities Act of 1941 (Lanham Act) provided federal funds for the construction of houses, schools, day care centers, hospitals, water and sanitation plants, and recreational facilities.

Lanham Act funds helped many communities, but many others suffered upheaval without federal funds to ease the problems of population movement. Local community chests and councils of social agencies took on some of the planning and financing of social services early in the war. Six major voluntary agencies* combined efforts through the United Service Organization for National Defense (USO) to provide services for military personnel, war workers, and transients. More than 1,000 USO centers were established.

Fundraising efforts in the voluntary sector were united by the National War Fund, which combined and regulated the money-raising campaigns of community chest funds with those of the war relief agencies so that traditional social services of local agencies could be financed. Overall control of the whole effort was exercised by the federal government through the War Relief Control Board, which licensed agencies and held authority over all secular wartime charities, except for the Red Cross.[40]

Wartime measures for education, like those for health, had implications for future developments. Army examinations had revealed an illiteracy rate of one in five among recruits. At the start of the war, the army asked the WPA to set up programs of adult and worker education and the National Youth Administration (NYA), a student vocational work program. Their activities were phased out or reduced as the army itself took on some of their tasks and after the U.S. Office of Education was expanded. Perhaps most important in the long run is the fact that federal aid was made available for elementary and secondary education in "impacted areas" and for agricultural extension services in rural areas. Education on the college level was also fostered as the federal government let out enormous contracts for research in engineering, science, and civil aeronautics, for education in defense industry management, and for Reserve Officers Training Corps (ROTC).

Veterans and the GI Bill

Over 16 million Americans participated in the war. Over 400,000 of them died and another 671,000 were wounded. The income needs of the dependents of members of the armed forces were met through a program of family allotments financed jointly

*YMCA, YWCA, National Catholic Community Service, Jewish Welfare Board, Salvation Army, and National Travelers Aid Society.

by the individual soldier, through a pay deduction, and by the federal government. The allowances were provided for by the Servicemen's Dependents Allowance Act of 1942[41] and were administered by the Office of Dependency Benefits of the War Department. During its first year of operation, ending June 30, 1943, a total of $797 million was disbursed, of which the government had contributed 50 percent. By 1945, allotment payments totaled $3 billion, with the government's contribution rising to $2 billion.[42]

All wives and children of soldiers in the six lowest pay grades of the armed forces qualified for family allotments regardless of income. In addition, soldiers received life and disability insurance as part of the National Life Insurance Act of 1940.[43]

Benefits for veterans of World War II included those available to veterans of previous wars. In the past, concern had been primarily with income security for dependents of the dead and disabled and with the vocational rehabilitation of the latter. There had long been dissatisfaction with the fact that "veterans without service-connected disabilities were left to their own devices in the matter of their readjustment to civilian life."[44] A first approach to help with readjustment problems was contained in the Selective Training and Service Act of 1940, which provided that inductees "be reemployed at the termination of their period of service in positions of like seniority, status and pay."[45] On November 13, 1942, President Roosevelt appointed the Armed Forces Committee on Postwar Education Opportunities for Service Personnel to study the educational problems that servicemen and servicewomen might encounter after the war. The president's appointment followed upon the urging of the resolution, adopted earlier in 1942, by the American Legion at its annual convention. The Servicemen's Readjustment Act of 1944[46]—the famous GI Bill of Rights—was largely the product of the American Legion.

The GI Bill was described by the Senate Finance Committee as "a fundamental bill of rights to facilitate the return of service men and women to civilian life."

> It is a comprehensive statement of the measures presently necessary and . . . represents the very least that should be done at this time in justice to veterans and in enlightened self-interest for the remainder of the country.[47]

The GI Bill represented the triumph of the "rehabilitation idea," that is, of "the idea that the country owes an obligation to the veteran to restore him to the civilian status and opportunities he would have enjoyed had there not been a war."[48] Restoration to civilian status was to be facilitated through provisions for education and training; loans for the purchase of a home, business, or farm; unemployment insurance payments; and veterans' employment services.

A number of factors converged to aid the passage of the GI Bill. There was, of course, very real concern for the welfare of veterans, especially as they returned to an uncertain economy in the midst of reconversion to peacetime operation. Involved, too, was a recognition of the educational and financial deficit suffered by men and women who had to delay customary educational and job pursuits for wartime service. Added to this, there was a concern over the stability of political and economic institutions, should large numbers of veterans be unable to find jobs. Pervading all was the fear of a postwar depression and the memory of the unemployment of the prewar period. The discharge of millions of veterans into the labor force at a time when war production had ended and thousands of workers were already looking for jobs was seen as a major problem. Thus, the GI Bill was designed to delay and ease entrance to the labor market. Actual federal government expenditures for veterans' services and benefits rose to about $3.4 billion for fiscal year 1946. They reached a peak of $9.3 billion, 23 percent of total federal expenditures, in 1950.[49]

Postwar Optimism

For a number of reasons, a widely expected postwar recession did not occur. The liberal monetary and educational provisions of the GI Bill and the beginning contribution of the provisions of the Social Security Act to economic stability were two cushioning factors. Even more important was the enormous backlog of demand for major consumer goods that had been unavailable during the war—new housing and automobiles, for example. The postwar spurt in marriages and births added to market demand for goods. The combination of needs and wartime savings stimulated the expansion of older industries and the development of such new products as television. The Depression-born fear of a "mature," "stagnating" economy was replaced with a new faith in the vigor of the economic system.

With concern about a return to economic recession and unemployment allayed, the United States entered a period of social complacency. Many in the country seemed pleased with continuing economic growth and intrigued with the promise of automation, of a cybernetic revolution that would provide affluence for all.

The desire for a return to "normalcy" often ran headlong into new realities. The war had given a boost to women's entry into the labor force—a trend that had begun during the Depression. Although many women were forced out of good-paying factory jobs to "make room" for returning GIs, working wives became a permanent part of the social landscape. Between 1940 and 1950, the share of all households that had a working wife increased from 7 to 13 percent.

However, despite this postwar air of social optimism, economic laissez-faire, and political conservatism, some new welfare programs were legislated: the National School Lunch Program in 1946; the Housing Act of 1949; the special Milk Program in 1954; the Indian Health Service in 1955; and finally, in 1960, the Kerr–Mills Act, which provided aid to the medically indigent. On a judicial level, at the height of the McCarthy period, a major decision on civil rights was handed down. In 1954, in Brown v. Board of Education,[50] the Supreme Court decided unanimously that in public school education, separate facilities for racial groups were "inherently unequal."

Public welfare had expanded early in the decade through incremental legislative changes that increased the number of potential program recipients and through benefit formula changes that liberalized payments. In 1956, disability insurance was added to the social security programs; a new category of public assistance—Aid to the Physically and Totally Disabled—was instituted; federal aid for medical expenses incurred by families receiving welfare was begun; and, in the ADC program, a caretaker provision was introduced whereby there was, for the first time, federal money to support the parent of a dependent child. Later in the decade, new groups were offered social insurance coverage and public assistance payments were raised as the federal government increased its contribution and attempted to equalize the payment efforts of poor and wealthy states. In 1956, federal funding for social services was added to ADC, and child welfare services were extended in 1958 from rural to urban areas.

For Native Americans, however, the postwar period was very difficult. In 1949, Congress began to shift Native American programs from the federal government to state governments and to back away from the federal protections of the 1934 Reorganization Act. By 1960, several dozen tribes were no longer protected by federal guardianship. While giving Native Americans equal rights with other citizens, the termination of protected status and the return of control to the states meant loss of social programs and aid as well as new taxes and sharp increases in unemployment. For some tribes, it was a disaster. In 1961, President Kennedy ended the termination policy, but not before it became a rallying point for Native American militancy.[51]

During the late 1940s and 1950s, employer-provided 'fringe benefits' became a central element of the American system of social welfare. Three trends converged to produce this shift. First, beginning with the Revenue Act of 1942, the Federal government began to encourage corporations to expand pensions and health coverage through the granting of generous tax incentives. In 1948, the Supreme Court ruled (Inland Steel v NLRB) that unions had the right to negotiate over benefits as well as wages. Finally, the significant organizing setbacks for labor unions after the War, especially "Operation Dixie"—a failed attempt to expand unionization in the South— convinced many unions that it was wiser to expand employer-based systems for health care and pensions than to count on the expansion of the Social Security system.

At the same time, the successes of Social Security had a decisive impact on the politics of social welfare. Historically, many of the 'deserving poor' had had to rely on public assistance. By the middle of the 1950s, however, the unemployed, older Americans, and people with disabilities, and widows and their children could all count on social insurance programs to protect them against poverty. Although the assistance programs for the elderly and people with disabilities were still important, the public assistance population was increasingly composed of groups that were considered undeserving. As widows qualified for survivors' benefits, Aid to Dependent Children recipients were more likely to live in families headed by a divorced or never-married woman. The departure of the unemployed from assistance programs meant that general assistance recipients were increasingly likely to have spotty work histories. Where in the 1930s, the various elements of the Social Security Act were supported by the same constituencies, by the 1950s, its social insurance and assistance programs for the elderly and people with disabilities had remained broadly popular while ADC could count on a much narrower constituency for political support.

Other social policies exacerbated the difference between well-off working families and the poor. The Housing Act of 1949 provided long-term mortgages for new, suburban construction while making it more difficult to gain financing for the purchase of homes in older urban neighborhoods. Rather, the Act provided two 'solutions' for declining cities: slum clearance that would eventually displace thousands of families and the expansion of public housing which concentrated the poorest urban residents in a few, high-rise projects. During the 1950s, Congress provided new funding for highway construction (but not for mass transit) fueling the abandonment of old urban neighborhoods by better-off workers.

All of these trends—the shift to employer-provided benefits, the split between social insurance and public assistance, and rapid suburbanization—included a racial dimension. African Americans had been concentrated in industries that were excluded from Social Security in the 1930s. Although this exclusion was eliminated, black workers were more likely than whites to work in jobs without unions or fringe benefits after the War. The plague of chronic joblessness meant that black workers and their families were less likely to qualify for social insurance than public assistance. By the end of the 1950s, politicians and the public increasingly saw black women and children as the primary beneficiaries of ADC. Finally, the move to the suburbs was almost wholly a white phenomenon. Black families—whatever their economic status—were largely confined to deteriorating urban neighborhoods. Even those African Americans who could purchase homes rarely could count on the appreciation of their value to the extent that whites could.

Although often pictured as a quiet decade of affluence and stability, the character of social welfare and its influence on American society had been transformed between 1950 and 1960. By the end of the decade, relatively affluent white suburban workers could count on tax-subsidized, employer-provided fringe benefits and Social Security to provide expanding protection against the risks of an industrial society. Black and Hispanic workers and families increasingly found themselves living in declining urban neighborhoods, threatened by 'slum clearance' or herded into public housing projects and dependent upon public assistance programs. As a result, the late 1950s saw increasingly virulent attacks on public welfare.

The Attack on Public Welfare

At the end of World War II, the elderly were the primary recipients of public assistance in the United States. Then, in 1950, a new public assistance program for the permanently and temporarily disabled was added to the Social Security Act. In addition, Congress added payments for the caretakers of dependent children under the ADC program.

Yet, the steady expansion of public assistance soon met with a backlash. The increased eligibility of the elderly for old age insurance led to a steady decline in recipients of old age assistance. In addition, recipients of ADC began to shift from the families of widows to those of unmarried mothers.

During the 1950s and early 1960s, "welfare reform" focused on restricting the eligibility of recipients.[52] State discretion was signaled by the Eisenhower administration's shift away from federal government centralization of authority and the reemergence of states' rights and local control. In state after state, punitive administrative policies were used to remove recipients from the welfare rolls and to deter new applications. State residency requirements were strictly enforced, so that black migrants who moved from the South to Northern cities, for example, were successfully prevented from receiving assistance. Drives to publicize the names of welfare recipients were widespread. As a way of weeding out suspected "frauds," entire caseloads were closed and all recipients required to undergo new application investigations. Beyond the overt intention of weeding out ineligible recipients was the covert hope that attrition would result from the unwillingness of many individuals to experience new eligibility investigations set up to deter them.

In a number of states, "suitable home" and "man-in-the-house" policies became bases for determining that the presence of an unrelated man made a home unsuitable for children. The presence of a man, even though unrelated, also was considered evidence that financial need did not exist. In the summer of 1960, the state of Louisiana was found to have used the "suitable home" pretext for closing 6,281 cases, involving 23,549 children. The practice was halted in 1961, when Secretary of Health, Education, and Welfare Arthur Fleming ruled that cases could no longer be closed as a result of unsuitable home findings, unless other suitable living arrangements had been made for the children.[53] Midnight raids to uncover men living with ADC mothers continued well into the 1960s, when they were effectively halted by the March 27, 1967, decision of the Supreme Court of California, which declared that public assistance workers could not be fired for refusing to participate in an unconstitutional invasion of privacy.[54]*

The most notorious example of attempts to reduce the welfare rolls—the effort that became symbolic of all—occurred at Newburgh, New York, during 1961. In that year, the Newburgh city manager promulgated a thirteen-point code of welfare regulations that included in one package many of the devices being used across the country to control the size of the welfare rolls and to reduce welfare expenditures. For example, applicants new to Newburgh were to give evidence of having come to the city with a concrete offer of employment; assistance was to be denied to applicants who had left a job voluntarily; all new cases were to be reviewed in the city manager's office prior to certification; active cases were to be reviewed monthly by the city's corporation counsel; work was to be mandated for all able-bodied males receiving money payments; and voucher payments were to be substituted for cash. State welfare officials in New York feared that Newburgh's behavior could threaten federal funding for the entire state system of welfare benefits. As a result, they successfully pressured the town's welfare administrators to ignore the city manager's directive.

The various attacks on public assistance programs highlighted a slowly changing perception of the adult recipient of public assistance. The image of that recipient was changing from the worthy, responsible aged or widowed beneficiary to the unworthy, unpopular, young, able-bodied, unemployed female or male. Most significantly, attention was focused on urban ADC mothers who were perceived as women who had children out of wedlock as a way of avoiding work and as blacks, despite the fact that residency requirements had effectively prevented black migrants from swelling the expanding rolls. During the 1950s, at least, increased expenditures for public

*Man-in-the-house rules and durational residence requirements were finally eliminated by *King* v. *King*, 392 U.S. 309 (1968), and by *Shapiro* v. *Thompson*, 364 U.S. 618 (1969), respectively.

welfare resulted from normal population growth, from expanded programs, and from liberalized benefits. Be that as it may, the new image of the welfare recipient meant that the base of public support for public welfare had eroded.

Poverty and the Reform of Welfare

By the 1960s, some of the optimism of the postwar era began to fade. A series of recessions started in 1948: 1948–1949, 1953–1954, 1957–1958, and 1961–1963. A renewed and growing concern with unemployment developed when unemployment rates approached 7 percent in 1958 and again in 1961. After each recession, the economy bounced back, but with less than full vigor. Indeed, each period of recovery was less energetic than that which preceded it; and definitions of full employment moved from the 2 percent of the 1940s to where some considered 4 percent as unrealistically low.

Despite this, the general view of the 1950s as the era of the affluent society held. What had changed was the view of poverty and of the poor. Kenneth Galbraith, writing in 1958, implied that poverty was spotty and scattered, not systemic. He identified two types of poverty: "insular" and "case." "Insular" poverty covered problems that arose from structural unemployment and differential unemployment rates—the special problems of the Appalachian region, for example. "Case" poverty denoted poverty arising from a personal deficiency, such as ill health, lack of education, or even racial or sexual discrimination.[55] Whether "insular" or "case" in nature, the problem was considered one of employability rather than of poverty per se. In fact, the United States rediscovered poverty as a serious social problem only in the early 1960s, when a series of studies and publications made reality unavoidable. The Social Security Administration, using 1959 data, established a poverty index and, for the first time, provided an official statistical measure of individuals and groups in poverty. Increased attention came with the publication of Michael Harrington's *The Other America: Poverty in the United States* in 1962 and Dwight MacDonald's "Our Invisible Poor" in 1963.[56] The 1964 *Annual Report* of the Council of Economic Advisors dealt with the situation at length and was transmitted to the Congress along with the *Economic Report of the President*.[57]

Slowly the response to poverty emerged, shaped by three factors: (1) the identification of depressed geographical areas, (2) the civil rights revolutions, and (3) the shift in the composition of public assistance rolls that began early in the 1960s. Overall, there was a programmatic emphasis on employment: the opening up of employment opportunities and the upgrading of labor market skills of the poor.

The first thrust of legislation was directed at the specialized problems of depressed areas. The Area Redevelopment Act of 1961 focused on problems of regional unemployment. If the poverty in an area was due to a depletion of natural resources and a decline in the demand for the traditional products of the area, then new industry was to be induced to move into the area. If the people of Appalachia suffered from the decrease of jobs in coal mining, then the expansion of factory employment seemed appropriate. In subsequent years, the 1961 legislation was expanded and a broader program, the Economic Development Act, was passed in 1965. Federal grants and loans provided aid to build industry in six depressed regions of the United States: Appalachia, New England, the Coastal Plains, the Ozarks, the Upper Great Lakes, and a poverty-stricken sector of the Southwest.

The statistical count of the poor made the special plight of the minority population dramatically clear. The risk of poverty for blacks was three times as great as that for whites. Discriminatory employment practices were scored as one major factor. The developing civil rights movement of the 1960s was increasingly forceful in pointing out areas of social, political, and economic discrimination and the consequences of this discrimination for unemployment and relief rolls. The Civil Rights Act of 1964 included a section prohibiting racial, sexual, or ethnic discrimination in employment[58] and established an enforcement mechanism, the Equal Employment Opportunity Commission.

The change in the public assistance rolls in the 1960s was the third major force behind the social legislation of the decade. During the previous decade, the number of unemployed had risen faster than the number of relief recipients, but the increases could be related to each other—they went up and down together. But, in 1963, this shifted, and from 1963 to 1970 unemployment rose by less than 300,000 while the number of public assistance recipients increased by more than 6 million.[59] The sharp rise in public assistance recipients was really a jump in ADC recipients, despite the fact that by 1960 the Survivor's Insurance program was covering 1.5 million children and 396,000 widows. A picture of ADC as harboring, and even creating, families broken by illegitimacy, divorce, and desertion developed. This new picture was brought into even sharper focus by the program's continuing emphasis on the unemployable female parent in the home—the worthy-widow halo—at a time when the larger society was insistently labeling that parent "unworthy" and employable.

Solutions to case poverty, whatever the cause, were sought in employment training, work incentives, and, above all, counseling services. The addition of federal funding for services to ADC recipients in 1956 was an expression of alarm at the new composition of the ADC rolls and of hope that services might lead to employment and financial independence. In 1962, the Manpower Development and Training Act was intended to provide training or retraining for workers displaced by economic or technological change. This reemphasis on labor market participation—on enhancing occupational potential—was, in part, an extension of the intent of the GI Bill. Regarding welfare recipients, however, it represented a shift from the cash programs of the New Deal to a service approach, which came to full development in the Public Welfare Amendments of 1962.

President Kennedy's assumption of office in January 1961 and the appointment of Abraham Ribicoff as secretary of health, education, and welfare provided the opportunity to get public assistance moving toward two new objectives: "Eliminating whatever abuses have crept into these programs and developing more constructive approaches to get people off assistance and back to useful roles in society."[60] In May 1961, the secretary appointed an Ad Hoc Committee on Public Welfare to study "the problems and prospects for public assistance in the next decade."[61] At about the same time, George K. Wyman, an administrator with experience in local, state, and federal welfare and in voluntary social welfare posts, was asked to make a report offering "recommendations and suggestions for administrative and program actions relating to procedures and operations in the Children's Bureau and the Bureau of Public Assistance."[62] The ad hoc committee was composed of twenty-five public and voluntary social welfare leaders, mostly social workers. Despite the fact that three members of the committee were deans of schools of social work, a fourth was appointed to be the committee's consultant. Wyman drew on essentially the same group in preparing his report. The similarity of recommendations is not surprising.

The recommendations of the committee were released in September and were "designed to reinforce and support family life through rehabilitation, prevention and protection." Basic to the committee's proposals were adequacy of financial assistance to needy persons and families, efficient administration and organization of public welfare programs, research into the causes of dependency and family breakdown, and, foremost, the provision of rehabilitative services by professionally trained personnel. In a statement reminiscent of Frederic Almy's 1912 warning against the provision of "untrained relief," the committee wrote: "Financial assistance to meet people's basic needs for food, shelter, and clothing is essential, but alone is not enough. Expenditures for assistance not accompanied by rehabilitation services may actually increase dependency and eventual costs to the community."[63] It was convinced that public welfare, through rehabilitation services, could become a "positive wealth-producing force in society" by contributing to an "attack on such problems as dependency, juvenile delinquency, family breakdown, illegitimacy, ill health, and disability."[64]

Of the committee's ten recommended immediate steps for change in public welfare, four were aimed directly at ADC. It was recommended:

1. that "Aid to Dependent Children Families" be strengthened by the initiation of an accelerated, intensive program of rehabilitation services offered by trained personnel;
2. that the temporary (1961) provisions of federal support for unemployed parents and for foster home care for ADC children be extended and a provision to include support for disabled and unemployed fathers living at home be added;
3. that measures for studying and dealing with the problems of illegitimacy be undertaken; and
4. that earnings of youths be exempted as a deduction from the amount of assistance granted a family.

Other recommendations for immediate action included appropriations for day care, the removal of residence requirements that conflict with "the freedom of movement . . . essential to economic progress," the limited use of voucher payments for persons with severe problems of money management, and the support of research and demonstration projects concerned with dependency and family breakdown. Although these recommendations were applicable to all public assistance programs, they, too, held special meaning for change in ADC.

The ad hoc committee strongly recommended that the role of professionally trained social workers in the program be considerably expanded. It urged "that one-third of all persons engaged in social work capacities in public welfare should hold masters' degrees in social work."[65] The significance of professionally trained social workers went beyond the direct provision of service. The committee had interpreted the occurrence of fraud in public welfare as a reflection of a "basic weakness in the standards of moral responsibility in modern society." Committee members thought that well-qualified social workers could offer knowledgeable, well-directed help to build self-respect and reinforce "capacities of persons to meet their problems and to behave responsibly."[66] No wonder then that the Public Welfare Amendments of 1962, which were largely based on the committee's recommendations, were familiarly known as the Social Services Amendments.

George K. Wyman's report had been submitted to Ribicoff one month before that of the ad hoc committee. Although Wyman's task was concentrated on administrative and procedural matters of concern to the Children's Bureau and the Bureau of Public Assistance, his recommendations were basically in line with those of the committee.

On December 6, 1961, Ribicoff addressed a memorandum to the Commissioner of Social Security setting forth a series of changes that would be made in public welfare programs. Along with encouraging the locating of deserting fathers and the detection of fraud, the changes were designed "to promote rehabilitation services and develop a family-centered approach." Each state was to be required to have "a statewide staff development plan which would include inservice training and opportunities for professional and technical education." And in order to emphasize that "our efforts must involve a variety of helpful services, of which giving a money payment is only one, and . . . that the object of our efforts must be the entire family," the name of the Bureau of Public Assistance was to be changed to the Bureau of Family Services.[67]

The reports of the ad hoc committee and of George K. Wyman, the memoranda of Ribicoff to the Commissioner of Social Security and to the administrators of state welfare departments, and a combined report of the state welfare administrators were all preludes to President Kennedy's message to Congress on February 1, 1962—the first presidential message entirely on the subject of public welfare. The president expressed concern about poverty that persisted in the midst of abundance and stated that the "reasons are often more social than economic."

> Merely responding with a relief check to complicated social or personal problems . . . is not likely to provide a lasting solution. Such a check must be supplemented, or in some cases made unnecessary, by positive services and solutions, offering the total resources of the community to meet the total needs of the family to help our less fortunate citizens help themselves.[68]

The legislative actions recommended by the president were those previously designated by Ribicoff as necessary to reduce the welfare rolls. He suggested, in addition, the appointment of an Advisory Council on Public Welfare to evaluate public welfare programs in the light of "the changing nature of the economic and social problems of the country."

President Kennedy's recommendations had considerable influence upon the substance of the amendments to the Social Security Act, the Public Welfare Amendments of 1962. Their promise of a new approach to the problems of dependency was based upon extensive advice from social welfare experts who implied future savings in public welfare expenditures. Yet, beneath its new rhetoric, the Kennedy administration's approach to public welfare had a long history. It proposed a return to seeking the cause of poverty within the individual—a return to helping individuals change themselves in order to operate successfully in an apparently well-functioning economy. This time, however, the personal counseling was to be buttressed by employment services—job training and job placement.

A significant outcome of this return to tradition was the president's recommendation that federal money be available for services not only for persons who are already dependent but also for those who might become dependent. The extent to which the prevention of dependency was focused on mothers with children was shown by the suggestion that Congress offer the states the option of combining into a single category of assistance their programs for the aged, blind, and disabled. The drive to simplify and coordinate the administration of public assistance programs did not extend to that category of assistance for families whose members were potentially employable.

Public Law 87-543, the Public Welfare Amendments of 1962, were signed by President Kennedy on July 25, 1962.[69] The new law, incorporating the recommendations of the president's message, encouraged the states to provide social services leading to self-care and self-support. Encouragement took the form of a change in the grant-in-aid formula, making the federal share of costs 75 percent of expenditures for services to reduce dependency and for training staff to achieve the intent of the law. In line with this intent, the law offered federal money for services not only to current recipients of public assistance but also to former recipients and to persons who were likely to become recipients. The intent was further strengthened by the provision of funding for demonstration projects aimed at experimenting with new methods for offering money payments and social services.

Although the amendments brought about change for all categories of public assistance and for the Child Welfare provisions of Title V of the Social Security Act, the most striking were those dealing directly or indirectly with Title IV, Aid to Dependent Children. The name of the program was changed to Aid and Services to Needy Families with Children and the program would henceforth be known as AFDC, Aid to Families with Dependent Children. The intent of public policy in providing assistance for needy families was expanded:

> For the purpose of encouraging the care of dependent children . . . by enabling each State to furnish financial assistance and rehabilitation and other services . . . to needy dependent children and the parents or relatives with whom they are living to help maintain and strengthen family life and to help such parents or relatives to attain or retain capability for the maximum self-support and personal independence consistent with the maintenance of continuing parental care and protection.[70]

The temporary legislation enacted in 1961 authorizing federal financial partici-pation in aid to children deprived of parental care and support because of the unem-ployment of a parent was extended, but assistance was denied to an unemployed par-ent who refused to accept retraining without good cause.[71] In providing for community work and training programs, the amendments attempted to heed Presi-dent Kennedy's suggestion that work projects "be an opportunity for the individual on welfare, not a penalty." The projects were to be "of a constructive nature, [geared to] the conservation of work skills and the development of new skills." The secretary was to ensure appropriate health, safety, and pay standards for those projects and ap-propriate arrangements for the care and protection of the child during the parent's absence. An additional work incentive provided that expenses reasonably attributable to work participation be considered in determining the amount of the family's assis-tance grant.[72] The technique of choice was a carrot, not a stick, to move people from the welfare rolls.

The 1962 amendments required that a service plan be developed and applied for each child recipient in the light of his or her particular home conditions. Such a plan would include the use of protective payments, if the assistance grant were being mismanaged. Funds for day care for children of working parents were authorized, as were funds for the extension of public child welfare services to all political subdivi-sions of the separate states, in effect paralleling the coverage of AFDC. The services were to be provided, to the extent feasible, by trained personnel.[73]

Social workers failed to pay sufficient attention to the challenge the Public Wel-fare Amendments posed for the profession. Social workers had promised not only that increased social service would improve the family life of the poor, but that this would reduce the number of recipients and the cost of public assistance. However, within a few years, the rolls expanded, leading to embarrassing questions about the effective-ness of social services. The 1962 amendments and their consequences undermined the credibility of the social work profession in public welfare policy.[74] The American Pub-lic Welfare Association, a national organization of people concerned with public wel-fare issues, had predicted such difficulties.[75] Social workers and social work services would never again wield significant influence in welfare policy.

For the moment, however, the enormous expansion in public services gave renewed attention to relationships between public and private agencies and between family and child welfare agencies. It became clear that developments in social welfare were being shaped by public welfare agencies. The development of a professional generic methodology of social work helping and the growing need for administrative economy had earlier sparked a series of mergers between volun-tary family and children's casework agencies. The enactment of the 1962 amend-ments to the Social Security Act (moving the public agency into the family and children's counseling services areas) and the voluntary agencies' continuing problem of funding raised questions about the necessity for voluntary agency services at all.[76]

The possibility for a new era of partnership had to await a new technique of funding. The purchase-of-service mechanism was embedded in the service amend-ments. The Social Security Act made federal funds available for contracting for services prescribed by the Secretary which in the judgment of the State agency cannot be as economically or as effectively provided by the staff of such State or local agency and are not otherwise reasonably available to individuals in need of them, and which are provided . . . (whether . . . by contract with public . . . or nonprofit private agencies).[77]

In 1962, whatever the problem with relationships between voluntary and public agencies, the future of social work as a profession seemed assured. The social service amendments had reversed Harry Hopkins's 1933 decision that public welfare not be a haven for professional social work practice. The extent of the reversal was indicated by the announcement of prescribed social services to be offered by "State public assistance agencies . . . in order to claim increased Federal funds." The commissioner of Social Security also announced the means by which services were to be made effective: "caseloads of no more than 60 per worker, 1 supervisor for each 5 workers, and home visiting as frequently as necessary."[78]

The War on Poverty

The "War on Poverty" is one of the most celebrated and maligned episodes in the history of American social welfare policy. The Johnson administration's initiative ultimately deserves neither the praise nor condemnation it received. Its origins in the "new economics" of the 1960s belied any radical intent. Yet, because it took place just as the civil rights movement of the 1960s was cresting, it became one of the most visible responses of the federal government to the demands of African Americans for full civil, political, and economic citizenship. Like the civil rights movement, its political popularity among white Americans was short-lived. As the nation distanced itself from the broader movement for African American equality, conservatives were able to cast the War on Poverty as one of the great failures of social policy. Three decades after its end, a conservative generation of welfare reformers saw themselves as undoing its work.

Poverty, which had been nearly invisible during the 1950s, became increasingly prominent in public discussions of the 1960s. The annual reports of the U.S. Department of Commerce were especially effective in identifying poverty groups, those individuals and families particularly vulnerable to the risks of an industrial society. Year after year, the poverty groups were identified as children, the aged, large families, and families headed by women. A double risk was suffered by rural families and people of color. Surprisingly, work—even full-time work—was no guarantee against poverty; the "working poor" became identified as a poverty group.

The War on Poverty had its origins in the Kennedy administration's economic policy advisors who believed that expanding Americans' capacity to consume was a key to sustained economic growth. The work of scholars like John Kenneth Galbraith had demonstrated that even after a generation of federal income support programs, a significant share of the population did not have even minimally adequate incomes. At the same time, concerns about juvenile delinquency and youth employment, centered in the Justice Department, led to experimenting with a new approach to youth engagement called "community action" as a means of overcoming the apathy and alienation that hampered poor urban residents.

Support for an attack on hunger and poverty was furthered by the growing strength of the civil rights movement. A demonstration climaxed by an historic speech by Reverend Martin Luther King Jr. brought an unprecedented 200,000 people to Washington, D.C., in a march for "jobs and freedom" and an interracial display of solidarity. President Lyndon B. Johnson's decision to include the elimination of poverty among his plans for a "Great Society" came at a fortuitous time. A tax cut in 1964 had succeeded in reversing a downward economic cycle, and a renewed faith in an affluent society made a successful War on Poverty seem feasible.

In his message urging Congress to "declare war on a domestic enemy which threatens the strength of our Nation and the welfare of our people," President Johnson wrote: "Today, for the first time in our history, we have the power to strike away the barriers to full participation in our society. Having the power, we have the duty."[79]

The Economic Opportunity Act was passed on August 20, 1964. Its declaration of purpose established public policy in relation to the elimination of poverty:

> The United States can achieve its full economic and social potential as a nation only if every individual has the opportunity to contribute to the full extent of his capabilities and to participate in the workings of our society. It is therefore the policy of the United States to eliminate the paradox of poverty in the midst of plenty in this Nation by opening to everyone the opportunity for education and training, the opportunity to work, and the opportunity to live in decency and dignity."[80]

The various titles of the act represented a continuation and intensification of the Kennedy thrust, that is, a further continuation of work training, work incentives, social services, and special programs for particular regions.

The Economic Opportunity Act provided, first of all, for a series of youth programs designed to give young people of low income and minority group families the education, skills, and experiences deemed necessary for success. The youth programs included federally established Job Corps training centers for out-of-school and unemployed youths requiring general and vocational education and help with social and physical difficulties; a work-training program supporting state and local governmental and private nonprofit activities aimed at preventing school dropouts; and a work-study program enabling young people to continue their education in secondary schools, colleges, and universities.

Titles III and IV provided for special programs to combat poverty in rural areas and for programs of employment and investment incentives in poverty areas beyond the reach of the provisions of the Area Redevelopment Act. Grants and loans to farmers and small businesses were the core of these titles. The aim of Title V, described as "Family Unity Through Jobs" by presidential assistant Sargent Shriver, was the development of short-term training and retraining courses leading to the transfer of trainees from relief rolls to jobs. Its central concern was for unemployed parents—fathers and mothers—receiving assistance through the AFDC–UP program. Title V was meant to "demonstrate that public assistance with work and training can be used as a positive instrument to keep families together, to increase employability, and to brighten our communities."[81] An important section created an adult volunteer corps—"Volunteers in Service to America" (VISTA)—to help with the rehabilitation and improvement of slums and other impoverished areas.

The most controversial—and important—provisions of the Economic Opportunity Act were those included in Title II, "Urban and Rural Community Action Programs." Community Action Programs (CAP) were defined as those that promised progress toward the elimination of poverty, that provided for "the maximum feasible participation" of residents of the geographic areas of group members covered, and that were conducted by public or private, nonprofit community action organizations. The initial popularity of the Office of Economic Opportunity (OEO) stemmed from its ability, through the CAP concept, to fund projects administered by public and voluntary agencies freed from the administrative control of city halls and united funds. Among the more popular programs funded were Head Start (a preparatory education program for preschool, low-income children), Upward Bound (an educational program meant to prevent school dropout and to encourage dropouts to return to school), day care centers, neighborhood recreation centers, and neighborhood health centers.

The Economic Opportunity Act reemphasized the 1962 view that work and jobs were the keys to strengthened family life. The act accelerated the spate of programs designed to remove parents and children from the home and from each other. Job training, job placement, and counseling for a variety of psychological and social ills represented a crash effort to reduce the welfare rolls. Day care, Head Start, Upward Bound, and so on served several purposes at once. For children, they were to be compensation for the failures of parental upbringing and enhancement of potential for adult economic independence. For parents, they represented an immediate freeing for job hunting. The act clearly indicated that employment as an American value was at least equal to the value placed on family life and family unity.

The OEO soon came under attack. Mayors of cities around the country were politically threatened by the federal funding of projects over which they had no control. Members of Congress were upset by legal suits brought by government-funded community legal services against federal programs. Communities were shaken by the aggressiveness and hostility of the poor who had found voice in the "maximum feasible participation" concept. Stories of mismanagement, radicalism, and fraud abounded. In time, President Johnson, increasingly enmeshed in the Vietnam War, became disenchanted with a War on Poverty that was not only costly but was creating political and social dissensions while seeming to make little direct contribution to its stated goal. The race riots of the summer of 1967 brought renewed attention to the problems of the ghetto poor. Nonetheless, the administration's overall support began to fade.

The Economic Opportunity Act and the War on Poverty did make important contributions to change. The "maximum feasible participation" concept opened new sources of psychological, financial, and political power as the poor found themselves having a say in, and in some instances even controlling, the programs and institutions that affected their lives. The concept became integral to other legislated social welfare programs, as in the Model Cities legislation of 1966, for example. The poor and other consumers of services became increasingly involved in education and health, as well as welfare, programs. As skills developed, their participation ranged from service to managerial to policy-making positions. Community action programs opened opportunities for large numbers of minority group members who were educationally prepared for executive and professional jobs but to whom such opportunities had been closed by discrimination. They helped make the poor and the members of minority groups not only visible but increasingly audible.

An equally significant legacy of community action programs was the development of community legal services. These services were not specifically mentioned in the Economic Opportunity Act as originally enacted. Once developed as community action programs, the importance of legal services for testing and securing the legal rights of the poor through a wide variety of class action suits became obvious, and amendments to the act made specific provision for inclusion. Community legal services, applying pressure for administrative action to implement judicial victories, appeared to be a most important governmental contribution to the welfare of the poor.

An unexpected result of the development of community action programs was a shift in social workers' views of social welfare, of social agencies, and of their profession. Originally ignored by officials of the Office of Economic Opportunity, social workers were soon brought into community action programs because of their competencies in community organizing, administration, and direct work with clients and client groups. The thrust of the War on Poverty and particularly of community action programs moved many social workers, and the profession itself, from a therapeutic to a reform approach, from a psychoanalytic to a social science base. The move led some to a seemingly antiprofessional stance as they pushed for community and consumer participation in policy making and decision making, for the input of nonprofessionals into service design and delivery, and for social action to "change the system." Social workers helped public assistance clients organize, and the Welfare Rights Organization became a substantial force for change.

Crosscurrents of opinion in regard to social welfare became sharper as Congress extended the federal government's role in social welfare. The Community Mental Health Act, which provided funds and set up community mental health centers, was passed in 1963. In 1964, Congress passed the Food Stamp Act to help meet the nutritional needs of the poor. Health insurance was provided for the elderly, a high-risk group in terms of vulnerability to illness and to poverty, and to the medically indigent by Title XVIII (Medicare) and Title XIX (Medicaid), respectively, amendments to the Social Security Act in 1965. Also in 1965, the Elementary and Secondary Education Act marked the first extension of federal aid for general purposes to local schools. In 1966, the Demonstration (Model) Cities Act proposed to demonstrate, through a concentration and coordination of housing, health, education, employment, and social services, the ability to transform decaying urban areas into settings for the good life. The Housing and Urban Development Act of 1968 gave impetus to President Johnson's intent to provide 6 million new dwellings for low- and moderate-income groups within the next ten years. Overall, the civil rights movement and the publicity it gave to the needs of the poor and of minority groups continued to push movement toward improved social well-being.

Expanded Benefits for the Aging

The aging in particular benefited from the prosperity of the postwar period. Social security benefits expanded steadily as professionals in the field pushed Congress to increase the number of workers covered and to liberalize payment levels. In 1940, only 58 percent of the work force was protected; by 1970, more than 90 percent of all workers were included. Coverage was extended to most self-employed, ministers, doctors, farmers, and domestic workers, employees of nonprofit organizations, members of the armed forces, and, optionally, state and municipal workers. The number of beneficiaries rose from only 220,000 in 1940 to 3.5 million in 1950 and to well over 25 million in 1970.

In the context of an expanding economy, with increased productivity and output, payment levels were raised throughout the period. In 1950, a large and redistributive increase had been enacted, averaging 77 percent, and ranging from 50 percent for those with the highest benefits to 100 percent for those with the lowest. There were more increments during the next twenty years, in response to an increased awareness of poverty among the older population. However, inflation protection still was not built into the program. Early retirement at age 62, with a reduced pension, was introduced in 1956 for women and in 1961 for men. In 1966, a special minimum benefit was enacted for those over the age of 72. The results showed in the data on poverty in the United States. In 1959, the first year for which there are "official" poverty data, more than 35 percent of the aged were counted poor; in 1970, the risk of poverty for those 65 or older had dropped to just below 25 percent. Concurrently, however, annual social security taxes rose by more than 1,100 percent—from $30 a year in 1940 to $374 a year by 1969.[82]

During the 1950s and 1960s, the concept of the social security funds shifted. The original view in 1935 was to establish a fund in accordance with accepted actuarial principles. A few years later, in 1940, the concern was that the funds might grow too large. Interest moved away from the full actuarial reserve to a contingency reserve fund. Now another shift occurred and we went to a pay-as-you-go system. It was done by expanding benefits—covering more workers, adding a new category of risk (disability), and making the benefit formula much more distributive. The program had started out in 1935 by emphasizing benefits on an insurance basis. Thirty years later there was much more concern about the social aspects. In addition we kept postponing scheduled tax increases. The fear of trust fund growth disappeared and instead the trustees were required to report to Congress when it thought the assets might become "unduly small." Many years of pay-as-you-go financing ensued.

The deprivation experienced by our older population was made more visible by the organization of senior clubs, the growth of organizations devoted to the needs of the elderly, and the strong coalition of the aged and labor that developed during the period from 1958 to 1965. Social insurance was designed to help provide economic protection, Medicare to meet urgent health needs, and food stamps to help with nutritional adequacy, but the special needs of the aging went beyond this. In 1961, the first special White House Conference on Aging was held, and, in 1965, the Older Americans

Act was passed to help meet the broad social service, legal, nutritional, and economic needs of older people. The act established the Administration on Aging within the federal government, state agencies on aging, and local Area Agencies on Aging to fund community services, coordinate and plan activities, sponsor research, help implement senior centers, and in general help with housing, transportation, and other services needed by the aging community. It not only provided money for many activities but institutionalized the voice of senior citizen groups in national policy making.[83]

Reform of Welfare: 1967

Not all groups fared as well as the aged. In particular, recipients of AFDC found themselves subject to increased monitoring. Neither the Public Welfare Amendments of 1962 nor the Economic Opportunity Act of 1964 succeeded in reducing the AFDC rolls. The number of recipients and total expenditures continued a steep climb. More of the poor were being helped, but not in the way Congress had intended. Despite this, the 1966 report of the Advisory Council on Public Welfare urged a continuation of the services approach to change.

The Advisory Council on Public Welfare had been appointed by the secretary of health, education, and welfare pursuant to the 1962 public welfare statutes. The overall tenor of the council's report *Having the Power, We Have the Duty* was that Congress should make public assistance more effective by seeing to the provision of more aid and more services "as a matter of right." The federal government should set nationwide standards for relief grants and assume their full cost above individually stipulated state shares. Discrepancies among state standards would thus be eliminated, and the states, freed of pressures to find new sources of revenues, would be able to concentrate on meeting human needs. Special legislation appropriating funds to encourage expansion and training of social workers and related personnel was deemed necessary.[84]

The recommendations of the Advisory Council have been cited as "the last hurrah of the social welfare professionals who had long dominated public assistance policy development."[85] And, indeed, those who influenced the shape of the report, despite its fresh declaration of a right to assistance and service, were in many ways out of touch with fellow professionals who were moving in a different direction.* For at the very moment that the council's report, supporting a continuing administrative tie between money payments and social services, was being released, a number of influential professionals were beginning to pressure for their separation. In fact, the proposal for separation had already been made in an unpublicized report by a special task force headed by James Dumpson, the New York City commissioner of welfare and a social worker.[86] Neither group, however, foresaw the congressional approach to be adopted in 1967.

---

*Although the council's report was open to criticism, it should be pointed out that among its recommendations were: (1) the introduction of a new public assistance program based on need alone and (2) the use of a simple client declaration form in establishing eligibility. Both were to become important elements in later proposals for welfare reform.

The Social Security Amendments of 1967 legislated both a stick and a carrot attack on the rising AFDC caseload. Using January 1967 as a base for purposes of federal withholding, a freeze was imposed on the number of children under 21 years who would be allowed to receive AFDC because of absence of a parent from the home. Second, a Work Incentive Program (eventually known as WIN, after having initially and disastrously been referred to as WIP) was instituted. The welfare freeze deliberately exempted AFDC cases attributable to a father's death or a parent's unemployment. Its aim, therefore, was to pressure state efforts against dependency due to divorce, desertion, and illegitimacy. WIN disqualified adults and out-of-school older children—female as well as male—for AFDC payments, if they refused to accept employment or to participate in training programs without good cause.

The most important revision in the 1967 amendments was the elimination of the 100 percent "tax" on the earnings of recipients. Before 1967, a mother's efforts toward self-sufficiency were "rewarded" with a dollar-for-dollar cut in her family's welfare check. After the 1967 amendments, recipients were allowed to keep the first thirty dollars of their earnings each month; their welfare check would only be reduced by two-thirds of any additional income. "Thirty and a third," as the policy was called, and the expansion of child care subsidies set a new path for welfare policy. No longer was welfare a "mother's pension" to allow mothers to focus on child rearing. Now, mothers on welfare would be encouraged, and eventually required, to look toward paid labor.

In contrast to the elderly, poor women with children soon faced a backlash. The punitive aspects of the 1967 welfare amendments caused dismay and then outrage among client groups interpreting the freeze as punishment of helpless children, among state administrations facing the prospect of increased and intolerable burdens on state budgets, and among social welfare professionals foreseeing state reductions in relief grants. President Johnson and his successor, President Richard M. Nixon, both delayed implementation of the freeze, which was repealed by congressional action in 1969.

The full effects of the WIN program were temporarily delayed by the administrative discretion permitted state and local departments of welfare in requiring recipient participation. Nevertheless, the intent of Congress and of the secretary of health, education, and welfare was proclaimed on August 15, 1967, in an announcement of a major administrative restructuring of the department. The Welfare Administration and Bureau of Family Services, established in 1962, were abolished, and a new agency, the Social and Rehabilitation Service (SRS), was created to administer public assistance, rehabilitation, and social services. The secretary's announcement indicated a planned deemphasis on family and community services and the substitution of "services aimed at rehabilitation in the broadest sense of the word."[87] The work orientation of SRS was further indicated by the appointment of the former commissioner of the Vocational Rehabilitation Administration as administrator of the new unit.

Gradually, through a series of administrative shifts, a new policy became clear: a national intent to separate money payments from services. It was the end of the service approach to public assistance. By 1969, the separation idea was the order of the day, and eventually federal regulations ordered that separation of money payments from services be achieved at state and local levels by January 1, 1974.

"Separation" was attractive on a number of counts. For those who were determined to infuse AFDC with a work orientation, separation quite literally meant separation of recipients from the requirement of services offered by professional social workers. In line with this, the institution of simple client declaration systems for establishing eligibility for cash benefits eliminated the need for professional skills in all aspects of the money payment process. For clients, separation meant the right to choose service voluntarily, when needed, without fear of losing a grant. For most professionals, separation meant a further delineation of the rights of clients and of the poor and of minority group members.

The National Association of Social Workers supported separation and pointed out that:

1. Service, when offered within the context of eligibility investigation, tends to become a condition for obtaining financial assistance. This undermines the concept of assistance as a right and . . . interferes with . . . self-determination in seeking and accepting service.
2. There is no reason to assume that financial need, in itself, necessarily calls for the provision of social services . . . Separation of assistance from social services will make it possible to organize services so that they reach those who have specific need for them.[88]

Social workers were now free to join other social scientists and social welfare theorists in a search for new forms of income transfers and for new ways of achieving a more equal distribution of income.

Civil Rights and Juvenile Justice

Social workers saw separation of money payments and services as a part of a new concern for the rights of the poor. This was well in line with a strand of social welfare that unraveled throughout the 1960s. Spurred by the civil rights revolution, questions about the rights of various groups in our society to social well-being were asked and answers were demanded. Judicial and administrative decisions strengthened the rights of the aged, the rights of the mentally ill, the rights of the retarded, the rights of tenants, the rights of prisoners, the rights of minority groups, and the rights of women.

Some legal rights of children were established by the Supreme Court's decision, In re *Gault*, of 1967. As originally conceived in 1899, the juvenile court sought to protect children from the impersonal legal processes of adult courts. Instead of an adversary approach, the child was to be offered the friendly help of a fatherly judge who would see to individualized treatment and, if necessary, rehabilitation. Seventy years of experience with juvenile courts had demonstrated the reality that services for rehabilitative purposes were a myth. In practice, the pretext of service was a substitute for justice. Children were incarcerated for indefinite periods. The rhetoric claimed training for a productive adult life; the actuality most often proved quite the contrary.

In 1967, the Supreme Court decided that children in trouble with the law had legal rights: to counsel, to confidentiality, to silence. Justice Abe Fortas, writing the majority decision, stated:

> While due process requirements will . . . introduce a degree of order and regularity to juvenile court proceedings to determine delinquency, and in contested cases will introduce some elements of the adversary system, nothing will require that the conception of the kindly juvenile judge be replaced by its opposite.[89]

The child could have both, justice and service. The juvenile's sudden right to "due process" galvanized the entire judicial and probation systems to a reconsideration of legal practices in regard to children. In addition, the fact that there are legal aspects to all child welfare programs and that workers in these programs have frequent contacts with courts and lawyers fostered a reawakening of interest in the law on the part of all social agencies and social welfare personnel engaged in services to children.

The *Gault* decision pointed out the need for a resolution of continuing value conflicts in all areas of social welfare.

Discussion Questions

1. How was the influence of World War II the same as or different from the influence of earlier wars in which the United States was involved?
2. Social workers' promise in 1962 to use social services to reduce the welfare rolls was disastrous for the profession's political influence on welfare policy. In what areas of social policy do social workers still have influence?
3. In what ways does the "War on Poverty" continue to influence contemporary social welfare policy and practice?

DOCUMENTS: War and Prosperity

The documents used to support post-World War II occurrences in social welfare are President Kennedy's *Message on the Public Welfare Program* (1962), excerpts from the *Economic Opportunity Act* (1964), and the Supreme Court decision, In the matter of *Gault* (1967). The documents are all products of the 1960s and represent the climax of post-World War II effort to bring economic affluence to bear on the promises of American democracy. The documents represent executive, legislative, and judicial responses to the social welfare issues of the period.

President Kennedy's message to Congress on public welfare programs was historic in its having been the first presidential message entirely devoted to the subject. The message, in effect, reiterates the thrust of Secretary of Health, Education, and Welfare Abraham Ribicoff's memorandum to the commissioner of Social Security. That memorandum bridged the efforts of the late 1950s to contain the growth of the public assistance rolls and the new approach to public welfare legislated by the 1962 Public Welfare Amendments. The secretary's concern was to eliminate fraud, but more than that to infuse public welfare—in reality, AFDC—with a philosophy geared to family stability and family independence. The approach implied a pathological base for poverty and dependence; therefore, the secretary pointed out the need for each state to assess its personnel and training needs to carry out the objectives of "a service-oriented program."

President Kennedy's message announces the new orientation to family welfare. It demonstrates administrative discretion at the federal level in shaping and regulating the public assistance programs. It shows, too, the need for congressional action for authorizing and funding new programs. In his leadership capacity, the president recommends congressional support of a new approach to public assistance by providing for the relief of unemployed parents, for community work and training projects, for the expansion and upgrading of social work personnel, and for a consultative Advisory Council on Public Welfare. The president's recommendation of the "rehabilitative road" to change in public welfare is couched in terms that plead for a demonstration of "the compassion of free men . . . in the light of . . . constructive self-interest."

The *Economic Opportunity Act* of 1964 and its heralded War on Poverty were President Johnson's extension of his predecessor's compassion for the poor. The act was also a response to a rediscovery of poverty, this time in the midst of economic plenty. The demand of the poor and particularly of the black minority for participation in the country's economic life, for a share of its wealth, seemed eminently reasonable. In 1964, the country was not yet so embroiled in the Southeast Asia conflicts that decisions about guns or butter had to be made. It seemed possible to have both, and the president, believing that we had the power to eliminate poverty, convinced the Congress that we had the duty to do so.

Ultimately, the *Economic Opportunity Act* was an abortive attempt to eliminate poverty. Nevertheless, it was historically important as an effort to do so. Additionally, the act made significant, perhaps permanent, contributions to social welfare in the United States through the introduction of the "maximum feasible participation" concept, which, at the least, led to some psychological and political gains in the power of minorities. This new power was demonstrated and furthered by the community action programs, among them Head Start and community legal services, funded by the act. It must be pointed out, however, that the overall thrust of the *Economic Opportunity Act* was one of "blaming the victim." The act was meant to change the poor and, in this way, open opportunities for them. Only incidentally did organizations for structural change in "the system" arise.

The War on Poverty was waged in the context of a civil rights revolution. Led by the black community, the United States was swept by demands for increased political, social, and economic equality. Other racial and ethnic groups, Puerto Ricans and Native Americans, for example, added their protests. Many other groups banded together in a fight for social justice. The Supreme Court decision, In re *Gault* represents a judicial response to demand on behalf of the rights of one group of children.

The juvenile court had been formed to provide individualized treatment for children. The erosion and subversion of the intent of the juvenile court is delineated in the opinion written for the Supreme Court by Justice Abe Fortas. In effect, the court's opinion requires attention to due process, to legal rights, as the path to individualized justice for children. The opinion denies that legal justice necessarily eliminates sympathy and compassion or attention to therapeutic and rehabilitative needs of children. In fact, suggests the opinion, "The essentials of due process . . . may be a more impressive and more therapeutic attitude so far as the juvenile is concerned."

The Fortas opinion had sweeping significance for children, for juvenile courts, and for professionals operating in juvenile courts. By extension, the opinion had significance for all of social welfare.

MESSAGE FROM PRESIDENT JOHN F. KENNEDY
PUBLIC WELFARE
February 1, 1962
H. Doc. No. 325

TO THE CONGRESS OF THE UNITED STATES:

Few nations do more than the United States to assist their least fortunate citizens—to make certain that no child, no elderly or handicapped citizen, no family in any circumstances in any State, is left without the essential needs for a decent and healthy existence. In too few nations, I might add, are the people aware of the progressive strides this country has taken in demonstrating the humanitarian side of freedom. Our record is a proud one—and it sharply refutes those who accuse us of thinking only in the materialistic terms of cash registers and calculating machines.

Our basic public welfare programs were enacted more than a quarter century ago. Their contribution to our national strength and well-being in the intervening years has been remarkable.

But the times, the conditions, the problems have changed—and the nature and objectives of our public assistance and child welfare programs must be changed, also, if they are to meet our current needs.

The impact of these changes should not be underestimated.

People move more often—from the farm to the city, from urban centers to the suburbs, from the East to the West, from the South to the North and Mid-west.

Living costs, and especially medical costs, have spiraled.

The pattern of our population has changed. There are more older people, more children, more young marriages, divorces, desertions, and separations.

Our system of social insurance and related programs has grown greatly: In 1940, less than 1 percent of the aged were receiving monthly old-age insurance benefits; today over two-thirds of our aged are receiving these benefits. In 1940, only 21,000 children, in families where the breadwinner had died, were getting survivor insurance benefits; today such monthly benefits are being paid to about 2 million children.

All of these changes affect the problems public welfare was intended to relieve as well as its ability to relieve it. Moreover, even the nature and causes of poverty have changed. At the time the Social Security Act established our present basic framework for public aid, the major cause of poverty was unemployment and economic depression. Today, in a year of relative prosperity and high employment, we are more concerned about the poverty that persists in the midst of abundance.

The reasons are often more social than economic, more often subtle than simple. Some are in need because they are untrained for work—some because they cannot work, because they are too young or too old, blind or crippled. Some are in need because they are discriminated against for reasons they cannot help. Responding to their ills with scorn or suspicion is inconsistent with our moral precepts and inconsistent with their nearly universal preference to be independent. But merely responding with a relief check to complicated social or personal problems—such as ill health, faulty education, domestic discord, racial discrimination, or inadequate skills—is not likely to provide a lasting solution. Such a check must be supplemented, or in some cases made unnecessary, by positive services and solutions, offering the total resources of the community to meet the total needs of the family to help our less fortunate citizens help themselves.

Public welfare, in short, must be more than a salvage operation, picking up the debris from the wreckage of human lives. Its emphasis must be directed increasingly toward prevention and rehabilitation—on reducing not only the long-range cost in budgetary terms but the long-range cost in human terms as well. Poverty weakens individuals and nations. Sounder public welfare policies will benefit the Nation, its economy, its morale, and, most importantly, its people.

Under the various titles of the Social Security Act, funds are available to help the States provide assistance and other social services to the needy, aged and blind, to the needy disabled, and to dependent children. In addition, grants are available to assist the States to expand and strengthen their programs of child welfare services. These programs are essentially State programs. But the Federal Government, by its substantial financial contribution, its leadership, and the standards it sets, bears a major responsibility. To better fulfill this responsibility, the Secretary of Health, Education, and Welfare recently introduced a number of administrative changes designed to get people off assistance and back into useful, productive roles in society.

These changes provided for:

The more effective location of deserting parents;

An effort to reduce that proportion of persons receiving assistance through willful misrepresentation, although that proportion is only a small part of the 1.5 percent of persons on the rolls found to be ineligible;

Allowing dependent children to save money for educational, employment or medical needs without having that amount deducted from their public assistance grants;

Providing special services and safeguards to children in families of unmarried parents, in families where the father has deserted, or in homes in danger of becoming morally or physically unsuitable; and

An improvement in the training of personnel, the development of services and the coordination of agency efforts.

In keeping with this new emphasis, the name of the Bureau of Public Assistance has been changed to the Bureau of Family Services.

But only so much can be done by administrative changes. New legislation is required if our State-operated programs are to be fully able to meet modern needs.

I. PREVENTION AND REHABILITATION

As already mentioned, we must place more stress on services instead of relief.

I recommend that the States be encouraged by the offer of additional Federal funds to strengthen and broaden the rehabilitative and preventive services they offer to persons who are dependent or who would otherwise become dependent. Additional Federal funds would induce and assist the States to establish or augment their rehabilitation services, strengthen their child welfare services, and add to their number of competent public welfare personnel. At the present time, the cost of these essential services is lumped with all administrative costs—routine clerical and office functions—and the Federal Government pays one-half of the total of all such costs incurred by the States. By separating out and identifying the cost of these essential rehabilitation, social work and other service costs, and paying the States three-fourths of such services—a step I earnestly recommend for your consideration—the Federal Government will enable and encourage the States to provide more comprehensive and effective services to rehabilitate those on welfare. The existing law should also be amended to permit the use of Federal funds for utilization by the State welfare agency of specialists from other State agencies who can help mount a concerted attack on the problems of dependency.

There are other steps we can take which will have an important effect on this effort. One of these is to expand and improve the Federal–State program of vocational rehabilitation for disabled people. Among the 92,500 disabled men and women successfully rehabilitated into employment through this program last year were about 15,000 who had formerly been receiving public assistance. Let me repeat this figure: 15,000 people, formerly supported by the taxpayers through welfare, are now back at work as self-supporting taxpayers. Much more of this must be done—until we are restoring to employment every disabled person who can benefit from these rehabilitation services.

The prevention of future adult poverty and dependency must begin with the care of dependent children—those who must receive public welfare by virtue of a parent's death, disability, desertion, or unemployment. Our society not only refuses to leave such children hungry, cold, and devoid of opportunity—we are insistent that such children not be community liabilities throughout their lives. Yet children who grow up in deprivation, without adequate protection, may be poorly equipped to meet adult responsibilities.

The Congress last year approved, on a temporary basis, aid for the dependent children of the unemployed as a part of the permanent aid-to-dependent-children program. This legislation also included temporary provisions for foster care where the child had been removed from his home, and an increase in Federal financial assistance to the aged, blind, and disabled. The need for these temporary improvements has not abated, and their merit is clear. I recommend that these temporary provisions be made permanent.

But children need more than aid when they are destitute. We need to improve our preventive and protective services for children as well as adults. I recommend that the present ceiling of $25 million authorized for annual appropriations for grants to the States for child welfare services be gradually raised, beginning with $30 million for 1963, up to $50 million for the fiscal year ending June 30, 1969, and succeeding years.

Finally, many women now on assistance rolls could obtain jobs and become self-supporting if local day-care programs for their young children were available. The need for such programs for the children, the children of working mothers has been increasing rapidly. Of the 22 million women now working, about 3 million have children under 6, and another 4 1/2 million have school-age children between 6 and 17. Adequate care for these children during their most formative years is essential to their proper growth and training. Therefore, I recommend that the child welfare provisions of the Social Security Act be changed to authorize earmarking up to $5 million of grants to the States in 1963 and $10 million a year thereafter for aid in establishing local programs for the day care of young children of working mothers.

II. PROMOTING NEW SKILLS AND INDEPENDENCE

We must find ways of returning far more of our dependent people to independence. We must find ways of returning them to a participating and productive role in the community.

One sure way is by providing the opportunity every American cherishes to do sound and useful work. For this reason, I am recommending a change in the law to permit States to maintain, with Federal financial help, community work and training projects for unemployed people receiving welfare payments. Under such a program, unemployed people on welfare would be helped to retain their work skills or learn new ones; and the local community would obtain additional manpower on public projects.

But earning one's welfare payments through required participation in a community work or training project must be an opportunity for the individual on welfare, not a penalty. Federal financial participation will be conditioned upon proof that the work will serve a useful community or public purpose, will not displace regular employees, will not impair prevailing wages and working conditions, and will be accompanied by certain basic health and safety protections. Provisions must also be made to assure appropriate arrangements for the care and protection of children during the absence from home of any parent performing work or undergoing training.

Moreover, systematic encouragement would be given all welfare recipients to obtain vocational counseling, testing, and placement services from the U.S. Employment Service and to secure useful training wherever new job skills would be helpful. Close cooperative arrangements would be established with existing training and vocational education programs, and with the vocational and on-the-job training opportunities to be created under the manpower development and training and youth employment opportunities programs previously proposed.

III. MORE SKILLED PERSONNEL

It is essential that State and local welfare agencies be staffed with enough qualified personnel to insure constructive and adequate attention to the problems of needy individuals—to take the time to help them find and hold a job—to prevent public dependency, and to strive, where that is not possible, for rehabilitation—and to ascertain promptly whether any individual is receiving aid for which he does not qualify, so that aid can be promptly withdrawn.

Unfortunately, there is an acute shortage of trained personnel in all our welfare programs. The lack of experienced social workers for programs dealing with children and their families is especially critical.

At the present time, when States expend funds for the training of personnel for the administration of these programs, they receive Federal grants on a dollar-for-dollar basis. This arrangement has failed to produce a sufficient number of trained staff, especially social workers. I recommend, therefore, that Federal assistance to the States for training additional welfare personnel be increased; and that in addition, the Secretary of Health, Education, and Welfare be authorized to make special arrangements for the training of family welfare personnel to work with those children whose parents have deserted, whose parents are unmarried, or who have other serious problems.

IV. FITTING GENERAL CONDITIONS OR SAFEGUARDS TO INDIVIDUAL NEEDS

In order to make certain that welfare funds go only to needy people, the Social Security Act requires the States to take all income and resources of the applicant into consideration in determining need. Although Federal law permits, it does not require States to take into full account the full expenses individuals have in earning income. This is not consistent with equity, common sense, or other Federal laws such as our tax code. It only discourages the will to earn. In order to encourage assistance recipients to find and retain employment, I, therefore, recommend that the act be amended to require the States to take into account the expenses of earning income.

Among relatives caring for dependent children are a few who do not properly handle their assistance payments—some to the extent that the well-being of the child is adversely affected. Where the State determines that a relative's ability to manage money is contrary to the welfare of the child, Federal law presently requires payments to be made to a legal guardian or representative, if Federal funds are to be used. But this general requirement may sometimes block progress in particular situations. In order to recognize the necessity for each State to make exceptions to this rule in a very limited number of cases, I recommend that the law be amended to permit Federal sharing to continue even though protective payments in behalf of children—not to exceed one-half of 1 percent of ADC recipients in each State—are made to other persons concerned with the welfare of the family. The States would be required to reexamine these exceptions at intervals to determine whether a more permanent arrangement such as guardianship is required.

When first enacted, the aid to dependent children program provided for Federal sharing in assistance payments only to the child. Since 1950, there has been Federal sharing in any assistance given to one adult in the household as well as to the child or children. Inasmuch as under current law, there may be two parents in homes covered by this program, one incapacitated or unemployed, I recommend in the interest of equity the extension of Federal sharing in assistance payments both to the needy relative and to his or her spouse when both are living in the home with the child.

V. MORE EFFICIENT ADMINISTRATION

Under present public assistance provisions, States may impose residence requirements up to 5 of the last 9 years for the aged, blind, and disabled. Increased mobility, as previously mentioned, is a hallmark of our times. It should not operate unfairly on either an individual State or an individual family. I recommend that the Social Security Act be amended so as to provide that States receiving Federal funds not exclude any otherwise eligible persons who have been residents of the State for 1 year immediately preceding their application for assistance. I also recommend that the law be amended to provide a small increase in assistance funds to those States which simplify their laws by removing all residence requirements in any of their federally aided programs.

In view of the changing nature of the economic and social problems of the country, the desirability of a periodic review of our public welfare programs is obvious. For that purpose I propose that the Secretary of Health, Education, and Welfare be authorized to appoint an Advisory Council on Public Welfare representing broad community interests and concerns, and such other advisory committees as he deems necessary to advise and consult with him in the administration of the Social Security Act.

No study of the public welfare program can fail to note the difficulty of the problems faced or the need to be imaginative in dealing with them. Accordingly, I recommend that amendments be made to encourage experimental, pilot or demonstration projects that would promote the objectives of the assistance titles and help make our welfare programs more flexible and adaptable to local needs.

The simplification and coordination of administration and operation would greatly improve the adequacy and consistency of assistance and related services. As a step in that direction, I recommend that a new title to the Social Security Act be enacted which would give to States the option of submitting a single, unified State plan combining their assistance programs for aged, blind and disabled, and their medical assistance programs for the aged, granting to such States additional Federal matching for medical payments on behalf of the blind and disabled.

These proposed far-reaching changes—aimed at far-reaching problems—are in the public interest and in keeping with our finest traditions. The goals of our public welfare programs must be positive and constructive—to create economic and social opportunities for the less fortunate—to help them find productive, happy, and independent lives. It must stress the integrity and preservation of the family unit. It must contribute to the attack on dependency, juvenile delinquency, family breakdown, illegitimacy, ill health, and disability. It must reduce the incidence of these problems, prevent their occurrence and recurrence, and strengthen and protect the vulnerable in a highly competitive world.

Unless such problems are dealt with effectively, they fester, and grow, sapping the strength of society as a whole and extending their consequences in troubled families from one generation to the next.

The steps I recommend to you today to alleviate these problems will not come cheaply. They will cost more money when first enacted. But they will restore human dignity; and in the long run, they will save money. I have recommended in the budget submitted for fiscal year 1963 sufficient funds to cover the extension of existing programs and the new legislation here proposed.

Communities which have—for whatever motives—attempted to save money through ruthless and arbitrary cutbacks in their welfare rolls have found their efforts to little avail. The root problems remained.

But communities which have tried the rehabilitative road—the road I have recommended today—have demonstrated what can be done with creative, thoughtfully conceived and properly managed programs of prevention and social rehabilitation. In those communities families have been restored to self-reliance, and relief rolls have been reduced.

To strengthen our human resources—to demonstrate the compassion of free men—and in the light of our own constructive self-interest—we must bring our welfare programs up to date. I urge that the Congress do so without delay.

THE WAR ON POVERTY
THE ECONOMIC OPPORTUNITY ACT OF 1964

88th Congress   Document
2d Session   No. 86

PUBLIC LAW 88-452—Aug. 20, 1964 [78 Stat.]

Public Law 88-452

AN ACT

August 20, 1964
(s 2642)

To mobilize the human and financial resources of the
Nation to combat poverty
in the United States

Be it enacted by the Senate and the House of Representatives of the United

Economic
Opportunity
Act of 1964

States of America in Congress assembled. That this Act may be cited as the
"Economic Opportunity Act of 1964."

FINDINGS AND DECLARATION OF PURPOSE

SEC. 2. Although the economic well-being and prosperity of the United States
have progressed to a level surpassing any achieved in world history, and although
these benefits are widely shared throughout the Nation, poverty continues to be the
lot of a substantial number of our people. The United States can achieve its full economic and social potential as a nation only if every individual has the opportunity to
contribute to the full extent of his capabilities and to participate in the workings of
our society. It is, therefore, the policy of the United States to eliminate the paradox
of poverty in the midst of plenty in this Nation by opening to everyone the opportunity for education and training, the opportunity to work, and the opportunity to live
in decency and dignity. It is the purpose of this Act to strengthen, supplement, and
coordinate efforts in furtherance of that policy.

TITLE I—YOUTH PROGRAMS

PART A—JOB CORPS

STATEMENT OF PURPOSE

SEC. 101. The purpose of this part is to prepare for the responsibilities of
citizenship and to increase the employability of young men and young women
aged sixteen through twenty-one by providing them in rural and urban residential
centers with education, vocational training, useful work experience, including
work directed toward the conservation of natural resources, and other appropriate
activities.

Part B—Work-Training Programs

STATEMENT OF PURPOSE

Sec. 111. The purpose of this part is to provide useful work experience opportunities for unemployed young men and young women, through participation in State and community work-training programs, so that their employability may be increased or their education resumed or continued and so that public agencies and private nonprofit organizations (other than political parties) will be enabled to carry out programs which will permit or contribute to an undertaking or service in the public interest that would not otherwise be provided, or will contribute to the conservation and development of natural resources and recreational areas. . . .

> Unemployed youth, work experience opportunities

Part C—Work-Study Programs

STATEMENT OF PURPOSE

Sec. 121. The purpose of this part is to stimulate and promote the part-time employment of students in institutions of higher education who are from low-income families and are in need of the earnings from such employment to pursue courses of study at such institutions. . . .

> Students, part-time employment

TITLE II—URBAN AND RURAL COMMUNITY ACTION PROGRAMS

Part A—General Community Action Programs

STATEMENT OF PURPOSE

Sec. 201. The purpose of this part is to provide stimulation and incentive for urban and rural communities to mobilize their resources to combat poverty through community action programs.

COMMUNITY ACTION PROGRAMS

Sec. 202. (a) The term "community action program" means a program—

(1) which mobilizes and utilizes resources, public or private, of any urban or rural, or combined urban and rural, geographical area (referred to in this part as a "community"), including but not limited to a State, metropolitan area, county, city, town, multicity unit, or multicounty unit in an attack on poverty;

(2) which provides services, assistance, and other activities of sufficient scope and size to give promise of progress toward elimination of poverty or a cause or causes of poverty through developing employment opportunities, improving human performance, motivation, and productivity, or bettering the conditions under which people live, learn, and work;

(3) which is developed, conducted, and administered with the maximum feasible participation of residents of the areas and members of the groups served; and

(4) which is conducted, administered, or coordinated by a public or private nonprofit agency (other than a political party), or a combination thereof. . . .

PART C—VOLUNTARY ASSISTANCE PROGRAM FOR NEEDY CHILDREN

STATEMENT OF PURPOSE

SEC. 219. The purpose of this part is to allow individual Americans to participate in a personal way in the war on poverty, by voluntarily assisting in the support of one or more needy children, in a program coordinated with city or county social welfare agencies.

AUTHORITY TO ESTABLISH INFORMATION CENTER

SEC. 220. (a) In order to carry out the purposes of this part, the Director is authorized to establish a section within the Office of Economic Opportunity to act as an information and coordination center to encourage voluntary assistance for deserving and needy children. Such section shall collect the names of persons who voluntarily desire to assist financially such children and shall secure from city or county social welfare agencies such information concerning deserving and needy children as the Director shall deem appropriate.

(b) It is the intent of the Congress that the section established pursuant to this part shall act solely as an information and coordination center and that nothing in this part shall be construed as interfering with the jurisdiction of State and local welfare agencies with respect to programs for needy children. . . .

TITLE III—SPECIAL PROGRAMS TO COMBAT POVERTY IN RURAL AREAS

STATEMENT OF PURPOSE

SEC. 301. It is the purpose of this title to meet some of the special problems of rural poverty and thereby to raise and maintain the income and living standards of low-income rural families and migrant agricultural employees and their families.

PART A—AUTHORITY TO MAKE GRANTS AND LOANS

SEC. 302. (a) The Director is authorized to make—

(1) loans having a maximum maturity of 15 years and in amounts not exceeding $2,500 in the aggregate to any low income rural family where, in the judgment of the Director, such loans have a reasonable possibility of affecting a permanent increase in the income of such families by assisting or permitting them to—

(A) acquire or improve real estate or reduce encumbrances or erect improvements thereon,

(B) operate or improve the operation of farms not larger than family sized, including but not limited to the purchase of feed, seed, fertilizer, livestock, poultry, and equipment, or

(C) participate in cooperative associations; and/or to finance nonagricultural enterprises which will enable such families to supplement their income.

(b) Loans under this section shall be made only if the family is not qualified to obtain such funds by loan under other Federal programs. . . .

TITLE IV—EMPLOYMENT AND INVESTMENT INCENTIVES

STATEMENT OF PURPOSE

SEC. 401. It is the purpose of this title to assist in the establishment, preservation, and strengthening of small business concerns and improve the managerial skills employed in such enterprises; and to mobilize for these objectives private as well as public managerial skills and resources. . . .

Small business concerns, assistance

TITLE V—WORK EXPERIENCE PROGRAMS

STATEMENT OF PURPOSE

SEC. 501. It is the purpose of this title to expand the opportunities for constructive work experience and other needed training available to persons who are unable to support or care for themselves or their families. In carrying out this purpose, the Director shall make maximum use of the programs available under the Manpower Development and Training Act of 1962, as amended, and Vocational Education Act of 1963. . . .

76 Stat. 23, 42 USC2571 note. 77 Stat. 403, 20 USC 35 note

VOLUNTEERS IN SERVICE TO AMERICA

SEC. 603. (a) The Director is authorized to recruit, select, train, and—

(1) upon request of State or local agencies or private nonprofit organizations, refer volunteers to perform duties in furtherance of programs combating poverty at a State or local level; and

(2) in cooperation with other Federal, State, or local agencies involved, assign volunteers to work (A) in meeting the health, education, welfare, or related needs of Indians living on reservations, of migratory workers and their families, or of residents of the District of Columbia, the Commonwealth of Puerto Rico, Guam, American Samoa, the Virgin Islands, or the Trust Territory of the Pacific Islands; (B) in the care and rehabilitation of the mentally ill or mentally retarded under treatment at non-profit mental health or mental retardation facilities assisted in their construction or operation by Federal funds; and (C) in furtherance of programs or activities authorized or supported under title I or II of this Act.

Recruitment and assignment

***

U.S. SUPREME COURT'S DECISION
In re Gault et al. No. 116
Argued December 6, 1966; Decided May 15, 1967

I

On Monday, June 8, 1964, at about 10 A.M., Gerald Francis Gault and a friend, Roland Lewis, were taken into custody by the Sheriff of Gila County. Gerald was then still subject to a six months' probation order which had been entered on Feb. 25, 1964, as a result of his having been in the company of another boy who had stolen a wallet from a lady's purse. The police action on June 8 was taken as a result of a verbal complaint by a neighbor of the boys, Mrs. Cook, about a telephone call made to her in which the caller or callers made lewd or indecent remarks. It will suffice for purposes of this opinion to say that the remarks or questions put to her were of the irritatingly offensive, adolescent, sex variety. . . .

The judge committed Gerald as a juvenile delinquent to the State Industrial School "for the period of his minority [that is, until 21], unless sooner discharged by due process of law." [Gerald was 15.] . . .

II

It is claimed that juveniles obtain benefits from the special procedures applicable to them which more than offset the substance of normal due process. As we shall discuss, the observance of due process standards, intelligently and not ruthlessly administered, will not compel the States to abandon or displace any of the substantive benefits of the juvenile process. But it is important, we think, that the claimed benefits of the juvenile process should be candidly appraised. Neither sentiment nor folklore should cause us to shut our eyes, for example, to such startling findings as that reported in an exceptionally reliable study of repeaters or recidivism conducted by the Stanford Research Institute for the President's Commission on Crime in the District of Columbia. This commission's report states:

"In fiscal 1966 approximately 66 per cent of the 16-and 17-year-old juveniles referred to the court by the Youth Aid Division had been before the court previously. In 1965, 56 per cent of those in the receiving home were repeaters. The S.R.I. study revealed that 61 per cent of the sample juvenile court referrals in 1965 had been previously referred at least once and that 42 per cent had been referred at least twice before."

Certainly, these figures and the high crime rates among juveniles could not lead us to conclude that the absence of constitutional protections reduces crime, or that the juvenile system, functioning free of constitutional inhibitions as it has largely done, is effective to reduce crime or rehabilitate offenders. We do not mean by this to denigrate the juvenile court process. . . .

But the features of the juvenile system which its proponents have asserted are of unique benefit will not be impaired by constitutional domestication. For example, the commendable principles relating to the processing and treatment of juveniles separately from adults are in no way involved or affected by the procedural issues under discussion.

Further, we are told that one of the important benefits of the special juvenile court procedures is that they avoid classifying the juvenile as a "criminal." The juvenile offender is now classed as a "delinquent. . . . " It is disconcerting, however, that this term has come to involve only slightly less stigma than the term "criminal" applied to adults. It is also emphasized that in practically all jurisdictions, statutes provide that an adjudication of the child as a delinquent shall not operate as a civil disability or disqualify him for civil service appointment. There is no reason why the application of due process requirements should interfere with such provisions.

Beyond this, it is frequently said that juveniles are protected by the process from disclosure of their deviational behavior. As the Supreme Court of Arizona phrased it in the present case, the summary procedures of Juvenile Courts are sometimes defended by a statement that it is the law's policy "to hide youthful errors from the full gaze of the public and bury them in the graveyard of the forgotten past."

This claim of secrecy, however, is more rhetoric than reality. Disclosure of court records is discretionary with the judge in most jurisdictions. Statutory restrictions almost invariably apply only to the court records, and even as to those the evidence is that many courts routinely furnish information to the F.B.I. and the military, and on request to government agencies and even to private employers. Of more importance are police records. In most states the police keep a complete file of juvenile "police contacts" and have complete discretion as to disclosure of juvenile records. Police departments receive requests for information from the F.B.I. and other law-enforcement agencies, the Armed Forces, and social service agencies, and most of them generally comply. . . .

In any event, there is no reason why consistently with due process, a State cannot continue, if it deems it appropriate, to provide and to improve provision for the confidentiality of records of police contacts and court action relating to juveniles. It is interesting to note, however, that the Arizona Supreme Court used the confidentiality argument as a justification for the type of notice which is here attacked as inadequate for due process purposes. The parents were given merely general notice that their child was charged with "delinquency." No facts were specified. The Arizona court held, however, that in addition to this general "notice," the child and his parents must be advised "of the facts involved in the case" no later than the initial hearing by the judge. Obviously, this does not "bury" the word about the child's transgressions. It merely defers the time of disclosure to a point when it is of limited use to the child or his parents in preparing his defense or explanation. . . .

The early conception of the juvenile court proceeding was one in which a fatherly judge touched the heart and conscience of the erring youth by talking over his problems, by paternal advice and admonition, and in which, in extreme situations, benevolent and wise institutions of the state provided guidance and help "to save him from a downward career."

Then, as now, goodwill and compassion were admirably prevalent. But recent studies have, with surprising unanimity, entered sharp dissent as to the validity of this gentle conception. They suggest that the appearance as well as the actuality of fairness, impartiality and orderliness—in short, the essentials of due process—may be a more impressive and more therapeutic attitude so far as the juvenile is concerned. . . .

It is not suggested that juvenile court judges should fail appropriately to take account, in their demeanor and conduct, of the emotional and psychological attitude of the juveniles with whom they are confronted. While due process requirements will, in some instances, introduce a degree of order and regularity to Juvenile Court proceedings to determine delinquency, and in contested cases will introduce some elements of the adversary system, nothing will require that the conception of the kindly juvenile judge be replaced by its opposite, nor do we here rule upon the question whether ordinary due process requirements must be observed with respect to hearings to determine the disposition of the delinquent child.

Ultimately, however, we confront the reality of that portion of the Juvenile Court process with which we deal in this case. A boy is charged with misconduct. The boy is committed to an institution where he may be restrained of liberty for years. It is of no constitutional consequence—and of limited practical meaning—that the institution to which he is committed is called an Industrial School. The fact of the matter is that, however euphemistic the title, a "receiving home" or an "industrial school" for juveniles is an institution of confinement. His world becomes "a building with white-washed walls, regimented routine and institutional hours. . . . "

Instead of mother and father and sisters and brothers and friends and classmates, his world is peopled by guards, custodians, state employees, and "delinquents" confined with him for anything from waywardness to rape and homicide.

In view of this, it would be extraordinary if our Constitution did not require the procedural regularity and the exercise of care implied in the phrase "due process." Under our Constitution, the condition of being a boy does not justify a kangaroo court. . . .

If Gerald had been over 18, he would not have been subject to Juvenile Court proceedings. For the particular offense immediately involved, the maximum punishment would have been a fine of $5 to $50, or imprisonment in jail for not more than two months.

Instead, he was committed to custody for a maximum of six years. If he had been over 18 and had committed an offense to which such a sentence might apply, he would have been entitled to substantial rights under the Constitution of the United States as well as under Arizona's laws and constitution. The United States Constitution would guarantee him rights and protections with respect to arrest, search and seizure, and pretrial interrogations. It would assure him of specific notice of the charges and adequate time to decide his course of action and to prepare his defense. He would be entitled to clear advice that he could be represented by counsel, and, at least if a felony were involved, the state would be required to provide counsel if his parents were unable to afford it.

If the court acted on the basis of his confession, careful procedures would be required to assure its voluntariness. If the case went to trial, confrontation and opportunity for cross-examination would be guaranteed. So wide a gulf between the State's treatment of the adult and of the child requires a bridge sturdier than mere verbiage, and reasons more persuasive than cliche can provide. . . .

III

Notice of Charges

Appellants allege that the Arizona juvenile code is unconstitutional or alternatively that the proceedings before the juvenile court were constitutionally defective because of failure to provide adequate notice of the hearings.

No notice was given to Gerald's parents when he was taken into custody, on Monday, June 8. On that night, when Mrs. Gault went to the Detention Home, she was orally informed that there would be a hearing the next afternoon and was told the reason why Gerald was in custody. The only written notice Gerald's parents received at any time was a note on plain paper from Officer Flagg delivered on Thursday or Friday, June 11 or 12, to the effect that the judge had set Monday, June 15, "for further hearings on Gerald's delinquency."

A "petition" was filed with the court on June 9 by Officer Flagg, reciting only that he was informed and believed that "said minor is a delinquent minor and that it is necessary that some order be made by the honorable court for said minor's welfare."

The applicable Arizona statute provides for a petition to be filed in juvenile court, alleging in general terms that the child is "neglected, dependent, or delinquent." The statute explicitly states that such a general allegation is sufficient, "without alleging the facts." . . .

We cannot agree with the court's conclusion that adequate notice was given to this case. Notice, to comply with due process requirements, must be given sufficiently in advance of scheduled court proceedings so that reasonable opportunity to prepare will be afforded, and it must "set forth the alleged misconduct with particularity." . . .

IV

Right to Counsel

Appellants charge that the Juvenile Court proceedings were fatally defective because the court did not advise Gerald or his parents of their right to counsel, and proceeded with the hearing, the adjudication of delinquency and the order of commitment in the absence of counsel for the child and his parents or an express waiver of the right thereto.

The Supreme Court of Arizona pointed out that "[t]here is disagreement [among the various jurisdictions] as to whether the court must advise the infant that he has a right to counsel." . . . It referred to a provision of the juvenile code which it characterized as requiring "that the probation officer shall look after the interests of neglected, delinquent and dependent children," including representing their interests in court. The court argued that "the parents and the probation officer may be relied upon to protect the infant's interests."

Accordingly it rejected the proposition that "due process requires that an infant have a right to counsel." It said that juvenile courts have the discretion, but not the duty, to allow such representation; it referred specifically to the situation in which the juvenile court discerns conflict between the child and his parents as an instance in which this discretion might be exercised.

We do not agree. Probation officers in the Arizona scheme are also arresting officers. They initiate proceedings and file petitions which they verify, as here, alleging the delinquency of the child; and they testify, as here, against the child.

The probation officer cannot act as counsel for the child. His role in the adjudicatory hearing is as arresting officer and witness against the child. Nor can the judge represent the child. There is no material difference in this respect between adult and juvenile proceedings of the sort here involved. In adult proceedings, this contention has been foreclosed by decisions of this court. A proceeding where the issue is whether the child will be found to be "delinquent" and subjected to the loss of his liberty for years is comparable in seriousness to a felony prosecution.

The juvenile needs the assistance of counsel to cope with problems of law, to make skilled inquiry into the facts, to insist upon regularity of the proceedings, and to ascertain whether he has a defense and to prepare and submit it. . . .

We conclude that the Due Process Clause of the Fourteenth Amendment requires that in respect of proceedings to determine delinquency which may result in commitment to an institution in which the juvenile's freedom is curtailed, the child and his parent must be notified of the child's right to be represented by counsel retained by them, or if they are unable to afford counsel, that counsel will be appointed to represent the child.

At the habeas corpus proceeding, Mrs. Gault testified that she knew that she could have appeared with counsel at the juvenile hearing. This knowledge is not a waiver of the right to counsel which she and her juvenile son had, as we have defined it. They had a right expressly to be advised that they might retain counsel. . . .

V

Confrontation, Self-Incrimination, Cross-Examination

Appellants urge that the writ of habeas corpus should have been granted because of the denial of the rights of confrontation and cross-examination in the Juvenile Court hearings, and because the privilege against self-incrimination was not observed. . . .

It would indeed be surprising if the privilege against self-incrimination were available to hardened criminals but not to children. The language of the Fifth Amendment, applicable to the states by operation of the 14th Amendment, is unequivocal and without exception. . . .

With respect to juveniles, both common observation and expert opinion emphasize that the "distrust of confessions made in certain situations" is imperative in the case of children from early age through adolescence.

In New York, for example, the recently enacted Family Court Act provides that the juvenile and his parents must be advised at the start of the hearing of his right to remain silent. The New York statute also provides that the police must attempt to communicate with the juvenile's parents before questioning him, and that a confession may not be obtained from a child prior to notifying his parents or relatives and releasing the child either to them or the Family Court. . . .

It is also urged, as the Supreme Court of Arizona here asserted, that the juvenile and presumably his parents should not be advised of the juvenile's right to silence because confession is good for the child as the commencement of the assumed therapy of the juvenile court process, and he should be encouraged to assume an attitude of trust and confidence toward the officials of the juvenile process.

United States Reports, Vol. 387, Cases Adjudged in the Supreme Court
(Washington, D.C.: U.S. Government Printing Office, 1967), pp. 1–81.

Notes

1. *Economic Report of the President: 1974, Together with the Annual Report of the Council of Economic Advisers* (Washington, D.C.: Government Printing Office, 1974), pp. 249, 259.
2. Ibid.

3. U.S. Bureau of the Census, *Statistical Abstract of the United States: 1973*, 94th ed. (Washington, D.C.: Government Printing Office, 1973), p. 328.

4. U.S. Bureau of the Census, *Current Population Reports*, Series P 60, No. 77, May 7, 1971.

5. *Economic Report of the President: 1974*, op. cit., p. 276.

6. For a good discussion see *Economic Report of the President: 1973* (Washington, D.C.: Government Printing Office, 1973), pp. 89–112.

7. U.S. Bureau of Labor Statistics, *Employment and Earnings*, monthly in *Monthly Labor Review*.

8. Mark J. Stern, "Did Poor Families Ever Act Strategically?" unpublished manuscript, pp. 26–29.

9. *Economic Report of the President: 1974*, op. cit., p. 219.

10. Roger Daniels, *Coming to America: A History of Immigration and Ethnicity in American Life* (New York: HarperCollins, 1990), p. 288; U.S. Bureau of the Census, Statistical Abstract 1992, 113th ed. (Washington, D.C.: Government Printing Office, 1992), p. 10.

11. Daniels, op. cit., p. 311.

12. David S. Wyman, *Abandonment of the Jews: America and the Holocaust: 1941–1945* (New York: Pantheon Books, 1984), p. 136.

13. An excellent review of this period in our immigration history may be found in Wyman, op. cit., passim, and Daniels, op. cit., pp. 294–304.

14. *Statistical Abstract: 1973*, op. cit., p. 51, and U.S. Department of Commerce, Bureau of the Census, *Historical Statistics of the United States: Colonial Times to 1957* (Washington, D.C.: Government Printing Office, 1960), p. 23 (hereafter cited as *Historical Statistics*). Data from U.S. National Center for Health Statistics, *Vital Statistics of the United States*, annual.

15. *Statistical Abstract: 1973*, op. cit., pp. 58–59.

16. Phyllis J. Day, *A New History of Social Welfare* (Englewood Cliffs, N.J.: Prentice Hall, 1989), p. 367.

17. *Statistical Abstract: 1973*, op. cit., pp. 30, 31.

18. U.S. Bureau of the Census, *Current Population Reports*, Series P 23, No. 29, February 1970.

19. Ibid.

20. U.S. Bureau of Economic Analysis, *Long Term Economic Growth, 1860–1970* (Washington, D.C.: Government Printing Office, 1973), p. 76.

21. Ibid., p. 185.

22. *Statistical Abstract: 1973*, op. cit., p. 585.

23. *Vital Statistics of the United States*, 1942, 1947.

24. *Statistical Abstract: 1973*, op. cit., p. 54. Data from U.S. National Center for Health Statistics.

25. Nathan E. Cohen, *Social Work in the American Tradition* (New York: Dryden Press, 1958), p. 226.

26. Ibid.

27. National Commission on Productivity, *Second Annual Report* (Washington, D.C.: Government Printing Office, 1973), p. 8.

28. *Long Term Economic Growth, 1960–1970*, op. cit., p. 76.

29. *Statistical Abstract: 1973*, op. cit., p. 250.

30. Ibid., p. 319.

31. *Economic Report of the President: 1949, Together with the Annual Economic Review, January 1949, by the Council of Economic Advisers* (Washington, D.C.: Government Printing Office, 1949), pp. 13–15.

32. *Historical Statistics*, p. 167.

33. *Economic Report of the President: 1974*, op. cit., p. 272.

34. Executive Order 8802 of June 25, 1941, Vol. 6, *Federal Register*, p. 3109.

35. For an excellent review of this period, see John Hope Franklin, *From Slavery to Freedom* (New York: Vintage, 1969), pp. 573–607; and Geoffrey Perrett, *Days of Sadness, Years of Triumph: The American People, 1939–1945* (New York: Coward, McCann, and Geoghegan, 1973), pp. 143–154, 310–324.

36. Day, op. cit., p. 360.

37. National Association of Social Workers, *Encyclopedia of Social Work* (New York: NASW, 1971), p. 554.

38. U.S. Congress, House Committee Print No. 4, *Medical Care of Veterans*, 90th Cong., 1st sess., April 17, 1967, p. 168. Prepared for the use of the House Committee on Veterans' Affairs.

39. *The Budget of the United States Government* (Washington, D.C.: Government Printing Office), fiscal years, annually.

40. *Social Work Year Book: 1945* (New York: Russell Sage Foundation, 1945), pp. 84–92, 163, 479–485, 502, 505.

41. U.S. Congress, Public Law No. 625, 77th Cong., 2nd sess., June 23, 1942.

42. Social Work Year Book: 1947 (New York: Russell Sage Foundation, 1947), p. 414.

43. U.S. Congress, Public Law No. 801, 76th Cong., 3rd sess., October 8, 1940.

44. President's Commission on Veterans' Pensions, *The Historical Development of Veterans' Benefits in the United States, A Report on Veterans' Benefits in the United States*, 84th Cong., 2nd sess., House Committee Print No. 244, May 9, 1956, p. 57.

45. Ibid., p. 52.

46. U.S. Congress, Public Law 346, 78th Cong., 2nd sess., June 22, 1944.

47. U.S. Senate, 78th Cong., Finance Committee, Report 755. Cited in the President's Commission on Veterans' Benefits, op. cit., p. 53.

48. President's Commission on Veterans' Benefits, op. cit., p. 55.

49. *Historical Statistics*, p. 740.

50. *Brown v. Board of Education of Topeka*, 347, U.S. 483 (1954).

51. Day, op. cit., pp. 322–323.

52. U.S. Department of Health, Education, and Welfare, *Social Security Bulletin*, monthly.

53. Winifred Bell, *Aid to Dependent Children* (New York: Columbia University Press, 1965).

54. *Benny Max Parrish* v. *The Civil Service Commission of the County of Alameda*, S.F. 22429, Supreme Court of California in Bank, March 27, 1967.

55. Michael Harrington, *The Other America: Poverty in the United States* (New York: Macmillan, 1962); Dwight MacDonald, "Our Invisible Poor," *New Yorker* (January 19, 1963): 37.

56. Ibid.

57. *Economic Report of the President, 1964, Together with the Annual Report of the Council of Economic Advisers* (Washington, D.C.: Government Printing Office, 1964), pp. 55–83.

58. The Civil Rights Act of 1964, Public Law 83–352, 78 Stat. 241, Title VII.

59. U.S. Bureau of the Census, *Statistical Abstract of the United States: 1964*, 85th ed. (Washington, D.C.: Government Printing Office, 1964), and U.S. Bureau of the Census, *Statistical Abstract of the United States: 1971*, 92nd ed. (Washington, D.C.: Government Printing Office, 1971).

60. Office memorandum, Abraham Ribicoff to W. L. Mitchell, commissioner of Social Security, December 6, 1961. To be found in U.S. Congress, House Committee on Ways and Means, *Hearings on H.R. 10032, Public Welfare Amendments of 1962*, 87th Cong., 2nd sess. February 7, 9, and 13, 1962, pp. 158–162.

61. *Hearings on H.R. 10032*, op. cit., p. 64.

62. George K. Wyman, "A Report for the Secretary of Health, Education, and Welfare," August 1961. To be found in *Hearings on H.R. 10032*, op. cit., p. 108.

63. Report of the Ad Hoc Committee on Public Welfare to the Secretary of Health, Education, and Welfare, September 1961. To be found in *Hearings on H.R. 10032*, op. cit., p. 78.

64. Ibid., p. 73.

65. Ibid., pp. 81–100.

66. Ibid., p. 74.

67. Office memorandum, op. cit.

68. President John F. Kennedy, "Message to Congress on Public Welfare," February 1962.

69. Public Law 87–543 had been considered as H. R. 10032 in public hearings held by the House Committee on Ways and Means, February 7, 9, and 13, 1962. It was introduced on March 8, 1962, in the House of Representatives as H.R. 10606 by Congressman Wilbur D. Mills.

70. U.S. Congress, House of Representatives, *Compilation of the Social Security Laws, including the Social Security Act, as Amended, and Related Enactments through December 31, 1962,* House Document No. 616, 87th Cong., 2nd sess., p. 132.

71. *Compilation of the Social Security Laws,* op. cit., Title IV, Sec. 407, p. 142.

72. *Compilation of the Social Security Laws,* op. cit., Sec. 409, pp. 144–146.

73. *Compilation of the Social Security Laws,* op. cit., Sec. 528, p. 158.

74. Gilbert Steiner, *Social Insecurity* (Chicago: Rand McNally, 1966), pp. 142–147. Steiner reviews the reasoning of professional social workers during this period.

75. American Public Welfare Association, statement submitted to the Advisory Council on Public Welfare, San Francisco, California, August 12, 1965, p. 6.

76. See, for example, Herman Levin, "The Essential Voluntary Agency," *Social Work* 11 (January 1966): 98–106. See also Ellen Winston, "A New Era of Partnership in Services for Children," *Child Welfare* 43 (May 1964): 221–225; and in the same issue, Leonard W. Mayo, "Discussion of a New Era of Partnership for Children," pp. 225–228.

77. *Compilation of the Social Security Laws,* op. cit., Title IV, Sec. 403, p. 136.

78. U.S. Department of Health, Education, and Welfare, Social Security Administration, Bureau of Family Services, press release, January 6, 1963.

79. President Lyndon B. Johnson, "Message on Poverty," March 16, 1964.

80. U.S. 88th Cong., 2nd sess., Public Law 88-452, Sec. 2.

81. Congressional presentation, March 17, 1964, prepared under the direction of Sargent Shriver. To be found in *The War on Poverty: The Economic Act of 1964, A Compilation of Materials Relevant to S. 2642, prepared for the Select Subcommittee on Poverty of the U.S. Senate Committee on Labor and Public Welfare,* 88th Cong., 2nd sess., Document No. 86, July 23, 1964, p. 65.

82. June Axinn, "Social Security: History and Prospects," *Current History* (August 1973): 52–56. Data are derived from the *Social Security Bulletin, Annual Statistical Summary* (Washington, D.C.: Government Printing Office, 1986).

83. For a detailed discussion of the politics of aging and the growth of special interest organizations in this period, see John B. Williamson, Linda Evans, and Lawrence A. Powell, *The Politics of Aging* (Springfield, Ill.: Charles B. Thomas, 1982), pp. 89–101, and Robert H. Binstock, "The Politics of Aging Interest Groups," in Robert D. Hudson, ed., *The Aging in Politics* (Springfield, Ill.: Charles B. Thomas, 1981), pp. 52–71.

84. U.S. Department of Health, Education, and Welfare, Welfare Administration, *Having the Power, We Have the Duty,* report of the Advisory Council on Public Welfare to the Secretary of H.E.W., June 29, 1966.

85. Gilbert Steiner, *The State of Welfare* (Washington, D.C.: The Brookings Institution, 1971), p. 109.

86. U.S. Department of Health, Education, and Welfare, "Report of the Task Force in Social Services," submitted to Assistant Secretary Lisle Carter, September 1, 1966, in the files of the department.

87. Quoted in National Association of Social Workers, *Washington Memorandum,* No. 90-1-9, August 30, 1967.

88. National Association of Social Workers, *Policy Statement on Separation of Social Services and Income Security Programs.* Approved by the Board of Directors, June 29, 1967.

89. U.S. Supreme Court, *In re Gault et al.,* No. 116, May 15, 1967.

8

Conservative Resurgence and Social Change: 1968–1992

In 1971, President Richard Nixon vetoed the amendments to the Economic Opportunity Act. The veto was not that surprising. After all, this legislation carried on many War on Poverty programs that Nixon and his party had opposed. What was startling was the tone of his objections. Nixon abandoned traditional mainstream conservative objections to the cost and potential waste associated with social welfare programs and instead focused on its potential for undermining the American family. In his veto message, Nixon asserted that "for the Federal Government to plunge headlong financially into supporting child development would commit the vast moral authority of the National Government to the side of communal approaches to child rearing over [and] against the family-centered approach."[1] Within a year, the battle over the family widened with the Supreme Court's decision in *Roe* v. *Wade* that American women had a constitutional right to abortion services. Congressional passage of the Equal Rights Amendment to the U.S. Constitution in 1972 set off another symbolic battle over the nature of gender and the relationship of the "public" and "private" spheres.

Two major forces framed the history of social welfare between 1968 and 1992. First, in contrast to the previous two decades, the economy grew at a much slower pace. The transition to a post-industrial, information economy combined with a deliberate effort to control inflation to keep economic growth slow and unemployment high. As a result, public welfare faced a host of new demands for services and benefits at a time when there was little economic growth to pay for them.

Second, the 1971 veto message marked the beginning of a sustained ideological attack on social welfare programs. The conservative New Right was deeply suspicious of all government programs and saw social welfare as connected to the declining competitiveness of the American economy, the weakening of its family structure, and the general decline of American moral character.

For a time the economic conservatism of the battle against inflation and the social conservatism of the battle over the family combined to form a powerful social movement that sought to reduce fundamentally the public commitment to social welfare. President Ronald Reagan used the early years of his presidency to lay out a new departure for social welfare, one that would shift power from the federal government to the states, from the public sector to voluntary associations, from open-ended "entitlements" to federal aid to limited block grants.

For the most part, "Reaganism" did not accomplish its goals. The structure of social welfare in 1992 looked more or less the way it had a decade earlier. However, the large tax cuts implemented by Congress and the president in 1981 combined with slow economic growth to limit the reach and effectiveness of existing programs. Rather than marking a new departure in social welfare, the 1980s were a period of declining effectiveness and the neglect of new, pressing social problems such as homelessness and the AIDS epidemic.

The United States was not unique. The welfare state came under attack throughout the Western world. One response to the poor performance of the economy was the abandonment of social welfare programs and efforts to mitigate the inequalities of the marketplace. In constant dollars, per capita expenditures for social welfare had increased at an annual rate of 6.5 percent in 1970, but fell to 4.2 percent a year by 1980. Despite an increase in poverty, the inequality of income distribution, and the startling visibility in the number of homeless in our major cities, social welfare expenditures increased only 1 percent in 1987. There were major cutbacks in many support and social service programs for the most vulnerable, and further cutbacks in social programs were proposed.[2]

Unemployment during the 1970s averaged 5.4 percent in the first half of the decade and jumped to 8.3 percent in the recession of 1975, recovering, but still at 5.8 percent in 1979. Consumer prices, driven by the sharp rise in oil prices, went up throughout the decade. Inflation remained out of control until the recession of 1982–1983. The recession slowed the inflation rate but at a heavy price for American workers. Unemployment rose to 9.5 percent and declined only slowly in the years following. By 1990, the unemployment rate stood at over 6 percent and inflation heightened.

Nowhere is the slowdown of economic growth and the shortfall in its distribution to American families from 1970 to 1990 clearer than in the data on gross national product (GNP) and on family income. GNP and median family income grew during the period but at a disappointing pace. After adjusting for inflation, the rise in GNP in the years between 1970 and 1990 was just over 40 percent. Household median income in constant dollars rose and fell during the period in response to changes in levels of unemployment and to price increases. But in 1990, it was at the same level as it had been in 1979 and only slightly higher than it was in 1970.[3] While median income remained level, the spread between the very rich and the very poor grew markedly. The number of billionaires quadrupled during the 1980s; the number of people below the poverty line increased by 35 percent.[4]

During the 1970s, the Organization of Petroleum Exporting Countries (OPEC) made dramatically clear the extent to which the American economy was subject to global pressures. Domestic inflation had disturbing implications for those who lived on fixed incomes especially, as well as for those who worked and found their ability to purchase goods and services declining. Rising prices combined with rising unemployment hit most heavily those least able to withstand wage and job loss.

The search for economic security has grown more intricate. The previous period, the era of the War on Poverty, had welcomed economic growth, consumerism, and affluence as panaceas for almost all economic and social problems. The environmental issues, urban decline, and globalization were problems without straightforward solutions. Union demands for wage and benefits increases to offset the erosions of inflation, decreased employment stability, industry's demand for tax relief as a stimulant to investment in new equipment and new ventures, taxpayer "revolts" against rising taxes and government expenditures, and the demand for restrained governmental budgets all contributed to the complexity of the economic situation.

Conservatives had long been suspicious of government action, but by the early 1970s they had been joined by many liberals. The war in Vietnam, government surveillance of protesters, and the Watergate affair had led many groups in American society to view the government in a less favorable light. Common Cause, a privately financed consumer's group, addressed its national constituency with the "plain and simple" truth:

> The reason the United States cannot solve the urgent problems that are plaguing our country, is because the government *is the problem.*[5]

From the start of the 1980 presidential campaign, the Republican candidate, Ronald Reagan, argued that the Democratic party had been unable to meet new and serious economic and social conditions. As president, Reagan acted to decrease the role of government in economic life. Arguing for "supply-side" economics, deregulation of business, and tax cuts as a means of stimulating economic growth, President Reagan attacked domestic social welfare programs. The first President Bush, while couching his arguments in a "kinder and gentler" manner, continued to allow his concern for interest rates and budget stability to take precedence over considerations of individual well-being. Changes in our economy, our political structure, family organization, and the age structure of our population combined to make large social welfare changes necessary. However, necessary social interventions took a back seat to tax cuts and budget restraint.

Changing Employment Patterns

The transition of the economy from an industrial to an informational base was complicated by government monetary policy and its implication for unemployment. Since 1946, the federal government had committed itself to pursuing maximum employment policies, a pledge it had reiterated with the passage of the Full Employment and Balanced Growth Act of 1978. Yet, with Paul Volker as its chairman, the Federal Reserve Board began using high interest rates as a means of slowing inflation. As a result, unemployment began a steady rise, reaching 11 percent in 1982, the highest level since the Great Depression. How could government commit itself both to "full employment" and to using unemployment to fight inflation? Economists had provided an answer with one acronym: NAIRU. The "nonaccelerating-inflation rate of unemployment" was defined as the lowest unemployment rate that was consistent with low inflation. This rate—which was estimated at around 6 percent during the 1980s—was redefined as the "natural" rate of full employment. Thus, for more than a decade, government policy defined a stagnant economy with more than 6 million unemployed workers as full employment.

The fight against inflation during the 1970s and 1980s harmed not only those who were unemployed; the loss of production because of slow economic growth harmed all Americans. Indeed, a conservative estimate of the lost production between 1974 and 1995 was equal to *$1.6 trillion*—nearly three months of the gross domestic product in 1995.[6] The years between 1968 and 1992 were characterized by a shift from an industrial economic base to a service economy. From 1970 to 1990 employment increased 47 percent, but manufacturing employment increased only 2 percent while the number of jobs in service industries rose 92 percent. More recently, more than 18 million new jobs were created between 1980 and 1990, but 88 percent of these were in services, finance, and sales. Factory employment

The recession of 1974–75 signaled a major restructuring of the American economy. Thousands of workers permanently lost their jobs and had to rely on unemployment compensation to weather economic hard times.

© Charles Gatewood/Pearson Education/PH College

declined during this period, although manufacturing productivity and output increased.[7]

For displaced workers of the industrial labor force, the result was unemployment and increased economic uncertainty. The new service jobs were likely to carry lower wages and be subject to involuntary temporary, part-time, and part-year employment. Social security—unemployment insurance, disability insurance, and old age insurance—were all adversely affected. With lower rates of unionization, the provision of corporate health and pension benefits had become serious social concerns. The expanding service sector had historically been a major source of employment for women and ethnic minorities, albeit one with generally low wages and poor working conditions.

In 1990, 45 percent of the work force was female, but 61 percent of those employed in services were women; 10 percent of those in the work force were black, 12 percent of those in services. And in the lowest paying sector of the service industry, personal services and hospitals, about 75 percent of the employees were female and 15 percent black; less than 10 percent were white men.

The Changing Family

Conservatives were right that family life *was* changing in important ways during the 1970s and 1980s, although they erred in seeing all of the trends as negative. At the start of the 1990s, family life was very different from the typical domestic family for whom our social programs had been designed fifty-five years earlier. In 1935, at the time of the passage of the Social Security Act, a nuclear family consisted of a mother who was a homemaker, a father who went to work, and perhaps three children. In contrast, the average household in 1990 was no longer a two-parent home with several children. This description applied to less than 30 percent of American households and 38 percent of families. Only 13 percent of families included two parents, one wage earner and one person home with the children. The median age of first marriage had risen during the 1980s and there were large increases in single persons, unmarried people having children, divorces, and desertions. The continuing popularity of marriage was countered by rising divorce rates.

The number of female-headed households rose sharply, with the fastest increase during the 1970s. In the 1980s, the increase in families headed by a single woman or by a grandmother continued, but at a slower pace. By 1990, 51 percent of all black children under age 18, 27 percent of Hispanic children, and 16 percent of white children were living with just one parent. In twenty years the proportion of families that were headed by women had doubled. The number of such families was up by 75 percent among blacks and by 106 percent among whites. The children in these households were being supported largely by their mothers.[8]

The average size of the U.S. household decreased about 21 percent in the twenty years from 1970 to 1990. However, this drop was not distributed equally throughout the population. There were more people who never married, more families that had no children, and more families that had just one child. In 1990, half of all American families had no current child-rearing responsibilities. There were also families that continued to have three, four, or five children. The result was that 80 percent of children were supported by only 30 percent of the population. This unequal distribution of the task of supporting children had a racial dimension. The birthrate was significantly higher in the black community than in the white; that part of the population least able to afford the responsibility of raising the next generation bore a disproportionate share of its cost.

The distribution of children had political implications. It became harder to obtain money for programs for the support of women and children that were seen as a less universal need than it was in the past. Some indications of this effect were seen in the increasing reluctance to support public education in some parts of the country and in the successful veto by President Bush of the Family and Medical Leave Act of 1990. That bill would have required employers with fifty or more employees to provide unpaid leave to new parents as well as to workers who needed to care for a sick family member. About fifteen states had legislation protecting jobs for workers when they needed extended time away for family or medical reasons, but for most American families there was no parental leave.[9]

Many Americans had fond memories of the "traditional" breadwinner family of the 1950s. Even though American families were better off because of women's earnings, and men and women shared the responsibilities of parenthood more equally, nostalgia prompted many Americans to decry the changes in family life. As a result, efforts by the Carter administration to reach a consensus on "family policy" foundered. Debates over abortion, equal rights, and the proper role of the federal government found no middle ground during these years.

In 1935, when the Social Security Act was passed, persons 65 years of age and over represented 6 percent of the total population; by 1970, the percentage had risen to 9.7; by 1990, more than 12 percent of the total population. By the year 2030, it was projected that 23 percent would be over the age of 65. The proportion of the working population—persons between 18 and 64 years of age—declined. Falling birthrates, combined with increased life expectancy, led to a new population pattern and a new set of social welfare needs. They also led to many concerns about the dependency ratio—the ratio between workers and nonworkers in society. The expectation that the working segment of the population could and would continue to finance the welfare of those not expected to work at the same level was questioned increasingly. With increased numbers, the aging became more politically effective. They needed and demanded new programs and expanded benefits, as the working population may have felt less able to provide them.[10]

This was offset in part by the increase of women in the labor force. The proportion of women working rose sharply in the twentieth century. In 1900, 20 percent of adult women worked. By 1960, on the eve of the civil rights and feminist revolutions, that proportion had increased to 30 percent; in 1970, it stood at 49 percent and by 1990, 69 percent of women of working age were in the labor force.[11] The reality of women in the workforce, and, consequently, the increased expectation that women hold jobs outside the home, had an impact not only on family social and economic status, but also on many social welfare programs. The social insurance system came under scrutiny for its treatment of working women. Issues of child care moved to the fore of public attention, while programs for poor women "not expected to work" became more suspect than in the past.

The decade of the 1970s brought a current of economic, social, and political malaise to American life. As in other eras leading to periods of reform, old values and old beliefs were scrutinized. But the frustrations and disappointments of the 1970s made "traditional" values more attractive to many Americans. Indeed, as distrust of government and of political leaders deepened, and the economic situation worsened, the general citizenry seemed to lose hope that positive change would occur for the country as a whole; individuals and self-interest groups began to look even more to their own. As faith in collective action faded, the traditional American confidence in the efficacy of individual effort prevailed. Ronald Reagan won the presidential election of 1980 on the promise of a return to conservative values that would restore the country's greatness.

The cost of high unemployment during the late 1970s and early 1980s fell disproportionately on low-income families. Their situation was further undermined by the budget policies of the Reagan administration. Although President Reagan failed to secure the large cuts in domestic programs he sought early in his administration, he did succeed in reducing federal income taxes, especially for those in high income brackets. As a result, throughout the 1980s, there was great pressure on the federal government to reduce spending. The resulting scramble to protect existing programs meant that new social needs—such as the increased visibility of the homeless and the emergence of the AIDS epidemic—had a hard time securing the funding they needed. Increasingly, government returned to a "residual" approach to the problems of the poor. Public programs acted only as a tattered safety net for those who could not fend for themselves.

Poverty and Income Distribution

Data from the Social Security Administration have traced a decline in the numbers of those counted poor from 39.5 million in 1959—the first year of the poverty count—to 31.9 million in 1988, a reduction in the poverty rate from 22.4 percent of the population to 13.1 percent. The rapid growth of in-kind programs—food stamps, housing subsidies, medical care payments—has, of course, increased the real income of the lowest income groups and further reduced the number of poor. Indeed, some observers have argued that, with the expansion of noncash transfers, and the suspected underreporting of income that occurs,

one can conclude that the goal of eliminating income poverty as stated by President Johnson in 1964 had been virtually achieved before the onset of the 1974–75 recession.[12]

Nonetheless, there were still grave poverty concerns in the United States. For one thing, poverty increased in the 1980s. The War on Poverty had led to a dramatic decrease in the late 1960s. During the 1970s, the poverty rate remained stable at about 11 to 12 percent. It rose to 15.2 percent during the Reagan recession of 1982–1983. Indeed, by 1990, 33.6 million people were counted poor—32 percent more than in 1970.

Second, the distribution of poverty was far from random. On the contrary, it was structured by race, ethnicity, sex, family situation, age, and employment status. For whites, the official poverty rate was about 11 percent in 1990; for Hispanics, 25 percent; for African Americans, 30 percent; and for Native Americans, 31 percent. The rate for households where the head worked full time was 4 percent; the rate for nonworking households, 25 percent.

Poverty among two-parent families decreased sharply while that of single-parent families rose. By the end of the period, 34 percent of one-parent, female-headed households were poor. During much of the 1970s, increased job opportunities and wage hikes helped. But much of the financial success was dependent upon the higher labor force participation of women, of working wives and mothers. Obviously, two-parent (and possibly two-earner) families were in better financial shape, but the implications of having both parents working and out of the home remained unexplored. Major questions about marriage, family life, and child care remained unanswered.

The biggest decline in poverty was among the aging. Between 1959 and 1970, the incidence of poverty among the elderly was reduced by about one-third, from 35 percent to 24 percent. It fell by more than one-third more by 1980, despite the increase in the number of persons who are 65 years and over in the population. By 1990, it was down to 12 percent. The exit from poverty experienced by the elderly was largely due to the effectiveness of income transfer programs, particularly of old age insurance. In 1972, an increase of 20 percent in old age insurance benefits was legislated; in 1974, it was an 11 percent increase. Starting in 1975, increases in retirement income were tied to increases in prices and average wages. Additionally, the passage of the Supplemental Security Act, which began operation in January 1974, provided a means-tested income transfer program guaranteeing a minimum income for the elderly and disabled. Furthermore, Supplemental Security Income (SSI) benefits, like social insurance, were indexed to keep pace with inflation. Automatic increases in transfer payments continued to help this group when food, heat, and housing costs did not outstrip gains. Nevertheless, the aging continued to be vulnerable to poverty. Many, if not "in poverty," lived *close* to poverty. More than 20 percent of the aged lived below 125 percent of the poverty line.

Children's poverty, in contrast, emerged as a major problem. In 1959, the poverty rate for children under the age of eighteen was 26 percent, about one-quarter higher than that for the population as a whole. During the 1960s, the poverty rate for children fell faster than that for the entire population to 15 percent in 1970. However, over the next twenty years, much of this improvement was lost. By 1990, the child poverty rate stood at 20 percent, nearly 1 1/2 times the total population figure of 13.5 percent.

A number of social realities increased the risk of poverty for American children. Changes in fertility rates meant that poorer groups in the population were having a larger share of all children. In addition, increased rates of divorce and single parent-hood meant that a larger proportion of children had to rely on the income of one parent. Finally, beginning in the middle of the 1970s, states began a concerted effort to restrict Aid to Families with Dependent Children. States used a variety of administrative barriers to restrict the growth of the welfare rolls and failed to adjust benefits for inflation, leading to a decline of more than a third in the "real" value of benefits. African American and Hispanic children suffered the most from all of these changes. By 1990, nearly 40 percent of them were living in poverty.

For Native Americans, the years of Presidents Nixon, Ford, and Carter were a mix of progress and retreat. There were improvements in health services and education. There was even some political representation in Western states. But the loss of land was still in progress, with only minimal repayments.

Reagan administration policies hit Native Americans very hard. Unemployment on the reservations reached 80 percent. In part in response to the leasing of tribal reservation land to white families, in part in response to the high unemployment rates and lack of opportunities on the reservations, many Native Americans migrated to urban areas. They still fared very poorly. High unemployment rates and very low incomes were typical. Native Americans were not eligible for state social services or support. They had to rely on federal programs for job training, housing assistance, and child welfare services. Thus, the social service cutbacks of the Reagan years affected this population with particular force. Poverty rates reached as high as 57 percent in some parts of the West.[13]

Frustration in regard to the eradication of poverty was aggravated by failure to agree on how to define it. Measuring poverty as an absolute dollar amount, as with the annually computed poverty index, was increasingly questioned. In 1959, the poverty line for a family of four was about one-half the median family income ($2,793 versus $5,417). As the growth of family incomes outstripped inflation, the gap between the two increased. In 1990, the median family income of $35,353 was nearly three times the poverty line for a family of four ($12,293). The deprivation of the poor resulted both from their lack of income and from the fact that they were falling behind the experience of average families.

Since the end of World War II, income distribution in the United States became less equal. As shown in Table 8.1, most of this change occurred after 1980. This happened despite economic growth, a War on Poverty, an increase in the labor-force participation of women, a liberalizing of social insurance benefits, and an expansion of social services. Basic control of income and of wealth in the United States became more concentrated at the top. The growth of wealth of the top income quintile, increased inequality of wages, rising regressive social security taxes and state and local sales taxes, and a decrease in the progressivity of federal income taxes all played their part. A combination of market factors and government policy led to a situation in which the rich became richer and the poor, poorer.[14]

Property and other assets were even less equally distributed than income. Whereas the top 1 percent of families controlled 4 percent of all income in 1988, they controlled 20 percent of all net financial assets, a larger share of the nation's wealth than the bottom *80* percent of the population. The economic gap between the races was

TABLE 8.1   *Distribution of Income*

	Percentage of National Income		
Income Class	*1947*	*1980*	*1990*
Lowest quintile	5.1%	5.1%	3.9%
Second quintile	11.8	11.6	9.6
Third quintile	16.7	17.5	16.0
Fourth quintile	23.2	24.3	24.1
Highest quintile	43.2	41.5	46.4

Source: Current Population Survey

more dramatic for wealth than income. African American married couples had a family income in 1988 that was about 80 percent that of white couples, but the net worth of the average black couple ($17,437) was just 27 percent that of white couples ($65,024).[15]

The Battle over "Rights"

The state of the economy was only one factor shaping social welfare. The concern of the 1960s with the rights of oppressed groups, paced by the militancy of the black community, led to advances in rights to privacy, due process, and equal protection. The emergence of many groups—women, students, children, the aging, Native Americans, prisoners, homosexuals, and others—demanding change resulted in their gaining at least some basic recognition. The historical value of individualism broadened to a demand for group-determined rights.

The American Indian Movement organized for militant defense of the rights of Native Americans. The 1970s saw the formation of a new Council of Energy Resources, which took to the courts to fight for rights to the development of the coal, oil, and other resources needed to promote industries on the reservations.

There were setbacks, but there were also victories. Some land claims were won, some land was put in trust for development for the benefit of Native Americans, and additional sums of money were appropriated to the Bureau of Indian Affairs for education. Nonetheless, Native Americans remained the poorest of the poor in the United States.

The period from 1970 to 1990 included conflicting trends in civil rights. In the 1970s, successes in extending civil liberties were scored in affirmative action programs and in efforts to replace institutionalization with community-based programs. Judicial decisions required the payment of reparations to groups who had been shown to have suffered from discriminatory pay and promotion differentials. In July 1980, the Supreme Court, in *Fullilove* v. *Klutznick*, upheld the use of quotas for minority contractors when it decided that Congress could award federal funds on the basis of race to redress past racial discrimination.[16] The courts seesawed on the issue of affirmative action throughout the decade. In 1984, the Supreme Court decided in a 6–3 decision that seniority overrules affirmative action concerns with regard to layoffs.[17] A May 1986 decision confirmed that position, but found that the adoption of hiring goals favoring minorities would be a permissible way for a government employer to redress its past discrimination.[18] In July 1986, in two cases, one involving New York City sheet metal workers and one involving firefighters in Cleveland, the use of affirmative action in the workplace to address past discrimination was endorsed when less drastic approaches would not work. In February 1987, in a 5–4 decision, the court endorsed "catch-up quotas" to counter severe past discrimination against blacks and the following month extended preferential hiring to women.[19]

By 1989, however, as its composition changed and conservatives achieved a majority, the Supreme Court began to back away from its support of affirmative action. In January, the court invalidated a Richmond law that set aside 30 percent of public works funds to minority-owned construction companies.[20] This was followed by a series of decisions against the use of racial or sex preferences to remedy past discrimination and making it increasingly difficult for plaintiffs to prove employment discrimination.

Against this background, Congress took action and passed the Civil Rights Act of 1990, which sought to reverse the Supreme Court's decisions and shift the burden of proof back to employers on discrimination issues. Employees did not have to demonstrate discrimination; employers would have to show that a practice that hurts women or minorities was necessary to the success of the business. The bill facilitated opportunities for employees to challenge court orders, granted victims of intentional discrimination the right to recover compensatory and punitive damages, and reaffirmed that any intentional job bias was illegal. President Bush vetoed the bill on October 22, 1990, on the grounds that it would force employers to adopt hiring and promotion quotas to avoid discrimination suits. The Senate failed by one vote to override the veto, leaving the expectation that the legislation would be reintroduced in future congressional sessions.

The same pattern of expansion and then a retrenchment applied to immigration policy. In 1965, the tie between the admission of immigrants and their ethnic origin was broken, and for over a decade it appeared that the U.S. fear of alien cultures was fading. Concerns about the economic success of a more open policy began arising during the early 1980s. By 1980, there were political, medical, and economic doubts about the entry of immigrants, who were seen by American labor as competitors for jobs, and about the participation of "foreigners" in education, health, and welfare services.

In addition to planned immigration, there were refugee admissions. Refugees from Indochina, from Haiti, and, in 1980, a new Cuban refugee population arrived in large numbers. Indeed, the anticipated ceilings on immigration of about 290,000 people annually were only a small part of the picture. Many more immigrants came into the country as close relatives of U.S. citizens or as refugees than were entering under the hemispheric quotas. Of the 1.5 million legal immigrants in 1990, fewer than 300,000 came under the immigration quotas; the remainder, 1.2 million, were exempt from numerical limitations.[21] Added to this were large numbers of illegal entrants, many from Mexico.

Both the refugees from Cuba and those from Haiti were greeted with less than open arms. It was rumored that President Fidel Castro of Cuba had been releasing prisoners and mental patients to come to the United States. The presence of the AIDS virus in both the Cuban and Haitian refugees was seen as another barrier to their admission. In the end, the Cuban refugees were admitted and the Haitians rejected. After much bureaucratic maneuvering, the political arguments in favor of embarrassing the communist regime overcame other objections and the Cuban refugees were admitted and given generous support by the U.S. government. The Haitian refugees were sent back to Haiti or placed in long-term detention because they were "only" seeking refuge from poverty, not from a political enemy. Many commentators have pointed to the role of racial prejudice in the decision.[22]

Immigration policy became dominated by two economic concerns. One was the fear for jobs. In 1965, we thought we needed more professional and more skilled labor to meet the demands of an expanding economy. But economic growth was slower than anticipated and, in addition, the industrial base of our economy was being replaced by a service base. As cheap labor, immigrants were viewed as competition for these jobs. Further, it was feared that immigrants would avail themselves too extensively of education services and public aid—cash welfare programs, food stamps, and Medicaid. In 1982, the Supreme Court ruled that all children regardless of immigration status had the right to attend public schools. But the benefits issue recurred throughout the period. Earlier in our history, immigrants were suspect for their religious and political ideas because they were feared as anarchists or communists or because of their possible allegiance to an enemy country. By 1990, however, economic issues had replaced political ones as the center of concern.

For children, too, there was a retreat from rights during the 1980s. The promise of the *Gault* decision of 1967, protecting the rights of children in trouble with the law, was compromised. There was visible return to giving priority to rehabilitation over justice in juvenile proceedings despite the paucity of resources that undermined the quality of services.

On a state level, the intent of laws such as Pennsylvania's Act 148, designed to support deinstitutionalization and community/own-home planning for children, was countered by a lack of supportive community services and by active efforts to legally cut the tie between dependent children and their mothers. The Office of Child Development's thrust toward "permanency planning," though overtly intended to protect children from the uncertainties of longtime foster care placements, unnecessarily risked the permanent separation of some children from their natural parents. The notion of going "beyond the best interest of the child"[23] to forge new permanent ties could, in the 1990s, prove an updated version of "binding out." People suffering from mental illness and mental retardation also saw their rights expand during the 1970s, but then fail to be fully realized. Since the early nineteenth century, institutions—first called 'insane asylums' and later called 'state hospitals'—had been the major policy response for this population. By the 1960s, innovations in therapy and research had led to the beginning of a community mental health system that would treat people with mental illnesses in their own communities.

But the institutions persisted, typically filled with individuals without resources or support to explore alternatives. In 1972, however, the Supreme Court (Wyatt v. Stickney) ruled that states could not continue to "warehouse" the mentally ill and mentally retarded. The court recognized a "right to treatment" that placed the burden on states to create noninstitutional alternatives to institutionalization that would reintegrate these populations into the community.

During the 1970s, lawsuits and public policy emptied many institutions. In 1955, more than five hundred thousand Americans lived in state psychiatric hospitals; by the 1990s, less than 60,000 did. In some states, massive efforts were made to provide services to reintegrate the mentally ill and mentally retarded while in other localities "dumping" was a more accurate description of the policy implementation. Concerns about cost, the hostility of current residents to the creation of community-based group homes (the acronym NIMBY—not in my back yard—came into common usage), and the largely untested strategies for community integration hampered efforts and led to mixed results.

During the 1980s, as fiscal constraints limited funding for new initiatives, even successful programs found themselves scrambling for funding. On the one hand, as with many voluntary social welfare efforts stretching back more than a century, advocates of community action were shown to be overly optimistic about the ability of voluntary efforts to reintegrate these populations. On the other hand, government found itself quite adept at first limiting and then cutting funding available for programs. Eventually, many mentally ill individuals found themselves reinstitutionalized, this time in prisons and jails instead of state hospitals.

The retreat on rights hit welfare families most severely. During the 1960s, the Supreme Court had strengthened the rights of welfare recipients by supporting their claims to due process, privacy, and the right to migrate. Between 1970 and 1990, a combination of legislation, court decisions, and administrative actions weakened these new, insecure rights. The federal government weakened its prohibitions on house searches while the New York state legislature used the failure to find standard housing as a means of denying welfare payments to new migrants.

Further changes in the requirement for AFDC moved us even closer toward mandatory workfare during the 1980s. With the passage of the Family Support Act in 1988, in every state AFDC recipients with children age six or older were required to work or attend a job training program or school. A state could require participation in work or education programs even for recipients with children as young as three years. If a recipient did not meet the state's behavioral rules, she might be "sanctioned," that is, her grant might be reduced or even eliminated. As the program was administered, evidence grew that it was severely punitive.[24]

Perhaps the most visible civil rights battle of the period was in the area of access to abortion. In two 1973 cases (*Roe* v. *Wade* and *Doe* v. *Bolton*), the Supreme Court established women's control over their own bodies by supporting their right to abortion during the first trimester of pregnancy. Since then there have been repeated attempts by "right-to-life" groups to argue the viability and rights of the fetus over the rights of the mother. While abortion was legal in the United States, proponents of abortion, the "pro-choice" groups, feared the implications for women of the changing composition of the Supreme Court. For poor women, the battle had already been lost, since the court ruled that the states were not required to make Medicaid funds available for abortions except in pregnancies resulting from rape or directly threatening their health.[25] By 1990, an uneasy balance had been reached on abortion. The public overwhelmingly supported abortion as part of the right to privacy, but was unwilling to pay the cost of this right for women who could not afford it. In reality, an increasing proportion of women were denied this reproductive right either because they could not afford it or because services were not accessible.

On the legislative and judicial fronts, one group—people with physical or mental disabilities—fared better. The Americans with Disabilities Act of 1990 established comprehensive civil rights. The law prohibited discrimination against people with physical or mental impairments in employment, transportation, and public accommodations. The regulations implementing the legislation required that new construction for public accommodations—schools, libraries, restaurants, and hospital and nursing home rooms, for example—be accessible. Existing businesses were required to make alterations to buildings to accommodate special needs unless they could show that expenses would be too great. The intent was to integrate those who have disabilities into all aspects of life.

Unfortunately, concern for the welfare of disabled people did not extend to their pension and public welfare rights. Despite repeated court rulings that disability insurance benefits could not be arbitrarily cut off, the Social Security Administration was slow to revise its eligibility procedures. The number of people receiving Disability Insurance (DI) or Supplemental Security Income was kept limited. For adults, the General Accounting Office (GAO) reported that over one-half of the applicants who had been denied benefits between 1984 and 1987 reported not working, and many reported they did not anticipate ever working again. Over two-thirds of those denied DI and not able to work reported serious income inadequacy, as did those denied benefits but working at least part-time.[26]

The right of children with disabilities to income support received a boost in 1990 when the Supreme Court ruled that the adult standard for establishing a disability applied to young people as well. As a result, eligibility for Supplemental Security Income for children began to expand after 1990. Yet, the results were mixed. No sooner did the Court decision take effect than budget-cutters in Congress looked to the incomes of children with disabilities as a source of "savings." The 1996 welfare reform law repealed this new entitlement.

Expenditures for Social Welfare

Total federal expenditures for social welfare continued to expand during the 1970s and 1980s, but the increase was not steady across the period. Government expenditures for health, education, and welfare rose from $3.9 billion in the predepression year of 1929 to $145.6 billion in 1970, then almost doubled to $290 billion by 1975. By 1978, expenditures stood at $394 billion. The difference between 1970 and 1978 was almost

$250 billion. Some of the increase was due to inflation and some to population growth. But, in 1987 prices, per capita welfare expenditures rose from $698 in 1950 to $1,952 in 1970 to $3,364 in 1978. In 1990, as in 1975, social welfare expenditures were 19.1 percent of GDP and 56.6 percent of total government outlays. The early 1970s represented a high point in the expansion of federal spending on social welfare as Social Security, public assistance, food, and community development programs all gained widespread support in Congress. After the middle of the 1970s, however, public support for welfare expansion declined. Only programs that included automatic cost-of-living increases were able to keep pace with the high inflation of the period.

The distribution of governmental welfare expenditures for 1990 indicates the areas of major concern. About half the $1,045 billion spent for social welfare purposes went for non–means-tested social insurances and government retirement programs and 25 percent went for education. Non–means-tested programs are programs for all income groups, not programs only for the poor. Less than 16 percent went to programs particularly targeted to the poor: public assistance, Medicaid, food stamps, and some service and employment training programs. The priority given the social insurances suggests again the value placed on work-related programs and the opportunities for political influence lost when human service workers fail to recognize the strength of social values.

The provision of health services has been a particular concern and health care spending has risen steadily. When all the health and medical services provided in connection with social insurance, public aid, public health, and veterans' programs are combined, this went from 13 percent of our social welfare dollars in 1950 to 26 percent in 1990.

Of special interest was the reversal by which federal government expenditures became the dominant element in public social welfare. In 1929, the federal government contributed 21 percent of total governmental outlays for social welfare. By 1970, the federal share had risen to more than 50 percent. It peaked at 63 percent in 1984 and by 1990 had dropped to just under 60 percent. With expenditures for education excluded, the federal government's share of the cost of public social welfare in 1990 was 76 percent.

The pressure to limit the federal budget highlighted the difference between *entitlement* programs—for which the government committed itself to providing funding for all those eligible for a program—and *discretionary* programs for which there were no such guarantees. In large measure, the increases in federal expenditures for social welfare were due to outlays that were not subject to administrative discretion. The bases of outlays for the social insurances, other governmental health and retirement programs, public assistance programs, and others are mandated by law. Discouraging applications so as to reduce benefit take-up rates and curbing error rates can save some tax dollars. But basically, barring congressional action to amend the laws, expenditures are subject only to the limits of the readiness or ability of beneficiaries and the various levels of government to participate.

Nevertheless, there were indications of effective restraint in the expansion of expenditures for social welfare. After years of rising importance in governmental budgets, welfare expenditures as a percentage of all governmental outlays were slightly lower in the 1980s than in the mid-1970s. This was true at the federal and at the state and local levels. Candidate Reagan promised cuts in social programs as part of reaching a balanced federal budget, and Presidents Reagan and Bush moved in that direction in planning their budgets.

Yet actual cuts in social welfare budgeting were not entirely easy to come by. The efforts of Richard Nixon in the budgets of 1974 and 1975 to eliminate social welfare programs that he deemed unsuccessful and wasteful met with limited success.[27] The campaign to abolish the Office of Economic Opportunity symbolized his effort. OEO itself was abolished, but its major programs—the community action programs, community legal services, and Head Start—were assigned to other agencies and continued with budgets essentially uncut. In the case of Head Start, the budget was even increased. Gerald Ford also discovered that executive pressure to cut programs is not easily accomplished. Notwithstanding the president's opposition, Congress refused to postpone salary increments for federal employees and resisted limiting the increase in veterans' benefits to the levels suggested by the Ford administration, even when these measures were touted as anti-inflationary. And President Carter found it necessary to yield to congressional pressures against withholding funds for a variety of local public works and to respond to the demands of black organizations and their leaders that funds for the employment of black youth be restored. The Reagan administration efforts to restructure and cut back some social security benefits were unsuccessful, as were his protracted efforts to eliminate community legal services. President Bush continued the effort to reduce health, education, and welfare benefits, but constituencies for social welfare measures were organized and acted effectively.

A discussion of social welfare expenditures must call attention to the rapid growth of the food stamp program. Starting with a relatively small appropriation of $550 million in 1970, it reached $17.7 billion in 1990.[28] The program is funded totally by the federal government. Food stamps are available on the basis of income, and their value varies inversely with the size of family income. This program and the energy assistance program are especially significant because they help the working as well as the nonworking poor and ease the inequity between those who work and those who do not. In addition, these in-kind programs helped equalize the value of grants in AFDC across the nation, since states with the smallest cash grants gave the largest in-kind benefits.

New Approaches to Income Security

Welfare Reform

In 1935, when provision was made in the Social Security Act for aid to dependent children, the conviction held that mothers, despite their poverty, should remain at home with their children. The 1967 amendments to the Social Security Act officially reversed that historic policy, reflecting the extent to which mothers of young children had moved, in public thinking, from unemployable to employable. Congress increased appropriations for day care programs and instituted the Work Incentive Program (WIN). WIN required that an assessment be made of the employability not only of unemployed fathers and out-of-school older children, but also of mothers. The transfer of administrative responsibility for OEO "work experience" programs from the Department of Health, Education, and Welfare to the Department of Labor further clarified the new congressional direction. Ideological support for this new approach came in 1971, when the House Ways and Means Committee extolled as a primary virtue of day care its ability to free mothers for work:

> Your committee is convinced that . . . the child in a family eligible under these programs will benefit from the combination of quality child care and the example of an adult in the family taking financial responsibility for him.[29]

The committee's thinking was translated into law by the compulsory work and supporting day care features of the Talmadge amendments of December 1971.[30]

New definitions of employability and unemployability had come into being and public income transfer policy shifted. Liberals and conservatives urged welfare reform, including more federal funding and more equitable standard setting and determination of terms of entitlement. State and local fiscal constraints, widely disparate state grants, and extensive discretionary and discriminatory practices made "federalization" attractive. The questions were of form and context.

Efforts to reform welfare during the 1970s and 1980s were caught in social and policy crosscurrents. For a time, the concept of a negative income tax (NIT)—in which low-income families would be guaranteed a minimum annual income—commanded broad support across the political spectrum. Yet, arguments about how high to set the minimum effectively blocked legislation from moving forward. Although both liberals and conservatives supported expanding the work opportunities of welfare recipients, conservatives were more interested in using "workfare" as a disincentive to keep people off the rolls whereas liberals favored the expansion of job training and education as a means of making recipients more employable.

The best opportunity for a shift toward a national, negative income tax system occurred during the early 1970s after President Nixon's address to the nation about his welfare reform plan in August 1969.[31] His proposals were incorporated in a bill known as H.R. 1 and were argued throughout 1970, 1971, and much of 1972, when some parts were finally adopted. The programs dealing with the adult categories of public assistance, Aid to the Aged, Aid to the Blind, and Aid to the Disabled, were to be combined in a new program, to be federally funded and federally administered. These groups of basically unemployable adult poor—the aged, the blind, and the disabled—posed no ideological problem. And on January 1, 1974, a new program, to be administered by the Social Security Administration and entitled "Supplemental Security Income," did come into being.

For those "American families who cannot care for themselves in whichever state they live," a new program, the Family Assistance Plan (FAP), was proposed as a substitute for AFDC. "Workfare" would replace welfare. A negative income tax mechanism was designed to set a floor on income while still encouraging people to work. A minimum guaranteed income—a subsidy—varying with family size, was set. Where working adults were involved, the subsidy was to be reduced as earned income went up, until a "breakeven point" in total income was reached. The program would, therefore, be available to the working as well as the nonworking poor. Mothers with very young children would be permitted to remain at home. In immediately employable families, however—that is, in two-parent families or in single-parent families with school-age children—financial aid would be conditioned upon the willingness of at least one adult to accept training or employment. In the president's words, FAP coupled "basic benefits to low-income families with children with incentives for employment and training to improve the capacity for employment of members of such families." In essence, "workfare" became the ideological base for different levels and plans of support for different groups of recipients. For poor families judged employable, inadequate grants were to be the incentive for work.

President Johnson's Commission on Income Maintenance Programs had been appointed in January 1968. Its report was released in November 1969, only four months after President Nixon's message on reform in welfare had been delivered to Congress. Like the Nixon plan, the commission's recommendations involved a negative income tax, although benefits were higher. The basic difference between FAP and the commission's proposal stemmed from their different views of the poor and of the circumstances of the poor. The commission wrote:

> It is often argued that the poor are to blame for their own circumstances and should be expected to lift themselves from poverty. The Commission has concluded that these are incorrect. Our economic and social structure virtually guarantees poverty for millions of Americans. Unemployment and underemployment are basic facts of American life. The risks of poverty are common to millions more who depend on earnings for their income. . . . The simple fact is that most of the poor remain poor because access to income through work is currently beyond their reach.[32]

The commission's report was ignored, and failure to obtain congressional approval for the Family Assistance Plan left unresolved many of the issues that had led to its proposal. The Nixon administration announced abandonment of plans to replace AFDC. President Ford's message to Congress on September 12, 1974, stating his legislative priorities, made no mention of welfare reform.

During the early 1970s, a number of factors combined to lessen the pressure to replace or reform the family welfare system. One was the initiation of the federal government's Supplemental Security Income (SSI) program for the elderly and disabled. Public interest in poor families receded once these unemployable groups, the most favored of the poor, had been cared for. Pressures from the states for reform in welfare lessened as the elimination of the Old Age Assistance, Aid to the Blind, and Aid to the Disabled categories of public assistance lowered demands on state treasuries. Pressures from the elderly and disabled diminished with SSI's guarantee of income. Additionally the introduction of "income disregards" as work incentive, and expansions of AFDC–UP and of in-kind programs that reduced inequalities between the working and nonworking poor, lowered the push toward change.

Several new suggestions for basic change in family welfare programs came to naught. They included presidential candidate George McGovern's 1972 proposal for a universal demogrant—a payment to be made to all persons—and the 1976 legislation introduced by Congresswoman Martha Griffith proposing a negative income tax plan that would favor married families.

A more elaborate negative income tax plan was introduced by President Carter in 1978. The Better Jobs and Income Program, as it was named, was similar to that proposed earlier by Nixon. A federal guarantee of minimum income was provided; benefit scales provided work incentives; job training and child care were planned. The Carter proposal moved beyond the Nixon Family Assistance Plan in that its coverage would have included individuals as well as families, and in its provision of jobs. But, like the Nixon proposal and the Griffith legislation, Carter's plan failed to receive congressional approval.

The failure to reach consensus on welfare reform during the 1970s had been attributed to several factors. Arguments had ensued as to whether to pursue an incremental or comprehensive strategy. Incrementalism was meant to improve the current system without changing its categorical nature and its divided administrative structure. Proponents of incrementalism pointed not only to the reality of a system in place but also to the more likely chance that piecemeal change could be achieved. Proponents of comprehensive reform held the many criticisms of public welfare to mean that a new package of programs, integrated toward common purposes, had to be devised.

The Carter proposal had hoped to achieve reform at no increase in costs beyond those of current public welfare programs. This goal had to be abandoned almost immediately. The job proposal became a source of difficulty too. Some criticized the plan for establishing the federal government as a true "employer of the last resort"; others saw in the offing a threat to private industry. And as with the Nixon plan, there was sharp disagreement about the level of grants. Political agreement among interest groups was impossible to come by.[33]

The historical opportunity for creating a negative income tax system had passed by the end of the 1970s. Welfare had become caught in the vortex of the battle over the "traditional family." Public support of single mothers through AFDC became a convenient target for conservatives who objected to the new values around gender equality and sexuality that were spreading through American society. At the same time, the findings on income maintenance experiments in New Jersey, Denver, and Seattle failed to put to rest concerns over the impact of higher welfare payments on family stability and work effort. Finally, the new reality of married women's involvement in the workplace undermined a welfare system based on the assumption that women's place was in the home.

Still, the Family Support Act of 1988—passed after arduous negotiations between Congress and the Reagan administration—should have laid the basis for a new approach to welfare. For social conservatives, the act included increased requirements for paternity establishment and child support enforcement. All welfare recipients except those with very young children were required to either find employment or make efforts to increase their self-sufficiency through education or training. To back up the work requirements of the Family Support Act, Congress made new funding available for training and education through the Jobs Opportunities and Basic Skills (JOBS) program. In addition, states were required to provide transitional child care, transportation, and health care benefits to women who had moved from welfare to work.

Yet, historical timing was not on the side of the Family Support Act. Within a year of its passage, the United States had fallen into recession. As unemployment increased, the number of welfare recipients began to rise for the first time since the early 1980s. The states found themselves having to contend with a 40 percent increase in welfare recipients as the total number of individuals on AFDC and general assistance increased from 10.4 million in 1987 to 14.9 million in 1992. Faced with the increased rolls, the states largely failed to comply with mandates around transitional transportation and child care and refused to commit the matching funds that were necessary to make use of the JOBS funding. By the early 1990s, the rise in recipients set off a backlash at the state level—tied to reducing the cost of the program—that shifted the welfare reform debate in a new, more conservative direction.

By 1990, there was a growing realization that the welfare system had to be thought of broadly to include the social insurances, the means-tested cash transfer programs, in-kind subsidies, health plans, and public employment programs, which together comprise an income security system. Discussions of the Nixon and Carter plans had assumed the imminent passage of universal health insurance, but this did not happen. Although the push toward "workfare" became more persistent than ever, there was a continuing reluctance to provide public jobs. Social insurance funding entered severe crises. The costs of support for an aging population led to a new look at the intent of retirement insurance and its place in a broadly based social security system. Throughout the 1950s and 1960s, the old age insurance program had become increasingly redistributive; now, with SSI in place, questions were being raised again about the relationship of individual contributions to the size of individual pensions.

Changes in family life and in the labor-force participation of women raised questions about the social insurance program, just as they had about the AFDC program. The social insurance program—old age insurance—was designed for a nuclear family with two parents and one (male) wage earner. For nonemployed women, in an era of widespread marital instability, problems arise in a system where benefits derive from the income of the employed spouse and are not portable. Employed women, too, appear dissatisfied with the way in which benefits are calculated, feeling that there are often inequities.[34]

The Aging

An increase in the number of people living to very old ages has meant an increase in the total amount of retirement benefits paid out and in the total costs of health care. In the context of inflation, rising unemployment, and falling birthrates, this raises questions for income and medical programs aimed at the aging population.

The 1979 Advisory Council on Social Security concluded that our social insurances were basically sound.

> The Council is unanimous in finding that the social security system is the government's most successful social program. It provides basic retirement, disability and survivorship protection which American workers can supplement with their own savings and private pensions, and it will continue to provide this protection for as far ahead as anyone can see.

> After reviewing the evidence, the Council is unanimously convinced that all current and future social security beneficiaries can count on receiving all the benefits to which they are entitled.[35]

Inflation and rising unemployment led to deficits in the Old Age Survivors and Disability Insurance (OASDI) funds in 1978, 1979, and 1980. There were some immediate financing problems to be addressed. In June 1980, the trustees recommended that the retirement trust fund be permitted to borrow from the other trust funds. For the longer run, there was widespread concern about the distribution of the payroll tax receipts among the health funds, the disability fund, and the retirement system, and a potential need to finance in part from general revenues if benefits were not to be cut below planned levels. The Advisory Council recommended that health insurance be financed from general revenues, thus preserving for Old Age Insurance (OAI) the image of "contributions" and "earned entitlements" to retirement income. Others recommended a change to an older age for entitlement as a way out of perceived financing problems.

President Reagan's initial reaction was to recommend major cuts in social security, including reductions in benefit payments for early retirement, elimination of the minimum benefit, and a postponement in the annual cost-of-living adjustment. In the face of widespread political opposition to these cutbacks and an urgent need for fiscal resolution, the president appointed a bipartisan National Commission on Social Security Reform in 1981 to examine the entire social insurance system and make recommendations that would lead to "long-term solvency" and ensure both "financial integrity" and "the provision of appropriate benefits."[36]

By January 1983, the commission had, it believed, resolved the system's funding problems and "saved" social security. It recommended, first of all, that "Congress . . . not alter the fundamental structure of the . . . program or undermine its fundamental principles." It was to remain a compulsory, non–means-tested, contributory program, which gave low-income workers a better return on their contributions than those who were higher up on the wage scale. To meet fiscal need, it proposed a partial taxation of higher-income retirees' benefits, a gradual increase in the retirement age (to 67), and increases in the contribution rate.[37]

The commission's recommendations were adopted and the deficit of the social security trust funds was eliminated. The balance went up immediately and the assets of the Old Age and Survivors Insurance (OASI) trust fund grew rapidly. At the time, projections were that the trust fund would rise to $12 trillion by 2030, the height of the impact of the retirement of baby-boomers.[38, 39]

The Social Security Act, as originally legislated, provided work-related benefits much in the way such benefits would have been provided through private insurance. The notion of equity was the tie among wages, tax contributions, and benefits. Amendments to the act have steadily altered this approach to reflect need and adequacy as well as equity. The passage of the SSI program in 1972 provided a means-tested income transfer program that guaranteed a minimum income for the elderly and disabled. Furthermore, SSI benefits, like OAI benefits, were indexed to keep pace with inflation. This change made it possible to rethink the extent to which the insurance programs should be used to redress inequities in wage and employment patterns.

While the health of the Old Age, Survivors, and Disability Insurance system was debated, fundamental changes in public policy influenced the expansion of private pensions. Economic slowdowns sent many companies into bankruptcy, often taking their employees' pension plan with them. These "defined benefit" plans were generally funded and controlled by companies. Although they received generous tax benefits for creating the programs, there was little government oversight of the plans' financial security.

In response to many well-publicized failures, Congress in 1974 passed the Employee Retirement Income Security Act (ERISA) that set out new regulations for pension plans and established a quasi-governmental insurance system—the Pension Benefit Guaranty Corporation—to cover losses associated with the termination of defined-benefit plans. However, the real impact the events of the early 1970s was to reorient pensions from defined-benefit to defined-contribution plans in which workers would have individual accounts into which they and their employer would contribute. Subsequent revenue acts developed a variety of special accounts—of which Individual Retirement Accounts and 401(k) accounts were the most popular—to facilitate this shift toward private pension accounts.

The implication of these changes during the 1970s was not immediately apparent. In contrast to the very public debate over the future of Social Security, these 'private' accounts typically passed "below the radar." Although they involved billions of dollars in tax breaks, few public policy analysts could assess their implications. Over time, however, it became clear that the mass of the tax breaks associated with these plans flowed to the richest Americans and largely bypassed those with greater need. Over time, even without efforts to 'privatize' Social Security, American retirement security began to tilt strongly toward private plans that increase income inequality among older Americans.

Concurrent with the debate about the balance of insurance and assistance programs in providing income for the aging was a debate about the level of support to be provided generally to the aged.

The issues were joined in the discussions about the provision of health benefits and long-term care. Medicare was designed to provide the aged with prepaid hospital insurance financed by payroll taxes and a medical insurance program to pay doctors' bills, outpatient hospital care, and some additional health services, financed by a combination of recipient payments and general tax revenues. It was intended to be a non–means-tested program.

With the rise in health care costs, efforts to contain expenses have increased. In 1983, Congress placed a lid on Medicare reimbursements for hospital stays with the introduction of the Diagnosis-Related Groups (DRGs) billing system. Patients were being discharged from hospitals "quicker but sicker." The concept of approved reimbursement rates was extended to physicians' services. In 1988, 37 percent of all Medicare-approved physicians were accepting Medicare-approved rates for fees. Unfortunately, there was evidence that patients might be experiencing cost shifting and restricted access to medical care. Premium increases and benefit cuts combined to increase the burden of health care on the aging. In 1980, the aged used 13 percent of their income for health care; that figure rose to 18.5 percent by 1990.[40]

In addition to cutting services, the effort to control public payment for health care for the aging meant a thrust toward placing a larger share of the cost on middle- and upper-income workers and beneficiaries. Thus, in 1990, while the maximum wages to be taxed for retirement, survivors, and disability income was set at $51,300 annually, workers with incomes up to $125,000 paid a Medicare tax of 1.45 percent. In 1988, Congress passed legislation, the Medicare Catastrophic Health Care Act, that extended hospital care for all under Medicare, to be paid for by a surtax on the incomes of middle- and upper-income aged. The bill was repealed just one year later when older Americans realized that the "catastrophic" health care bill did not cover long-term custodial care and was a substantial tax on a small part of the population. The increased number of Americans over the age of eighty made long-term care a pressing issue. Yet, in the absence of public insurance for nursing home care, the federal government backed into its policy. Increasingly, Medicaid—the health care program for low-income Americans—became the chief funder of nursing home care. However, to qualify for Medicaid, the elderly were required to "spend down" their assets. Often, senior citizens would see their life savings quickly evaporate before they became poor enough to receive Medicaid. In reality, we had a policy for the public funding of nursing home care, but it was one that required some wrenching economic choices for older Americans and their families.

The Unemployed

Although the debate over welfare and the fiscal crisis of Social Security attracted the greatest headlines, some of the sharpest policy changes of the 1970s and 1980s involved provisions for the unemployed. Unemployment remained a problem throughout the period, largely because of the deliberate use of high unemployment as a means of fighting inflation. Yet, even though government policy increased the number of unemployed Americans, the government took less responsibility for their economic security during the 1970s and 1980s than it had in earlier decades.

Changes in the workplace contributed to the decreasing effectiveness of unemployment insurance. The economic transition underway during the 1970s and 1980s meant that fewer of the unemployed experienced temporary layoffs and more were displaced from their jobs. In addition, a greater share of Americans were working part-time or temporary jobs. Many who held these jobs failed to qualify for unemployment insurance.

The sharpest changes in the unemployment system occurred in the early years of the Reagan administration. Before 1981, when the national unemployment rate went above a certain level, all of the eligible unemployed were entitled to collect unemployment for an additional thirteen weeks after their twenty-six weeks of basic coverage expired. As part of his "economic recovery" plan in 1981, President Reagan proposed and Congress enacted limits on the availability of extended benefits except in individual states that were experiencing high unemployment.

The combination of a changing labor market and deliberate government policy took its toll on the unemployed. In 1980, 44 percent of the unemployed had received unemployment compensation. By 1985, the percentage had fallen to 32 percent.

When the economy again fell into recession in 1989, less than a third of the unemployed were eligible for unemployment compensation.[41]

At the same time, public employment—another means of reducing unemployment—was shrinking. During the early 1970s, Congress passed the Comprehensive Employment and Training Act (CETA) which, in addition to providing funding for job training, funded public service employment for city governments. During the recessions of 1974–1975 and 1980, CETA public service employment provided many jobs and helped to keep down the unemployment rate in many metropolitan areas. Yet, the program was widely unpopular in Congress and was terminated in 1981. Cuts in federal funding for public service employment combined with the shrinking tax base of many American cities to severely reduce the availability of public employment. Because public employment was the primary source of white-collar employment for African Americans in American cities, the cuts to public employment fell disproportionately on the black community.

The last line of defense for the unemployed—general assistance—was also in eclipse during these years. In 1990, twenty-two states had statewide programs; seventeen more had programs in some counties, and in six states there was a program of small emergency grants in some counties. In seven states there was no program at all. General assistance was concentrated in large cities and provided financial and medical assistance to low-income individuals and families who were not eligible for federally funded assistance programs. Maximum cash benefits ranged from a low of 5 percent of the poverty line in Charleston County, South Carolina, to a "high" of 77 percent in Portland, Maine. Overall, support under this program ran well below half of the poverty line.[42]

Most of the programs emphasized the necessity to work for clients deemed employable, but the meaning of employability was not clear. Were those classified as employable truly capable of sustaining employment? Second, even if they were employable, were they getting realistic help in a job search? For those who were not immediately employable, what kinds of training programs were to be provided and who would be admitted?

Women

A staff report of the United States Commission on Civil Rights charged that federal and state welfare programs, federal job training programs, and social insurance and private pension plans all discriminated against women. AFDC and its work programs were subject to special attack. Not only were low AFDC benefits keeping women and their families in poverty, but WIN, when it did succeed in placing women in jobs, had done so at discriminatory, low-entry wage levels in jobs that offered little chance for advancement. Significantly, a staff member of the United States Commission on Civil Rights had this to say about the commission's first hearings on women's rights:

> The value of having low income women in these hearings is that they educate us and tell us problems. They also find . . . there are laws that cover them. . . . And these hearings get action . . . because they draw attention.[43]

That hearing took place in 1974. A Department of Justice Task Force on Sex Discrimination issued a report in 1979 with a broad overview of sexual discrimination in our pension system.[44]

Many studies and reports on the changing position of women were issued in the late 1970s. The Department of Labor held a major conference analyzing "Women's Changing Roles at Home and on the Job" in 1977.[45] That same year, the social security amendments legislated that the secretary of health, education, and welfare, in consultation with the Task Force on Sex Discrimination in the Department of Justice, make a detailed study of unequal treatment of men and women under the Social Security Act, and started an exploration of ways of eliminating dependency as a factor in the determination of spouse's benefits.[46] The Task Force on the Treatment of Women was appointed, and its report was issued early in 1978.[47] Secretary Joseph A. Califano Jr. also requested that the Advisory Council on Social Security "consider the criticism that the present benefit structure does not recognize the changing role of women in our society."[48] Reactions to the 1978 Task Force report and letters sent to the Advisory Council became basic data for the 1979 HEW report, *Social Security and the Changing Roles of Men and Women.* Although the 1979 report analyzed options for change and did not make definite recommendations, it did serve a basic purpose: "to focus public debate on concerns about the way social security relates to the present complex and diversified structure of American society."[49] Later in 1979, the Advisory Council stated the issue thus:

> Two new objectives [for social security] are commanding increasing attention. First, from the recognition that women are important contributors to the economic well being of the family, whether they work inside or outside the home, comes the desire that women be entitled to benefits in their own right, not simply or primarily as economic dependents of their spouses. Second, in addition to individual equity, equity is now also tested by whether couples with the same total earnings receive the same protection, regardless of which partner earned what share.[50]

The Social Security Amendments of 1983 pursued the matter further with a directive for the secretary of health and human services to report on earnings sharing and for the Congressional Budget Office to examine the analysis.[51] Most of the attention during the 1980s, however, was focused on the fiscal soundness of the social security funds, and issues of adequacy and equity in women's benefits were given much less attention.

Issues of women's rights were raised on many fronts: the courts, Congress, the administration, the women's movement, and the public generally. But change for women generally and for poor women in particular did not occur with the predicted swiftness. Ambivalence about ways to help poor women combined with a broader ambivalence about the proper role of all women in our society. The failure to achieve ratification of the Equal Rights Amendment by the required approval of two-thirds of the states and the rescinding of approval by several states indicate the indecision of the period.

Veterans

It was hoped that the coming together of women, black and white, "rich" and "poor," on problems of discrimination might result in common demand for change—change reflected in the welfare of poor families. Thirty-five years earlier some observers thought veterans would play such a catalytic role. The 1956 report of the President's Commission on Veterans' Pensions analyzed the meaning of the special status accorded veterans:

> Veterans and their families will eventually be a majority of the population of the United States. Veterans in modern times are better off economically than nonveterans in similar age groups.[52]

The 1956 commission pointed to the extent to which basic needs of "all citizens, veterans and non-veterans alike, for economic security are being increasingly met through federal, state and private programs." In summary, the commission concluded: "Military service in time of war or peace is the obligation of citizenship and should not be considered inherently a basis for future Government benefits," and "all veterans' benefits should be meshed with the nation's general security system."

The commission's report of 1956 wielded little influence. But the benefits awarded in 1966 to veterans of the Korean War (retroactively) and the Vietnam War suggested some policy shifts. Certainly, the educational benefits for these groups did not compare favorably with those provided for veterans in 1944. Veterans of Vietnam in particular paid the price of our unhappiness with that war. President Franklin D. Roosevelt, signing the GI Bill on June 22, 1944, stated: "This law gives emphatic notice to the men and women of our armed forces that the American people do not intend to let them down."[53] Americans seemed to agree—albeit with serious hesitation—that veterans are a group apart who deserve special consideration.

For services the Reagan and Bush administrations opted for a safety net approach with increasing selectivity in all areas of social services and in-kind benefits. Selectivity—namely, limiting services to the low-income population and creating programs for the poor only—resulted in vulnerable programs. Nevertheless, governmental provisions for medical care, mental health and mental retardation, foster care, legal aid, housing, and so on fostered such a policy. In regard to the personal social services—homemaker service, child care services, counseling, and so on—the Social Service Amendments of 1974 (Title XX of the Social Security Act) made some public services available on a fee-for-service basis to a limited group above the poverty level. But overall, there was not an egalitarian force in the United States strong enough to move the country toward universality in social services.

In 1970, social welfare seemed open to new endeavors, new efforts to help those in need. But by 1990, the attention to federal budget deficits dampened the interest not only in social services but also in any expansion of programs for retirees, for women, or for the unemployed. Welfare reform too was put on hold. President Carter had urged Congress to consider the establishment of a national minimum benefit level pegged at 65 percent of the poverty threshold, as well as additional allocations for job development,[54] but President Reagan moved toward social welfare cutbacks.

Combined with budget restraints was the desire to narrow the role of the federal government. Revenue sharing, block grants, and the proposed return to the states of responsibility for many job training, education, community development, justice, and health programs were a retreat from the longtime trend toward centralized—that is, federal—responsibility for social welfare. Behind the Reagan drive to return responsibility for many programs to the states was a desire to cut total expenditures for social welfare. Funding for social programs was contained by the device of expanding block grants so that they had to cover more programs. Expansion of any one program then comes at the expense of a reduction in another. President Bush was inclined to further President Reagan's move toward block grants with the states making the allocation decisions.

Discussion Questions

1. How did the rights revolutions of this period expand the rights of specific groups in the population? Did it have an effect on the lives of Americans not specifically covered by these legal changes?
2. Efforts to formulate a family policy failed during the 1970s. Can you imagine what elements might constitute a viable family policy? How would this policy fit with the ideas about gender equality?
3. Americans appear to have a high tolerance of economic inequality. Why is this? Are there ideas about distributive justice that might support high economic inequality?

DOCUMENTS: Conservative Resurgence and Social Change

President Richard M. Nixon's *Message on Reform in Welfare* (1969) is one of two documents used to illustrate social welfare events during the 1970s and 1980s. Although the message was written in 1969, it was considered as H.R. 1 in 1970. The debate that swirled around the message and the bill highlighted the major issues in public welfare.

The Family Assistance Plan (FAP) proposed in the message was the center of controversy. In the initial debate, attacks came from both liberals and conservatives. The merits of the negative income tax approach to helping poor families, the sufficiency of the guaranteed basic allowance, the work-incentive features, and the inclusion of benefits for the working poor were all subject to scrutiny by proponents and opponents. Liberals generally approved the plan to federalize aid for poor families. They were dismayed, however, by the seemingly punitive "workfare" aspects of the message and by the low guaranteed basic allowance of $1,600 a year for a family of four. Conservatives were frightened by the possibility that an income transfer program guaranteeing benefits for the working poor would attract people to the welfare rolls and weaken their attachment to the labor force.

What comes through forcefully in the message is the switch from a service approach to welfare to an income-workfare approach. Moreover, the message makes clear that mothers are now to be considered employable—or potentially employable. The implication was a reversal of the "own home" philosophy of child care proclaimed by President Theodore Roosevelt at the first National Conference on Children and Youth in 1909.

As criticisms of H.R. 1 became more volatile, the Nixon administration and Congress responded with changes in the original proposal. The basic guaranteed allowance was raised, but supplementation through food stamps was eliminated. Even more serious from the point of view of welfare recipients in the more generous North was the threat of a cutback in their grants. The plan, as originally devised, offered protection against such a loss by requiring the states to supplement the guaranteed allowance. This was also eliminated. Work requirements became more stringent, specifying that mothers with children over three years old be available for work. Three-quarters of the minimum wage was stipulated as acceptable pay.

On the one side were those who worried about the inadequacies and injustices of the program. On the other side was a group concerned with mounting costs. Analyses of multiple program benefits and their overlap increased the anxiety of those who feared the erosion of work incentives. Stalemate ensued and the proposal was quietly abandoned.

President Jimmy Carter's Better Jobs and Income Program was, in its essential thrust, similar to the FAP. The two plans differed in two major aspects: (1) The Carter plan provided universal coverage, whereas the Nixon proposal was for families only; and (2) the Carter proposal included job creation. Despite the differences, the Carter plan also failed to achieve approval.

The increased interest in work-force participation and a desire to reduce the number of people receiving government income transfer payments led, by the late 1970s, to renewed vigor in removing people from the disability rolls. The administration pursued a disability review process that required claimants to show that there had not been sufficient improvement to stop their disability payments. Claimants sued, holding that although they had the burden of coming forward with some evidence of disability initially, in review the administration had the burden of showing that they were no longer disabled.

The administration lost many individual cases on this issue. They announced a policy of non-acquiescence: They would obey the court in a particular case, but would not generalize the principle to apply it to other claimants. They chose not to seek review of these cases in the Supreme Court.

Congress moved to resolve the matter when it passed new regulations for termination of disability benefits based on medical improvement. The standard established by Congress in 42 U.S.C.S. § 423f requires that, in order to cease paying disability benefits, there be substantial evidence demonstrating that there has been sufficient medical improvement that the individual is now well enough to "engage in substantial gainful activity."[55]

The text of this statute applies to Title II benefits (Disability Insurance). A similar statute[56] with identical language applies to Supplemental Security Income. The law also provides for continuation of disability benefits during an administrative appeal in a termination case. Slowly, benefits were being restored to some people with disabilities.

REFORM IN WELFARE
MESSAGE FROM PRESIDENT RICHARD M. NIXON

August 11, 1969

TO THE CONGRESS OF THE UNITED STATES:

A measure of the greatness of a powerful nation is the character of the life it creates for those who are powerless to make ends meet.

If we do not find the way to become a working nation that properly cares for the dependent, we shall become a Welfare State that undermines the incentive of the working man.

The present welfare system has failed us—it has fostered family breakup, has provided very little help in many States and has even deepened dependency by all too often making it more attractive to go on welfare than to go to work.

I propose a new approach that will make it more attractive to go to work than to go on welfare, and will establish a nationwide minimum payment to dependent families with children.

I *propose that the Federal government pay a basic income to those American families who cannot care for themselves in whichever State they live.*

I propose that dependent families receiving such income be given good reason to go to work *by making the first sixty dollars a month they earn completely their own, with no deductions from their benefits.*

I propose that we *make available an addition to the incomes of the "working poor,"* to encourage them to go on working and to eliminate the possibility of making more from welfare than from wages.

I propose that these payments be made upon certification of income, with demeaning and costly investigations replaced by simplified reviews and spot checks and with *no eligibility requirements that the household be without a father.* That present requirement in many States has the effect of breaking up families and contributes to delinquency and violence.

I propose that all employable persons who choose to accept these payments be required to register for work or job training and *be required to accept that work or training,* provided suitable jobs are available either locally or if transportation is provided. Adequate and convenient day care would be provided children wherever necessary to enable a parent to train or work. The only exception to this work requirement would be mothers of pre-school children.

I propose *a major expansion of job training and day care facilities,* so that current welfare recipients able to work can be set on the road to self-reliance.

I propose that we also *provide uniform Federal payment minimums for the present three categories of welfare aid to adults*—the aged, the blind and the disabled.

This would be total welfare reform—the transformation of a system frozen in failure and frustration into a system that would work and would encourage people to work.

Accordingly, we have stopped considering human welfare in isolation. The new plan is part of an overall approach which includes a comprehensive new Manpower Training Act, and a plan for a system of revenue sharing with the State to help provide all of them with necessary budget relief. Messages on manpower training and revenue sharing will follow this message tomorrow and the next day, and the three should be considered as parts of a whole approach to what is clearly a national problem.

NEED FOR NEW DEPARTURES

A welfare system is a success when it takes care of people who cannot take care of themselves and when it helps employable people climb toward independence.

A welfare system is a failure when it takes care of those who *can* take care of themselves, when it drastically varies payments in different areas, when it breaks up families, when it perpetuates a vicious cycle of dependency, when it strips human beings of their dignity.

America's welfare system is a failure that grows worse every day.

First, it fails the recipient: In many areas, benefits are so low that we have hardly begun to take care of the dependent. And there has been no light at the end of poverty's tunnel. After four years of inflation, the poor have generally become poorer.

Second, it fails the taxpayer: Since 1960, welfare costs have doubled and the number on the rolls has risen from 5.8 million to over 9 million, all in a time when unemployment was low. The taxpayer is entitled to expect government to devise a system that will help people lift themselves out of poverty.

Finally, it fails American society: By breaking up homes, the present welfare system has added to social unrest and robbed millions of children of the joy of childhood; by widely varying payments among regions, it has helped to draw millions into the slums of our cities.

The situation has become intolerable. Let us examine the alternatives available:

—We could permit the welfare momentum to continue to gather speed by our inertia; by 1975 this would result in 4 million more Americans on welfare rolls at a cost of close to $11 billion a year, with both recipients and taxpayers shortchanged.

—We could tinker with the system as it is, adding to the patchwork of modifications and exceptions. That has been the approach of the past, and it has failed.

—We could adopt a "guaranteed minimum income for everyone," which would appear to wipe out poverty overnight. It would also wipe out the basic economic motivation for work, and place an enormous strain on the industrious to pay for the leisure of the lazy.

—Or, we could adopt a totally new approach to welfare, designed to assist those left far behind the national norm, and provide all with the motivation to work and a fair share of the opportunity to train.

This administration, after a careful analysis of all the alternatives, is committed to a new departure that will find a solution for the welfare problem. The time for denouncing the old is over; the time for devising the new is now.

RECOGNIZING THE PRACTICALITIES

People usually follow their self-interest.

This stark fact is distressing to many social planners who like to look at problems from the top down. Let us abandon the ivory towers and consider the real world in all we do.

In most States, welfare is provided only when there is no father at home to provide support. If a man's children would be better off on welfare than with the low wage he is able to bring home, wouldn't he be tempted to leave home?

If a person spent a great deal of time and effort to get on the welfare rolls, wouldn't he think twice about risking his eligibility by taking a job that might not last long?

In each case, welfare policy was intended to limit the spread of dependency; in practice, however, the effect has been to increase dependency and remove the incentive to work.

We fully expect people to follow their self-interest in their business dealings; why should we be surprised when people follow their self-interest in their welfare dealings? That is why we propose a plan in which it is in the interest of every employable person to do his fair share of work.

THE OPERATION OF THE NEW APPROACH

1. *We would assure an income foundation throughout every section of America for all parents who cannot adequately support themselves and their children.* For a family of four with less than $1,000 income, this payment would be $1,600 a year; for a family of four with $2,000 income, this payment would supplement that income by $960 a year.

Under the present welfare system, each State provides "Aid to Families with Dependent Children," a program we propose to replace. The Federal government shares the cost, but each State establishes key eligibility rules and determines how much income support will be provided to poor families. The result has been an uneven and unequal system. The 1969 benefits average for a family of four is $171 a month across the nation, but individual State averages range from $263 down to $39 a month.

A new Federal minimum of $1,600 a year cannot claim to provide comfort to a family of four, but the present low of $468 a year cannot claim to provide even the basic necessities.

The new system would do away with the inequity of very low benefits levels in some States, and of State-by-State variations in eligibility tests, by establishing a Federally-financed income floor with a national definition of basic eligibility.

States will continue to carry an important responsibility. In 30 States, the Federal basic payment will be less than the present levels of combined Federal and State payments. These States will be required to maintain the current level of benefits, but in no case will a State be required to spend more than 90% of its present welfare cost. The Federal government will not only provide the "floor," but it will assume 10% of the benefits now being paid by the States as their part of welfare costs.

In 20 States, the new payment would exceed the present average benefit payments, in some cases by a wide margin. In these States, where benefits are lowest and poverty often the most severe, the payments will raise benefit levels substantially. For 5 years, every State will be required to continue to spend at least half of what they are now spending on welfare, to supplement the Federal base.

For the *typical "welfare family"*—a mother with dependent children and no outside income—the new system would provide a basic national minimum payment. A mother with three small children would be assured an annual income of at least $1,600.

For *the family headed by an employed father or working mother,* the same basic benefits would be received, but $60 per month of earnings would be "disregarded" in order to make up the costs of working and provide a strong advantage in holding a job. The wage earner could also keep 50% of his benefits as his earnings rise above that $60 per month. A family of four, in which the father earns $2,000 in a year, would receive payments of $960, for a total income of $2,960.

For *the aged, the blind* and *the disabled,* the present system varies benefit levels from $40 per month for an aged person in one State to $145 per month for the blind in another. The new system would establish a minimum payment of $65 per month for all three of these adult categories, with the Federal government contributing the first $50 and sharing in payments above the amount. This will raise the share of the financial burden borne by the Federal government for payments to these adults who cannot support themselves, and should pave the way for benefit increases in many States.

For the *single adult* who is not handicapped or aged, or for the *married couple without children,* the new system would not apply. Food stamps would continue to be available up to $300 per year per person, according to the plan I outlined last May in my message to the Congress on the food and nutrition needs of the population in poverty. For dependent families there will be an orderly substitution of food stamps by the new direct monetary payments.

2. *The new approach would end the blatant unfairness of the welfare system.* In over half the States, families headed by unemployed men do not qualify for public assistance. In no State does a family headed by a father working full-time receive help in the current welfare system, no matter how little he earns. As we have

seen, this approach to dependency has itself been a cause of dependency. It results in a policy that tends to force the father out of the home.

The new plan rejects a policy that undermines family life. It would end the substantial financial incentives to desertion. It would extend eligibility to *all* dependent families with children, without regard to whether the family is headed by a man or woman. The effects of these changes upon human behavior would be an increased will to work, the survival of more marriages, the greater stability of families. We are determined to stop passing the cycle of dependency from generation to generation.

The most glaring inequity in the old welfare system is the exclusion of families who are working to pull themselves out of poverty. Families headed by a non-worker often receive more from welfare than families headed by a husband working full-time at very low wages. This has been rightly resented by the working poor, for the rewards are just the opposite of what they should be.

3. *The new plan would create a much stronger incentive to work.* For people now on the welfare rolls, the present system discourages the move from welfare to work by cutting benefits too fast and too much as earnings begin. *The new system would encourage work by allowing the new worker to retain the first $720 of his yearly earnings without any benefit reduction.*

For people already working, but at poverty wages, the present system often encourages nothing but resentment and an incentive to quit and go on relief where that would pay more than work. The new plan, on the contrary, would provide a supplement that will help a low-wage worker—struggling to make ends meet—achieve a higher standard of living.

For an employable person who just chooses not to work, neither the present system nor the one we propose would support him, though both would continue to support other dependent members in his family.

However, a welfare mother with pre-school children should not face benefit reductions if she decides to stay home. It is not our intent that mothers of pre-school children must accept work. Those who can work and desire to do so, however, should have the opportunity for jobs and job training and access to day care centers for their children: this will enable them to support themselves after their children are grown.

A family with a member who gets a job would be permitted to retain all of the *first $60 monthly income*, amounting to $720 per year for a regular worker, *with no reduction of Federal payments.* The incentive to work in this provision is obvious. But there is another practical reason: Going to work costs money. Expenses such as clothes, transportation, personal care, Social Security taxes and loss of income from odd jobs amount to substantial costs for the average family. Since a family does not begin to *add* to its net income until it surpasses the cost of working, in fairness this amount should not be subtracted from the new payment.

After the first $720 of income, the *rest* of the earnings will result in a systematic reduction in payments.

I believe the vast majority of poor people in the United States prefer to work rather than have the government support their families. In 1968, 600,000 families left the welfare rolls out of an average caseload of 1,400,000 during the year, showing a considerable turnover, much of it voluntary.

However, there may be some who fail to seek or accept work, even with the strong incentives and training opportunities that will be provided. It would not be fair to those who willingly work, or to all taxpayers, to allow others to choose idleness when opportunity is available. Thus, they must accept training opportunities and jobs when offered, or give up their right to the new payments for themselves. No able-bodied person will have a "free ride" in a nation that provides opportunity for training and work.

4. *The bridge from welfare to work should be buttressed by training and child care programs.* For many, the incentives to work in this plan would be all that is necessary. However, there are other situations where these incentives need to be supported by measures that will overcome other barriers to employment.

I propose that *funds be provided for expanded training and job development programs* so that an additional 150,000 welfare recipients can become job worthy during the first year.

Manpower training is a basic bridge to work for poor people, especially people with limited education, low skills and limited job experience. Manpower training programs can provide this bridge for many of our poor. In the new Manpower Training proposal to be sent to the Congress this week, the interrelationship with this new approach to welfare will be apparent.

I am also requesting authority, as a part of the new system, to provide child care for the 450,000 children of the 150,000 current welfare recipients to be trained.

The child care I propose is more than custodial. This Administration is committed to a new emphasis on child development in the first five years of life. The day care that would be part of this plan would be of a quality that will help in the development of the child and provide for its health and safety, and would break the poverty cycle for this new generation.

The expanded child care program would bring new opportunities along several lines: opportunities for the further involvement of private enterprise in providing high quality child care service; opportunities for volunteers; and opportunity for *training and employment in child care centers of many of the welfare mothers themselves.* I am requesting a total of $600 million additional to fund these expanded training programs and child care centers.

5. *The new system will lessen welfare red tape and provide administrative cost savings.* To cut out the costly investigations so bitterly resented as "welfare snooping," the Federal payment will be based upon a certification of income, with spot checks sufficient to prevent abuses. The program will be administered on an automated basis, using the information and technical experience of the Social Security Administration, but, of course, will be entirely separate from the administration of the Social Security trust fund.

The States would be given the option of having the Federal government handle the payment of the State supplemental benefits on a reimbursable basis, so that they would be spared their present administrative burdens and so a single check could be sent to the recipient. These simplifications will save money and eliminate indignities; at the same time, welfare fraud will be detected and lawbreakers prosecuted.

6. *This new department would require a substantial initial investment, but will yield future returns to the Nation.* This transformation of the welfare system will set in motion forces that will lessen dependency rather than perpetuate and enlarge it. A more productive population adds to real economic growth without inflation. The initial investment is needed now to stop the momentum of work-to-welfare, and to start a new momentum in the opposite direction.

The costs of welfare benefits for families with dependent children have been rising alarmingly the past several years, increasing from $1 billion in 1960 to an estimated $3.3 billion in 1969, of which $1.8 billion is paid by the Federal government, and $1.5 billion is paid by the States. Based on current population and income data, the proposals I am making today will increase Federal costs during the first year by an estimated $4 billion, which includes $600 million for job training and child care centers.

The "start-up costs" of lifting many people out of dependency will ultimately cost the taxpayers far less than the chronic costs—in dollars and in national values—of creating a permanent underclass in America.

FROM WELFARE TO WORK

Since this Administration took office, members of the Urban Affairs Council, including officials of the Department of Health, Education and Welfare, the Department of Labor, the Office of Economic Opportunity, the Bureau of the Budget, and other key advisers, have been working to develop a coherent, fresh approach to welfare, manpower training and revenue sharing.

I have outlined our conclusions about an important component of this approach in this message; the Secretary of HEW will transmit to the Congress the proposed legislation after the summer recess.

I urge the Congress to begin its study of these proposals promptly so that laws can be enacted and funds authorized to begin the new system as soon as possible. Sound budgetary policy must be maintained in order to put this plan into effect—especially the portion supplementing the wages of the working poor.

With the establishment of the new approach, the Office of Economic Opportunity will concentrate on the important task of finding new ways of opening economic opportunity for those who are able to work. Rather than focusing on income support activities, it must find means of providing opportunities for individuals to contribute to the full extent of their capabilities, and of developing and improving those capabilities.

This would be the effect of the transformation of welfare into "workfare," a new work-rewarding system:

For the first time, all dependent families with children in America, regardless of where they live, would be assured of minimum standard payments based upon uniform and single eligibility standards.

For the first time, the more than two million families who make up the "working poor" would be helped toward self-sufficiency and away from future welfare dependency.

For the first time, training and work opportunity with effective incentives would be given millions of families who would otherwise be locked into a welfare system for generations.

For the first time, the Federal government would make a strong contribution toward relieving the financial burden of welfare payments from State governments.

For the first time, every dependent family in America would be encouraged to stay together, free from economic pressure to split apart.

These are far-reaching effects. They cannot be purchased cheaply, or by piecemeal efforts. This total reform looks in a new direction; it requires new thinking, a new spirit and a fresh dedication to reverse the downhill course of welfare. In its first year, more than half the families participating in the program will have one member working or training.

We have it in our power to raise the standard of living and the realizable hopes of millions of our fellow citizens. By providing an equal chance at the starting line, we can reinforce the traditional American spirit of self-reliance and self-respect.

***

STANDARD OF REVIEW FOR TERMINATION
OF DISABILITY BENEFITS

A recipient of benefits under this subchapter or subchapter XVIII of this chapter based on the disability of any individual may be determined not to be entitled to such benefits on the basis of a finding that the physical or mental impairment on the basis of which such benefits are provided has ceased, does not exist, or is not disabling only if such finding is supported by—

    (1) substantial evidence which demonstrates that—
        (A) there has been any medical improvement in the individual's impairment or combination of impairments (other than medical improvement which is not related to the individual's ability to work), and
        (B) (i) the individual is now able to engage in substantial gainful activity, or
        (ii) if the individual is a widow or surviving divorced wife under section 402(e) of this title or a widower or surviving divorced husband under section 402(f) of this title, the severity of his or her impairment or impairments is no longer deemed, under regulations prescribed by the Secretary, sufficient to preclude the individual from engaging in gainful activity; or

(2) substantial evidence which—

(A) consists of new medical evidence and (in a case to which clause (ii)(II) does not apply) a new assessment of the individual's residual functional capacity, and demonstrates that—

(i) although the individual has not improved medically, he or she is nonetheless a beneficiary of advances in medical or vocational therapy or technology (related to the individual's ability to work), and

(ii)(I) the individual is now able to engage in substantial gainful activity, or

(II) if the individual is a widow or surviving divorced wife under section 402(e) of this title or a widower or surviving divorced husband under section 402(f) of this title, the severity of his or her impairment or impairments is no longer deemed under regulations prescribed by the Secretary sufficient to preclude the individual from engaging in gainful activity, or

(B) demonstrates that—

(i) although the individual has not improved medically, he or she has undergone vocational therapy (related to the individual's ability to work), and

(ii) the requirements of subclause (I) or (II) of subparagraph (A)(ii) are met; or

(3) substantial evidence which demonstrates that, as determined on the basis of new or improved diagnostic techniques or evaluations, the individual's impairment or combination of impairments is not as disabling as it was considered to be at the time of the most recent prior decision that he or she was under a disability or continued to be under a disability, and that therefore—

(A) the individual is able to engage in substantial gainful activity, or

(B) if the individual is a widow or surviving divorced wife under section 402(e) of this title or a widower or surviving divorced husband under section 402(f) of this title, the severity of his or her impairment or impairments is not deemed under regulations prescribed by the Secretary sufficient to preclude the individual from engaging in gainful activity; or

(4) substantial evidence (which may be evidence on the record at the time any prior determination of the entitlement to benefits based on disability was made, or newly obtained evidence which relates to that determination) which demonstrates that a prior determination was in error.

Nothing in this subsection shall be construed to require a determination that a recipient of benefits under this subchapter or subchapter XVIII of this chapter based on an individual's disability is entitled to such benefits if the prior determination was fraudulently obtained or if the individual is engaged in substantial gainful activity (or gainful activity in the case of a widow, surviving divorced wife, widower, or surviving divorced husband), cannot be located, or fails, without good cause, to cooperate in a review of the entitlement to such benefits or to follow prescribed treatment which would be expected to restore his or her ability to engage in substantial gainful activity (or gainful activity in the case of a widow, surviving divorced wife, widower, or surviving divorced husband). Any determination under this section shall be made on the basis of all the evidence available in the individual's case file, including new evidence concerning the individual's prior or current condition which is presented by the individual or secured by the Secretary. Any determination made under this section shall be made on the basis of the weight of the evidence and on a neutral basis with regard to the individual's condition, without any initial inference as to the presence or absence of disability being drawn from the fact that the individual has previously been determined to be disabled. For purposes of this subsection, a benefit under this subchapter is based on an individual's disability if it is a disability insurance benefit, a child's, widow's, or widower's insurance benefit based on disability, or a mother's or father's insurance benefit based on the disability of the mother's or father's child who has attained age 16.

Public Law 98–460, 98th Congress, September 15, 1984

Notes

1. Gilbert Y. Steiner, *The Children's Cause* (Washington, D.C.: The Brookings Institution, 1976), p. 113.

2. All data on social welfare expenditures in this chapter are from U.S. Social Security Administration, *Social Security Bulletin*, Vol. 52, No. 11 (1989), and Vol. 53, No. 12 (1990), unless otherwise indicated. Poverty data are from U.S. Bureau of the Census, *Current Population Reports*, Series P-60, *Characteristics of the Population Below the Poverty Level*, selected years. Data on the income of households, families, and persons are from U.S. Bureau of the Census, *Current Population Reports*, Series P-60, *Money Income of Households, Families and Persons in the U.S.*, selected years.

3. U.S. Bureau of Economic Analysis, *The National Income and Product Accounts of the United States: 1929–1982*, and *Survey of Current Business*, July issues.

4. For an extended analysis of the changes in the distribution of income and wealth during this period, see Kevin Phillips, *The Politics of Rich and Poor* (New York: Random House, 1990).

5. David Cohen, president of Common Cause, membership letter, June 1980.

6. William Baumol and Alan S. Binder, *Macroeconomics: Principles and Policy*, 7th ed. (New York: The Dryden Press, 1998), p. 118.

7. U.S. Department of Labor, Bureau of Labor Statistics, *Employment and Earnings*, January issues.

8. All demographic data in this chapter are derived from U.S. Bureau of the Census, *Current Population Reports*, Series P-20, *Population Characteristics*, selected years, unless otherwise indicated.

9. *New York Times*, July 26, 1990, p. A16.

10. June Axinn and Mark J. Stern, *Dependency and Poverty: Old Problems in a New World* (Lexington, Mass.: Lexington Books, 1988), pp. 31–49.

11. U.S. Department of Labor, Bureau of Labor Statistics, *Employment in Perspective: Working Women*, monthly; and *Historical Statistics of the United States: Colonial Times to 1970*.

12. Robert J. Lampman, "Changing Patterns of Income, 1960–1974," in David Warner, ed., *Toward New Human Rights: The Social Policies of the Kennedy and Johnson Administrations* (Austin: The University of Texas Press, 1977), p. 122.

13. Phyllis J. Day, *A New History of Social Welfare* (Englewood Cliffs, N.J.: Prentice Hall, 1989), pp. 366–370.

14. U.S. Bureau of the Census, "Household Wealth and Asset Ownership: 1988," *Current Population Reports*, Series P-70, No. 22 (Washington, D.C.: Government Printing Office, 1990).

15. Melvin L. Oliver and Thomas M. Shapiro, *Black Wealth, White Wealth: A New Perspective on Racial Inequality* (New York and London: Routledge, 1995), p. 69.

16. *Fullilove* v. *Klutznick*, 448, U.S. 448, 1980.

17. *Firefighters' Local Union #1784* v. *Stotts*, June 11, 1984. Opinion excerpted in the *New York Times*, June 13, 1984, p. B12.

18. *Wygant* v. *Jackson Board of Education* (476 U.S. 267), May 19, 1986.

19. *Local Number 28, Sheet Metal Workers' International Association* v. *Equal Employment Opportunity Commission* (478 U.S. 421), July 2, 1986; *Local Number 93, International Association of Firefighters* v. *City of Cleveland and Cleveland Vanguards* (478 U.S. 501), July 2, 1986. Opinions excerpted in the *New York Times*, July 3, 1986, p. B8; *United States* v. *Paradise* (480 U.S. 149), February 25, 1987; *Johnson* v. *Transportation Agency of Santa Clara County* (480 U.S. 616), March 25, 1987.

20. *New York Times*, January 24, 1989, p. A18.

21. U.S. Immigration and Naturalization Service, *Statistical Yearbook*, 1991.

22. An excellent review of the shifts in immigration policy during the period may be found in Pastora San Juan Cafferty, Barry R. Chiswick, Andrew M. Greeley, and Teresa A. Sullivan, *The Dilemma of American Immigration Policy: Beyond the Golden Door* (New Brunswick, N.J.: Transaction Books, 1983), pp. 3–37, and in Roger Daniels, *Coming to America* (New York: Harper Collins, 1990), pp. 328–349, 378–380.

23. Joseph Goldstein, Anna Freud, and Albert J. Solnit, *Beyond the Best Interest of the Child* (New York: Free Press, 1979).

24. Frances Piven and Richard Cloward, "Eroding Welfare Rights," *Civil Liberties Review* (Winter–Spring 1974): 41–51; Laurie Udesky, "Welfare Reform and Its Victims," *The Nation* (Vol. 251, No. 9, September 24, 1990): pp. 302–306.

25. *Harris* v. *McRae*, 448, U.S. 297, 1980.

26. U.S. General Accounting Office, *Social Security Disability* (Washington, D.C.: Government Printing Office, November 1989).

27. Edward R. Fried et al., *Setting National Priorities: The 1974 Budget* (Washington, D.C.: The Brookings Institution, 1973), pp. 170–232; Barry M. Blechman et al., *Setting National Priorities: The 1975 Budget* (Washington, D.C.: The Brookings Institution, 1974), pp. 18–42, 166–206.

28. Library of Congress, Congressional Research Service, "Cash and Noncash Benefits for Persons with Limited Income: Eligibility Rules, Recipient and Expenditure Data, FY 1988–90."

29. *Report on H.R. 1*, U.S. Congress, House Committee on Ways and Means, 92nd Cong., 1st sess., 1971, p. 163.

30. U.S. 92nd Cong., 2nd sess., Public Law 92–223, December 28, 1971.

31. President Richard M. Nixon, "Message on Reform in Welfare," August 11, 1969.

32. U.S. Department of Health, Education, and Welfare, *Poverty Amid Plenty: The American Paradox*, report of the President's Commission on Income Maintenance Programs, November 1969.

33. For a detailed description of discussions of welfare reform, see Gordon L. Weil, *The Welfare Debate of 1978* (White Plains, N.Y.: Institute for Socioeconomic Studies, 1978); and Irving Garfinkel, "Welfare Reform: Two Views," *Journal/The Institute for Socioeconomic Studies* 4 (4, 1979): pp. 58–72.

34. U.S. Department of Health, Education, and Welfare, *Social Security and the Changing Roles of Men and Women*, February 1979.

35. Reports of the 1979 Advisory Council on Social Security, p. 1.

36. Executive Order 12335, December 16, 1981. Published in *Weekly Compilation of Presidential Documents* 17, December 21, 1981: 137–194.

37. Axinn and Stern, op. cit., pp. 121–151.

38. June Axinn and Mark Stern, "Social Security Policy Reconsidered," *Challenge* 33:4, July/August 1990, pp. 22–27.

39. See, for example, the proposal in 1989 of Senator Moynihan to reduce payroll taxes for all and the proposal of Democratic congressional leaders in 1991 to reduce the tax rate for low income workers and to raise the tax base for high salaried wage earners, *New York Times*, February 17, 1991, p. 36.

40. U.S. House of Representatives, Select Committee on Aging, *The President's 1986 Budget: An Assault on America's Aged and Poor*, Comm. Pub. No. 99–481 (Washington, D.C.: Government Printing Office, 1985). For a review of the changes in social insurance and Medicare, see the two articles by John L. Hess, "Confessions of a Greedy Geezer," *The Nation*, April 2, 1990, and "The Catastrophic Health Care Fiasco," *The Nation*, May 21, 1990.

41. U.S. Employment and Training Administration, *Unemployment Insurance Statistics* (Washington, D.C.: Government Printing Office, monthly), and U.S. Department of Labor, *Annual Report of the Secretary of Labor* (Washington, D.C.: Government Printing Office, annual).

42. Lewin/ICF and James Bell Associates, *State and Local General Assistance Programs: Issues and Changes* (Prepared for the assistant secretary for planning and evaluation, Department of Health and Human Services, November 1990).

43. Lucy Edwards, assistant general counsel, U.S. Commission on Civil Rights. Quoted in the *New York Times*, June 20, 1974, p. 44.

44. U.S. Department of Justice, Task Force on Sex Discrimination, *The Pension Game: American Pension System from the Viewpoint of the American Woman* (Washington, D.C.: Government Printing Office, 1979).

45. U.S. Department of Labor, National Commission for Manpower Policy, *Women's Changing Roles at Home and On the Job*, Special Report No. 26, September 1978.

46. U.S. Congress, Public Law 95-216, Sec. 341.

47. U.S. Department of Health, Education, and Welfare, *Social Security and the Changing Roles of Men and Women*, February 1979.

48. Ibid., p. 4.
49. Ibid., p. 7.
50. Advisory Council, op. cit., p. 91.
51. U.S. Congress, Congressional Budget Office, *Earnings Sharing Options for the Social Security System* (Washington, D.C.: Government Printing Office, January 1986).
52. To be found in U.S. Congress, House Committee Print No. 4, *Medical Care of Veterans*, 90th Cong., 1st sess., April 17, 1967, p. 255. Prepared for the use of the Committee on Veterans' Affairs.
53. U.S. Congress, *Congressional Record*, 78th Cong., 2nd sess., 1944, 90 pt. 5:6588.
54. Weil, op. cit., p. 98.
55. 42 U.S.C.S. § 1382.
56. U.S. Congress Public Law 98-460, § 2(a).

9

Social Welfare and the Information Society: 1992–2007

The 1990s began in the shadow of a recession. After falling to 5.3 percent of the labor force in 1989, the unemployment rate rose to 7.5 percent in 1992. Yet, the economic gloom of the early 1990s rapidly dissolved. By 1996, the unemployment rate had fallen to under 5.5 percent, the figure that many economists had claimed was the lowest unemployment could go without sparking inflation. In the years that followed, it fell even lower, reaching just over 4 percent by the end of the 1990s, even though inflation remained relatively low.

In spite of the remarkable economic growth of the 1990s, however, the business cycle still existed. Beginning in 2000, the American economy began to falter. Within three years, unemployment had increased to over 6.4 percent of the civilian labor force; the federal government—which had experienced its first years of budget surpluses in two generations—was forecasting record deficits; and the economy could do no better than anemic growth.

Although the economic slowdown of the early 2000s was mild by historical standards, the American public's confidence was shaken by other events. In 2001, the worst terrorist attack on American soil destroyed the World Trade Center in New York and heavily damaged the Pentagon. In the next several years, America launched wars in Afghanistan and Iraq that the Bush administration claimed were connected to the "war against terrorism." At home, a set of unpopular tax cuts was enacted by Congress and the second President George Bush, raising the prospect that the old Reagan gambit—using high deficits as a way of cutting social programs—would again be used by a conservative president.

After two decades of sluggish economic growth, the robust economy of the 1990s puzzled policymakers and scholars. Although many reasons for the turnaround were suggested, the most compelling explanation linked economic growth to the transition of the United States (and much of the world) to an information-based economy. By the middle of the 1990s, technological discoveries in biotechnology, communications, and computers had pushed the world economy in a new direction.

New products, new markets, and higher efficiency led to increases in productivity and the standard of living that had not been seen since the early 1970s.

Yet, social policy ideas failed to keep up with economic growth. The new economic and social realities of the 1990s undermined some of the old ways of addressing social problems. Social welfare programs between the 1930s and 1980s had sought to promote stability in the workplace and in family life. Although workers and families still found stability attractive, American business and domestic life failed to deliver. Increasingly, the American workplace was organized along *flexible* lines; there was more turnover, more part-time workers, and more temporary employees. At the same time, the decline of the traditional family—spurred by increases in divorce rates, single motherhood, and the increased visibility of gay and lesbian populations—made many assumptions of twentieth-century social welfare programs obsolete.

Powerful interests blocked many attempts to address the new realities at work and at home. Attempts to reform the health care system foundered because of opposition from the insurance and pharmaceutical industries. Although a Family and Medical Leave Act passed and was signed into law in 1993, more ambitious plans to provide support to families failed. In their everyday life, more and more Americans were living new realities, but social policy failed to keep pace with these changes.

Americans did unite, however, around one "reform," a restructuring of the federal public assistance program that ended the *entitlement* to aid, required recipients to seek work, and set a five-year time limit on the receipt of aid. Although the real impact of welfare reform on the lives of poor people was unclear, it marked a major change in the way the federal government articulated its responsibility for addressing poverty and dependency.

The Economy: Productivity, Growth, and Employment

Since 1970, the federal government had struggled to use monetary and fiscal policy to ensure sustained economic growth. During the 1970s, the economy swung between periods of rapid growth and recession. After the economic slowdown of 1981–1982, the economy grew, but unemployment remained stubbornly high.

During the 1990s, it appeared the economy finally got it right. After the recession of 1991, the economy expanded for the remainder of the decade. Gross domestic product grew every quarter between 1992 and 2000, increasingly by 31 percent in real terms between 1993 and 2000. Productivity moved ahead as well. Although output per hour for all persons had only increased by 1 percent between 1992 and 1995, productivity accelerated during the last half of the decade. Output per hour in the business sector rose by 17 percent between 1993 and 2000.[1]

Much of the robust economic expansion could be linked to the technological revolutions of the 1980s and 1990s. After many years of investment, the application of computers and communications innovations began to make the economy more efficient and productive. In manufacturing, computers assumed a greater role in production and the management of inventories. In the burgeoning service sector, the expansion of the Internet created new industries and made existing services more efficient. Even as unemployment declined as low as 4.0 percent at the end of the decade, the threat that inflation would short-circuit the expansion seemed distant.

But the new economy carried new costs. The success of the restructuring of the American economy was based on a newly "flexible" labor force. More workers found themselves working without fringe benefits. The risks of displacement were higher. More workers found themselves permanently working in "temporary" jobs. Thus, even as incomes went up and unemployment declined, workers faced a new world of insecurity that neither the private sector nor government was prepared to address.

At the bottom of the economic ladder, an old phenomenon gained greater prominence. An "informal economy" composed of businesses and workers who operated in a twilight zone between the established economy and the world of crime became a more important part of all productive activities. The informal economy was particularly important for low-income workers. Many jobs in the personal and domestic service sector—house and office cleaners, child care workers—operated in the informal economy, avoiding Social Security and other taxes.[2]

Welfare provided one motivation for workers to enter the informal economy. Because a large share of earnings was subtracted from one's benefits under Aid to Families with Dependent Child (AFDC) and other public assistance programs, welfare mothers often constructed survival strategies that included "off the books" work. At the same time, the growth of the informal economy provided a safety valve for welfare reform. Poor women on welfare often had more sources of income than official statistics suggested. As states moved to restrict welfare payments, poor women were likely to expand their efforts in other areas.[3]

Unemployment fell, but it remained unequally distributed. Among whites, unemployment fell from 4.8 to 3.6 percent between 1990 and 1999, but the unemployment rate of African Americans fell from 11.4 to 8.3 percent over the same period. Teenagers who were in the labor force in 1999 still had a unemployment rate of 15 percent.

In the previous two decades, government policymakers had used unemployment to keep inflation down. As a result, even as the economy improved, low-wage workers hardly benefited. Finally in the late 1990s, a sustained period of low unemployment improved the economic position of low-wage workers. Low-wage workers—whose incomes had hardly increased at all during the 1980s—enjoyed the first real increase in their wages as the century came to a close. Only in 1997 did the upper limit for the bottom 20 percent of the income distribution reach its 1990 level.[4]

The Rich and the Poor

The gap between the rich and poor continued to expand. Although families with the lowest wages saw some improvement during the 1990s, the large share of the expanding economic pie continued to go to the most affluent. The growing inequality of income and wealth was exacerbated by the government's fiscal policies. Supply-side economics, reminiscent of aspects of President Herbert Hoover's policies during the Great Depression and President Reagan's policies during the early 1980s, framed the budget debates of the era. To "get the economy going," the federal budget was to be balanced, to a considerable extent by cutting back on food, health, housing, job training, and income programs for the poor while simultaneously cutting taxes for upper-income groups hoping to increase their investments. Looking at the impact of federal fiscal policy on income distribution, we see that expenditures made for social security in 1992 decreased the poverty gap by about 45 percent and means-tested benefits by almost 25 percent. In contrast, federal taxes increased the gap slightly. Despite the positive impact of the earned income tax credit (a wage supplement for the working poor), federal taxes increased the poverty gap overall by 0.8 percent.[5]

In 1990, the income cutoff for the top 5 percent of the population ($118,163) was just over 7.5 times as large as the cutoff for the bottom 20 percent ($15,589). This ratio increased sharply during the decade, reaching a peak of 8.22 in 1997 before declining slightly. Only the top 5 percent showed substantial gains. (See Figure 9.1.) Whereas in 1947 the poorest 20 percent of households had received 5.1 percent of the income, by 1998 they had only 3.6 percent. In contrast, the top 20 percent in 1998 received 49.1 percent; almost half of that, 21.2 percent, went to the top 5 percent of households.

Poverty

The good economic conditions of the 1990s reduced poverty, but it still remained higher than it had been twenty years earlier. Although the national income grew rapidly, the proportion of the population below the poverty line declined slowly. After rising from 12.8 to 15.1 percent between 1989 and 1993, poverty fell steadily, reaching 11.3 percent in 2000, its lowest level since 1979. In the wake of recession, the poverty rate jumped to 11.7 percent in 2001. Children, African Americans, Hispanics, and female-headed households continued to have significantly greater risks of poverty than the population as a whole.

African Americans enjoyed the most rapid declines in poverty. Between 1990 and 2001, the black poverty rate fell from 31.9 to 22.7 percent, its lowest level in American history. Although the white poverty rate in 1998—10.5 percent—was significantly lower than the black rate, white poverty was far more common than it had been in the early 1970s. Hispanic poverty rates also dropped at the end of the decade, but they were at risk of becoming the poorest ethnic group in the United States at the start of the new century.[6]

Although President Clinton had been elected on a promise to "make work pay," the number of Americans whose work did not pay enough to get them out of poverty increased during his administration. The expansion of low-wage employment and the informal economy combined with welfare reform to increase the importance of the working poor. In 1990, 2 million persons worked full-time for the full year, but remained in poverty. By 1998, 2.8 million Americans were in this unenviable condition.

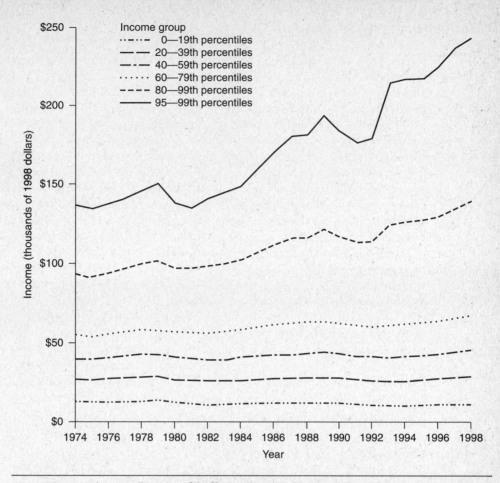

FIGURE 9.1 *Average Income of Different Income Groups, United States, 1974–1998.* For most American families, incomes did not change very much for the last 25 years of the twentieth century. However, for the wealthiest 5 percent of the population, it was a different story. Families in this income group saw their average income rise by over 80 percent during these years.

Source: U.S. Census Bureau, *Current Population Surveys, 1975–1999*

Children, however, continued to bear the real cost of social change and public neglect. Although their poverty rate fell from 20.6 to 16.3 percent between 1990 and 2001, they still remained more likely to be poor than either the working-age population or the aged. The expansion of female-headed households was one contributor to children's difficulties. In 2001, 24 percent of female-headed households still lived in poverty. Although the risk of child poverty remained high for black children, it fell from 44.8 to 30.2 percent between 1990 and 2001.

Changes in Family Composition

The population of the United States is expanding at the fastest rate in the industrialized world. At a growth rate of 1 percent a year, we are exceeding the increases of the 1980s by significant numbers. Part of the increase is attributable to immigration and part to the increase in birthrates as the baby boom generation has children.

Accompanying the increase is a slight stabilization in the structure of the American family. The number of two-parent households with children increased by 700,000 from 1990 to 1995. This came after a twenty-year decline. The divorce rate decreased from 23 divorces per 1,000 married women in 1980 to 20.5 in 1995. But the median age of marriage continued to rise as did the number of people who never marry. Births to unmarried mothers were still going up, albeit at a slower rate.[7] It is too early to tell whether the trend toward more single households and more single-parent families and the threat to the traditional American family may be coming to a halt.

Women's labor-force participation—irrespective of race, ethnicity, marital status, or the presence of children—continued to rise. In 1992, 66 percent of all single women and 60 percent of all married women were in the labor force. Two-earner families as well as single-parent working households were typical.[8]

Rising life expectancy and falling fertility rates meant that the U.S. population continued to age. Median age went from 32.8 years in 1990 to 35.8 in the year 2000. As the population aged, more two-earner families were finding themselves caught in a time bind. By 1996, some 10 to 12 percent of the work force had responsibility for the care of an aging parent. By the year 2020, that rose to 33 percent. The earners are pushed to care both for children and for less independent parents.

The Family and Medical Leave Act: One Response to Changes in Family Structure

One of the first pieces of legislation signed by President Clinton was the Family and Medical Leave Act of 1993. The act requires employers to grant workers up to twelve weeks of unpaid leave annually for the birth or adoption of a child, to care for an ill family member, or to recover from serious illness. Although the leave is unpaid, health benefits remain intact throughout the period. When workers return to their jobs, they are guaranteed an equivalent position with seniority maintained. The legislation applies to private and public employers with fifty or more workers.

Regulations issued in early 1995 defined family members for whose care a worker might take leave as a spouse, a child, or a parent. Leave is not granted to care for the parent of a spouse, nor is it to be applicable for the care of a partner. The definition of covered illness has been extended so that it is clear that problems connected with pregnancy are included and that the leave need not be for consecutive days. Substance abuse as well as stress are covered if they constitute mental illness.[9]

That the leave is unpaid clearly limits its usefulness in meeting the needs of most workers. In general, women with higher incomes have received more family benefits. A 1990 national child care survey found, for example, that 39 percent of women in professional occupations but only 15 percent of women in production, 11 percent of women in services, and none in agriculture were offered at least one child care benefit by their employers. Two-career families were most likely to make use of the offered benefit, single parents the least likely.[10] The Family Leave Act is a step forward in meeting the needs of working families—but it is a small step.

Population Shifts

The racial and ethnic mix of the United States continues to swing—from white to red, brown, and black. In 1980, the non-Hispanic white population was 80 percent of the total; in 1995, it was 74 percent. Overall, changing immigration patterns as well as differential birthrates are creating one of the largest racial and ethnic shifts in U.S. history.[11]

The Census Bureau estimates that the proportion of people of color will continue to rise. In the year 2000, the American population was 12 percent African American, 3.6 percent Asian, and 0.9 percent Native American. The 2000 census, for the first time, allowed individuals to identify themselves as multiracial, a choice taken by 2.4 percent of the population. In addition, 15 million people (5.5 percent of the population) were unsatisfied with the racial categories provided by the census. By 2050, the estimates indicate that the proportion of African Americans will remain fairly constant while that of Native Americans will be up slightly. Those of Asian extraction will increase to 8 percent of the population, and 25 percent of us will be of Hispanic origin. Slightly over half of the population—53 percent—will be non-Hispanic whites. These dramatic shifts have had major implications for social welfare in the United States. Immigration policy, affirmative action, public welfare, social services, education, health care, and social security are just some of the areas affected as the color, the culture, and the age mix of the population changes.

Health Programs

The Problems

During the 1990s, the nation experienced a great deal of furor, many proposals, and little action toward health care reform. Two major concerns have driven the movement: expenditures have been rising rapidly, and there are an increasing number of American families who do not have health insurance.

For more than thirty years, health care costs have risen. One reason is that the steady stream of new technologies has made health care more expensive as well as more effective. Additionally, demand for health care has risen as the population has aged and as public and private insurance provide a ready market for health and medical services. Prices, incomes, and profits in the industry have gone up. In 1965, before Medicare and Medicaid, health expenditures absorbed just under 6 percent of our gross national product; in the mid-1990s, they absorbed 14 percent.[12]

The number of individuals who do not have any health insurance has risen, however. In 1987, about 31 million people were uninsured throughout the year; by 1994, this was up to 40 million people. This increase in the health insurance gap occurred despite the large expansion of Medicaid coverage and the increasing proportion of the population eligible for and covered by Medicare. In 1987, 76 percent of the population had employment-related coverage for health; in 1994, only 70 percent were so insured. The change in our labor market—the downsizing of large manufacturing and communication corporations—was largely responsible.[13] Estimates are that about one in every four people will lose their insurance coverage for some time during the next 2 1/2 years, either because they have changed jobs or because they have developed a serious illness.

Having insurance does not guarantee adequate health care. The lack of coverage of preventive services in most health plans combined with a ceiling on lifetime benefits increases the risk of bankruptcy in the event of major illness. And the growth of health maintenance organizations (HMOs) and managed care is limiting and unsatisfactory to many.

The government safety net—Medicare, Medicaid, and the Veterans' Administration health system—meets many of the health care needs of the aging, the poor, and veterans with service-connected problems. But Medicare does not cover prescriptions, a major expense for many elderly, nor does it cover long-term care. Medicaid does cover long-term care for the poor, who make up about half of all people in nursing homes. But only about 47 percent of poor people receive it, and for those it does cover, it pays doctors less for services than many are willing to accept, making availability of care a major problem. Hospital emergency rooms often substitute for doctors' offices. Access to care is an issue for many poor and elderly patients.

Overall, the United States does not do as well as other developed countries. We spend more per capita and have less satisfactory results. Infant mortality is higher, life expectancy lower. This is particularly true for people of color—African Americans, non-white Hispanics, and Native Americans—whose poverty is accompanied by poor health and shorter lives. Public health, environmental programs, and medical research take up a small percentage of health care expenditures as compared to personal health care expenses.

The Failure of Comprehensive Reform

Debates about our health care system, or, more precisely, about the financing and the availability of health care, occupied center stage during much of the early years of Clinton's presidency. The thirty-five working groups that made up the Hillary Rodham Clinton Task Force on Health Care Reform produced a detailed health plan more than 1,300 pages long. The bill, the Health Security Act (S1757), was introduced in Congress in the fall of 1993. It provided for universal access to a comprehensive package of benefits, using managed care to control utilization and costs. The plan involved many regional health alliances, each of which would have three different plans to offer consumers. It was a highly complex bill with an enormous amount of detail on eligibility, coverage, premiums, and benefits. During much of 1993 and

1994 it was explained, debated, ridiculed, defended, and finally defeated. This was the sixth time this century that reformers thought they might achieve comprehensive national health insurance and failed.[14]

A piecemeal approach, in the Congress and at the state level, replaced the effort to achieve a major overhaul of health care financing in the United States. Congress began to consider a number of proposals for smaller expansions of Medicare and Medicaid, and for the regulation of private health insurance plans to keep insurance companies from dropping people. For the elderly, proposals to cover the costs of prescriptions under Medicare were discussed. There was consideration of the extension of Medicaid to all children in families with incomes under 200 percent of the poverty line.[15]

The states also embraced incremental reform. But a year after passing legislation extending and reforming health services, they retreated.

In the face of congressional inaction, the private sector undertook its own form of "health care reform." Although opponents of government reform had raised the specter of bureaucratic controls of the patient-doctor relationship to defeat the Health Security Act (HSA) in 1994, the rise of managed care did just that, but without the protections that HSA had included. Exclusion of pre-existing conditions, routine denial of expensive treatment, and the frantic effort to get people out of hospitals faster and faster reignited the demands for reform as the decade came to a close. "Patients' Bill of Rights" legislation that protected consumers from some of the more overt abuses of the managed care industry gained the support of a majority of Americans and was passed by the Senate in 2001, but was again frustrated by special interests.[16]

Health care for the poor followed a similar pattern. Although Republican proposals to turn Medicaid funding into a block grant failed, more Medicaid recipients found themselves unwillingly pushed into managed care plans. Because poor people often lacked the knowledge and skill to negotiate the complex regulations that governed these plans, they were likely to find themselves denied needed services and frustrated when they were sick. The costs and benefits of managed care remained difficult to assess. Did managed care encourage companies to offer preventative care to keep the cost of treating more serious illnesses down or did they simply use administrative hurdles to make it more difficult for recipients to receive the care they needed? It was clear that one group—corporate executives—benefited handsomely when winning public contracts boosted private managed care companies' stock prices.

The decline in the welfare rolls because of the improved economy and welfare reform reduced the number of working-age Americans on Medicaid. Those who left the welfare rolls were supposed to have access to transitional medical coverage, but many states failed to inform former recipients of this right. In Pennsylvania, for example, the state was forced to sign a consent decree in 1999 in which it promised to preserve the medical coverage of all welfare recipients who had left the rolls, a reversal of the routine cutoff which had been implemented in 1997. The passage of a national children's health insurance program (CHIP) in 1997 added many new children to the rolls, but much of this increase was canceled out by the number of children losing Medicaid coverage.[17]

Capital Hill rally against Medicare Cuts, October 18, 1995.
National Council of Senior Citizens

The elderly were vulnerable to changes in health policy. The aging already pay much more for their own health care than they did prior to the passage of Medicare. Further increasing costs and reducing coverage would be a serious drain on the incomes of many. The elderly are worried, too, about the availability and ease of access to doctors and health care providers, and they feel threatened by HMOs and managed care. A more extreme proposal would offer a privatization alternative. Recipients could elect to have the government set up individual medical savings accounts and have private health insurance with high deductibles.

Even when Congress appeared to make progress on health care, the results were often confusing. In 1997, a bill was signed into law to require insurers to provide parity between coverage for physical and behavioral health. Although the intent of the bill was to expand the coverage of individuals and families for behavior health services, insurers were able to use managed care as a means of restricting patients' access to these services.[18]

In 2003, Congress passed legislation to add prescription drug coverage to Medicare. Consistent with the ideological foundation of the Republican Congress, the legislation gave a major role to private insurance companies in offering coverage to senior citizens and people with disabilities. While the legislation offered *choice* to recipients, it was less clear that Medicare Part D provided the optimal protection. Most notably, the structure of the program required recipients to make substantial out-of-pocket co-payments when their annual drug cost exceeded $2,250. Only when their annual costs exceed six thousand dollars, did Part D again pay most of the cost. In addition, the legislation explicitly forbade Medicare from attempting to negotiate cheaper price for drugs, again adding to the cost of the plan. Although the President heralded prescription drug coverage as this administration's major domestic legislative achievement, it raised as many doubts as it addressed about the Republican's market-based approach to health care.

The congressional inaction on health care reform in 1994 was an important defeat of the idea that government had a responsibility to ensure that all Americans had access to medical coverage. Yet, even in defeat, the issue refused to fade away. The set of social problems that had originally sparked public interest in health care reform—the number of uninsured, the increased restrictiveness of available plans—continued to plague the system. At the same time, the shift to managed care and the attempts of government to limit the cost of health care introduced a new set of problems. As America moved into a new century, health care reform and the half-century quest for universal coverage remained very much on the social reform agenda.

Addressing Poverty and Dependency: The Scope of Welfare Reform

The most lasting change in American social welfare during the 1990s was the reform of programs for low-income Americans. As in previous decades, middle-class Americans had a distorted view of the size of the welfare population, how long recipients stayed on the rolls, and the cost of public programs. The massive entry of women into the labor force in the previous three decades had undermined a major assumption of public assistance: that mothers should stay home with their children. Finally, new research results suggested that long-term dependency was a much more significant problem than had previously been believed.

The welfare population of the 1990s was sharply divided into two strata. The vast majority of women who *ever* collected welfare did so for less than two years. Yet, a significant minority stayed on welfare for more than eight years. Thus, depending on how one phrased it, welfare could be seen as a temporary program or a permanent trap. During the early 1990s, the second image of the welfare population—that it was dominated by a permanent dependent population—drove the welfare debate.

The new alarm with long-term dependency was supported as well with a healthy dose of self-interest and ideology. The driving force behind welfare reform during the early 1990s was cost, not so much for the federal government, but for the states. In reality, the federal government spent $20 billion on AFDC in its peak year, less than 2 percent of the federal budget of over $1 trillion in the early 1990s.[19]

For the states, however, the rise in welfare rolls had a more severe fiscal impact. In 1992, more than 20 percent of expenditures by the states went to public welfare—including AFDC and Medicaid. Increased welfare rolls, declining state revenues (because of the recession), and the requirement that states balance their budgets combined to focus attention on reducing the cost of the program.

The first indicator of the fiscal problem was the fate of the Family Support Act which had been enacted in 1988. Although the FSA refocused AFDC on the goal of self-sufficiency, much of the federal financing for the job-training program (JOBS) went unused because it required state matching funds. In the stringent budget years of the early 1990s, state legislatures were unwilling to spend their own dollars to promote self-sufficiency, even if the federal government offered to match their effort.

The Changing Dynamics of the Welfare Debate

Concerns about cost combined with worries about morality. During the late 1980s and early 1990s, the proportion of children born out of wedlock rose. Part of this rise was a statistical artifact—the fall of the marital fertility rate meant that a larger share of births occurred out of wedlock. Although the out-of-wedlock birthrate rose by 37 percent between 1985 and 1992, the percent of all births that occurred outside of marriage increased from 22 to 30 percent. Moreover, illegitimacy became more visible in the white community. As late as 1980, African Americans had accounted for more out-of-wedlock births than whites. By 1992, however, 59 percent of out-of-wedlock births were to whites and only 38 percent were to blacks.[20]

The increased strength of the New Right within the Republican party put pressure on legislators to focus on the problem of "illegitimacy." Yet, instead of asking complex questions about the opportunity structure for poor teenagers, the availability of sex education, and the adequacy of reproductive services, conservatives dwelt on the supposed incentive that AFDC provided for young women to have children out of wedlock. Whatever the merits of their arguments, the battle against illegitimacy had a major impact on the politics of welfare.

As conservatives focused on the role of costs and morality in welfare reform, many liberals and moderates—many of whom called themselves "New Democrats"—were rethinking their position on public assistance. Mainstream academic thought had become more skeptical about the effects of welfare on the poor. First, David Ellwood and Mary Jo Bane concluded that previous research had understated the importance of long-term dependency. The nineteenth-century belief that welfare was a trap that fostered dependency and undermined efforts at self-sufficiency took on a new shine in light of their findings.[21] Ellwood and Bane also suggested that welfare bureaucracies at the state and local level had become a barrier to the reduction of dependency. Second, William J. Wilson, the eminent African American sociologist, gave new credence to the belief that poor neighborhoods had become seedbeds for dependency and other "pathologies." Again, a nineteenth-century image—that the poor lived in a different social and moral universe than the mainstream—found intellectual support.[22]

This line of academic research found a responsive chord among many liberal politicians. For three decades, liberals had been pilloried by conservatives because of their "permissiveness," their unwillingness to stand up for traditional moral positions on family, work, and gender. A new position of welfare—one that stressed responsibility, work, and self-sufficiency—could provide a means for liberals and moderates to defend themselves against charges of permissiveness.

David Ellwood again provided the crucial synthesis. In his book *Poor Support*, Ellwood was able to articulate an analysis of poverty that moved together traditional liberalism with the "New Democratic" concern with responsibility. Ellwood argued that changes in welfare had to be teamed with efforts to improve the status of low-wage workers. By "making work pay," through the expansion of tax credits and increases in the minimum wage, Ellwood's plan would increase the incentives of welfare recipients to enter the work force. Time limits and work requirements would give them additional incentives to get off welfare.[23]

Ellwood's proposals became the core of Bill Clinton's welfare reform agenda during the 1992 presidential election. During the first year of his presidency, Clinton was able to get Congress to agree to a critical part of his plan, the expansion of the earned income tax credit (EITC) as part of the Omnibus Budget Reconciliation Act. The EITC had first been enacted in the 1970s to provide a small wage subsidy for low-income workers with children. The 1993 legislation increased both the size of the tax credit and the number of families who were eligible for it.

The Clinton administration moved more slowly on the reform of public assistance. In the meantime, many states had received "waivers" from the federal government to adopt experimental schemes for welfare. A few of these actually expanded cash assistance. For example, a number of states increased the earnings disregard, so that welfare recipients could earn more without having their welfare benefits reduced. For the most part, however, the waiver programs tested a set of initiatives to reduce benefits. These included more aggressive efforts to require welfare recipients to work or face sanctions, and a set of *behavioral* reforms focusing on the supposed immoral behavior of welfare recipients. Welfare recipients in some states were faced with cuts in their benefits if their children missed school too often, if they failed to document their children's vaccination records, or if they missed a rent payment.

The most widely debated of these behavioral reforms was the "family cap." Until 1996, welfare benefits were tied to family size. If a welfare recipient had an additional child while on welfare, her check would rise to reflect the increase in family size. The family cap froze the family's payment at its level before the new baby was born. To many Americans, the image of a welfare recipient having additional children brought together all of the negative stereotypes of the poor—irresponsibility, promiscuity, dependency, and rising costs. The family cap became the shorthand for an increased focus on "personal responsibility" in the welfare debate.

By the time President Clinton released his plan for welfare reform in the summer of 1994, events had largely overtaken the administration. Clinton's efforts to reform health care were in the last stage of their slow death. Efforts at the state level had moved the welfare debate in a more conservative and harsh direction. Finally, that fall, the Republicans achieved a resounding electoral victory in congressional elections, capturing majorities in both the Senate and the House of Representatives. If welfare reform were to occur during the 1990s, it would take the ideas of congressional Republicans as its starting point.

Welfare reform was a key tenet of the Contract with America, which many Republicans credited with their electoral victory in 1994. The Personal Responsibility Act (H.R. 4) introduced in 1995 outlined a radical shift in welfare policy.[24] The entitlement to welfare would be ended and a host of welfare programs, including AFDC, food stamps, federal child welfare spending, and Medicaid would be transformed into a block grant to the states. Welfare recipients would be required to work and limits would be set on the time one could collect welfare. In addition, a number of groups of mothers and children would be defined as undeserving and ineligible of aid: teen mothers, those who refused to work, immigrants, and convicted drug felons.

The New Consensus over Welfare Reform

Although the debate over welfare reform during 1995 and 1996 was acrimonious, there was much that the two sides held in common. Both the Clinton administration and Congress wanted stronger work requirements and supported the idea of time limits. In addition, although they squabbled over the nature of federal–state cooperation, both sides anticipated that welfare reform would give the states more discretion in charting welfare policy. In addition, adopting time limits implied that the "entitlement" to cash assistance would be weakened.

The Clinton administration and Congress used the popularity of welfare reform as a cover for policy changes that could not be enacted on their own. For example, the Supreme Court decision of 1990 had extended Supplemental Security Income (SSI) to children who suffered from a set of behavioral disabilities. Both the administration and Congress were willing to include a reversal of this decision in the welfare reform legislation.

The battle over welfare waxed and waned during 1995 and 1996 as the president and congressional Republicans played an elaborate game of chicken. The public backlash over the budget deadlock of 1995–1996 and the resulting "shutdown" of the federal government gave the president and congressional Democrats the upper hand through most of 1996. As a result, they were able to make significant changes in the Republicans' original plan. Food stamps, Medicaid, and child welfare services were removed from the block grant. The amount of money available for child care increased substantially. Many of the behavioral reforms—such as the family cap—changed from a national mandate to a state option. In addition, Congress agreed to "maintenance of effort" stipulations that required states to continue their welfare spending.

Yet, as the 1996 elections approached it was clear that President Clinton and many Democrats feared that they would be blamed if no welfare reform was enacted. As a result, after President Clinton vetoed several versions of the bill, the Personal Responsibility and Work Opportunity Reconciliation Act of 1996 (PRWORA) was passed and signed into law in August 1996.

The welfare reform debate ended where it had started: with a preoccupation with reducing the cost of welfare. The new legislation ended the entitlement to cash assistance. Temporary Assistance for Needy Families (TANF) was substituted for AFDC. Combined with the adoption of time limits and work requirements, the states were able to use their new authority to discourage families from applying for welfare and to raise barriers to their receiving benefits. The major "liberal" element in the law was a dramatic expansion in the size of the child care and development block grant which provided a large increase in subsidized child care for low-income families.[25]

The most glaring omission of the welfare reform law was its failure to require states to offer educational and training opportunities to welfare recipients. Pennsylvania was representative of many states in its adoption of a "rapid attachment" strategy which put an incentive on getting welfare recipients into low-wage jobs and off welfare as quickly as possible. Although congressional supporters might claim that they wished to break the cycle of dependency, the lack of substantial job training opportunities ensured the cycle of poverty.

In 2005, Congress reauthorized TANF. The new legislation included two major changes. First, in line with the Bush administration's efforts to politicize the debate over family life, the new bill included funding for 'marriage promotion' efforts. Second, the bill tightened the work requirements governing state plans to compel states to place more welfare recipients into work programs.

The Impact of Welfare Reform

If the purpose of welfare reform was primarily to reduce the cost of public assistance, it was a stunning success in its first several years. When PRWORA was signed in 1996, the average AFDC caseload nationally was about 12.5 million individuals. By March 1999, the TANF caseload had fallen to 7.3 million recipients. By 2004, fewer than five million Americans were served by TANF. Yet, the wide variations of declines from state to state suggested that these data were not the result of the overall improvement in the economic status of the poor, but rather testimony to the states' increased ability to use welfare rules to push poor families off the rolls or to discourage them from entering. Thus, while Minnesota recorded a 13 percent decline between January 1997 and March 1999, Wisconsin—with the most publicized efforts to reduce their rolls—recorded a 78 percent decline.[26]

In some states, like general assistance before it, public assistance for needy families began to disappear, in spite of "maintenance of efforts" requirements. Idaho, which had provided aid to 24,000 individuals in 1996, had only 2,461 on its TANF rolls in March 2002. In the South, Florida and Georgia had a million people on welfare in 1996, but only a quarter of that number in 2002.[27]

The evidence on the well-being of former recipients, however, hardly provided a cause for celebration. Most of those who left welfare, although earning more than they would have collected from welfare, continued to live in poverty. The failure of welfare reform to provide much incentive to the state to train and educate recipients meant that as recipients left the rolls, they found themselves in low-wage jobs that could not lift them out of poverty.

Female heads of household and their children were especially hard hit. Between 1993 and 1995, they had benefited as a group by the improving economic conditions, their average earning rising from $14,668 to just under $17,000. But as welfare reform pushed millions of poorly educated women into the labor force, it exerted a downward pressure on their wages. Between 1995 and 1997, as the economy soared and unemployment dropped below 5 percent, the wages of female heads of household stalled, increasing by only a few hundred dollars per year. After 1998, even these gains ceased.[28]

Careful analyses of evidence on low-wage, female-headed families suggested that as public assistance became a smaller share of family income, women scrambled to make ends meet. Old survival strategies—accepting "off the books" employment, obtaining resources from friends and families, doubling up to reduce housing costs— had again become permanent parts of the family economy of the poor. During the 1960s, it had been said that welfare policy should provide "floors and doors"—a safety net and opportunities to escape poverty. By 2006, the welfare system, serving an ever-smaller share of families in need, seemed to offer neither.

The impact of welfare reform on children's well-being is still unknown. Although the welfare reform law had expanded funding for child care, the Department of Health and Human Services estimated that the child care and development block grant provided funding for only 1.25 million children out of the 10 million who were income eligible for child care subsidies. The experience of states that made a real effort to provide adequate child care provides one indication of the gap between the demand for child care and the available resources. In Illinois, for example, the use of subsidized child care expanded by 80 percent between 1997 and 1999.[29]

Welfare Reform and "Immigration Control"

The welfare reform law targeted the cutoff of aid to immigrants as a major policy focus. Despite voluminous data demonstrating that the availability of public assistance and social services had little to do with the dynamics of migration, lawmakers viewed welfare reform as an easy way to promote a popular cause. In 1994, California Proposition 187 demonstrated the popular appeal of limiting the availability of educational and social services for immigrants and undocumented migrants. The initiative barred undocumented migrants from using schools, hospitals, and public assistance and sought to give teachers, social workers, and hospital personnel responsibility for identifying ineligible individuals. Although the major provisions of the initiative were blocked by the courts, "Prop 187" became a model for congressional action. Some of the harshest changes in the welfare law were directed at preventing noncitizens from receiving means-tested programs. In 1996, Congress also passed legislation that raised the income threshold required to sponsor new immigrants, enacted new penalties against those who overstayed temporary visas, limited the due process rights of migrants who could not demonstrate they were in the United States legally, and put new money into the militarization of the border between the United States and Mexico.[30]

By 1997, congressional Republicans—many chastened by their electoral defeats in the 1996 election—moved to restore some of the benefits denied immigrants. Yet, the true irony of the immigrant bashing of the 1990s was that it accelerated the pace at which immigrants attained citizenship. With even legal immigrants finding themselves denied benefits and at risk for harassment, many Americans who had been born in other countries decided that their future was more secure as citizens.

The punitive approach to immigration provoked a backlash. During 2006, the Republican–controlled Congress debated legislation to criminalize undocumented workers and build 700 miles of walls along the Rio Grande to keep Latin American, undocumented workers out, a proposal opposed even by the President. In the heat of the 2006 midterm elections, the President abandoned the search for a more comprehensive approach to immigration reform and ultimately signed a bill authorizing the construction of the wall. In the face of Republican hostility, Latin American voters, many of whom supported George W. Bush for re-election, voted in greater numbers for Democrats in 2006, a major reason why they retook both houses of Congress.

The Return to Voluntarism and the Rise of Privatization

Since the 1980s, many conservatives had argued that one consequence of the expansion of social welfare programs had been to discourage voluntarism. Thus, as the federal government began to limit social programs, advocates tried to demonstrate the vitality of the voluntary sector and its capacity to take up the slack created by a shrinking government role. During the 1980s, these efforts had often appeared as little more than window dressing designed to deflect criticism of program cuts.

Certainly, the fate of homelessness policy during the 1980s and 1990s suggested that the claims of voluntarists rarely were consistent with realities. As the homeless became a more visible part of the social landscape during the 1980s, public attention focused on the role of voluntary organizations, including churches and other religious organizations, in responding to the needs of this population. Yet, it was only with the passage of federal legislation that adequate funding for homeless programs became available.

Inconvenient realities did not weaken the enthusiasm of budget-cutters for the possibilities of voluntary activity. The welfare reform law provided new opportunities for voluntary organizations to become involved in the routine provision of services to the poor. In addition, PRWORA opened up the opportunities for religious congregations to become eligible for welfare funding. Supported by a body of research on the importance of churches in aiding the poor, federal and state policy encouraged religious congregations to take a more active role in poverty policy.[31] The expanding role of religion in public policy affected educational policy as well. In contrast to the 1960s, when Congress took special care in defining a role for religious schools in funding for elementary and secondary education, by the 1990s, many federal and state policymakers were willing to move aggressively to make public funding available for church schools. A number of states and localities adopted "voucher" plans that made certificates available to low-income parents that they could use either for public or private education. Although the courts had not yet reached a decision on the constitutionality of vouchers as the century drew to a close, the issue underlined the increased prominence of religion in social welfare policy.

The cause of faith-based social welfare received a big boost from the inauguration of George W. Bush in 2001. The President claimed that his "compassionate conservatism" could be implemented by expanding the role of religious institutions in providing social services. Although Congress resisted his proposals, the Bush administration used a number of executive orders to expand religion's role in public social welfare in spite of the constitutional concerns raised by these policies.

The September 11 tragedy highlighted both the strengths and weaknesses of voluntary social welfare. There was a huge outpouring of concern for the victims of terrorism with more than 2.4 billion dollars being donated to private charities. Yet, the coordination of aid was poor with help not always reaching those most in need. The Red Cross drew particular criticism because it was slow to distribute aid and used September 11 funds for purposes not directly connected to the disaster. As a result, an August 2002 poll reported that 42 percent of respondents had lost confidence in private charities as a result of September 11, while only 19 percent had gained confidence.

The efficacy of voluntary charity was dealt a blow in August 2005 when Hurricane Katrina blasted through the Gulf Coast and New Orleans, leaving that city almost entirely submerged for three days. The Bush administration's approach to social welfare was cast in dramatic relief as actually helping victims of the tragedy took a back seat to a public-relations effort to show that the President "cared" about what had happened. Yet, as government failed in its most basic responsibilities—providing food and water, searching for survivors, caring for the sick, and burying the dead—the administration's claims ran headlong into a monstrous reality. The fact that a large number of the victims of the hurricane were poor and black only served to underline the limits of voluntarism and the failure of conservative governance.

Yet, Hurricane Katrina did benefit many. In an age of privatization and outsourcing, private contractors who provided the food, housing, social services, and transportation for the hurricane's victims often were handsomely rewarded for their work, even when it was shoddy or failed to reach victims. Although "personal responsibility" was the hallmark of conservative social policy, this principle did not extend to private contractors, or for that matter, to the President.

Private, for-profit businesses had a larger role in social welfare by the late 1990s. The availability of third-party reimbursements under private health insurance, Medicare, and Medicaid had greatly expanded the role of for-profit enterprises in some fields of social welfare during the 1970s and 1980s. Child care, nursing homes, hospitals, and residential treatment facilities all expanded. Between 1977 and 1987, the for-profit share of establishments increased by 80 percent in child care, 22 percent in individual and family services, and 45 percent in residential care.[32]

This trend accelerated during the 1990s. PRWORA, for example, enabled for-profits to enter the child welfare field in greater numbers. In addition, businesses discovered a new set of "profit centers" in certain areas of social welfare, for example, in data processing and research and evaluation.

The entry of for-profit enterprises into child welfare took on particular urgency because of other changes in policy. After a decade of supporting 'family preservation' as the chief approach to child welfare, Congress in 1997 passed the Adoption and Safe Families Act (ASFA) which placed additional pressure on child welfare agencies to find permanent homes for children removed from homes because of abuse or neglect. After three decades of increased effort to preserve the link between children and their parents, ASFA was a shift back to an older tradition of child rescue, harking back to the approach of nineteenth-century 'child savers.'

Welfare reform meant more than changes in a handful of means-tested programs. It was a symbol of a whole set of changes affecting social welfare during the 1990s. From the New Deal until the 1970s, government had moved steadily to expand the right of ordinary citizens to protection against the risk of poverty and to not suffer from discrimination. Yet, the cost of providing these rights set off a strong backlash. As the public sector sought to reduce taxes and the programs supported by them, policy was increasingly farmed out to nonpublic institutions. The expanded role of nonprofits, religious institutions, and for-profit businesses was much a part of welfare reform as the death of AFDC and the birth of TANF.

Although welfare reform offered new opportunities to for-profit business, Old Age, Survivors' and Disability Insurance (OASDI), the core of the Social Security program, offered the most lucrative target. The trust funds for the program ran persistent deficits during the 1970s and early 1980s. After the Social Security reform of 1983, however, the program had been put on a path toward surpluses for the remainder of the twentieth century and into the first decades of the next.

Yet, the specter of a "Social Security crisis" remained. In many respects, the politics of Social Security policy were the reverse of the health care reform experience. In health care reform, a popular reform proposal was sidetracked because it would threaten the power and profits of insurance companies, hospitals, and other health care providers. With Social Security, the potential profits of privatization kept "reform" alive even though the public embraced the existing system.

During the 1990s, however, Social Security faced a new challenge: the interests of the financial services industry. The major conservative proposal for "privatizing" Social Security was to allow individuals to create their own retirement account in lieu of paying Social Security taxes. If such a proposal were enacted, literally billions of dollars that is currently collected in payroll taxes would instead filter through banks, stock brokers, and other financial institutions. The financial services industry spent much of the decade spreading a message that workers could not count on Social Security when they retired. Over time, these coordinated attacks increased public concern about the system.

In spite of these efforts, however, support of the existing system continued to frustrate those who wished to undermine it. President Clinton's proposal to commit a large share of future budget surpluses to Social Security was warmly received by the public. The future of Social Security, however, was put in jeopardy by the actions of the second Bush administration and Congress between 2001 and 2003. With the support of the president, Congress passed a series of tax cuts heavily tilted toward the richest Americans. As a result, the federal budget—excluding Social Security taxes—went from a surplus of 236 billion dollars in the 2000 fiscal year to a projected deficit of 455 billion dollars in 2003, before the impact of the 2003 tax cuts had been felt.

Where the Clinton administration had proposed that the budget surplus of his administration be used to insure Social Security's economic well-being, President Bush chose the exact opposite strategy; he planned to use ballooning deficits in the budget to force a restructuring of the system in the coming years.

At least in the short term, however, President Bush again miscalculated. His 2005 proposal to shift Social Security to private accounts met with such a chilly reception from the public and Congress that it never came for a vote. Yet, the first decade of the twenty-first century continued the pattern of the previous thirty years with tax-subsidized private pensions accounting for a larger share of retirement income.

In some ways, those backing private pensions had already won the battle. Since the resolution of the Social Security crisis in 1983, most public policy around the income security of the aged had been directed to private plans. The expansion of Individual Retirement Accounts (IRAs), 401(k) accounts, and other "defined-contribution" plans had far exceeded increases in public pensions.

During the 1990s, the proportion of the population that depended on these private plans increased dramatically, reaching more than half of the elderly by 2000. Yet, this growth was spread unequally across the population; two-thirds of the richest fifth of the population had pensions, but less than 20 percent of the bottom fifth did. As a result, of the 88 billion dollars of pensions distributed in 1990, 57 percent went to the richest fifth of the population.

The rise of publicly subsidized private pensions had both economic and political implications. Thanks to the Social Security system, the distribution of income among the elderly had become more equal between 1960 and 1990. During the 1990s, however, inequality among the elderly increased because of the rapid rise in pensions.

More significantly, the increased role of private pensions puts the political support for Social Security in jeopardy. When the next Social Security "crisis" comes, it will be easier to convince the affluent elderly to support proposals that hurt older people of more modest means.

The Continuing Civil Rights Battle

Americans continued to struggle with the definition of rights and responsibilities during the 1990s. Welfare reform had been justified as a means of righting this balance by requiring poor people to be more responsible; at the same time, many of them lost any right to assistance from the federal government. Although policies that were meant to correct social inequality were under attack, those tied to the right of privacy gained more support from the political and legal system.

Education

Educational programs have been the target of a great deal of backlash against people of color and of different ethnic groups. The drive to require all teaching to be done in English seems to be particularly targeted at Hispanic-speaking children, a growing group in the United States. For immigrants, legal and illegal, there are now many challenges to their right to public education.

The elimination of remedial courses, in the name of economy, at colleges and universities hurt black, Hispanic, and Native American students particularly hard. In the 1992–1993 school year, 11 percent of whites but 15 percent of Native Americans and 19 percent of black, Hispanic, and Asian American undergraduates took remedial courses. Changing college admission standards and cutting the number of remedial courses, or offering them only at junior colleges, operates against the efforts of students to correct inadequate education at the elementary and secondary school level.[33]

The Supreme Court ruled against a school desegregation program in Kansas City where magnet city schools were used to bring white students from the suburbs into the inner city. There have been a raft of court decisions limiting the responsibilities of schools to promote desegregation. The black community appeared split on the issue. Some saw the retreat from integrated schooling as a retreat from equality, while others urged a return to neighborhood schools with an equalization of facilities and opportunities.

Large cuts in the budget for the Bureau of Indian Affairs have led to what the Office of Indian Education Programs called "a major, major problem," putting children in physical danger in buildings with inadequate ventilation, plumbing, and fire-escape routes. The quality of education provided is reflected in the level of spending. Although the Bureau of Indian Affairs is required to finance tribal schools at the per student average for their state, the rule was ignored because insufficient funding was provided by Congress. Congress had, in effect, opted to continue separate and unequal education for Native Americans.[34]

In our colleges and universities, consideration of race, ethnicity, and gender as part of admission decisions has been attacked vigorously. Objections have been particularly vociferous in California and in Texas. In California, Governor Pete Wilson urged that there be no preferential admission. Shortly thereafter, a suit was filed against the medical and law schools of the University of California attacking preferential consideration. The University of California banned admissions that used race or gender as a criterion. Other state legislatures, governors, and university boards were considering and acting to eliminate preferential admissions on the basis of race or ethnicity. A major decision banning preferential admissions came in a 1996 University of Texas case in the Fifth Circuit Court of Appeals that clearly banned race-based admissions. In 2003, however, the Supreme Court—in *Gratz* v. *Bollinger* and *Grutter* v. *Bollinger*—ruled that promoting racial diversity in education settings was a legitimate criterion for college admissions. Although the decisions restricted the practices that could be used to promote diversity and called for a time limit on the use of affirmative action, proponents of affirmative action saw these decisions as significant victories.

Affirmative Action in the Marketplace

The courts, which in the past had supported the drive of vulnerable groups, particularly blacks and women, to seek a redress of the opportunity structure they faced in the market, have now moved against preferential hiring and contracting.

Almost any set of data that is examined shows the subordinate position of women and of people of color in our economy. Wages, incomes, promotion rates, middle management, top management, number of contractors, number of independent manufacturing firms: the numbers all tell the same story. Women and minorities suffer severely because of their gender and their race. And yet there is a growing series of objections from white men who claim to have suffered because of affirmative action programs.

A National Opinion Research Center survey in 1990 found that only 7 percent of white Americans had personally experienced reverse discrimination and 16 percent knew of someone who had. On the other hand, 70 percent thought that whites were being hurt by affirmative action programs.[35]

Efforts to eliminate affirmative action programs are gaining ground at the state and the federal level. In California, an initiative to outlaw affirmative action received strong support in the fall of 1996. Other states were attempting similar actions, with varying results. The Supreme Court ruled in 1995 in a 5–4 decision that the federal government was highly restricted in its use of affirmative action programs applied to contractors with the federal government. Federal "set-aside" provisions were not ruled out completely, but they were ordered to meet the more stringent requirements already set for the states. The Pentagon, rather than providing a set-aside provision for minority contractors in long-distance telephone services, gave them a pricing advantage in their bids. The program appeared to be successful, but now officials are backing away from it.

President Clinton ordered a review of the federal government's affirmative action programs. A report, released in May 1995, concluded that race or sex could be acceptable as one of several factors in such programs, and that programs involving "goals" rather than quotas should be used.[36] The president supported reform, but not abolition, of affirmative action programs.

Abortion and the Right to Privacy

In the early 1990s, the right to abortion that the Supreme Court had established in 1973 seemed to be at risk. The appointment of conservative justices to the Court during the 1980s and early 1990s had decisively changed its ideological complexion. In spite of strong support for abortion rights in public opinion polls, state legislators became increasingly willing to enact restrictions on reproductive services.

The Webster decision, announced by the Court in 1989, provided an equivocal reassertion of *Roe* v. *Wade*. The Court agreed that the right to abortion was constitutionally guaranteed, but the decision expanded the ability of states to limit that right through notification procedures, waiting periods, and the regulation of providers. Although abortion rights advocates were relieved that the Court did not overturn *Roe*, the decision made that "right" seem less real. In fact, it became more and more difficult for a majority of women to gain access to abortion services, as clinics closed their doors and few hospitals offered abortions. In addition, an underground network of terrorists targeted abortion clinics and physicians for violence at the same time that civil disobedience campaigns like "Operation Rescue" impeded women's ability to exercise reproductive choice safely and peaceably.[37]

At the same time, the foundation of *Roe* v. *Wade* in the "right to privacy" first articulated in the Supreme Court's *Griswold* decision in 1965 made steady progress. In 2003, to the surprise of many, the Supreme Court took the unusual step of claiming that an earlier Court decision on the rights of adults to engage in consensual sex—whatever their gender—had been incorrect. The decision in *Lawrence* v. *Texas* was notable because it used evolving thought in Europe and recent scholarship in gay and lesbian history to support the decision. (See the end of this chapter for excerpts from this decision.)

The *Lawrence* decision was notable as well because the rights of sexual minorities had become a major flashpoint in the culture wars. By the early twenty-first century, virtually no Americans defended the morality of racial and gender discrimination; the struggles were primarily about how much needed to be done to remedy them. In contrast, a significant minority of Americans continued to view gay, lesbian, bisexual, and transgender people as "sinful." The legitimacy of discrimination against sexual minorities affected many social policies from the debate over civil unions or "gay marriage" to the rights of domestic partners to work-related benefits to the funding of HIV/AIDS drugs and services. As the twenty-first century began, activists were developing new strategies for mobilizing public sentiment about these issues.

In 2004, the debate over gay civil rights took a public turn when the supreme court of Massachusetts found that the commonwealth's constitution provided the legal basis for same-sex marriage. Congress had already acted in the 1990s to "defend marriage" against the progress of civil unions. Now, conservatives demanded a constitutional amendment to prevent same-sex marriage (and perhaps recognized civil unions as well). Although many states passed bans of same-sex marriage, over time it was hard for most Americans to reconcile their dislike of discrimination with the advocacy of a same-sex marriage ban. In 2006, New Jersey's high court also backed same-sex unions on equal protection grounds.

The Great Lockup

The biggest retreat on human rights occurred largely out of the public's view. During the 1990s, a larger share of Americans found themselves under the control of the criminal justice system. As prison construction boomed, imprisonment became the most common American response to behavior that was out of the mainstream. By the end of the century, the United States had locked up a larger share of its population than any democracy ever had.

In many ways, the imprisonment boom was curious. Victimization rates—the number of Americans who had actually suffered from a criminal act—declined steadily during the 1990s. In 1993, 5.2 percent of Americans over the age of 12 had experienced some personal crime and 31 percent had experienced a crime against property. By 1998, both of these rates had declined significantly, to 3.8 percent for personal crimes and to 21.7 percent for property crimes.[38]

Yet, this decline in real criminal behavior had little impact on the number of arrests. In 1990, there were 12 arrests for every 1,000 Americans. By 1997, this rate had only declined to 10.4. The disparity between victimization and arrests was even greater for personal crimes. Although the victimization rate for violent crimes had declined from 4.9 to 3.7 percent between 1993 and 1998, the number of arrests for violent crimes only fell from 2.9 to 2.7 per thousand during the 1990s.[39]

While actual crime plummeted and arrests remained stable, the number of Americans under correctional supervision—in prison, on probation, or on parole— exploded. In 1990, 4.3 million adults were under correctional supervision. In 1996,

As the twentieth century drew to a close, new pressing social issues—such as the AIDS epidemic—stimulated new social movements. Although many of these movements borrowed methods from past social movements, including the civil rights movement, they also created new ways of dramatizing their concerns and influencing public policy.

AP/World Wide Photo

the number had reached 5.5 million. Men's involvement in the criminal justice system expanded rapidly, but women's rose even more steeply. Between 1990 and 1997, the proportion of men under correctional supervision rose from 4.2 to 4.9 percent, but the proportion for women rose from 0.6 to 0.8 percent.[40]

The real focus of the great lockup, however, was racial minorities. By 1996, 2 percent of all whites in the United States were under correctional supervision, but 9 percent of African Americans were. At every stage of the criminal justice system, African Americans found themselves likely to suffer more harsh punishments than whites.

The great lockup of the 1990s carried huge implications for the future of social welfare in the United States. As the amount of prison construction expanded, the amount of school construction languished. The cost of incarcerating such a large share of the population restricted funding for programs that might reduce crime further. Truly frightening was the fact that the costs paled in comparison to what would happen in the future. The popularity of "three strikes" laws, which required life sentences without parole for repeat offenders, made it likely that the prison system of the twenty-first century would be home to a large, aging population.

But the implications of criminal justice policy went beyond prison walls. A criminal record made it more difficult for former inmates to reintegrate in American society. As a result, the great lockup added incentives for former inmates to enter the informal economy, in either criminal or quasi-criminal activities. At the same time, the lockup of so many men meant that the chances of poor women to find stable partners declined. Even as conservatives called for reinforcing the traditional family, their advocacy of harsh criminal justice policy worked to remove men from poor neighborhoods.

Conclusion

American society during the 1990s and early twenty-first century was buffeted by crosscurrents. As revolutions in technology and economic restructuring pushed individuals and families into a brave, new world of computers, genetic engineering, and instantaneous global communications, the fear of change provided a large audience for those who appealed to tradition. The solutions that Americans had developed earlier in the century for the problems of industrial society were less effective at addressing the problems of an information society. As a result, Americans experimented with new ideas at the same time that they hoped the old ones could get them through.

Most important, the implications of the new social and economic realities had yet to penetrate government and the political system. Much like the late nineteenth century, public policy could not keep up with the rapid changes that Americans were experiencing. The public looked to government for solutions to the new realities it faced: less stable jobs, more frequent need for retraining, the challenges of dual-earner families, and acceptance that "life without father" was now the common experience for many children. Yet, the political system seemed intent on rehashing a set of ideological disputes from the previous twenty years. At a time when business seemed interested in managing the realities of a new, diverse work force, the political system used affirmative action as a wedge issue to divide the public. Where most Americans had come to accept new sexual mores and wanted policy that would prevent these behaviors from leading to illness and death, politicians wanted to discuss the need for "abstinence" and to block the the distribution of condoms and family planning information.

The first decade of the new century posed a great challenge to American democracy. Buffeted by many new challenges—globalization, international terrorism, the wars in Iraq and Afghanistan, a new wave of immigration, and Hurricane Katrina—many asked if the American people could disenthrall themselves from the comfortable, simplistic view of the world marketed by conservative politicians and develop new answers for a new century. As they staggered forward, the answer to that question remained very much up in the air. Americans seemed torn between a pessimistic, defensive posture toward change and an optimistic openness to its new possibilities. Only time would tell which side of their character would prevail.

Discussion Questions

1. As we know, many fewer poor people receive public assistance today than a decade ago. How has this changed the settings in which social workers now encounter poor people?
2. Should we think about welfare reform as continuous or discontinuous with the history of social welfare?
3. Is there a single social work position on immigration? What services do immigrants need? Does current legislation make providing these services easier or harder?

DOCUMENTS: Social Welfare and the Information Society

The single most important policy innovation of the 1990s was the "reform" of the public assistance system brought about by the Personal Responsibility and Work Opportunity Reconciliation Act of 1996. This act changed federal funding for cash assistance to poor families from an open-ended entitlement to a block grant. The act focused the new cash assistance program—*Temporary* Assistance for Needy Families—on the short-term relief of need; assistance was limited to five years and states were allowed to impose stricter time limits if they wished. In addition to pushing the states to require welfare recipients to work, the act identified a set of groups—unmarried teen mothers, drug felons, and immigrants—for even greater restrictions on their ability to qualify for assistance.

In order to justify this new departure, the 104th Congress began the act with a set of "Findings" which sought to connect welfare dependency, illegitimacy, and the "crisis" of the American family. As often occurs, advocates of welfare reform drew selectively on a large and complex body of data to support their position. The findings reproduced here are as notable for what they leave out as for what they include. For example, no mention is made of the increasingly unequal distribution of income, worker displacement, or high unemployment that sparked the increase in the welfare rolls during the early 1990s.

Undocumented foreign workers, or "illegal aliens" as many conservatives chose to call them, were also a focus of the supporters of California Proposition 187. This citizen initiative was proposed by Governor Pete Wilson in August 1995 and passed into law on November 4 of that year. The proposal was a response to the fear of Californians that a large number of immigrants—legal and illegal—would threaten wage rates, increase the costs of public welfare, and lead to overcrowding in the schools. The legislation barred all undocumented workers and their families from using public social services, publicly funded health care services, public elementary or secondary schools, or public postsecondary educational institutions. The institutions involved were required to notify the attorney general of California and the U.S. Immigration and Naturalization Service of the presence of any "illegal alien."

Emergency health care, the Supplemental Food Program for Women, Infants, and Children (WIC), school lunches and breakfasts, and public education are the only federally mandated benefits available to undocumented workers. Thus, this act effectively would have removed any safety net. In response to a suit brought by the American Civil Liberties Union, the Mexican American Legal Defense and Education Fund, and other immigrant rights groups, most of Proposition 187 was declared unconstitutional in California just one year after it was enacted. It will be years before the case reaches the Supreme Court. Meanwhile, however, the intent to discourage Mexican immigration is clear.

Changes in Americans' ideas about gender and sexuality were at the heart of social transformations of the 1990s and early twenty-first century. The Supreme Court entered this debate in its 2003 decision overruling Texas's anti-sodomy law. The Court had to reverse its 1986 decision that upheld a similar law in Georgia. Justice Kennedy did so by drawing on recent work by scholars who found that legal discrimination against gays and lesbians is a relatively recent development. He also cited the findings of European courts to rebut the belief that "Western civilization" had a long-standing antipathy to gays and lesbians.

The legal strategy used by the Court majority, however, could come to haunt pro-choice forces in the future. Justice Scalia, in a characteristically forceful dissent, noted that the Court had chosen not to overrule *Roe* v. *Wade* in 1992 because of its respect for precedents, *stare decisis.* If the Court were willing to overturn precedents in this case, Scalia suggested, it might eventually revisit whether *stare decisis* needed to be respected in the case of abortion.

UNITED STATES PUBLIC LAWS
104th CONGRESS—SECOND SESSION

PUBLIC LAW 104-193 [H.R. 3734]
AUGUST 21, 1996

PERSONAL RESPONSIBILITY AND WORK
OPPORTUNITY RECONCILIATION ACT
OF 1996

104 P.L. 193; 110 Stat. 2105;
1996 Enacted H.R. 3734;
104 Enacted H.R. 3734

An Act

To provide for reconciliation pursuant to section 201(a)(1) of the concurrent resolution on the budget for fiscal year 1997.

Be it enacted by the Senate and House of Representatives of the United States of America in Congress assembled,

SECTION 1. SHORT TITLE

This Act may be cited as the "Personal Responsibility and Work Opportunity Reconciliation Act of 1996."

TITLE I—BLOCK GRANTS FOR TEMPORARY ASSISTANCE FOR NEEDY FAMILIES

Sec. 101. FINDINGS.
The Congress makes the following findings:

(1) Marriage is the foundation of a successful society.

(2) Marriage is an essential institution of a successful society which promotes the interests of children.

(3) Promotion of responsible fatherhood and motherhood is integral to successful child rearing and the well-being of children.

(4) In 1992, only 54 percent of single-parent families with children had a child support order established and, of that 54 percent, only about one-half received the full amount due. Of the cases enforced through the public child support enforcement system, only 18 percent of the caseload has a collection.

(5) The number of individuals receiving aid to families with dependent children (in this section referred to as "AFDC") has more than tripled since 1965. More than two-thirds of these recipients are children. Eighty-nine percent of children receiving AFDC benefits now live in homes in which no father is present.

(A) (i) The average monthly number of children receiving AFDC benefits—

(I) was 3,300,000 in 1965;

(II) was 6,200,000 in 1970;

(III) was 7,400,000 in 1980; and

(IV) was 9,300,000 in 1992.

(ii) While the number of children receiving AFDC benefits increased nearly threefold between 1965 and 1992, the total number of children in the United States aged 0 to 18 has declined by 5.5 percent.

(B) The Department of Health and Human Services has estimated that 12,000,000 children will receive AFDC benefits within 10 years.

(C) The increase in the number of children receiving public assistance is closely related to the increase in births to unmarried women. Between 1970 and 1991, the percentage of live births to unmarried women increased nearly threefold, from 10.7 percent to 29.5 percent.

(6) The increase of out-of-wedlock pregnancies and births is well documented as follows:

(A) It is estimated that the rate of nonmarital teen pregnancy rose 23 percent from 54 pregnancies per 1,000 unmarried teenagers in 1976 to 66.7 pregnancies in 1991. The overall rate of nonmarital pregnancy rose 14 percent from 90.8 pregnancies per 1,000 unmarried women in 1980 to 103 in both 1991 and 1992. In contrast, the overall pregnancy rate for married couples decreased 7.3 percent between 1980 and 1991, from 126.9 pregnancies per 1,000 married women in 1980 to 117.6 pregnancies in 1991.

(B) The total of all out-of-wedlock births between 1970 and 1991 has risen from 10.7 percent to 29.5 percent and if the current trend continues, 50 percent of all births by the year 2015 will be out-of-wedlock.

(7) An effective strategy to combat teenage pregnancy must address the issue of male responsibility, including statutory rape culpability and prevention. The increase of teenage pregnancies among the youngest girls is particularly severe and is linked to predatory sexual practices by men who are significantly older.

(A) It is estimated that in the late 1980's, the rate for girls age 14 and under giving birth increased 26 percent.

(B) Data indicates that at least half of the children born to teenage mothers are fathered by adult men. Available data suggests that almost 70 percent of births to teenage girls are fathered by men over age 20.

(C) Surveys of teen mothers have revealed that a majority of such mothers have histories of sexual and physical abuse, primarily with older adult men.

(8) The negative consequences of an out-of-wedlock birth on the mother, the child, the family, and society are well documented as follows:

(A) Young women 17 and under who give birth outside of marriage are more likely to go on public assistance and to spend more years on welfare once enrolled. These combined effects of "younger and longer" increase total AFDC costs per household by 25 percent to 30 percent for 17-year-olds.

(B) Children born out-of-wedlock have a substantially higher risk of being born at a very low or moderately low birth weight.

(C) Children born out-of-wedlock are more likely to experience low verbal cognitive attainment, as well as more child abuse, and neglect.

(D) Children born out-of-wedlock were more likely to have lower cognitive scores, lower educational aspirations, and a greater likelihood of becoming teenage parents themselves.

(E) Being born out-of-wedlock significantly reduces the chances of the child growing up to have an intact marriage.

(F) Children born out-of-wedlock are 3 times more likely to be on welfare when they grow up.

(9) Currently 35 percent of children in single-parent homes were born out-of-wedlock, nearly the same percentage as that of children in single-parent homes whose parents are divorced (37 percent). While many parents find themselves, through divorce or tragic circumstances beyond their control, facing the difficult task of raising children alone, nevertheless, the negative consequences of raising children in single-parent homes are well documented as follows:

(A) Only 9 percent of married-couple families with children under 18 years of age have income below the national poverty level. In contrast, 46 percent of female-headed households with children under 18 years of age are below the national poverty level.

(B) Among single-parent families, nearly 1/2 of the mothers who never married received AFDC while only 1/5 of divorced mothers received AFDC.

(C) Children born into families receiving welfare assistance are 3 times more likely to be on welfare when they reach adulthood than children not born into families receiving welfare.

(D) Mothers under 20 years of age are at the greatest risk of bearing low birth weight babies.

(E) The younger the single-parent mother, the less likely she is to finish high school.

(F) Young women who have children before finishing high school are more likely to receive welfare assistance for a longer period of time.

(G) Between 1985 and 1990, the public cost of births to teenage mothers under the aid to families with dependent children program, the food stamp program, and the medicaid program has been estimated at $ 120,000,000,000.

(H) The absence of a father in the life a child has a negative effect on school performance and peer adjustment.

(I) Children of teenage single parents have lower cognitive scores, lower educational aspirations, and a greater likelihood of becoming teenage parents themselves.

(J) Children of single-parent homes are 3 times more likely to fail and repeat a year in grade school than are children from intact 2-parent families.

(K) Children from single-parent homes are almost 4 times more likely to be expelled or suspended from school.

(L) Neighborhoods with larger percentages of youth aged 12 through 20 and areas with higher percentages of single-parent households have higher rates of violent crime.

(M) Of those youth held for criminal offenses within the State juvenile justice system, only 29.8 percent lived primarily in a home with both parents. In contrast to these incarcerated youth, 73.9 percent of the 62,800,000 children in the Nation's resident population were living with both parents.

(10) Therefore, in light of this demonstration of the crisis in our Nation, it is the sense of the Congress that prevention of out-of-wedlock pregnancy and reduction in out-of-wedlock birth are very important Government interests and the policy contained in part A of title IV of the Social Security Act (as amended by section 103(a) of this Act) is intended to address the crisis. . . .

PART A—BLOCK GRANTS TO STATES
FOR TEMPORARY ASSISTANCE FOR NEEDY FAMILIES

401 Sec. 401. PURPOSE.

(a) In General.—The purpose of this part is to increase the flexibility of States in operating a program designed to—

(1) provide assistance to needy families so that children may be cared for in their own homes or in the homes of relatives;

(2) end the dependence of needy parents on government benefits by promoting job preparation, work, and marriage;

(3) prevent and reduce the incidence of out-of-wedlock pregnancies and establish annual numerical goals for preventing and reducing the incidence of these pregnancies; and

(4) encourage the formation and maintenance of two-parent families.

(b) No Individual Entitlement.—This part shall not be interpreted to entitle any individual or family to assistance under any State program funded under this part. . . .

***

NOVEMBER ELECTION PROPOSITIONS

INITIATIVE STATUTE—ILLEGAL ALIENS—PUBLIC SERVICES, VERIFICATION, AND REPORTING

PROPOSITION 187

PROPOSED LAW

The People of California find and declare as follows:
SECTION 1. Findings and Declaration.

That they have suffered and are suffering economic hardship caused by the presence of illegal aliens in this state.

That they have suffered and are suffering personal injury and damage caused by the criminal conduct of illegal aliens in this state.

That they have a right to the protection of their government from any person or persons entering this country unlawfully.

Therefore, the People of California declare their intention to provide for cooperation between their agencies of state and local government with the federal government, and to establish a system of required notification by and between such agencies to prevent illegal aliens in the United States from receiving benefits or public services in the State of California.

SECTION 2. Manufacture, Distribution or Sale of False Citizenship or Resident Alien Documents: Crime and Punishment.

Section 113 is added to the Penal Code, to read:

113. Any person who manufactures, distributes or sells false documents to conceal the true citizenship or resident alien status of another person is guilty of a felony, and shall be punished by imprisonment in the state prison for five years or by a fine of seventy-five thousand dollars ($75,000).

SECTION 3. Use of False Citizenship or Resident Alien Documents: Crime and Punishment.

Section 114 is added to the Penal Code, to read:

114. Any person who uses false documents to conceal his or her true citizenship or resident alien status is guilty of a felony, and shall be punished by imprisonment in the state prison for five years or by a fine of twenty-five thousand dollars ($25,000).

SECTION 4. Law Enforcement Cooperation with INS.

Section 834b is added to the Penal Code, to read:

834b. (a) Every law enforcement agency in California shall fully cooperate with the United States Immigration and Naturalization Service regarding any person who is arrested if he or she is suspected of being present in the United States in violation of federal immigration laws.

(b) With respect to any such person who is arrested, and suspected of being present in the United States in violation of federal immigration laws, every law enforcement agency shall do the following:

(1) Attempt to verify the legal status of such person as a citizen of the United States, an alien lawfully admitted as a permanent resident, an alien lawfully admitted for a temporary period of time or as an alien who is present in the United States in violation of immigration laws. The verification process may include, but shall not be limited to, questioning the person regarding his or her date and place of birth, and entry into the United States, and demanding documentation to indicate his or her legal status.

(2) Notify the person of his or her apparent status as an alien who is present in the United States in violation of federal immigration laws and inform him or her that, apart from any criminal justice proceedings, he or she must either obtain legal status or leave the United States.

(3) Notify the Attorney General of California and the United States Immigration and Naturalization Service of the apparent illegal status and provide any additional information that may be requested by any other public entity.

(c) Any legislative, administrative, or other action by a city, county, or other legally authorized local governmental entity with jurisdictional boundaries, or by a law enforcement agency, to prevent or limit the cooperation required by subdivision (a) is expressly prohibited.

SECTION 5. Exclusion of Illegal Aliens from Public Social Services.

Section 10001.5 is added to the Welfare and Institutions Code, to read:

10001.5. (a) In order to carry out the intention of the People of California that only citizens of the United States and aliens lawfully admitted to the United States may receive the benefits of public social services and to ensure that all persons employed in the providing of those services shall diligently protect public funds from misuse, the provisions of this section are adopted.

(b) A person shall not receive any public social services to which he or she may be otherwise entitled until the legal status of that person has been verified as one of the following:

(1) A citizen of the United States.

(2) An alien lawfully admitted as a permanent resident.

(3) An alien lawfully admitted for a temporary period of time.

(c) If any public entity in this state to whom a person has applied for public social services determines or reasonably suspects, based upon the information provided to it, that the person is an alien in the United States in violation of federal law, the following procedures shall be followed by the public entity:

(1) The entity shall not provide the person with benefits or services.

(2) The entity shall, in writing, notify the person of his or her apparent illegal immigration status, and that the person must either obtain legal status or leave the United States.

(3) The entity shall also notify the State Director of Social Services, the Attorney General of California, and the United States Immigration and Naturalization Service of the apparent illegal status, and shall provide any additional information that may be requested by any other public entity.

SECTION 6. Exclusion of Illegal Aliens from Publicly Funded Health Care.

Chapter 1.3 (commencing with Section 130) is added to Part 1 of Division 1 of the Health and Safety Code, to read:

CHAPTER 1.3. PUBLICLY-FUNDED HEALTH CARE SERVICES

130. (a) In order to carry out the intention of the People of California that, excepting emergency medical care as required by federal law, only citizens of the United States and aliens lawfully admitted to the United States may receive the benefits of publicly-funded health care, and to ensure that all persons employed in the providing of those services shall diligently protect public funds from misuse, the provisions of this section are adopted.

(b) A person shall not receive any health care services from a publicly-funded health care facility, to which he or she is otherwise entitled until the legal status of that person has been verified as one of the following:

(1) A citizen of the United States.

(2) An alien lawfully admitted as a permanent resident.

(3) An alien lawfully admitted for a temporary period of time.

(c) If any publicly-funded health care facility in this state from whom a person seeks health care services, other than emergency medical care as required by federal law, determines or reasonably suspects, based upon the information provided to it, that the person is an alien in the United States in violation of federal law, the following procedures shall be followed by the facility:

(1) The facility shall not provide the person with services.

(2) The facility shall, in writing, notify the person of his or her apparent illegal immigration status, and that the person must either obtain legal status or leave the United States.

(3) The facility shall also notify the State Director of Health Services, the Attorney General of California, and the United States Immigration and Naturalization Service of the apparent illegal status, and shall provide any additional information that may be requested by any other public entity.

(d) For purposes of this section "publicly-funded health care facility" shall be defined as specified in Sections 1200 and 1250 of this code as of January 1, 1993.

SECTION 7. Exclusion of Illegal Aliens from Public Elementary and Secondary Schools.

Section 48215 is added to the Education Code, to read:

48215. (a) No public elementary or secondary school shall admit, or permit the attendance of, any child who is not a citizen of the United States, an alien lawfully admitted as a permanent resident, or a person who is otherwise authorized under federal law to be present in the United States.

(b) Commencing January 1, 1995, each school district shall verify the legal status of each child enrolling in the school district for the first time in order to ensure the enrollment or attendance only of citizens, aliens lawfully admitted as permanent residents, or persons who are otherwise authorized to be present in the United States.

(c) By January 1, 1996, each school district shall have verified the legal status of each child already enrolled and in attendance in the school district in order to ensure the enrollment or attendance only of citizens, aliens lawfully admitted as permanent residents, or persons who are otherwise authorized under federal law to be present in the United States.

(d) By January 1, 1996, each school district shall also have verified the legal status of each parent or guardian of each child referred to in subdivisions (b) and (c), to determine whether such parent or guardian is one of the following:

(1) A citizen of the United States.

(2) An alien lawfully admitted as a permanent resident.

(3) An alien admitted lawfully for a temporary period of time.

(e) Each school district shall provide information to the State Superintendent of Public Instruction, the Attorney General of California, and the United States Immigration and Naturalization Service regarding any enrollee or pupil, or parent or guardian, attending a public elementary or secondary school in the school district determined or reasonably suspected to be in violation of federal immigration laws within forty-five days after becoming aware of an apparent violation. The notice shall also be provided to the parent or legal guardian of the enrollee or pupil, and shall state that an existing pupil may not continue to attend the school after ninety calendar days from the date of the notice, unless legal status is established.

(f) For each child who cannot establish legal status in the United States, each school district shall continue to provide education for a period of ninety days from the date of the notice. Such ninety day period shall be utilized to accomplish an orderly transition to a school in the child's country of origin. Each school district shall fully cooperate in this transition effort to ensure that the educational needs of the child are best served for that period of time.

SECTION 8. Exclusion of Illegal Aliens from Public Postsecondary Educational Institutions.

Section 66010.8 is added to the Education Code, to read:

66010.8 (a) No public institution of postsecondary education shall admit, enroll, or permit the attendance of any person who is not a citizen of the United States, an alien lawfully admitted as a permanent resident in the United States, or a person who is otherwise authorized under federal law to be present in the United States.

(b) Commencing with the first term or semester that begins after January 1, 1995, and at the commencement of each term or semester thereafter, each public postsecondary educational institution shall verify the status of each person enrolled or in attendance at that institution in order to ensure the enrollment or attendance only of United States citizens, aliens lawfully admitted as permanent residents in the United States, and persons who are otherwise authorized under federal law to be present in the United States.

(c) No later than 45 days after the admissions officer of a public postsecondary educational institution becomes aware of the application, enrollment, or attendance of a person determined to be, or who is under reasonable suspicion of being, in the United States in violation of federal immigration laws, that officer shall provide that information to the State Superintendent of Public Instruction, the Attorney General of California, and the United States Immigration and Naturalization Service. The information shall also be provided to the applicant, enrollee, or person admitted.

SECTION 9. Attorney General Cooperation with the INS.

Section 53069.65 is added to the Government Code, to read:

53069.65. Whenever the state or a city, or a county, or any other legally authorized local governmental entity with jurisdictional boundaries reports the presence of a person who is suspected of being present in the United States in violation of federal immigration laws to the Attorney General of California, that report shall be transmitted to the United States Immigration and Naturalization Service. The Attorney General shall be responsible for maintaining on-going and accurate records of such reports, and shall provide any additional information that may be requested by any other government entity.

SECTION 10. Amendment and Severability.

The statutory provisions contained in this measure may not be amended by the Legislature except to further its purposes by statute passed in each house by rollcall vote entered in the journal, two-thirds of the membership concurring, or by a statute that becomes effective only when approved by the voters.

In the event that any portion of this act or the application thereof to any person or circumstance is held invalid, that invalidity shall not affect any other provision or application of the act, which can be given effect without the invalid provision or application, and to that end the provisions of this act are severable.

SUPREME COURT OF THE UNITED STATES

No. 02-102

JOHN GEDDES LAWRENCE AND TYRON GARNER, PETITIONERS

v.

TEXAS

ON WRIT OF CERTIORARI TO THE COURT OF APPEALS OF TEXAS,

FOURTEENTH DISTRICT
[June 26, 2003]

JUSTICE KENNEDY delivered the opinion of the Court.

Liberty protects the person from unwarranted government intrusions into a dwelling or other private places. In our tradition the State is not omnipresent in the home. And there are other spheres of our lives and existence, outside the home, where the State should not be a dominant presence. Freedom extends beyond spatial bounds. Liberty presumes an autonomy of self that includes freedom of thought, belief, expression, and certain intimate conduct. The instant case involves liberty of the person both in its spatial and more transcendent dimensions.

I

The question before the Court is the validity of a Texas statute making it a crime for two persons of the same sex to engage in certain intimate sexual conduct. In Houston, Texas, officers of the Harris County Police Department were dispatched to a private residence in response to a reported weapons disturbance. They entered an apartment where one of the petitioners, John Geddes Lawrence, resided. The right of the police to enter does not seem to have been questioned. The officers observed Lawrence and another man, Tyron Garner, engaging in a sexual act. The two petitioners were arrested, held in custody over night, and charged and convicted before a Justice of the Peace.

The complaints described their crime as "deviate sexual intercourse, namely anal sex, with a member of the same sex (man)." App. to Pet. for Cert. 127a, 139a. The applicable state law is Tex. Penal Code Ann. §21.06(a) (2003). It provides: "A person commits an offense if he engages in deviate sexual intercourse with another individual of the same sex." . . .

The petitioners exercised their right to a trial *de novo* in Harris County Criminal Court. They challenged the statute as a violation of the Equal Protection Clause of the Fourteenth Amendment and of a like provision of the Texas Constitution. Tex. Const., Art. 1, § 3a. Those contentions were rejected. The petitioners, having entered a plea of *nolo contendere*, were each fined $200 and assessed court costs of $141.25. App. to Pet. for Cert. 107a–110a.

The Court of Appeals for the Texas Fourteenth District considered the petitioners' federal constitutional arguments under both the Equal Protection and Due Process Clauses of the Fourteenth Amendment. After hearing the case en banc the court, in a divided opinion, rejected the constitutional arguments and affirmed the convictions. 41 S. W. 3d 349 (Tex. App. 2001). The majority opinion indicates that the Court of Appeals considered our decision in *Bowers v. Hardwick*, 478 U. S. 186 (1986), to be controlling on the federal due process aspect of the case. *Bowers* then being authoritative, this was proper.

We granted certiorari, 537 U. S. 1044 (2002), to consider three questions:

(1) Whether Petitioners' criminal convictions under the Texas "Homosexual Conduct" law— which criminalizes sexual intimacy by same-sex couples, but not identical behavior by different-sex couples—violate the Fourteenth Amendment guarantee of equal protection of laws?

(2) Whether Petitioners' criminal convictions for adult consensual sexual intimacy in the home violate their vital interests in liberty and privacy protected by the Due Process Clause of the Fourteenth Amendment?

(3) Whether *Bowers v. Hardwick*, 478 U. S. 186 (1986), should be overruled? Pet. for Cert. i.

The petitioners were adults at the time of the alleged offense. Their conduct was in private and consensual.

II

We conclude the case should be resolved by determining whether the petitioners were free as adults to engage in the private conduct in the exercise of their liberty under the Due Process Clause of the Fourteenth Amendment to the Constitution. For this inquiry we deem it necessary to reconsider the Court's holding in *Bowers*.

There are broad statements of the substantive reach of liberty under the Due Process Clause in earlier cases, including *Pierce v. Society of Sisters*, 268 U. S. 510 (1925), and *Meyer v. Nebraska*, 262 U. S. 390 (1923); but the most pertinent beginning point is our decision in *Griswold v. Connecticut*, 381 U. S. 479 (1965).

In *Griswold* the Court invalidated a state law prohibiting the use of drugs or devices of contraception and counseling or aiding and abetting the use of contraceptives. The Court described the protected interest as a right to privacy and placed emphasis on the marriage relation and the protected space of the marital bedroom. *Id.*, at 485.

After *Griswold* it was established that the right to make certain decisions regarding sexual conduct extends beyond the marital relationship. In *Eisenstadt v. Baird*, 405 U. S. 438 (1972), the Court invalidated a law prohibiting the distribution of contraceptives to unmarried persons. The case was decided under the Equal Protection Clause, *id.*, at 454; but with respect to unmarried persons, the Court went on to state the fundamental proposition that the law impaired the exercise of their personal rights, *ibid*. It quoted from the statement of the Court of Appeals finding the law to be in conflict with fundamental human rights, and it followed with this statement of its own:

"It is true that in *Griswold* the right of privacy in question inhered in the marital relationship. . . . If the right of privacy means anything, it is the right of the *individual*, married or single, to be free from unwarranted governmental intrusion into matters so fundamentally affecting a person as the decision whether to bear or beget a child. *Id.*, at 453.

The opinions in *Griswold* and *Eisenstadt* were part of the background for the decision in *Roe v. Wade*, 410 U. S. 113 (1973). As is well known, the case involved a challenge to the Texas law prohibiting abortions, but the laws of other States were affected as well. Although the Court held the woman's rights were not absolute, her right to elect an abortion did have real and substantial protection as an exercise of her liberty under the Due Process Clause. The Court cited cases that protect spatial freedom and cases that go well beyond it. *Roe* recognized the right of a woman to make certain fundamental decisions affecting her destiny and confirmed once more that the protection of liberty under the Due Process Clause has a substantive dimension of fundamental significance in defining the rights of the person.

In *Carey v. Population Services Int'l*, 431 U. S. 678 (1977), the Court confronted a New York law forbidding sale or distribution of contraceptive devices to persons under 16 years of age. Although there was no single opinion for the Court, the law was invalidated. Both *Eisenstadt* and *Carey*, as well as the holding and rationale in *Roe*, confirmed that the reasoning of *Griswold* could not be confined to the protection of rights of married adults. This was the state of the law with respect to some of the most relevant cases when the Court considered *Bowers v. Hardwick*.

The facts in *Bowers* had some similarities to the instant case. A police officer, whose right to enter seems not to have been in question, observed Hardwick, in his own bedroom, engaging in intimate sexual conduct with another adult male. The conduct was in violation of a Georgia statute making it a criminal offense to engage in sodomy. One difference between the two cases is that the Georgia statute prohibited the conduct whether or not the participants were of the same sex, while the Texas statute, as we have seen, applies only to participants of the same sex. Hardwick was not prosecuted, but he brought an action in federal court to declare the state statute invalid. He alleged he was a practicing homosexual and that the criminal prohibition violated rights guaranteed to him by the Constitution. The Court, in an opinion by Justice White, sustained the Georgia law. Chief Justice Burger and Justice Powell joined the opinion of the Court and filed separate, concurring opinions. Four Justices dissented.

. . .

In academic writings, and in many of the scholarly *amicus* briefs filed to assist the Court in this case, there are fundamental criticisms of the historical premises relied upon by the majority and concurring opinions in *Bowers.* . . . We need not enter this debate in the attempt to reach a definitive historical judgment, but the following considerations counsel against adopting the definitive conclusions upon which *Bowers* placed such reliance.

At the outset it should be noted that there is no longstanding history in this country of laws directed at homosexual conduct as a distinct matter. Beginning in colonial times there were prohibitions of sodomy derived from the English criminal laws passed in the first instance by the Reformation Parliament of 1533. The English prohibition was understood to include relations between men and women as well as relations between men and men. See, *e.g.*, *King v. Wiseman*, 92 Eng. Rep. 774, 775 (K. B. 1718) (interpreting "mankind" in Act of 1533 as including women and girls). Nineteenth-century commentators similarly read American sodomy, buggery, and crime-against-nature statutes as criminalizing certain relations between men and women and between men and men. . . . The absence of legal prohibitions focusing on homosexual conduct may be explained in part by noting that according to some scholars the concept of the homosexual as a distinct category of person did not emerge until the late 19th century. See, *e.g.*, J. Katz, The Invention of Heterosexuality 10 (1995); J. D'Emilio & E. Freedman, Intimate Matters: A History of Sexuality in America 121 (2d ed. 1997) ("The modern terms *homosexuality* and *heterosexuality* do not apply to an era that had not yet articulated these distinctions"). Thus early American sodomy laws were not directed at homosexuals as such but instead sought to prohibit nonprocreative sexual activity more generally. This does not suggest approval of homosexual conduct. It does tend to show that this particular form of conduct was not thought of as a separate category from like conduct between heterosexual persons.

Laws prohibiting sodomy do not seem to have been enforced against consenting adults acting in private. A substantial number of sodomy prosecutions and convictions for which there are surviving records were for predatory acts against those who could not or did not consent, as in the case of a minor or the victim of an assault. As to these, one purpose for the prohibitions was to ensure there would be no lack of coverage if a predator committed a sexual assault that did not constitute rape as defined by the criminal law

. . .

In summary, the historical grounds relied upon in *Bowers* are more complex than the majority opinion and the concurring opinion by Chief Justice Burger indicate. Their historical premises are not without doubt and, at the very least, are overstated.

. . .

Of even more importance, almost five years before *Bowers* was decided the European Court of Human Rights considered a case with parallels to *Bowers* and to today's case. An adult male resident in Northern Ireland alleged he was a practicing homosexual who desired to engage in consensual homosexual conduct. The laws of Northern Ireland forbade him that right. He alleged that he had been questioned, his home had been searched, and he feared criminal prosecution. The court held that the laws proscribing the conduct were invalid under the European Convention on Human Rights. *Dudgeon v. United Kingdom*, 45 Eur. Ct. H. R. (1981) ¶52.

Authoritative in all countries that are members of the Council of Europe (21 nations then, 45 nations now), the decision is at odds with the premise in *Bowers* that the claim put forward was insubstantial in our Western civilization.

In our own constitutional system the deficiencies in *Bowers* became even more apparent in the years following its announcement. The 25 States with laws prohibiting the relevant conduct referenced in the *Bowers* decision are reduced now to 13, of which 4 enforce their laws only against homosexual conduct. In those States where sodomy is still proscribed, whether for same-sex or heterosexual conduct, there is a pattern of nonenforcement with respect to consenting adults acting in private. The State of Texas admitted in 1994 that as of that date it had not prosecuted anyone under those circumstances.

. . .

In explaining the respect the Constitution demands for the autonomy of the person in making these choices, we stated as follows: "These matters, involving the most intimate and personal choices a person may make in a lifetime, choices central to personal dignity and autonomy, are central to the liberty protected by the Fourteenth Amendment. At the heart of liberty is the right to define one's own concept of existence, of meaning, of the universe, and of the mystery of human life. Beliefs about these matters could not define the attributes of personhood were they formed under compulsion of the State." Persons in a homosexual relationship may seek autonomy for these purposes, just as heterosexual persons do. The decision in *Bowers* would deny them this right.

. . .

To the extent *Bowers* relied on values we share with a wider civilization, it should be noted that the reasoning and holding in *Bowers* have been rejected elsewhere. The European Court of Human Rights has followed not *Bowers* but its own decision in *Dudgeon v. United Kingdom*. See *P. G. & J. H. v. United Kingdom*, App. No. 00044787/98, ¶56 (Eur. Ct. H. R., Sept. 25, 2001); *Modinos v. Cyprus*, 259 Eur. Ct. H. R. (1993); *Norris v. Ireland*, 142 Eur. Ct. H. R. (1988). Other nations, too, have taken action consistent with an affirmation of the protected right of homosexual adults to engage in intimate, consensual conduct. See Brief for Mary Robinson et al. as *Amici Curiae* 11-12. The right the petitioners seek in this case has been accepted as an integral part of human freedom in many other countries. There has been no showing that in this country the governmental interest in circumscribing personal choice is somehow more legitimate or urgent.

. . .

Bowers was not correct when it was decided, and it is not correct today. It ought not to remain binding precedent. *Bowers v. Hardwick* should be and now is overruled.

The present case does not involve minors. It does not involve persons who might be injured or co-erced or who are situated in relationships where consent might not easily be refused. It does not involve public conduct or prostitution. It does not involve whether the government must give formal recognition to any relationship that homosexual persons seek to enter. The case does involve two adults who, with full and mutual consent from each other, engaged in sexual practices common to a homosexual lifestyle. The petitioners are entitled to respect for their private lives. The State cannot demean their existence or control their destiny by making their private sexual conduct a crime. Their right to liberty under the Due Process Clause gives them the full right to engage in their conduct without intervention of the government. "It is a promise of the Constitution that there is a realm of personal liberty which the government may not enter." *Casey*, supra, at 847. The Texas statute furthers no legitimate state interest which can justify its intrusion into the personal and private life of the individual.

Had those who drew and ratified the Due Process Clauses of the Fifth Amendment or the Fourteenth Amendment known the components of liberty in its manifold possibilities, they might have been more spe-cific. They did not presume to have this insight. They knew times can blind us to certain truths and later generations can see that laws once thought necessary and proper in fact serve only to oppress. As the Consti-tution endures, persons in every generation can invoke its principles in their own search for greater freedom.

The judgment of the Court of Appeals for the Texas Fourteenth District is reversed, and the case is remanded for further proceedings not inconsistent with this opinion. It is so ordered.

. . .

JUSTICE SCALIA, with whom THE CHIEF JUSTICE and JUSTICE THOMAS join, dissenting. "Liberty finds no refuge in a jurisprudence of doubt." *Planned Parenthood of Southeastern Pa. v. Casey*, 505 U. S. 833, 844 (1992). That was the Court's sententious response, barely more than a decade ago, to those seeking to overrule *Roe v. Wade*, 410 U. S. 113 (1973). The Court's response today, to those who have en-gaged in a 17-year crusade to overrule *Bowers v. Hardwick*, 478 U. S. 186 (1986), is very different. The need for stability and certainty presents no barrier.

Most of the rest of today's opinion has no relevance to its actual holding—that the Texas statute "furthers no legitimate state interest which can justify" its application to petitioners under rational-basis re-view. *Ante*, at 18 (overruling *Bowers* to the extent it sustained Georgia's anti-sodomy statute under the rational-basis test). Though there is discussion of "fundamental proposition[s]," *ante*, at 4, and "fundamen-tal decisions," *ibid*. nowhere does the Court's opinion declare that homosexual sodomy is a "fundamental right" under the Due Process Clause; nor does it subject the Texas law to the standard of review that would be appropriate (strict scrutiny) if homosexual sodomy *were* a "fundamental right." Thus, while overruling the *outcome* of *Bowers*, the Court leaves strangely untouched its central legal conclusion: "[R]espondent would have us announce . . . a fundamental right to engage in homosexual sodomy. This we are quite un-willing to do." 478 U. S., at 191. Instead the Court simply describes petitioners' conduct as "an exercise of their liberty"—which it undoubtedly is—and proceeds to apply an unheard-of form of rational-basis review that will have far-reaching implications beyond this case. *Ante*, at 3.

I

I begin with the Court's surprising readiness to reconsider a decision rendered a mere 17 years ago in *Bowers v. Hardwick*. I do not myself believe in rigid adherence to *stare decisis* in constitutional cases; but I do believe that we should be consistent rather than manipulative in invoking the doctrine. Today's opin-ions in support of reversal do not bother to distinguish—or indeed, even bother to mention—the paean to *stare decisis* coauthored by three Members of today's majority in *Planned Parenthood v. Casey*. There, when *stare decisis* meant preservation of judicially invented abortion rights, the widespread criticism of *Roe* was strong reason to *reaffirm* it:

"Where, in the performance of its judicial duties, the Court decides a case in such a way as to resolve the sort of intensely divisive controversy reflected in *Roe*[,] . . . its decision has a dimension that the resolution of the normal case does not carry. . . . [T]o overrule under fire in the absence of the most compelling reason . . . would subvert the Court's legitimacy beyond any serious question." 505 U. S., at 866–867.

Today, however, the widespread opposition to *Bowers*, a decision resolving an issue as "intensely divisive" as the issue in *Roe*, is offered as a reason in favor of *overruling* it. See *ante*, at 15–16. Gone, too, is any "enquiry" (of the sort conducted in *Casey*) into whether the decision sought to be overruled has "proven "unworkable,"" *Casey*, *supra*, at 855.

Today's approach to *stare decisis* invites us to overrule an erroneously decided precedent (including an "intensely divisive" decision) *if*: (1) its foundations have been "eroded" by subsequent decisions, *ante*, at 15; (2) it has been subject to "substantial and continuing" criticism, *ibid*.; and (3) it has not induced "individual or societal reliance" that counsels against overturning, *ante*, at 16. The problem is that *Roe* itself—which today's majority surely has no disposition to overrule—satisfies these conditions to at least the same degree as *Bowers*.

. . .

It seems to me that the "societal reliance" on the principles confirmed in *Bowers* and discarded today has been overwhelming. Countless judicial decisions and legislative enactments have relied on the ancient proposition that a governing majority's belief that certain sexual behavior is "immoral and unacceptable" constitutes a rational basis for regulation. See, *e.g., Williams v. Pryor*, 240 F. 3d 944, 949 (CA11 2001) (citing *Bowers* in upholding Alabama's prohibition on the sale of sex toys on the ground that "[t]he crafting and safeguarding of public morality . . . indisputably is a legitimate government interest under rational basis scrutiny"); *Milner v. Apfel*, 148 F. 3d 812, 814 (CA7 1998) (citing *Bowers* for the proposition that "[l]egislatures are permitted to legislate with regard to morality . . . rather than confined to preventing demonstrable harms"); *Holmes v. California Army National Guard* 124 F. 3d 1126, 1136 (CA9 1997) (relying on *Bowers* in upholding the federal statute and regulations banning from military service those who engage in homosexual conduct); *Owens v. State*, 352 Md. 663, 683, 724 A. 2d 43, 53 (1999) (relying on *Bowers* in holding that "a person has no constitutional right to engage in sexual intercourse, at least outside of marriage"); *Sherman v. Henry*, 928 S. W. 2d 464, 469–473 (Tex. 1996) (relying on *Bowers* in rejecting a claimed constitutional right to commit adultery). We ourselves relied extensively on *Bowers* when we concluded, in *Barnes v. Glen Theatre, Inc.*, 501 U. S. 560, 569 (1991), that Indiana's public indecency statute furthered "a substantial government interest in protecting order and morality," *ibid*., (plurality opinion);

. . .

State laws against bigamy, same-sex marriage, adult incest, prostitution, masturbation, adultery, fornication, bestiality, and obscenity are likewise sustainable only in light of *Bowers'* validation of laws based on moral choices. Every single one of these laws is called into question by today's decision; the Court makes no effort to cabin the scope of its decision to exclude them from its holding . . . The impossibility of distinguishing homosexuality from other traditional "morals" offenses is precisely why *Bowers* rejected the rational-basis challenge. "The law," it said, "is constantly based on notions of morality, and if all laws representing essentially moral choices are to be invalidated under the Due Process Clause, the courts will be very busy indeed."

JUSTICE THOMAS dissenting. I join JUSTICE SCALIA'S dissenting opinion.
I write separately to note that the law before the Court today "is . . . uncommonly silly." *Griswold v. Connecticut*, 381 U. S. 479, 527 (1965) (Stewart, J., dissenting). If I were a member of the Texas Legislature, I would vote to repeal it. Punishing someone for expressing his sexual preference through noncommercial consensual conduct with another adult does not appear to be a worthy way to expend valuable law enforcement resources.

Notwithstanding this, I recognize that as a member of this Court I am not empowered to help petitioners and others similarly situated. My duty, rather, is to "decide cases "agreeably to the Constitution and laws of the United States."" *Id.*, at 530. And, just like Justice Stewart, I "can find [neither in the Bill of Rights nor any other part of the Constitution a] general right of privacy," *ibid.*, or as the Court terms it today, the "liberty of the person both in its spatial and more transcendent dimensions," *ante*, at 1.

Notes

1. "Economic Indicators," June 2003. Prepared for the Joint Economic Committee by the Council of Economic Advisors (Washington, D.C.: Government Printing Office, 1999).
2. Saskia Sassen, "The Informal Economy," in John H. Mollenkopf and Manuel Castells, eds. *Dual City: Restructuring New York* (New York: Russell Sage Foundation, 1991), pp. 79–102.
3. Kathryn Edin and Laura Lein, *Making Ends Meet: How Single Mothers Survive Welfare and Low-Wage Work* (New York: Russell Sage Foundation, 1997).
4. U.S. Census Bureau, "Money Income in the United States, 2001," Current Population Report 60–206 (Washington, D.C.: Government Printing Office, 2002).
5. Derived from U.S. House of Representatives, Committee on Ways and Means, *Overview of Entitlement Programs: 1994 Green Book*, July 15, 1994, Table H-11, p. 1171.
6. U.S. Census Bureau, "Historical Poverty Tables—People," calculated from the Current Population Survey, Annual Demographic Files (March), 1960–1999, http://www.census.gov/hhes/poverty/histpov/hstpov3.html.
7. Carol J. De Vita, *The United States at Mid-Decade* (Washington, D.C.: Population Reference Bureau, Inc., 1996).
8. U.S. Bureau of Labor Statistics, Bulletin 2307.
9. Mary Rowland, "A Clearer Picture of Unpaid Leave," *New York Times*, "Money" section, January 29, 1995, p. 13.
10. Carol Kleiman, "Study Shows Job Status Skews Family Benefits," *Chicago Tribune*, February 8, 1993.
11. U. S. Bureau of the Census, *Current Population Reports*, Series P-25, "Population Projections of the U. S. by Age, Sex, Race, and Hispanic Origin: 1995–2050. (Washington D.C.: Government Printing Office, 1996).
12. Unless otherwise specified, data on health care are from U.S. Health Care Financing Administration, Office of National Health Statistics.
13. Center on Budget and Policy Priorities, *Number without Health Insurance Remains at Record Level*, October 6, 1995, pp. 1–2.
14. Paul Starr, *The Social Transformation of American Medicine* (New York: Basic Books, 1982), provides an excellent review of this history.
15. Abigail Trafford and Spencer Rich, "Health Care Reform in Congress?" *Washington Post*, September 20, 1994, pp. 12–14; Robert P. Hey, "Reform Drive Fights for Life," *AARP Bulletin*, September 1994, 35, 8, pp. 1–10.
16. U.S. Congress, "Patients' Bill of Rights Act of 1999," H.R. 358.
17. Families USA, "One Step Forward, One Step Back: Children's Health Coverage after CHIP and Welfare Reform" (October, 1999).
18. United States Congress, 105 P.L. 34: 111 Stat. 788; 1997 Enacted H.R. 2014; 105 Enacted H.R. 2014. "Mental Health Parity Act of 1996," August 5, 1997.
19. U.S. Census Bureau, *Statistical Abstract of the United States 1998* (Washington, D.C.: Government Printing Office, 1998), p. 312.
20. Ibid., p. 76.
21. Mary Jo Bane and David T. Ellwood, *Welfare Realities: From Rhetoric to Reform* (Cambridge, Mass.: Harvard University Press, 1994), pp. 28–66.

22. William J. Wilson, *The Truly Disadvantaged: The Inner City, the Underclass, and Public Policy* (Chicago: University of Chicago Press, 1987), pp. 20–62.
23. David T. Ellwood, *Poor Support: Poverty in the American Family* (New York: Basic Books, 1988), pp. 231–244.
24. U.S. Congress, 104th Congress, "Personal Responsibility Act of 1995," H.R. 4.
25. U.S. Congress, 104th Congress, "The Personal Responsibility and Work Opportunity Reconciliation Act of 1996," Public Law 104–193 [H.R. 3734].
26. U.S. Department of Health and Human Services, *Temporary Assistance for Needy Families (TANF) Program.* Fifth Annual Report to Congress (August 2002), pp. 20–21.
27. Ibid., pp. 20–21.
28. Ibid., p. 44.
29. Ibid., pp. 132–133.
30. Douglas S. Massey, "March of Folly: U.S. Immigration Policy after NAFTA," *The American Prospect* 37 (March–April 1998): 22–33.
31. Ram Cnaan, "Our Hidden Safety Net," *Brookings Review* 17:2 (Spring 1999): 50.
32. Lester M. Salamon, "The Marketization of Welfare: Changing Nonprofit and For-Profit Roles in the American Welfare State," *Social Service Review* (March 1993): 32.
33. "Report Warns Against Reducing Remedial Classes in Colleges," *New York Times*, February 13, 1996, p. A12.
34. "Schools on Reservation Crumbling for Lack of Repair Money," *New York Times*, September 3, 1995, p. 17.
35. Orlando Patterson, "Affirmative Action on the Merit System," *New York Times*, August 9, 1995, p. 13.
36. Robert Pear, "Report to Clinton Faults Programs to Aid Minorities," *New York Times*, May 31, 1995, p. A1.
37. "Abortion: The Rate vs. the Debate," *New York Times*, February 25, 1996, p. 4.
38. U.S. Department of Justice, Bureau of Justice Statistics, *Sourcebook of Criminal Justice Statistics*, 26th ed. (Washington, D.C.: Government Printing Office, 1999), p. 173.
39. Ibid., p. 329.
40. Ibid., p. 462.

Index